A Publication Sponsored by
the Society for Industrial and Organizational Psychology, Inc.,
A Division of the American Psychological Association

Other books in the Professional Practice Series sponsored
by the Society and published by Jossey-Bass include:

Employees, Careers, and Job Creation
Manuel London, Editor

Organizational Surveys

Organizational Surveys

Tools for Assessment and Change

Allen I. Kraut, *Editor*

Foreword by Manuel London

Jossey-Bass Publishers • San Francisco

Substantial discounts on bulk quantities of Jossey-Bass books are available to corporations, professional associations, and other organizations. For details and discount information, contact the special sales department at Jossey-Bass Inc., Publishers.
(415) 433–1740; Fax (800) 605–2665.

Jossey-Bass Web address: http://www.josseybass.com

 Manufactured in the United States of America on Lyons Falls Pathfinder Tradebook. This paper is acid-free and 100 percent totally chlorine-free.

Library of Congress Cataloging-in-Publication Data

Organizational surveys : tools for assessment and change / Allen
   I. Kraut, editor ; foreword by Manuel London.
      p.   cm. — (Jossey-Bass business and management series)
   (Jossey-Bass social and behavioral science series)   (Society for
   Industrial and Organizational Psychology professional practice
   series)
   Includes bibliographical references and index.
   ISBN 0-7879-0234-9
   1. Organizational effectiveness—Evaluation.   2. Employee attitude
surveys.   3. Consumers—Attitudes.   I. Kraut, Allen I.   II. Series.
III. Series: Jossey-Bass social and behavioral science series.
IV. Series: Professional practice series.
HD58.9.O737   1996
658.4—dc20   96-7804

FIRST EDITION
HB Printing 10 9 8 7 6 5 4 3

A *joint publication in*
The Jossey-Bass Business & Management Series
and
The Jossey-Bass Social & Behavioral Science Series

Society for Industrial and Organizational Psychology Professional Practice Series

Contents

Foreword

Organizational Surveys is part of the Professional Practice Series sponsored by the Society for Industrial and Organizational Psychology. The books in the series address contemporary ideas and problems, focus on how to get things done, and provide state-of-the art technology based on theory and research from industrial and organizational psychology. We try to satisfy the needs of practitioners and those being trained for practice.

Four earlier volumes in this series, under the senior editorship of Douglas W. Bray, were published by Guilford Press and are now distributed by Jossey-Bass. Douglas W. Bray edited the first book: *Working with Organizations and Their People* (1991). The book examines the role of industrial and organizational psychologists as practitioners involved in evaluation, training, and organization development.

The second book, *Diversity in the Workplace* (1992), edited by Susan E. Jackson, offers cases and methods for creating and assessing a diverse workplace, managing workplace diversity through personal growth and team development, and strategic initiatives to manage workplace diversity.

Abraham K. Korman's *Human Dilemmas in Work Organizations: Strategies for Resolution* (1994) considers the expanding world of the human resource practitioner. Chapters describe programs for employee assistance, stress management, marginal performers, reorganizations, employee ethics, and elder care.

Ann Howard's book *Diagnosis for Organizational Change* (1994) focuses on organizational diagnosis for design and development. The contributors examine the assessment of human talent for staffing and training. They also provide an overview of the high-involvement workplace with a consideration of organization cultures, reward systems, and work teams.

As the new senior editor of the Professional Practice Series under our new publisher, Jossey-Bass, I edited *Employees, Careers, and Job Creation* (1995). This book examines ways human resource development programs contribute to an organization's viability and growth in tough economic times. It describes programs that help employees maintain their value to their firms or find new employment after organizational downsizing. It shows how organizations, government, and universities can work together to help employees create new ventures and career opportunities.

When I began conversations with my editorial board about possible topics for next volumes, everyone was enthusiastic about a book on organizational surveys. An up-to-date examination of survey methods and applications is long overdue. Allen I. Kraut, a member of the editorial board, was the ideal person to develop the idea and edit the volume. As a leading expert and practitioner at IBM, Allen spearheaded innovations in survey design and implementation. Equally important, he was responsible for an organizational survey that worked! He helped build a survey process used for many years to track the corporation's progress on key issues pertaining to management, work environment, and human resource policies. Moreover, the survey was a component in evaluating managers' success as managers.

Now a member of the Baruch College faculty, Allen began this editorial effort by contacting a group of practitioners to test their reactions about the need for an up-to-date volume on organizational surveys. They agreed strongly with our editorial board that the field needed such a book. Allen recognized that human resource practitioners did not need a "how to" book, but rather one that would address contemporary issues of how surveys promote individual, group, and organizational change and development. The current volume lives up to this goal.

Organizational Surveys demonstrates the value of surveys for diagnosing individual and organizational strengths and weaknesses, communicating organizational culture and expectations, and evaluating human resource policies and programs. This volume describes best practices and methods by which organizations share items and compare results. It links survey results to indexes of organization effectiveness, such as customer satisfaction, financial performance, and employee turnover. It also addresses tough issues, such as holding managers accountable for survey results and avoiding treating survey results as necessarily reliable and valid data about individual capabilities.

Our previous board was instrumental in the conceptualization of the current book, and I appreciate their contribution. They were Warner Burke, Pat Dyer, Nita French, Ann Howard, Allen Kraut, Walter Tornow, and Victor Vroom. With this volume, we make the transition to a new editorial board. Work on future volumes is under way by our new board: Lawrence Fogli, Nita French, Catherine Higgs, Allen Kraut, Edward Levine, Kenneth Pearlman, and Walter Tornow.

April 1996   Manuel London
                                                 State University of New York
                                                 Series Editor

Preface

Organizational surveys are a major area of practice for industrial and organizational psychologists. Yet, although texts about constructing surveys are available, very little literature exists about the actual *practice* of designing and conducting surveys and using them in organizations. *Organizational Surveys* is an attempt to fill that gap.

The typical terms used to describe the surveys used within organizations are *employee opinion surveys* or *employee attitude surveys,* but they seem a bit old-fashioned. I have deliberately chosen a more contemporary label, *organizational surveys,* for the title of this book, not only to be up to date but also to avoid some unintended and negative meanings. The term *employee survey* may imply that the survey covers only a select group of organizational members, as when employees (meaning only lower-level workers) are distinguished from managers or executives. This is an invidious distinction that is neither realistic nor desirable. In addition, the words *opinion* and *attitude* are sometimes used as though to divide mere feelings and perceptions from an objective *reality.* In fact, feelings and perceptions represent our world, and we act upon them just as if they were our objective reality because we believe them to be our reality. Also, the term *opinion survey* is often taken to connote a public opinion poll, which is a far narrower meaning than this book intends.

Although terms like employee attitude survey or employee opinion survey are popularly used to describe much of the survey work in the area of organizational and industrial psychology, for many executives such terms conjure up images of "smile tests" or measures of employee "happiness." But in many organizations, today's surveys often ask for reports and perceptions of key behaviors, such as management's emphasis on customer satisfaction and better service, organizational support of efforts for better quality, sufficiency of training, individuals' empowerment to make decisions, and so on. Survey participants are asked to report on various aspects of organizational functioning and on the success of change efforts. The information given by respondents in these surveys goes far beyond mere attitudes. Therefore, the term organizational survey seems more accurate because it specifies the entire organization as its realm and virtually any topic as fair game.

Nevertheless, some of our chapter authors use the term *employee survey* through force of habit. From my conversations with them, it is clear that they intend the same broad and nonpejorative meaning I try to convey with the term *organizational survey.* In a few cases, the term *employee survey* is used to avoid possible confusion with other surveys done by the organization, such as surveys of customers.

Audience

This book is intended to look at surveys as they are currently practiced in organizations, and as they are evolving. It is written by experienced practitioners, who have a strong scientific orientation. The chapter authors and I have three specific audiences in mind.

- Practitioners in industrial and organizational psychology or closely related fields who direct organizational surveys or are in some other way involved in them
- Academics who are preparing others to design and conduct surveys or to use survey results, and their students
- Human resource professionals and executives who want a broader understanding of how to use surveys as powerful sets of tools

In a sense, *Organizational Surveys* is a report from the field, from accomplished and thoughtful survey researchers. They share their successes (as well as a few regrets). They also report the leading edge of today's practices, and most share their hopes, predictions, and recommendations for the future.

Overview of the Contents

This book covers organizational surveys from three standpoints.

Part One reviews *why* organizations employ surveys. The chapters in this section cover such different survey aims as providing leverage for organizational and cultural change, assessing employee views, conducting research, and stimulating and evaluating management and organizational development.

Applications of organizational surveys are reviewed generically rather than in particular content areas. While important content areas to which surveys are being applied (such as quality or workforce diversity) are used as examples, no attempt is made to review findings on such topics. Instead, the focus is on organizational reasons for using surveys and the purposes and activities to which surveys are applied.

Part Two focuses on the survey process, *how* surveys are designed and conducted, or "done." This section examines such critical elements of the survey process as setting expectations with management and following through to take action on the data. It also discusses practical issues that are key to an effective survey, such as preparing codes that make feedback to organizational units possible, dealing with write-in comments, and using advanced technology to administer a survey.

Part Three considers a number of special topics related to surveys, such as multicompany survey consortia, doing international surveys, linking data to bottom-line outcomes, and ethical issues.

This volume is *not* a methodological tome. There already exist a number of excellent texts on how to select scientific samples, test for statistical significance, construct surveys, write items, devise scales, conduct conscientious administrations, and other related topics. (Many of these texts are noted in the Introduction.) Nevertheless, such topics do get a good deal of attention in this volume, and the reader will find a lot here that illustrates and extends the basic methodological issues into the arena of practice.

Still, this book is primarily for practitioners who, presumably, already have or can get the scientific grounding on which surveys are based. Each chapter attempts a comprehensive and integrative review of what is known about its topic. This includes program descriptions and evaluations where possible, along with examples or cases and the historical bases for today's practices. The emphasis is on the description of good current practice in organizational surveys and implications for better future practice.

Acknowledgments

I was delighted to be invited to prepare this volume, as much of my professional life has been centered around the use of organizational surveys. Many of the people I have worked with over the years have added greatly to my understanding and deserve to be acknowledged.

They include the staff of the Institute for Social Research at the University of Michigan, where I studied, and particularly my adviser, Robert L. Kahn. In my early years at IBM, I was privileged to work with several distinguished survey researchers who were both colleagues and tutors: S. William Alper, Richard A. Dunnington, Fred Goldner, John R. Hinrichs, Geert Hofstede, Stuart M. Klein, Richard R. Ritti, David Sirota, and Alan D. Wolfson.

In the 1970s and 1980s, I saw firsthand at IBM the extraordinary strength of organizational surveys in helping management at all levels to assess employee viewpoints and to shape and guide firmwide change. No one deserves more credit for the success of these efforts than Walton E. Burdick, the visionary chief human resources executive through most of that era. His unfailing acceptance, support, and encouragement of surveys was greatly helped by the leadership of two talented directors of personnel research: Charles E. Hawkins and Thomas F. Cummings.

During those years, I was fortunate enough to work with (and learn from) several other highly talented professionals at IBM who have also helped directly in this volume by suggesting topics and by reviewing and commenting on one or more chapters: Norman D. Costa, William E. Dodd, Andrea Goldberg, Sarah Johnson, Steven Marcus, Patricia Pedigo, and Gillian Peppercorn. Other friends and associates who have helped by reviewing one or more chapters include Raymond Johnson, George Hollenbeck, Frank Papotto, Melvin Sorcher, Carol Timmreck, and Anna Marie Valerio. Maria V. Park and Ian Scott have also been helpful with their insights on the use of organizational surveys.

My colleagues at Baruch College have been very generous in reviewing a number of chapters and providing constructive reactions and comments to the authors. I thank Denise Bane, Mingwei Guan, Michael Judiesch, Richard Kopelman, Abraham Korman,

Karen Lyness, Steven Pappamarcos, Hannah Rothstein, Cynthia Thompson, and Donald Vredenburgh.

As might be expected, the members of the Professional Practice Series editorial board at the time this volume was proposed were generous with their comments and quite helpful in their advice. They include Warner Burke, the late Patricia Dyer, Nita French, Ann Howard, Walter Tornow, and Victor Vroom. The series editor, Manuel London, was particularly supportive.

My greatest appreciation is extended to the authors of the chapters in this book. All of them are busy and successful practitioners with significant accomplishments in the field of organizational surveys. I can testify that they worked very hard (and through several drafts each) to produce the chapters in this book. Our profession is indebted to them for sharing their experience and knowledge.

It has been a major growth experience for me to edit and contribute to *Organizational Surveys*. It has enriched my own thinking and understanding of the power and potential of organizational surveys. It has also been an honor for me to lead this effort, and I am thankful to have been asked to do it.

This book is dedicated to my loving long-term partner, Florence Reiss Kraut, an exemplar of survey skills: an expert in interviewing, empathetic understanding, insightful data analysis, helpful and supportive feedback, creative problem solving; and an energetic catalyst for change.

Rye, New York   Allen I. Kraut
April 1996

The Authors

ALLEN I. KRAUT is professor of management at Baruch College, City University of New York. He spent much of his professional career at IBM, where he held managerial posts in personnel research and management development until 1989. He directed major studies of how employees balance work and family life issues, along with other research designed to enhance the flexibility of the firm's workforce. As president of Kraut Associates, a human resource consulting firm, he has specialized in opinion surveys. He earned his Ph.D. degree in social psychology in 1965 at the University of Michigan, where he was affiliated with the Institute for Social Research. He is a fellow of the American Psychological Association and a diplomate of the American Board of Professional Psychology. In 1995, he received SIOP's Distinguished Professional Contributions Award.

Steven D. Ashworth is senior research manager in human resource research at the Allstate Research and Planning Center, Allstate Insurance Company. In addition to managing a staff of HR research professionals, he has been directly involved in developing and managing large-scale employee survey research programs for Allstate. His particular interest is the application of technology to research and the impact of technology on work and workers. A 1983 graduate of the University of Houston with a Ph.D. degree in industrial and organizational psychology, he is a member of the Society for Industrial and Organizational Psychology, the Academy of Management, and the Mayflower Group. He is on the editorial review boards of *Personnel Psychology* and the *Journal of Applied Psychology*.

David W. Bracken is a performance management consultant with Towers Perrin in its Minneapolis, Minnesota, office. He has over sixteen years of experience in organizational assessment as a researcher, practitioner, and consultant. Prior to joining Towers Perrin, he was director of organizational assessment and research at Personnel Decisions, Inc. He has also held positions at National Computer Systems, BellSouth, Assessment Designs International, and Xerox. He received his Ph.D. degree in industrial and organizational psychology in 1983 from the Georgia Institute of Technology. He is a licensed psychologist in the state of Georgia and a member of the American Society for Training and Development, the American Psychological Association, and the Society for Industrial and Organizational Psychology.

W. Warner Burke is professor of psychology and education and director of the graduate program in organizational psychology at Teachers College, Columbia University. He is also president of W. Warner Burke Associates, Inc., an organizational consulting firm. He is a fellow of both the Academy of Management and the Academy of Human Resource Development and the author of more than ninety articles and book chapters on organizational development, training, and social and organizational psychology and the author, coauthor, editor, or coeditor of thirteen books. Currently he serves on the Committee on Techniques for the Enhancement of Human Performance, National Research Council of the National Academy of Sciences. He holds a Ph.D. degree (1963) in social psychology from the University of Texas.

Allan H. Church is a principal of W. Warner Burke Associates, Inc., specializing in the design, analysis, and implementation of advanced individualized feedback systems for executive, leadership, and management development programs. He also has considerable experience conducting large-scale organizational surveys. Prior to joining Burke Associates, he worked for IBM in both the Communications Measurement and Research and the Corporate Personnel Research departments. He has published over thirty articles and is an active member, as both presenter and reviewer, in a variety of professional associations. Currently he is coediting a special issue for *Group and Organization Management* on multisource (360-degree) feedback systems. He received his Ph.D. degree in organizational psychology in 1994 from Columbia University.

Celeste A. Coruzzi is director in the Change Integration Practice at Price Waterhouse LLP. She was a principal of W. Warner Burke Associates, Inc., and remains a trustee of the Organization Development Network and editor of the *OD Practitioner.* Having worked for over a decade as a consultant to a variety of organizations, she focuses on the areas of empowering employees, managing large-scale change, benchmarking quality improvement efforts, and developing consulting skills competencies among HR and OD professionals. Prior to joining Burke Associates, she worked at IBM in the area of personnel research and, before that, at NASA, doing survey research designed to identify the managerial competencies that promote highly effective teams. She has published several articles on management and organizational change. She received her Ph.D. degree in organizational psychology from Columbia University in 1988.

Marilyn K. Gowing is director of the Personnel Resources and Development Center of the U.S. Office of Personnel Management. The center conducts basic, applied, and innovative research in every area of human resource management for federal, state, and local government agencies. She received her Ph.D. degree in industrial and organizational psychology in 1981 from the George Washington University, which honored her in 1991 with its Distinguished Alumna Award. She is a past secretary of the Society for Industrial and Organizational Psychology (SIOP) and a past president of the Personnel Testing Council of Metropolitan Washington. She has coauthored *Taxonomies of Human Performance* (with E. A. Fleishman), and has written more than thirty articles and book chapters, including chapters in the SIOP scientist and practitioner series.

A. Catherine Higgs is senior research director for strategic business research at the Allstate Research and Planning Center, Allstate Insurance Company. For over a decade, she has directed research staff pursuing a wide range of topics, including management policy and practices, workforce strategy and forecasting, organizational design and effectiveness, measurement of organizational performance, management and employee selection and performance, compensation, and communication programs. She is a member of the Professional Practice Series editorial board for the Society for Industrial and Organizational Psychology (SIOP) and was chair of SIOP's Continuing Education and Workshop Committee from 1993 to 1995. She is on the executive advisory panel for the Academy of Management's *Executive* and is a former member of the Mayflower Group board of governors. She is a 1974 graduate of the University of Maryland, with a Ph.D. degree in social and quantitative psychology.

John R. Hinrichs has over thirty years survey-related experience as a consultant, business entrepreneur, college professor (Cornell University), and corporate staff psychologist (IBM, Mobil, and Exxon). He is the author of three books and over ninety articles, book chapters, and papers in both the professional and popular press, including chapters in the *Annual Review of Psychology* and the *Handbook of Industrial and Organizational Psychology*. He is a fellow of the Society for Industrial and Organizational Psychology and the American Psychological Society and former president of the Metropolitan New York Association for Applied Psychology. He is an American Board of Professional Psychology diplomate in industrial and organizational psychology and a licensed psychologist in Connecticut and has served on the board of governors of the Center for Creative Leadership. He is a graduate of Johns Hopkins and Purdue universities and earned his Ph.D. degree in industrial and labor relations at Cornell University in 1962.

Raymond H. Johnson is education and training manager, Process Leadership Office, Ford Motor Company. For twenty years prior to taking this position, he was a senior internal consultant, responsible for Ford's worldwide employee survey program and representing Ford in various leadership positions in the Mayflower Group—an employee survey consortium consisting of forty-one major U.S. companies. He received his Ph.D. degree in industrial and organizational psychology from Michigan State University in 1973.

Sarah Rassenfoss Johnson is program director, Worldwide Human Resources Research, IBM Corporation. She is responsible for the employee opinion survey strategy at IBM and is also involved in benchmarking and research projects on a variety of HR topics. She has worked on many surveys of the worldwide IBM employee population. She received her Ph.D. degree in industrial and organizational psychology from Ohio State University in 1985.

Karl Kuhnert is associate professor of industrial and organizational psychology at the University of Georgia, with a special interest in leadership and change within large organizations in both the public and private sector. He received his Ph.D. degree in industrial and organizational psychology in 1985 from Kansas State University. Over the past decade, he has authored or coauthored over thirty articles and fifteen book chapters and has made over fifty conference presentations. He currently consults with the Federal Law Enforcement Training Center and United Parcel Service on their survey and feedback systems.

Anita R. Lancaster has been assistant director at Defense Manpower Data Center (DMDC) since 1991, responsible for program formulation and execution for DMDC's Washington, D.C., office. These programs support the Office of the Secretary of Defense and include market research, program evaluation, personnel surveys, media advertising, and development and maintenance of personnel databases. From 1984 to 1991, she was assistant director for accession policy, Office of the Secretary of Defense, where she had policy oversight for military entrance requirements (for example, aptitude testing), enlistment processing, and development of military occupational and training information. She received her Ph.D. degree in educational guidance and counseling from Wayne State University in 1978. She is a recipient of the Secretary of Defense Medal for Meritorious Civilian Service.

Dan P. McCauley is associate project director at International Survey Research Corporation's headquarters in Chicago. Over his career, he has worked on the survey systems of numerous companies, including Amoco, AT&T, John Hancock, Nestlé USA, and United Parcel Service. He received his Ph.D. degree in industrial and organizational psychology from the University of Georgia in 1994.

William H. Macey is president of the consulting firm Personnel Research Associates, Inc. His work as a consultant for the past seventeen years has emphasized the development, administration, and analysis of survey programs and feedback systems, including the design of computer software for these purposes. Prior to this, he worked for Miller Brewing Company, where he was responsible for the development and implementation of personnel research strategies affecting managerial, professional, clerical, and skilled trades occupational groups. He received his Ph.D. degree in psychology from Loyola University in 1975.

David A. Nadler is president and chief executive officer of the Delta Consulting Group, Inc., a management consulting firm that provides services related to the management of strategic-level organizational change. Earlier he was a faculty member of the Graduate School of Business at Columbia University. His specialties include large-scale organizational change, executive leadership, organizational design, and senior team development. He has written numerous articles and book chapters and authored or edited nine books, including *Feedback and Organization Development, Organizational Assessment, Managing Organizational Behavior, Strategic Organization Design, Organizational Architecture,* and *Prophets in the Dark: How Xerox Reinvented Itself and Drove Back the Japanese* (with David T. Kearns). His most recent book is *Discontinuous Change: Leading Organizational Transformation.* He received his Ph.D. degree in organizational psychology from the University of Michigan in 1975.

Erich P. Prien is an industrial and organizational psychologist in private practice in Memphis, Tennessee. He has been a faculty member at several universities, retiring recently from Memphis State University. He is a fellow of the Society for Industrial and Organizational Psychology and the American Psychological Association and holds certification in industrial and organizational psychology from the American Board of Professional Psychology. He received his Ph.D. degree in industrial psychology from Case Western Reserve University in 1959.

Marshall Sashkin is professor of human resource development at George Washington University. He has developed and published numerous organizational survey instruments and is also an active consultant, having conducted or assisted in various survey projects for organizations such as General Electric, American Express, and Sara Lee. He received his Ph.D. degree in organizational psychology from the University of Michigan in 1970.

William A. Schiemann is president of Wm. Schiemann & Associates, Inc., a Somerville, New Jersey, firm specializing in organizational effectiveness and change management. He has consulted extensively on corporate cultural changes, quality and productivity improvement, and employee relations issues and has worked with senior management to enhance corporate performance, communication, and culture. He has conducted hundreds of employee and customer surveys, focus groups, and interviews. Prior to founding his firm, he was senior vice president with Sirota & Alper Associates and vice president of Opinion Research Corporation. He received his Ph.D. degree in organizational psychology from the University of Illinois in 1976.

Janet L. Spencer is director at Delta Consulting Group, Inc., working in the areas of strategic organizational diagnosis and change, senior team development, and executive leadership. In her consulting work, she has led the design, development, and execution of several large survey efforts, using the results to inform and steer change processes. Prior to joining Delta, she worked as a principal consultant for W. Warner Burke Associates, Inc. She has also worked for AT&T, specializing in assessment center design and implementation. She received her Ph.D. degree in organizational psychology from Columbia University in 1991. She is a member of the Academy of Management and the American Psychological Association.

David B. Wagner is director at Delta Consulting Group, Inc., working in the areas of strategic organizational diagnosis and change, strategic human resource management, and senior team development. Prior to 1995, he was responsible for Delta's applied research activities, including survey research, working with numerous clients on organizational diagnosis, cultural change, and organizational effectiveness. Before joining Delta, he held internal and external consulting positions in various companies, focusing on organizational diagnosis, survey design and implementation, cultural change, and management and executive development. He received his Ph.D. degree in industrial and organizational psychology from New York University in 1990. He is a member of the Academy of Management and the American Psychological Association.

Jack W. Wiley is president of Gantz Wiley Research, a consulting firm specializing in employee opinion and customer satisfaction surveys for both domestic and international corporate clients. Previously he was director of organizational research for Control Data and held personnel research positions at National Bank of Detroit and Ford Motor Company. He has nationally recognized expertise in linking employee survey results to measures of customer satisfaction and business performance. He developed WorkTrends USA, a national normative database of employee opinions, and has made numerous presentations on survey research to professional associations around the country. He received his Ph.D. degree in organizational psychology from the University of Tennessee in 1978.

An Overview of Organizational Surveys

Allen I. Kraut

Surveys of employee opinions and perceptions seem quite popular nowadays, but it was not always so. In 1953, noted industrial psychologist Morris Viteles wrote *Motivation and Morale in Industry,* and this "comprehensive account of the latest studies and attitude surveys bearing upon the wants and needs of workers" (in the words of the dust jacket) reported that Conference Board studies of thousands of U.S. companies found barely 50 doing attitude surveys in 1944, rising to 245 in 1947. A later Conference Board study, in 1951, found 223 companies that had done surveys, of which only 3 had done them before 1940.

In Viteles's view (p. 246), the fourfold central purpose of the "employee-attitude survey" is to (1) learn the importance employees attach to different aspects of the work situation, (2) assess the level of employee satisfaction and morale to enable management to respond in units that require attention, (3) identify the factors determining employee satisfaction and morale, and (4) extend motivational theory. Reflecting interests of the postwar era, Viteles's comments show a great concern about ways to increase productivity and to maintain "industrial harmony" (between management and workers and their unions). Yet, even now, his writing seems remarkably sophisticated in describing the scientific use of surveys and their practical side. He notes that surveys raise employee expectations and quotes one executive as saying: "An attitude survey is like a hand grenade—once you pull the pin you have to do something with it. Otherwise it may hurt you rather than help you" (p. 394).

Obviously, we have come a long way in favor of surveys since then. Recent data suggest that in the 1990s, more than half of U.S. companies are using surveys of employees. A study by Delaney, Lewin, and Ichniowski (1988) surveyed 7,000 executives and received data representing 495 business units. The executives used surveys in from 38 percent to 51 percent of their units, depending on the type of employees in each unit. Another large poll, by Gallup (1988), found seven out of ten companies reporting they had done a survey of employees within the last ten years. Kraut and Freeman (1992) found survey usage reported by 78 percent of the human resource directors from seventy-five large well-managed firms.

These studies do not indicate how well or successfully the surveys are done. On anecdotal evidence, they seem to vary widely in size, frequency, types of questions, sampling strategy, form of administration, and use of the collected data. Still, by virtue of their visibility, surveys get a lot of attention and have the potential for broad impact in a company.

The term *organizational survey* describes a number of methods of systematically gathering data from the members of an organization. These methods include questionnaires, interviews, and even (unobtrusive) observation. Most questionnaires are self-administered and often paper and pencil, although this medium is rapidly being supplanted by such other media as telephones and computers. Interviews may be carried out individually (face-to-face or not) or even in focus groups.

A survey will usually have a theme, evidenced in standardized, usually close-ended questions, perhaps with some open-ended items also included. Later, the data will be formally processed, analyzed, and reported to the survey sponsors. Although there are many variations, the unifying component of organizational surveys is that they are a methodical way of gathering data from people in an organization for specific purposes.

Origins

A short history of sample surveys in general (Rossi, Wright, & Anderson, 1983) shows they came into wide use in the 1920s and 1930s, primarily to determine public opinion (and political views) and to perform market research. During World War II, the U.S. government used surveys extensively to seek opinions from civilians and military personnel. The work by Samuel Stouffer and Associates, *The American Soldier* (1947–1950), was an awesome example of using survey research for policy purposes.

After the war, many of the people involved in such government survey activities moved to university centers and set up survey research centers, such as the University of Michigan's Institute for Social Research, whose staff included Rensis Likert, Angus Campbell, and Leslie Kish. Although much of the effort of such groups was devoted to social science research, part of their work led to research in private-sector organizations, and gradually some of their staff and graduates left to conduct internal survey research within and for different companies.

Methodologies

With these origins, it should be no surprise that the published craft and science of survey research has been dominated by fields outside of industrial and organizational psychology. Much of what has been written comes from sociologists, public opinion pollsters, market researchers, and social psychologists, mainly for application to their own fields. Largely from academic bases, the authors cover topics like the logic of the science, research designs, sampling and multivariate statistics, question-writing, index construction, data analysis, and reporting.

One of the first comprehensive texts, *Survey Research,* authored by Charles Backstrom and Gerald Hursh-Cesar, was published in 1963 and intended for political scientists and political sociologists. A second edition came out almost two decades later, in 1981, but seems to be out of print. The popular *Survey Research Methods,* by Earl Babbie, came out in 1973 and is now in its second edition (1990). Focusing on the "logic and skills" of survey research, it has also spawned a larger text, *The Practice of Social Research,* now in its sixth edition (1992).

Along the way, we have seen some paperback texts produced primarily for public opinion pollsters, like *The Sample Survey: Theory and Practice,* written by Donald Warwick and Charles Lininger (1975), and Floyd J. Fowler's slim *Survey Research Methods* (rev. ed., 1988).

Some books, such as sociologist Donald Dillman's *Mail and Telephone Surveys: The Total Design Method* (1978), aim to present the "step-by step details" of doing a survey. A more recent text, *Designing and Conducting Survey Research* (1992), authored by public administration faculty Louis Rea and Richard Parker, also provides step-by-step instruction for survey research.

Still other books have focused on subparts of survey research, such as market researcher Stanley Payne's classic *The Art of Asking Questions* (1951) or the more recent *Asking Questions: A Practical Guide to Questionnaire Design,* by public opinion researchers Seymour Sudman and Norman Bradburn (1982). In this vein are two other classics, Robert Kahn and Charles Cannell's *The Dynamics of Interviewing* (1957) and Leslie Kish's *Survey Sampling* (1965). A more comprehensive work, using many contributors and directed at social science research, can be found in the *Handbook of Survey Research,* edited by Peter Rossi, James Wright, and Andy Anderson (1983).

All the works just cited, along with the standard research methodology texts, have been the foundation for training industrial and organizational psychologists in survey research. Practical experience has been afforded through university-based survey research centers and graduate internships in industry. However, very few books have been written by or for those doing organizational surveys, although there have been some articles in various journals. A notable exception is Randall Dunham and Frank Smith's slender 1979 paperback, *Organizational Surveys.* Based largely on surveys done at Sears, Roebuck, it was written for managers, with the stated goal of presenting "the practical application of survey techniques" in order to provide managers "with the expertise necessary to conduct surveys properly and to use the results effectively" (p. iv). At a pragmatic level, it also served researchers well as a primer for understanding the operational and nonscientific aspects of surveys as they might be used within organizations.

Changing Purposes

In a general sense, the purposes of organizational surveys center around the themes distinguished by David Nadler in Chapter Eight: assessment and change. As Viteles's remarks showed, the early years of organizational surveys were dominated by an interest in the *assessment* of employee opinions, an interest also signalled by the subtitle of Dunham and Smith's 1979 book on organizational surveys: *An Internal Assessment of Organizational Health.* A similar theme is echoed by the title of another volume issued at about the same time, *Organizational Assessment: Perspectives on the Measurement of Organizational Behavior and the Quality of Work Life,* which was authored by three influential academically based industrial and organizational psychologists, Edward Lawler, David Nadler, and Cortlandt Cammann (1980). Signalling an emerging new emphasis, their book was part of a series on "organizational assessment and change." This shift toward an interest in change was aided by another work from the same era, titled *Feedback and Organization Development: Using Data-Based Methods,* by Nadler (1977). Although surveys were not mentioned in the title, they were obviously the source of the data being used to fuel change. Several examples and models for using survey data were detailed.

In my experience over three decades, I have seen organizational surveys performed for several different reasons, although most fit neatly under the umbrella terms of assessment or change. It is also worth noting that any particular survey may try to achieve several different purposes, which can overlap or even conflict with one another.

The major purposes of organizational surveys are described below. The order of listing begins with the purposes that are primarily assessment related and ends with the purposes that are primarily change related. The reader will note that some reasons for performing these surveys are a mix of both assessment and change.

To Pinpoint Areas of Concern

It is common for companies to have a generalized interest in knowing what aspects of the work setting are satisfying or dissatisfying to employees. They have a wish to "see how things are going," that is, to do an assessment in the organization. This type of evaluation may be aimed at particular issues to see what people feel good or bad about. There may be particular concerns on the minds of management, such as pay or benefits or supervision. In other cases, the interest may be in a particular group of people rather than a topic.

Here the reason is to learn what groups may be "problem" units. This kind of survey can come about if poor labor relations are manifested, for example. In nonunion companies, a group petition may represent a threat of collective action, which can be very upsetting and spark management to learn what pleases or displeases different groups. Efforts may be taken to identify the attitudes associated with pro-union behaviors (the study by Hamner and Smith, 1978, is an example).

The units of interest may also be demographic groups. Unexpected increases in turnover among recent college recruits or in critical skill groups (like programmers, scientists, or engineers) can create an interest in how group staff feel about various issues. In recent years, many companies have been driven by diversity concerns to seek out the opinions of employees grouped by gender and ethnicity.

To Observe Long-Term Trends

Keeping tabs on relevant issues and significant groups over time requires multiple surveys done in comparable ways. The desire for long-term trend data may come out of interest in the impact of management attempts to make meaningful change in response to earlier survey inputs. Or it may arise from an interest in assessing changes caused by shifts in the firm's environment. Such changes can come about from sources as varied as the impact of inflation on people's evaluations of their pay, the effects of competition on feelings of job security, or people's perception of management's competence to deal with technological changes.

To some executives, such surveys are analogous to an annual physical examination. Even if one feels well, it may be worthwhile to check the status of one's vital elements of function against prior data. Here, the orientation is to prevent problems or nip them in the bud. Articles in the popular press suggesting, for example, that "employee morale" is deteriorating generally can also provoke a company's interest in surveys of trends.

To Monitor Program Impact

In a similar fashion, measuring reactions to earlier changes is a legitimate purpose of employee surveys. Such changes include reorganizations, reductions in force, relocations, and the introduction of new personnel practices (like different performance appraisals, career paths, or pay systems).

Other changes that some firms measure include the effects of shifts in ongoing programs. These shifts might include changed methods of parts distribution, different phasing of technical training, increases in pay levels, or alterations in staffing ratios. The impact of such changes may show up more starkly in some employee groups than in others or influence the ratings of some issues more than others, occasionally in unexpected ways. For example, in one company, a change in the "holidays" plan that designated three existing minor holidays as "personal choice" days, allowing them to be taken at any time an employee chose, resulted in more favorable ratings of both the holiday and vacation plans.

These after-the-fact measurements can reveal if organizational changes have had the desired or expected effects, as opposed to negative or unanticipated impacts, and can thus form a basis for making data-based corrections where needed.

To Provide Input for Future Decisions

In some organizations, surveys gather useful data to influence future management decisions. For example, one might want to know which benefit plans the employees would most like to see improved. And even if one does not want to ask this or a similar question of the staff directly, the survey can at least assess which of several plans employees are least satisfied with.

Surveys can uncover employee preferences, such as for a particular geographical location or work hours. They can also analyze needs in areas like training, tools or administrative support, support systems for balancing work and family life, and so on. Again, organizational decisions driven by systematically gathered data are more likely to be on target than someone's pet program unguided by meaningful input.

To Add a Communication Channel

As organizations grow larger or more widespread, management often expresses the need for communication systems that supplement already existing ones. The opinion survey can play that communication system role, getting around the filtering out of negative reports often seen in large organizations.

Surveys are also a means to assess if a plaintive voice is merely a squeaky wheel or really the tip of an iceberg. In addition, the practice of reporting back survey results to participants can encourage a pattern of two-way communication and can be the basis for ongoing dialogues on key issues.

To Perform Organizational Behavior Research

As the training of most organizational survey researchers is in the social sciences, it should be no surprise that many of them use surveys, at least in part, for research on topics of importance in the field of organizational behavior. The landmark leadership studies associated with Ohio State University (Stodgill & Coons, 1957) and the University of Michigan (Likert, 1961) were based on surveys done in various organizations, and other researchers have followed their example. Professional journals are full of studies on the relationship of attitudes and perceptions to outcomes like absenteeism, turnover, pro-union behaviors, and work accidents. Most of these studies are based on data from organizational surveys. The relevant questions are often only a small part of a firm's survey and may be tied to outside criteria. The research topic may be defined by the firm's interest in that topic or by the interests of the researcher. In any case, even a casual reading of the professional literature shows that organizational surveys are often used for organizational behavior research.

Progressive firms are often aware of other groups' research and will use their own regular surveys, or even specially designed surveys, to address similar issues. Although each firm's aim is to serve its own interests, such research sometimes adds substantially to general knowledge.

To Assist Organizational Change and Improvement

In progressive organizations, surveys can evolve into a way of life that encourages change through continuous organizational improvement. By using surveys for self-assessment and then to stimulate and guide desirable changes, organizations make surveys a basis for deliberate efforts at better organizational functioning.

When surveys report data for individual units, the findings focus attention on those units and their problems, sometimes known euphemistically as "opportunities for improvement." Comparisons among units, invidious or not, encourage diagnosis of and action on apparent problems. Such comparisons often focus attention on smaller units as well as larger ones and increase the possibility of unit accountability and responsiveness.

Surveys, if properly done, can thus be seen as a *discipline* in the sense that they can become a system for regularly attending to important issues, unit by unit. The discipline can extend to regular and formal systems for taking actions and reporting them. We may think of this as a discipline in the same sense that an individual's health-promoting habits—such as regularly brushing his or her teeth, getting exercise, and taking care of social and emotional needs that are at risk of being crowded out by the pressure to do more urgent tasks—are a discipline.

An investment of energy and resources is needed to produce organizational improvement built on surveys, and this investment can also pay dividends later. Obviously, time and attention must be given to the total survey process. One aspect of desirable preparation and infrastructure development is the training of managers to deal with the survey data when they receive them. Some of this training, such as how to hold an effective feedback meeting and how to diagnose and solve problems, can have an enormous spillover effect and result in managers who are more effective in many other aspects of their supervisory roles. (For example, see reports by Dodd and Pesci, 1977, and also Smith, 1976.)

The striving for organizational improvement also focuses management attention on particular aspects of organizational functioning. Many firms now use surveys as a way to measure aspects of their functioning that make them more competitive, including quality, customer satisfaction, and internal efficiencies.

Over the last decade or so, there has been a sea change in the types of issues covered in most organizational surveys. My impression, based on scores of surveys, is that "people" issues such as morale, satisfaction with various aspects of work, and industrial relations were the most popular (and sometimes exclusive) topics in the past. Work and family issues and diversity issues are more recent additions. However, it is in the business issues labelled cultural change, quality, and customer satisfaction that we see the biggest increase. The items covered under such rubrics deal with issues vital to organizational success. Their use in surveys is intended to drive and measure *changes* in the ways firms operate and succeed or fail. (A corroboration of these trends may be seen in the Chapter Twelve discussion of the new items added to the Mayflower Group's core set of survey questions over the last two decades.)

To Provide Symbolic Communication

Perhaps the most important, and least understood, strategic purpose of the organizational survey is that of symbolic communication. This function is especially important in attempts at organizational change. Although symbolic communication is sometimes obvious, it is often what sociologists call a latent (or underlying and not always obvious) function. Like it or not, every aspect of the survey process sends a message to the people involved in it. Both the content and the conduct of a survey carry enormous meaning.

When a firm's staff are asked questions about their satisfaction with pay, benefits, and careers, they presume that those areas of satisfaction are important to management. If a survey asks questions about how managers are behaving, both the managers and their staffs are put on notice that those behaviors are important aspects of the manager's role.

We must recognize that the contents of a survey signal and highlight what the firm's leaders want to know about (whether it is customer satisfaction, quality, empowerment, innovation, or a similar topic). In fact, when new signals need to be called because the organization is trying to stimulate different ways of functioning, survey topics and items are powerful educational tools. They communicate to all: "This is what management is interested in. These are the issues management is paying to learn more about."

Unfortunately, when surveys are poorly done, the messages strongly communicated may be unintended ones. This often happens through the conduct (as opposed to the content) of the survey. If no feedback is given to employees, the (perhaps unintended) message that they perceive may be that management does not want to get into a meaningful dialogue, is trying to cover up the results, or has no desire to include employees in dealing with the findings.

A lack of visible action may send the message, "We don't really care what you say."

Ignoring the data, taking no action, or not communicating any actions taken might seem to send no message. But a lack of a visible response to survey results actually communicates a negative message. This message may be interpreted in various ways, that employees lack importance, that the survey was a charade or ruse, or that management does not care about employees' perceptions and opinions. In any case, lack of response is a powerful, if negative, symbolic communication to employees.

However, it seems that more and more executives are using survey measures to see how their change efforts are going. They report out the results and use them to push their change agendas further. Some even use the measures as part of a scorecard for evaluating and rewarding management at different levels.

Conclusion

In the last half century, organizational surveys have grown from rarities to popular and potentially powerful tools for management to use. They can serve a variety of purposes, from being tools for numerous types of assessment to being levers for far-reaching organizational change.

In a fundamental shift, more organizations than ever are using surveys as strategic tools to drive and measure organizational change. Going beyond the traditional measures of morale and employee satisfaction, many firms have fashioned their surveys to carry new messages and gather new data. These innovations try to gauge how well the organization comprehends new circumstances and acts in appropriately different ways. Such measurements, providing useful knowledge on which to base and judge action, have become part of many firms' efforts to succeed in an increasingly competitive and demanding environment.

As we shall see later in this volume, the technology for administering surveys, processing and analyzing data, and communicating the results has become enormously sophisticated. Still, we must recognize that technical and methodological skills and tools are necessary but not sufficient for organizational surveys to be successful.

A recent poll (Management Decisions Systems, 1993) of one hundred firms using surveys shows several obstacles to effective practice. The leading obstacle is reported to be "failure to provide feedback and lack of action planning and follow-through." This is followed closely by "lack of middle and senior management commitment." The third obstacle, "low perceived value of the surveys," may be caused by the other two (p. 6).

The critical ingredient for fruitful organizational surveys is a wise and committed leadership. Using surveys well requires a deep understanding by top management of its reasons for doing a survey in the first place. Top management must have the will and energy to make use of the survey process. Organizations take their cues from their leaders and act accordingly.

The full magnitude of an organizational survey reveals itself over time; a survey is a process and not an event. Top management can play an important part at several points. True leaders can speak out early and shape the social reality and meaning of surveys for others in the organization. They can force attention to the results, against competing priorities. They can monitor and follow up on actions in response to survey findings. They can reward and recognize successful users of the data and act as role models.

Survey researchers working in organizations must have the professional and practical skills to conduct surveys well. But they cannot simply wait for a wise and committed executive leadership to emerge. Successful survey professionals also tutor and coach top managers on their roles in the survey process. Acting as ghostwriters, survey professionals will sometimes even draft speeches and letters from the management to support the process. Often, as part of a human resource management group, survey professionals will set up the procedures for line managers at various levels to review survey results, the action plans taken in response, and the follow-through on such plans. Although these are line management responsibilities, the survey researchers must often do behind-the-scenes work to energize and maintain the process.

It is important to recognize that survey professionals must have the understanding, interpersonal skills, and personal drive to educate and forge a partnership with top management if organizational surveys are to be well used. If the professional community is successful in creating such bonds with top management, the coming years will be very exciting indeed.

References

Babbie, E. (1990). *Survey research methods* (2nd ed.). Belmont, CA: Wadsworth.

Babbie, E. (1992). *The practice of social research* (6th ed.). Belmont, CA: Wadsworth.

Backstrom, C. H., & Hursh-Cesar, G. (1981). *Survey research* (2nd ed.). New York: Wiley.

Delaney, J. T., Lewin, D., & Ichniowski, C. (1988). *Human resource management policies and practices in American firms.* New York: Industrial Relations Research Center, Graduate School of Business, Columbia University.

Dillman, D. A. (1978). *Mail and telephone surveys: The total design method.* New York: Wiley.

Dodd, W. E., & Pesci, M. L. (1977, June). Managing morale through survey feedback. *Business Horizons,* pp. 36–45.

Dunham, R. B., & Smith, F. J. (1979). *Organizational surveys: An internal assessment of organizational health.* Glenview, IL: Scott, Foresman.

Fowler, F. J., Jr. (1988). *Survey research methods* (Rev. ed.). Newbury Park, CA: Sage.

Gallup, G. (1988). Employee research: From nice to know to need to know. *Personnel Journal, 67,* 42–43.

Hamner, W. C., & Smith, F. J. (1978). Work attitudes as predictors of unionization activity. *Journal of Applied Psychology, 63,* 143–421.

Kahn, R. L., & Cannell, C. F. (1957). *The dynamics of interviewing: Theory, technique, and cases.* New York: Wiley.

Kish, L. (1965). *Survey sampling.* New York: Wiley.

Kraut, A. I., & Freeman, F. (1992). *Upward communications: Programs in American industry* (Tech. Rep. No. 152). Greensboro, NC: Center for Creative Leadership.

Lawler, E. E. III, Nadler, D. A., & Cammann, C. (1980). *Organizational assessment: Perspectives on the measurement of organizational behavior and the quality of work life.* New York: Wiley.

Likert, R. (1961). *New patterns of management.* New York: McGraw-Hill.

Management Decisions Systems. (1993). *Employee surveys: Current and future practices.* Darien, CT: Author.

Nadler, D. A. (1977). *Feedback and organization development: Using data-based methods.* Reading, MA: Addison-Wesley.

Payne, S. (1951). *The art of asking questions.* Princeton, NJ: Princeton University Press.

Rea, L. M., & Parker, R. A. (1992). *Designing and conducting survey research: A comprehensive guide.* San Francisco: Jossey-Bass.

Rossi, P. H., Wright, J. D., & Anderson, A. B. (1983). *Handbook of survey research.* San Diego, CA: Academic Press.

Smith, P. E. (1976). Management modeling training to improve morale and customer satisfaction. *Personnel Psychology, 29,* 351–359.

Stodgill, R. M., & Coons, A. E. (1957). *Leader behavior: Its description and measurement.* Columbus: Ohio State University, Bureau of Business Research.

Stouffer, S. A., & Associates. (1947–1950). *The American soldier: Studies in social psychology in World War II* (Vols. 1–4). Princeton, NJ: Princeton University Press.

Sudman, S., & Bradburn, N. M. (1982). *Asking questions: A practical guide to questionnaire design.* San Francisco: Jossey-Bass.

Viteles, M. S. (1953). *Motivation and morale in industry.* New York: Norton.

Warwick, D. P., & Lininger, C. A. (1975). *The sample survey: Theory and practice.* New York: McGraw-Hill.

PART 1

Purposes and Uses

In Part One, we take an in-depth look at how organizational surveys are used and the purposes to which they are put. Each author or set of authors looks at a different purpose or group of related purposes, showing the broad variety of purposes served by organizational surveys, from assessment to organizational and individual change.

In Chapter One, Catherine Higgs and Steven Ashworth cover an interesting mix of traditional and novel uses of survey data for assessment and research. Although some of the uses and purposes they describe are "plain vanilla" evaluations of employee opinions and attitudes, much in these assessments goes to issues that are quite topical, such as the balance between work and family life and workplace diversity. Higgs and Ashworth make the useful clarification that much of what is called *assessment* is also straightforward, if descriptive, *business research*. It is the process of obtaining and producing usable information to help an organization achieve its purposes. They also list a wide array of topics that can be researched through an ongoing survey program. It is an impressively wide-ranging array, satisfying many management data needs. As shown in the case study they present, a program of periodic organizational surveys also permits (and encourages) programmatic research, with later surveys building on the findings and actions taken after earlier surveys.

Warner Burke, Celeste Coruzzi, and Allan Church use a diagnostic model in Chapter Two to illustrate how surveys can be used as significant interventions for organizational change. Their model provides a set of concepts with which researchers can explore the key variables of organizational behavior and outputs. It also provides a language and set of concepts that can be used to communicate with management about what the survey measures and why what is measured is important. To illustrate their mode of working, Burke, Coruzzi, and Church present a case study featuring a survey that was repeated during a period of great organizational upheaval. Changes in the survey results showed shifts in employees' perceptions and even shifts in the relationships among the major variables. The authors explain how these relationships can be used by management as *levers* for future change.

Using organizational surveys for cultural change is the topic covered by David Wagner and Janet Spencer in Chapter Three. After defining cultural change, they give clear examples of how each stage of an organizational survey is an opportunity to help change a firm's culture. These experienced practitioners see each step, from questionnaire design to administration to the reporting of results and the survey feedback process, as an opportunity to foster change. Two notions stand out in this chapter. One is the need for a process that transforms survey data into information, then to knowledge, and ultimately into action. The other is the desirability of creating new *metrics*, the measures used by an organization to gauge and analyze performance in relation to the achievement of the organization's strategic goals.

A broader view yet is given by William Schiemann in his chapter on driving organizational change by understanding the impacts on multiple stakeholders. His thesis is that organizations must have alignment between their strategies and the impact on employees and also on other key groups, such as customers, communities, shareholders, and even regulators. In integrating the work of others, Schiemann provides some models for examining the links between survey data from various groups. These models can help us evaluate the strategic alignment of critical stakeholders with organizational performance. He also makes a strong case for employee data as an indicator of current and future organizational performance.

The use of survey technology, and multisource feedback in particular, for individual assessment and change is discussed by David Bracken in Chapter Five. Popularly known as 360-degree feedback, multisource feedback is an attempt to get systematic, integrated data from subordinates, peers, and superiors. Judging by current promotional materials, it is a timely topic indeed. In many respects, these feedback tools are built on the success of organizational surveys, but they also draw on concepts of management development to a great degree. In doing so, they raise many critical questions about topics to be covered on surveys, issues around data collection and reporting, and potential abuses. This chapter is an extensive and informative discussion of a process deceptively simple in appearance and one with strong implications for other organizational surveys.

Organizational Surveys
Tools for Assessment and Research

A. Catherine Higgs
Steven D. Ashworth

Employee surveys can be an excellent means for conducting organizational research. Certainly not everyone holds this view; some would separate scientific research from the more pragmatic aspects of employee opinion survey research. Hippocrates may have started the controversy when he wrote, "There are in fact two things, science and opinion; the former begets knowledge, the latter ignorance." While employee surveys do not always advance basic science (and while we are not prepared to refute Hippocrates!), they often contribute to important organizational decisions. In this chapter, we review and provide examples of employee opinion surveys used as tools for applied business research, and we suggest a direction for the future evolution for employee survey research. Our emphasis is a pragmatic one—how to address both practical and scientific questions simultaneously. In other words,

Note: We would like to acknowledge the collaborative efforts of our colleagues at the Allstate Research and Planning Center in the preparation of this chapter: Wendy Abbott, Wendy Arendt, Linda Carr, Tanny Joyce, Timothy Oleno, Ellen Papper, Marion Silar, and Pauline Velez. It has been a pleasure to work with so many talented people, and each one has been a partner in learning. We also acknowledge the many colleagues in other organizations who have shared their work with us over the years, and who have assisted and advised us with the design of our own research.

how to generate information for real decisions by the organization and, at the same time, contribute to the general field of knowledge about effective organizational management.

In this chapter, we make use of Zikmund's concept of *business research,* defined as the "systematic and objective process of gathering, recording, and analyzing data for aid in making business decisions" (Zikmund, 1988, p. 6). As described by Zikmund, there are three levels of research: exploratory, descriptive, and causal.

Exploratory research is research in its early stages of development. Often the researcher is gathering information that will lead to further, higher-level research. An example of an exploratory survey question is, "How many children do you have in your household who require child care arrangements?"

Descriptive research requires a little more knowledge and understanding of the research domain but often simply elicits characteristics of the topic of interest. For example, a descriptive research question might ask, "Are you satisfied with the company's child care referral program?" This question would be aimed at measuring the impact of the company's program from the employee's perspective.

The *causal level* of research requires the testing of cause-and-effect relationships among study variables. In our child care example, a causal research study might develop hypotheses based on the economics of the family situation and test whether economic condition predicts a preference for on-site versus at-home child care arrangements.

In organizations, research flows from one level to another, usually beginning with exploratory or descriptive research and sometimes leading to causal research. Often exploratory or descriptive research is all that is required or supported by organizational decision makers, with causal research seen by these executives as an interesting luxury. Nevertheless, exploratory and descriptive research often serve as the evolutionary groundwork for a network of follow-up studies that in their totality represent a causal research program.

We also adopt a broad definition of organizational surveys in this chapter. While surveys of employee *opinions* may have formed the bulk of organizational research done in the past, current survey programs are as likely to gather attitudes, preferences, and even behavioral intentions and observations as they are to gather merely opinions. Survey methods are core research tools, particularly valuable in large and geographically dispersed organizations. Surveys are often used for research studies that are sponsored by industry groups, academic affiliations, or commercial enterprises and that compare workers across dozens or hundreds of organizations.

Evolution of Organizational Surveys

The evolution of the use of surveys within organizations basically parallels the development of the fields of industrial and organizational psychology and human resource management. The changing topics and uses of organizational surveys also reflect broad trends and issues within society that affect the world of work.

Although surveys based on self-report questionnaires were used in studies of both individual workers and jobs in the first few decades of the twentieth century, formal programs of employee opinion surveys were not undertaken until the 1930s (Lawler, 1986). In 1938, Sears, for example, began its survey program, which continues to be active today, having been periodically updated as company strategy and structure have changed. The early focus of many employee opinion survey programs in the 1930s was the worker groups who were possible candidates for union organizing drives. This focus broadened through the next thirty years to an emphasis on worker satisfaction and on work environment factors affecting satisfaction (Barmash, 1993; Dunham & Smith, 1979).

The early 1970s witnessed a shift in organizational survey research from concrete and job-specific inquiries to climate studies (such as those of Schneider, 1975). Climate studies were broader in scope, dealt with people's perceptions of a great variety of organizational practices and procedures, and frequently included an organizational level of inquiry. Similarly, formal employee opinion surveys also began to shift to include questions about job characteristics, work styles, and such organizational issues as managerial effectiveness, job stress, and job design or productivity.

The 1980s brought an emphasis on participative management in organizations and, with it, questions about participative management style and employee involvement and an interest in feedback mechanisms in formal employee opinion survey programs.

As a result, many companies substantially redesigned their survey programs. A common principle for redesign was to focus the survey on questions that made sense at the work group level and were actionable in work group feedback meetings. To support the work group component, companies developed survey feedback guides, training materials, and other aids. For example, IBM, Bank of America, and the Boeing Company all did exceptional work in this area in the 1980s.

During the 1990s, surveys continue to reflect both changing social and organizational trends and the evolution of research knowledge. Expanding organizations such as Intel and Microsoft have begun employee opinion survey research programs. In both high-tech and more traditional business sectors, there is a common and dominant theme to recent changes in formal organizational survey programs in the attempt to establish a linkage between employee survey results and organizational outcomes such as customer satisfaction, process efficiencies, and financial returns. (*Human Resource Planning* devoted a special issue in 1991 to a series of articles on these potential linkages; see Tornow, 1991). Surveys are also being used as part of organizational change efforts called, variously, reengineering, reinvention, process redesign, and so on.

Table 1.1 summarizes these historical trends and future projections in the purpose, content, focus, and methodology of the organizational survey. The table is derived from reviews of the literature cited in this chapter and from our personal knowledge of unpublished results of studies conducted in many companies.

In the remainder of this chapter, we review and give examples of organizational survey research. Unless otherwise identified, the examples cited are drawn from work we are familiar with through our professional affiliations (like the Society for Industrial and Organizational Psychology and the Academy of Management) and benchmarking organizations (like the Mayflower Group and various industry-specific and geographical location–specific groups).

Although employee survey research is under way in many organizations, much of it is unpublished, and some is considered to be proprietary. In fact, because of the practitioner emphasis of this book, we have concentrated on examples that are unpublished (and perhaps unlikely ever to be published) but that demonstrate the actual use of employee surveys to address organizational questions. Indeed, some of what we consider to be business research

Table 1.1. Summary of Changes in Organizational Survey Research Since the 1930s.

	1930s–1940s	1950s–1960s	1970s–1980s	1990s–Present	Future
Purpose	Measure employee morale and emotional adjustment; decrease unionization activities	Measure job satisfaction, presumably to improve organizational productivity	Predict important organizational outcomes: turnover, absenteeism, and stress	Provide linkage to key company strategies: quality, customer satisfaction, and HR strategic focus	Increased focus on business strategy; measurement of bottom-line impact of HR and readiness for change
Content	Morale	Job satisfaction	Job satisfaction, attitudes toward specific programs, and job characteristics	Employees as participant observers, behavioral intentions, and actual behavior	Even more behavioral, perceptions of company strategy
Focus	Individual worker	Individual worker	Individual worker, job level, and total organization	Organizational, job level, business unit, and team	Teams, other new organizational structures, nonemployee workforce, and customers
Methodology utilized	Interviews and questionnaires	Paper and pencil questionnaires	Standardized paper and pencil or scannable forms	Scannable forms, computer-administered questionnaires, computer-aided interviews, and interactive response pads	Computers, e-mail, and Internet

may not be "publishable," given the requirements of academic journals. Nevertheless, within the definition of business research, all the studies we cite have provided valuable exploratory or descriptive information for business decision making and have sometimes tested causal hypotheses.

Survey Purpose

Organizational surveys may be conducted for a variety of purposes. Many organizations still use surveys for traditional employee relations and employee participation purposes, but others have extended the techniques to additional topics. The following section highlights some research that has been done within traditional organizational survey programs and reviews some actual surveys that demonstrate the flexibility of the techniques and the range of research that can be pursued. It concludes with a detailed case example of a long-term organizational survey research program.

To Measure Employee Relations, Morale, and Involvement

The traditional employee opinion survey is often geared to identifying employee morale concerns or to involving employees and managers in joint problem solving. In fact, what many people mean when they refer to "employee opinion surveys" is this traditional approach, which is by far the widest use of surveys within organizations. In most companies, a standard set of questions is used over time and given to most units. The survey is administered throughout the entire organization at least once every two or three years, either at a single designated time or with units participating on a rolling basis over the two- or three-year period. Results are summarized by unit or division. Reports are supplied to managers and often to all other employees as well. Feedback or discussion meetings are held among managers and employees to perform action planning to address the problems identified. Research within this formal program structure usually concerns the basic employment satisfaction issues addressed in the survey (for example, jobs, managers, pay, benefits, and working conditions) and sometimes concern the survey process or questionnaire itself.

To Predict Organizational Outcomes

Some innovative researchers have tied organizational survey results to actual consequences for the organization itself. An example of using survey results to develop models to predict future organizational outcomes is the work of Frank Smith. Smith developed a variety of indices using employee opinions to predict outcomes such as absenteeism or union activity (Dunham & Smith, 1979). More recently, researchers have developed models based on employee surveys to predict other organizational outcomes, such as future levels of customer satisfaction (Schneider, 1991) and company branch effectiveness (Johnson, Ryan, & Schmit, 1994).

To Segment Employees

Another example of research accomplished with organizational survey program data is the approach that treats survey data much like a market research database. Employees are regarded as the customers and the company and the job are regarded as the products or services purchased. From this perspective, a wide range of market research segmentation questions become appropriate (for example, demographic analyses by tenure, job level, division, business strategy, compensation plan, gender, racial or ethnic group, and age are used to segment different groups).

For this kind of research, useful data analysis techniques include classification and segmentation methods like CHAID (chi-square automatic interaction detection) or CART (classification and regression tree analysis) (Breiman, Freidman, Olshen, & Stone, 1984). These two techniques have been extensively used in marketing research and are particularly useful for organizational survey data as well (Magidson, 1988). Their real beauty is their ability to discover interactions and configurational effects that cannot be easily discovered through linear techniques such as regression.

To Compare Employee Perspectives Across Organizations

Significant research based on survey data across multiple organizations is possible when the organizations ask basically the same questions in their opinion surveys. This situation can occur when organizations participate in a consortium, agree to participate in multiorganizational academic research, or are all clients of the same consulting firm.

Kraut, Manfredo, and Kelley's study (1995) of intrinsic and extrinsic satisfaction factors across thirty different companies is a good example of a multiorganizational approach to employee survey research. Their study required not only multiorganizational data but also a survey reflecting employee views about what was recognized and rewarded in each employee's own organization.

Organizational Survey Research for Other Purposes

Experience with formal organizational survey programs and the sensitivity of survey information have tended to make organizations cautious about using survey approaches to research other employment issues. For example, we know of several companies that did employee turnover studies in the mid to late 1980s, when employee turnover rates generally were much higher than most companies are experiencing in the mid 1990s. One company reported being apprehensive about how former employees would react to survey telephone calls to their homes; however, in this case, the company's concerns were unfounded; interviewers could not get respondents off the phone!

Based on similar experiences, other companies have since undertaken employee surveys on other sensitive topics such as affirmative action and diversity. Many of these surveys are not single events but part of a series of related studies over several years. The wide range of topics now addressed in organizational survey research is illustrated by the following list of topics researched by many U.S. companies over the past ten years.

- *Benefits, pay, and company programs.* Examples include
   Comprehensive benefits surveys focusing on awareness, understanding, and use of current benefits and projected future needs and interests.
   Pay and incentives surveys determining understanding of pay and incentives programs, the extent to which they are perceived as fair and motivating, and whether appropriate information and management explanation have been provided.

Affirmative action and equal employment opportunity surveys asking how company efforts were perceived, how individuals felt they were treated, and whether programs were perceived as fair.

Similar surveys on specific company programs, including those relating to family and child care, diversity, community and charities, nonsmoking programs, employee assistance, job posting, substance abuse testing, new work sites, transportation regulations or van pools, work schedule flexibility, office security procedures, and so on.

- *Surveys about employment functions or events.* Examples include
  Recruitment and selection surveys determining the factors that attracted people to the company, which factor was most important, and how the recruiting process was perceived. This category includes traditional job analysis studies conducted by survey methods.

  Performance appraisal surveys asking for perceptions of performance appraisal policy, descriptions of how the policy is perceived to work and what events occur, and reports of frequency of specific actions exhibited by workers, managers, and teams.

  Training and program evaluation surveys, including traditional studies of satisfaction with training studies, reports of on-the-job changes after training for both self and others, and reports of specific events or behaviors occurring as part of program implementation.

  Career development and succession-planning surveys asking which factors are seen to be the ones that help people "get ahead."

  Retention and turnover surveys focusing on why employees leave the organization, employees' perceptions of managers and work climate and how a new environment is different, and whether employees would return after they have "seen the other side."

- *Surveys about organizational processes and change.* Examples include
  Employee involvement and total quality initiative surveys measuring employee awareness and understanding and asking for reports of key events that have occurred, assessment of success of such programs, recommendations for change, and satisfaction with the company's efforts.

Internal customer satisfaction surveys, which may be one of two types, focusing on overall impressions of services from a particular group or department or on satisfaction with a particular transaction, product, or service provided by an employee or small team of employees.

Job and organizational design surveys eliciting descriptions of characteristics of jobs and job duties, descriptions of workflow and work bottlenecks, satisfaction with work tools and environment, and characteristics of teams.

- *Surveys about the impact of business strategies.* Examples include

Communication effectiveness surveys asking whether employees are aware of, understand, and agree with the organization's stated strategies or operational goals and whether employees have modified their behavior to support implementation of those strategies or goals.

Strategy implementation surveys determining whether, in employees' view, what the company intends in its interactions with customers actually occurs as designed.

Competitive market intelligence surveys focusing on the trends that employees are observing among local competitors and that customers are reporting.

Public image and political context surveys asking about employees' impressions of how the company appears to customers, employees' impressions of political or public issues, employees' suggestions about how to influence the public, and employees' willingness to play a role in public information campaigns.

Effects of mergers, acquisitions, restructuring, or downsizing surveys asking how employees feel, asking what their issues of concern are, and contrasting rumors and facts.

This list illustrates that organizational surveys can be used to investigate a wide range of companywide issues and research concerns. To view an organizational survey as merely a traditional assessment of morale is a very limited interpretation.

Case Study

The following case study illustrates how one organization used organizational survey research as a tool for practical decision making. It also illustrates the point that survey research is often evolutionary—one study leads to another and the resulting network of valuable information collected not only aids in business decisions but also begins to form a body of research leading to causal hypotheses.

The research program in this case consists of a series of studies conducted over seven years; each study derived from the previous work, and each used organizational survey methods in some respect. The first study was a mail survey of approximately 4,000 employees, who answered open- and close-ended questions about affirmative action processes within the company and stated their views of their own work and career options. In spite of the organization's twenty-year experience with affirmative action, executives were surprised by the contrasts between the views of different groups.

The second study focused on employees' understanding of the concepts of affirmative action and diversity and the perceived differences between these two concepts. It was an internally developed survey, mostly open-ended, mailed to 5,500 employees, and receiving responses from approximately 2,200. An effort was made to determine if employees saw diversity as a business or strategic issue for the company as well as a personal issue for themselves.

Based on the results of this second study, the company began a substantial diversity education effort. The education centered on diversity as a concept and defined diversity as a business issue, highlighting the diversity of the company's customer base.

The third study was undertaken as part of the second phase of diversity education, which was development of the actual skills and behaviors to be used in a diversity-aware workplace. The research component was part of a 360-degree profile instrument used in the educational process, in which all managers participated. In addition to providing individual feedback to every training participant, the data were also analyzed for a companywide view, known as a human resource planning analysis, which profiled the various sectors of the workforce according to their strengths and vulnerabilities. At the same time, the fourth study was collecting survey data that included answers to a series of questions on diversity topics.

A fifth research study is being planned that will correlate both skill profiles and survey data with organizational measures such as specific observed behavioral changes, customer satisfaction by customer segment, and operational and financial measures. This organization's commitment to its policy direction is substantial. When asked about the impact of recent U.S. political trends on company policy, the organization's senior executive was quoted as saying, "We had good business reasons for starting this, and we have no plans to change. Our commitment to diversity will be a factor in our future success." (Survey results are unlikely to be published outside the organization.)

Changes in Question Format

Approaches that use open-ended responses are sometimes more effective for gathering employee input than are rating-scale or fixed-response surveys. For example, in a study of how well employees understand a company's diversity program, an open-ended question like, "If you were explaining diversity to someone, what would you tell them?" might be effective. When measuring the specific level of knowledge about a company program, however, a question might look more like a test item: for example, "Match the following program names with their explanations." A survey that uses a variety of question types enables research that goes beyond mere awareness or attitude; it is often necessary, for example, to ascertain employees' basic understanding of a topic before further questions are pursued about how their understanding of that topic affects their decisions or actions. In cases where the goal is to distinguish among employee preferences (for example, in benefits or training), questions that involve rankings or modified versions of trade-off analyses can be used.

In recent years, many researchers have moved to the use of behavioral reports or observations, basing their shift on the theory that employees are both participants in and observers of a company's strategy, policies, and practices (Schneider & Chung, 1994). For this type of research, researchers are less likely to ask employees how satisfied they are with a company practice (for example, "How satisfied are you with the performance appraisal process?") and more likely to ask about behaviors or observations related to the practice (for example, "How many times in the past year have you had a performance appraisal meeting with your manager?"). Certainly the frequency of an appraisal may not indicate an employee's satisfaction level with the practice. New employees may desire more frequent appraisals than longer-term employees, for example. But when the process being measured is well established, accurate measurement of whether an action occurred is critical. As Schneider and Bowen (1995) put it: "Employees are . . . terrific and accurate at identifying the kinds of *internal* service issues to which attention must be paid. They know, for example, the ways in which marketing and operations management fail to coordinate their efforts; they know the problems human resources management has in keeping a well-trained staff coming to work on time and not quitting; they know the ins and outs of what must happen to facilitate the efforts of those who deal with the end-user consumer" (p. 247).

Research on Methods and Measurement

An extensive array of research has been conducted by scientists investigating such issues as order effects, scale variations, response tendencies and biases, group differences, and a variety of other survey methodology and measurement topics (Schuman & Presser, 1981). Although some of this research has been laboratory study, much of it has been conducted within the context of ongoing surveys. Research aimed at survey improvement can often be embedded within a survey without affecting the primary survey goals. Research on item-ordering effects, item-wording effects, neutral response categories, data aggregation, and item scale reversals can be conducted simply by distributing different survey forms to selected samples of respondents. For example, a study of how item readability affects responses found that the higher the reading level of a survey item, the more likely a respondent is to answer using the middle or neutral response category (Velez, 1993). Research of this type is usually aimed at improving the quality of data gathered by the survey program.

Not all research leads to easily implemented solutions. For example, in one of our studies, we found that respondents answered an overall summary item differently when it was located early in the questionnaire as opposed to being the final item. This research indicated that we needed to hold item positions constant in the survey program, since we were interested in comparing trends over time. While order effects have been found in other studies (see, for example, Kraut, Wolfson, & Rothenberg, 1975), few pragmatic general suggestions have been made concerning optimal positioning of survey items, other than holding their positions constant, and even that is not always easy to do. Survey instruments are often dynamic tools, increasing or decreasing in size over time and subject to many political and organizational pressures (try arguing with the company executive who wants his or her favorite item placed at the beginning of the survey!).

Item or scale variation is also a very important research area for researchers engaged in an active and ongoing organizational survey program. There is constant pressure in such programs to change item wording, scale formats, and so on to meet changing organizational needs. While it may be tempting to allow organizational clients to change item wording from, say, "my manager" to "my team leader," research in other social science disciplines suggests that even minor wording changes can cause dramatic shifts in response patterns. Schuman and Presser (1981) cite research that showed that changing the phrase "should forbid" to "should not allow" caused a 17-point shift in positive responses to a question on public support of communism.

Further, there is often pressure to compile historical trend information on items, especially when survey systems are being used to measure organizational progress or continuing success of a program. Without research to establish the equivalency of changed items, a great deal of continuity can be lost when item responses change due to wording differences.

Lessons from Other Research Specialties

Survey research has a long history in several disciplines in addition to industrial and organizational psychology. In fact, many of the research findings on item effects, item framing, and context effects were discovered by sociologists and social psychologists working in the areas of public opinion polling and political science (see Achen, 1975). Other research specialties, such as marketing research, have contributed greatly to methodological innovations in conducting and analyzing survey research. These innovations include the use of conjoint analysis or perceptual mapping techniques (used on consumer survey results) to measure preferences accurately and to cluster respondents into groups with similar attitude patterns (Segal, 1982).

Organizational researchers can learn yet another lesson from market researchers, who are often quite effective at communicating study results through colorful use of language. Descriptive terms such as "young urban professional" or "empty nester" convey research results in an intuitive, understandable way that encourages broad understanding of the concepts being measured. Research that is designed and communicated in a way that is useful to decision makers has led to many effective marketing, economic, and political decisions.

Internal Versus External Researchers

The various types of organizational survey research are often performed by different types of individuals. Organizations such as Allstate, Ford, Microsoft, and dozens of others have a staff of research professionals who conduct survey and other research as internal consultants. Other organizations rely heavily on external consultants or academicians for research. Survey research can be successfully implemented in a wide variety of ways—by using internal staff only, by hiring external consultants, or by collaborating with academics. In deciding between internal and external research professionals, several questions should be considered: What skills are demanded by the research? To what extent will organizational savvy be required to successfully implement the research? How unusual is the organization or the research topic to be addressed?

Skills

For the most part, the skills required to conduct successful survey research inside a corporation are not a function of the researcher's work setting. This is not to say, however, that anyone can conduct a successful organizational research project. The ability to develop an effective survey instrument (or other research tool) usually comes from experience in conducting surveys, not just from education about surveys or survey methods. If research requires knowledge of a corporation's culture or management practices, internal professionals may be better able to meet the organization's research needs. Conversely, if the research calls for the use of a standardized or published research tool such as the Job Descriptive

Index (JDI) (Smith, Kendall, & Hulin, 1969), consultants and/or academics will often be most experienced in the instrument's use. With the current emphasis on quality and benchmarking, companies may choose consulting arrangements because they offer access to sources of benchmarking information for companies that are not members of large consortia such as the Mayflower Group (see Bracken, 1992; the Mayflower Group is described in Chapter Eleven).

Organizational Savvy

Skill requirements for successful research are not limited to survey development abilities. Successful research may begin with a carefully developed research tool, but it will not be totally successful unless the researchers are skilled at communicating results, identifying action plans, consulting on implications, and planning implementation of indicated remedies. There are times, in other words, when organizational savvy is the most important requirement. Knowledge of how an organization works, who makes decisions, potential barriers to implementation, and even the current state of labor relations is critical to the ultimate success of research, since use of research results often involves the development and deployment of action plans.

Our experience has been that external researchers can be successful in implementing organizational research but that they are usually more successful when collaborating with organizational insiders. Some of the most effective research we have conducted in our own organization has involved extensive collaboration with academic researchers (for example, Ashworth, Higgs, Schneider, Shepherd, & Carr, 1995; Campion, Medsker, & Higgs, 1993), and this pattern seems apparent in other organizations as well (for example, Ford (see Johnson, Ryan, & Schmit, 1994), IBM (see Kraut, Pedigo, McKenna, & Dunnette, 1989), Sears (see Dunham & Smith, 1979), and undoubtedly many others.

Organizational Uniqueness and Survey Design

Organizational researchers sometimes assume that customization of a survey instrument or research design is required when the company or situation is unique, and often this customization is requested or even demanded by research clients when it is not necessary. There is a long history of successful research using standard research tools, especially when the research topic is well understood (as job satisfaction, job stress, and turnover are, for example).

However, when organizational researchers are asked to measure a company-specific topic such as the corporate vision or a benefit plan, internal resources can be invaluable. If the program to be measured has never been tried before or if the organization is structured completely differently from others in the same industry, it is likely that internal support will be needed.

Why Survey Research Programs Prosper in Some Organizations and Not in Others

Although successful organizational survey research programs have prospered in some organizations for decades, in other organizations, research efforts come and go, and in yet others, they never get started. What accounts for success?

To our knowledge, the success of organizational survey research programs has never been a formal research topic. To begin addressing that topic, we interviewed managers of several successful programs. The following key factors for an effective organizational survey research program are based on their assessments.

Research is used as a business tool. The organization supports business research in general—as evidenced by its support for research in a variety of other areas such as marketing, investments, product development, and so on—and understands the value of research in yielding fact-based business decisions.

Research demonstrates that the workforce is valued. The organization values its employees and recognizes that its strategy is implemented by the sum total of individual employees' acts.

Research is practical and useful. Each organizational survey research project or program has an immediate practical use to someone, and results often play a direct role in the company's decisions. Usefulness of results is enhanced by the research group's consistent follow-up and consulting.

The research program has vision. Leaders of the survey research program have a broad vision of how it fits into the organization's business strategy. The research group has established itself as competent and objective. Reporting study results is managed with objectivity and candor.

Organizational development tools are used in the implementation of research. The research group understands the importance of communicating and marketing its capabilities. In fact, the most successful research groups operate on a consulting model, modified for an internal market. The research group understands organizational change processes and how they work and also understands the range of potential influence techniques, and it uses these tools in its work.

Efficient project management is utilized. Finally, whatever management model it uses, whether a team of self-managed colleagues or a more traditional model, the research group also demonstrates effective project management skills. Group members know which resources to assign to various tasks and how to sequence tasks and projects. They can juggle dozens of potentially conflicting project demands. Their management efforts are geared to giving clients clear expectations and meeting client commitments.

A successful organizational survey research program is not an accident. It depends on many of the same skills as other organizational influence and change programs. None of the managers interviewed mentioned professional publication of results as a factor in organizational sponsorship of their research. That finding is probably the best explanation of why only a portion of study results are ever published. Usually organizational leaders see no benefit to the company or impact on business results from publishing.

There is no publication performance requirement for the company's researchers and often no organizational support for publication. Researchers' daily workloads leave no time available for preparing publications. Moreover, the skills researchers have developed to be successful within organizations can be different than those needed for successful publication. Appeals for scholarship can get lost in the whirl of daily business activity. When publication occurs, often an academic colleague has supplied the motivation and helped with the work.

The Future of Organizational Survey Research

The future of survey research in organizations is solid. One trend we have noticed is the vast proliferation of surveys that a typical employee is subjected to as the result of reengineering efforts, Total Quality Management endeavors, diversity programs, and other human resource innovations (Rollins, 1994). In a 1992 survey of human resource professionals, 73 percent reported that their human resource department would have greater involvement than before in implementing business strategies over the next two to three years, suggesting an increasing demand for employee information (Caudron, 1994, p. 58).

At the same time, technological advances such as electronic mail, groupware, and the Internet are giving organizations the ability to communicate very quickly even with a widely distributed workforce. The frequency of organizational surveys made possible by technology does raise concerns about whether adequate time will be spent using the results of one survey before another is undertaken. Also, if results come so quickly after one another that they cannot be effectively utilized and communicated, employees may become annoyed with extensive surveys and not respond to future ones, making studies increasingly difficult to complete.

Additional indirect effects will come about as technology changes the nature of the organization itself. The professional and popular press have popularized the concept of "virtual organizations," where the physical workspace is no longer a vital element of the work. Future research in organizations will need to consider a very different looking workplace (O'Hara-Devereaux & Johansen, 1994).

Organizational Trends Driving Survey Research

In the future, a researcher who desires to gather the opinions of the workforce may need to gather data from traditional employees, employees working at home, contract workers inside the organization, and perhaps even employees of another organization working in a strategic alliance with the host company. The trend toward increasing categories of workforce members creates both challenges and opportunities for organizations in the area of survey research.

In addition, future surveys will need to look not only at individual attitudes but at the shared attitudes and values of work teams. Organizations completely committed to the team approach may even stop measuring attitudes at the individual worker level.

Who will be the customer or client of organizational survey research in the future? How will survey findings be summarized if job categories or work units no longer exist? Organizational change is becoming so widespread and rapid that survey research in the future will likely precede and contribute to subsequent theory and causal studies.

The future is also uncertain for corporate managers, who seem to be the first casualties of the new organizational trends. These same trends will require changes in the implementation of survey findings in the organization that positions its managers as the main customers of survey research but may present an opportunity for the organization that uses surveys to hold people accountable for their behavior toward others.

These trends also bring opportunities for researchers interested in using survey research to influence the future of their organizations. More and more, research is conducted to link employee attitudes to corporate strategies (Higgs, Ashworth, & Crist, 1995; Hinrichs, Kraut, & Schiemann, 1995) or to important organizational outcomes such as customer service (Schneider & Bowen, 1995) or organizational financial performance (Johnson, Ryan, & Schmit, 1994). Whatever form future organizations take, researchers will continue to be interested in what satisfies people at work and what keeps them coming back to work every day. It is likely that one source of that information will continue to be the organizational survey.

References

Achen, C. H. (1975). Mass political attitudes and the survey response. *American Political Science Review, 69,* 1218–1231.

Ashworth, S. D., Higgs, A. C., Schneider, B., Shepherd, W., & Carr, L. S. (1995, May). *The linkage between customer satisfaction data and employee-based measures of a company's strategic business intent.* Paper presented at the Tenth Annual Conference of the Society for Industrial and Organizational Psychology, Orlando, FL.

Barmash, I. (1993). More substance than show. *Across the Board, 30,* 43–46.

Bracken, D. W. (1992). Benchmarking employee attitudes. *Training and Development Journal, 46*(6), 49–53.

Breiman, L., Freidman, R. A., Olshen, C. J., & Stone, C. J. (1984). *Classification and regression trees.* Belmont, CA: Wadsworth.

Campion, M. A., Medsker, G. J., & Higgs, A. C. (1993). Relations between work group characteristics and effectiveness: Implications for designing effective work groups. *Personnel Psychology, 46,* 823–850.

Caudron, S. (1994). HR leaders brainstorm the profession's future. *Personnel Journal, 73,* 54–61.

Dunham, R. B., & Smith, F. J. (1979). *Organizational surveys: An internal assessment of organizational health.* Glenview, IL: Scott, Foresman.

Higgs, A. C., Ashworth, S. D., & Crist, R. C. (1995, May). *Development of a quarterly employee survey linked to a company's key business strategies: Researcher and client perspectives.* Paper presented at the Tenth Annual Conference of the Society for Industrial and Organizational Psychology, Orlando, FL.

Hinrichs, J., Kraut, A. I., & Schiemann, W. A. (1995, March). *Using surveys to drive change.* Paper presented at the meeting of the New York Metropolitan Association for Applied Psychology, New York.

Johnson, R. H., Ryan, A. M., & Schmit, M. (1994, April). *Employee attitudes and branch performance at Ford Motor Credit.* Paper presented at the Ninth Annual Conference of the Society for Industrial and Organizational Psychology, Nashville, TN.

Kraut, A. I., Manfredo, P. A., & Kelley, S.K.H. (1995). *Profiles of employee satisfaction: A cross-corporate comparison of situational influence.* Unpublished manuscript.

Kraut, A. I., Pedigo, P. R., McKenna, D. D., & Dunnette, M. D. (1989). The role of the manager: What's really important in different management jobs. *Academy of Management Executive, 3,* 286–293.

Kraut, A. I., Wolfson, A. D., & Rothenberg, A. (1975). Some effects of position on opinion survey items. *Journal of Applied Psychology, 60,* 774–776.

Lawler, E. E. III (1986). *High-involvement management: Participative strategies for improving organizational performance.* San Francisco: Jossey-Bass.

Magidson, J. (1988). Improved statistical techniques for response modeling. *Journal of Direct Marketing, 2,* 6–18.

O'Hara-Devereaux, M., & Johansen, R. (1994). *Globalwork: Bridging distance, culture, and time.* San Francisco: Jossey-Bass.

Rollins, T. (1994). Turning employee survey results into high-impact business improvements. *Employee Relations Today, 21,* 35–44.

Schneider, B. (1975). Organizational climates: An essay. *Personnel Psychology, 28,* 447–479.

Schneider, B. (1991). Service quality and profits: Can you have your cake and eat it, too? *Human Resource Planning, 14,* 151–157.

Schneider, B., & Bowen, D. E. (1995). *Winning the service game.* Boston: Harvard Business School Press.

Schneider, B., & Chung, B. (1994, April). *Market-focused I/O: Conceptualization for service industries.* Paper presented at the Ninth Annual Conference of the Society for Industrial and Organizational Psychology, Nashville, TN.

Schuman, H., & Presser, S. (1981). *Questions and answers in attitude surveys.* San Diego: Academic Press.

Segal, M. N. (1982). Reliability of conjoint analysis: Contrasting data collection procedures. *Journal of Marketing Research, 19,* 139–143.

Smith, P. C., Kendall, L. M., & Hulin, C. L. (1969). *The measurement of satisfaction in work and retirement.* Skokie, IL: Rand McNally.

Tornow, W. W. (Ed.). (1991). Service quality and organizational effectiveness (Special issue). *Human Resource Planning, 14*(2).

Velez, P. (1993). *The neutral response on attitudinal measures: An attribute of the item.* Unpublished master's thesis, San Jose State University.

Zikmund, W. G. (1988). *Business research methods.* Fort Worth, TX: Dryden.

CHAPTER 2

The Organizational Survey as an Intervention for Change

W. Warner Burke
Celeste A. Coruzzi
Allan H. Church

It might be difficult to prove, but apparently more and more organizations are using surveys. If our experience serves as a barometer, this observation is true. As other chapters in this book demonstrate, organizational surveys serve many purposes. They are often used simply to get a fix on "where we stand" and what needs to be addressed to improve matters. Currently benchmarking is in vogue. Organizational executives want to know how their company compares with the "best in class." A survey may tell them (Spendolini, 1992).

Less often found, perhaps, but more in line with our own practice, is the use of *organizational surveys as interventions for change*. Feedback from an organizational survey was used during the SmithKline Beecham merger, for example, to aid in monitoring the degree of progress the company was making toward achieving its new "Simply Better" culture (Burke & Jackson, 1991). In another pharmaceuticals organization, survey results were used as part of a larger change effort to diagnose issues related to senior leadership, teamwork, and management behaviors and to determine the impact of these issues on employee outcomes (see, for example, Church, Margiloff, & Coruzzi, 1995).

The particular use of a survey as an intervention for change is not mutually exclusive of other uses; the particular use is more a matter of focus and emphasis. In other words, a single organizational survey may serve multiple purposes. Our purpose in this chapter is to provide a detailed case example of how a survey in questionnaire form and the survey feedback process can be used in an overall change effort.

First, then, we very briefly describe the diagnostic model that guides our work and provides our perspectives about organizational performance and change. Second, we describe an actual case, showing how we use the model as a guide and change or modify it with each organizational survey. The model sets the standard for survey conceptualization and for what to measure, but the relationships among the model elements will vary as a function of the particular survey conducted in a particular organization at a particular moment in time. In other words, the arrows in the model (Figure 2.1) can take different directions, depending on the results of a given survey. Finally, we discuss lessons learned and provide suggestions for using organizational surveys as change interventions.

Diagnostic Models of Organizational Performance and Change

In organizational consulting work, and especially when a survey instrument is required, numerous models exist to guide the consultation. For example, McKinsey & Company's 7-S model is highly popular and apparently used widely. More sophisticated models, such as those of Tichy (1983) and Nadler and Tushman (1977), are also available to consultants. (For a summary of these and other models used diagnostically in organizational development efforts, see Burke, 1994a.) The point we wish to make here is that a model that is comprehensive and based on sound theory and research enhances the efficacy of an organizational diagnosis and serves as a guide to actions to take as a consequence of the diagnosis.

Our own change work is guided by the Burke-Litwin model of organizational performance and change (Burke & Litwin, 1992). While our surveys are tailored for each organization with respect to some of the items, we use a core set of questions based on the model. Our reasons for this procedure are (1) to ensure that the primary and critical dimensions of organizational performance and change are assessed and (2) to provide for each organization a set of survey items that may be compared with survey items from other organizations.

The Burke-Litwin model is based on two distinct sets of organizational dynamics. One set concerns primarily the *transactional* level of human behavior in organizations; that is, the everyday interactions and exchanges that ultimately affect performance. The second set of dynamics addresses processes of organizational *transformation;* that is, significant changes in behavior, especially those associated with direction, leadership, and organizational culture. The thinking underlying this distinction between transactional and transformational dynamics in organizations has been influenced by the writing of James McGregor Burns (1978), who described transforming and transacting leaders. However, the distinction has also been derived from practice, that is, from our consulting efforts to change organizations. Thus, the Burke-Litwin model attempts, first, to specify the interrelationships of organizational variables and, second, to distinguish transformational and transactional dynamics in organizational behavior and change. Figure 2.1 summarizes the model.

Mission and strategy, leadership, and organizational culture (the top boxes in the model) are the transformational variables and the remaining items, or factors, are the transactional variables. The top eleven factors, including the external environment, interact and influence performance, the twelfth factor (at the bottom of the figure). The feedback loop completes the model, highlighting the fact that the fundamental underlying theory of the model is open-systems theory (Katz & Kahn, 1978).

In summary, the model portrays

- The twelve primary variables that need to be considered in any attempt to predict and explain the total behavioral output of an organization
- The most important interactions among the twelve variables
- How the variables affect change

**Figure 2.1. Burke-Litwin Model of
Organizational Performance and Change.**

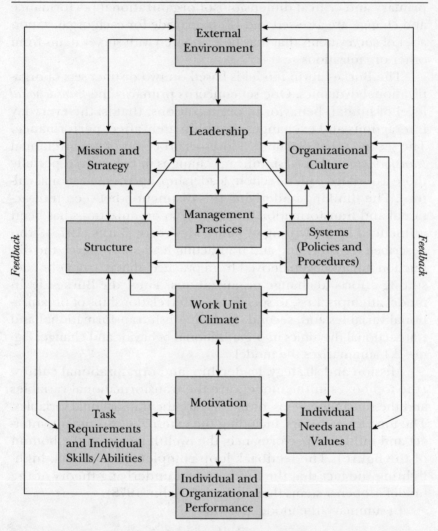

Source: Burke & Litwin, 1992, p. 528. Used by permission.

Using the Model: Data Gathering and Analysis

Distinguishing transformational and transactional issues in organizations has implications for planning organizational change. Unless one is conducting a total organizational diagnosis, preliminary interviews will result in enough information to construct a reasonably focused survey. Survey targets will be determined from the interview results and, most likely, will be focused on either transformational or transactional issues or both. Transformational issues call for a survey that probes external environment, mission and strategy, leadership, and culture and their impact on performance. Transactional issues need a focus on structure, systems, management practices, work unit climate, and performance. Other transactional probes might involve motivation, including job/skills matches and individual needs and values. For example, part or all of the Job Diagnostic Survey (Hackman & Oldham, 1980) might be appropriate.

A consultant helping to manage change would conduct preliminary interviews with, say, fifteen to thirty representative individuals in the organization. If a summary of these interviews revealed that significant organizational change was needed, additional data related to the transformational (or top) part of the model would be collected. In major organizational change, transformational variables represent the primary levers, those areas in which change must be focused. The following are examples of organizations facing transformational change:

- An acquired or merged organization whose culture, leadership, and business strategy are dramatically different from those of the acquiring or original organization (even if both organizations are in the same industry), thereby necessitating a new, merged organization. (For an example of how the model has been used to facilitate a merger, see Burke & Jackson, 1991.)
- A federal agency in which the mission has been modified and the structure and leadership changed significantly, yet the culture remains in the past.
- A high-tech firm whose leadership has changed recently and is perceived negatively, whose strategy is unclear, and whose

internal politics have moved from minimal (before) to pre-dominant (after). The hue and cry here is, "We have no direction from our leaders and no culture to guide our behavior in the meantime."

For an organization in which the presenting problem requires a fine-tuning or improving process rather than a transformational process, the transactional, or second, layer of the model serves as the point of concentration. Examples include changes in an organization's structure, modification of a reward system, management development (perhaps in the form of a program that concentrates on behavioral practices), and the administration of a climate survey to assess progress toward changes in job stratification, job clarity, degree of teamwork, and so on.

To summarize, the Burke-Litwin diagnostic model emphasizes that organizational change is either transformational—requiring radical leaps if not fundamental changes in the way things are done—or transactional—requiring fine-tuning and improving of the organization's existing behavior. Additionally, considering the model from a cause-and-effect perspective entails hypothesizing and testing relationships among the factors and assuming that the weight of change is top-down; that is, the heaviest or most influential organizational dimensions for change are, first and foremost, the external environment, then mission and strategy, leadership, culture, and so on.

As we stated above, there are many other useful models. We use the Burke-Litwin model for its comprehensiveness and its implications about what causes what in organizations. (For a more detailed description of the Burke-Litwin model, see Burke & Litwin, 1989, 1992; Burke, 1994a, 1994b.)

We now present a detailed case study of organizational change, in which the model and a survey based on the model are used in the consultative process as significant interventions. More specifically, this case illustrates (1) the use of a model-based questionnaire and the survey feedback process as a change intervention and (2) the elasticity of the model; that is, how it becomes a slightly different framework from the standard version displayed in Figure 2.1 when survey data are analyzed and applied to the various factors and interactions that compose the model.

Using the Diagnostic Model to Survey a Financial Services Organization

The following financial services example provides a rich case study of the diagnostic model in practice. It shows a change effort that started out as a transformational effort and moved itself into a transactional effort over a four-year period. The model provided a foundation for our consultation, which helped the company's managers link how they managed the organization to achieving the results they desired.

The Pressure to Change

In 1992, a major financial services corporation that was on the brink of disaster turned itself around, becoming a company whose performance reached record levels in 1995. The company brought in a new leadership team that was committed to a vision of the company as a dominant player in the financial services industry in its geographical domain. The team's goal was to move the organization from a mind-set of simply making transactions to a mind-set of being business advisers to its customers. The team worked hard to strengthen the business and to serve the financial needs of customers and the communities in which the company did business. This involved expanding the company's lines of products and services, training employees in the new product lines, and creating a fundamental shift in the minds of employees about what it means to deliver outstanding customer service.

Articulating the Future State

The company's new leadership team spent its first year crafting and communicating its vision to employees. At employee conventions and off-site meetings, these executives attempted to provide employees with examples of what the best companies in customer service industries were doing to provide high-quality service. They actively recruited employees from customer service industries (not just from other financial services organizations) to help create a shift in the culture, the premise being that financial people could learn from these other folks about what it means to provide exceptional customer service.

Measuring Progress

After the first year of change, one that was characterized by a major reorganization, technology upgrades, renovations of facilities, and an aggressive marketing campaign designed to change the company's public image, a survey effort was launched. The first organizationwide survey of employees during a time of great change and pressure to perform was undertaken primarily to determine what was and was not working with regard to the change. Another equally important goal of the survey was to translate the articulated vision into a set of observable and measurable behaviors against which employees could measure themselves year after year.

Development of the Diagnostic Survey

Using the framework of the diagnostic model, we queried a representative sample of 300 employees to help us translate the vision statement into day-to-day behaviors. We arranged a series of twenty focus groups, stratified by geographical domain and organizational level, and we asked questions about how people perceived the change effort—what was working and what was not, the pressures they experienced from the external environment, and their perceptions of the vision statement, the leadership of the company, the new versus the old culture, structure, management practices, systems, work group climate, job/skills match, motivation, individual needs and values, and performance. The results of the focus group sessions allowed us to generate a clear picture of the future and a clear picture of the present state and what was needed to move toward the vision. As one employee stated: "We understand where we need to go, and judging by where we are now, . . . the future is an island and we are on the main shore with a boat that has no oars. We need help in figuring out how we can get there from here." The focus group sessions were instructive in helping us determine employees' issues regarding change. The challenge ahead was to determine the extent to which the issues raised were significantly affecting progress.

In order to answer the latter question, we designed a structured rating-scale questionnaire to measure the issues raised in the focus groups more precisely and to determine which aspects of the organization were most affecting customer service levels and overall performance. The focus group results were used to formulate this companywide survey, which had 150 questions organized according to the twelve factors in the diagnostic model.

In this case, the diagnostic model was used as the basic framework for data gathering, and it also provided a common language for use between management and other employees. The survey was an opportunity for management to convey to people what was important to focus on in the coming year, and it was equally useful in surfacing employees' issues about what was and was not working in the change effort. Some of the issues addressed included the following.

- *External environment.* How does the company compare with the competition? How do people characterize their relationships to the parent company? To what extent do people understand the customers', communities', and shareholders' concerns?
- *Mission and strategy.* How familiar are people with the stated vision and the strategies decided upon for achieving that vision? Are people clear about what they are trying to achieve and how they are supposed to achieve it? Are the mission and strategy relevant, meaningful, and achievable? How appropriate is the rate of change, and to what extent do people perceive they are making progress?
- *Leadership.* To what extent are leaders unequivocally supporting the new direction, acting with inspiration, acting as a cohesive team, and being trustworthy and ethical in their treatment of people? Do leaders communicate enough about changes that affect people and their jobs, and do their actions match their words?
- *Organizational culture.* To what extent are people attempting new approaches to doing their work, anticipating problems rather than fighting fires, soliciting diverse opinions and perspectives before decisions are made, treating one another with trust and respect, and freely sharing information across units—both the good news and the bad?
- *Structure.* To what extent does the structure help people cooperate to get the job done? Do people understand the rationale behind structural changes and reorganizations, and to what extent are reorganizations managed effectively?

- *Management practices.* Do managers inspire people to act, involve people in decisions that affect their work, encourage openness and candid communication, develop people in both formal and informal ways, foster innovation, and act with integrity toward others?
- *Systems.* To what extent do the technology, communication, compensation and benefits, and training and career development initiatives throughout the company help people accomplish their work?
- *Work unit climate.* To what extent do people perceive teamwork, trust, recognition, openness, cooperation, and appreciation of diversity to exist in their own work groups?
- *Job/skills match.* Are people clear about what they need to do to be successful? Is their work challenging? To what extent do their skills match their jobs?
- *Motivation.* How empowered are people? What is the level of employee morale and of the significance and satisfaction people experience in their work?
- *Individual needs and values.* To what extent are people's needs for balance in their work and personal lives met? Do people feel a sense of pride in the organization as well as a sense of security about their jobs?
- *Performance.* To what extent does the company achieve the highest level of employee performance of which it is capable? Is the company profitable? Does it maintain a good reputation with customers and the communities in which it exists? Does the company have a strong future—will it survive?

The customized survey instrument contained 150 questions as well as a host of employee demographic questions. All the diagnostic questions were positively worded (for example, "To what extent are structural changes and reorganizations effectively managed?"), and they were all answered on a 5-point Likert rating scale (1 being "to a very small extent" and 5 being "to a very great extent"), with a "don't know" option included. Thus, the higher the score, the more positive or favorable the response. At the end of the questionnaire, four questions requiring write-in answers provided respondents with an opportunity to comment on and/or identify any issues or concerns not specifically addressed in the questionnaire itself. Additionally, the insights obtained from write-in comments are often invaluable for understanding why a given pattern of ratings is observed in the results. The four questions were (1) "What is exciting about your work?" (2) "What are the blocks/hindrances you experience in your work?" (3) "If you could recommend one thing to improve satisfaction and effectiveness at work, what would it be?" and (4) "What is the most significant issue facing the company during this time of change?"

The survey document and an accompanying letter from the CEO were sent to every employee. In total, 1,712 individuals responded to the survey, representing a 45 percent response rate. Of those who responded, 86 percent also completed the write-in comments sheet, raising particular points about which they felt strongly. A comparison of the respondent demographic profile with company demographics overall showed very similar percentage breakdowns across locations, levels, gender, and years with the company. Thus, from a demographic point of view, this was indeed a representative sample from which we could draw conclusions.

Results

The findings illustrated an organization in transition, an organization in which the raw materials for growth and high performance were clearly present. There was dedication, energy, excitement, and a willingness to do whatever it took to make this change a success. Figure 2.2 depicts some of the survey highlights. (Actual values for each factor of the diagnostic model are shown in Figure 2.5.)

The *external environment* was placing great pressure on people to change (the score for this item was 3.73). The change was seen as significant for survival yet manageable, perhaps because the parent company was supportive of people's efforts and there was a heightened awareness of customers' needs and expectations. However, in an environment where new players were entering and old players leaving, there was also a preoccupation with jobs—who had them, who did not, who would not, and so forth, and a feeling of inadequacy in ability to respond to the expectations management was setting for customer service.

In terms of achieving the *vision* and its related *mission and strategy,* overall, employees reported significant change to be occurring. More than half the people were making significant change

Figure 2.2. A Financial Services Organization: 1993 Description.

	External Environment + Change significant yet manageable + Supportive parent + Understand customers' needs − Concerned about jobs and job market − Lack tools to service customers	

Mission and Strategy	**Leadership**	**Organizational Culture**
+ Vision/mission clear, relevant, accepted − Strategy unclear, ambiguous	+ Committed + Supportive − Not participative	+ Risk taking + Experimental + Break up of "old" culture − Uncertain of new rules of game − Lack inclusion in decision making − Differences not valued

Structure	**Management Practices**	**Systems**
− Interdepartmental competition, roles unclear − Support functions not supportive	*(Highest-rated category)* + Knowledgeable + Entrepreneurial − Not participative − Intolerant of bad news	+ Training high quality but limited access − Outdated technology and MIS − Too much paperwork − Customer service not rewarded

	Work Unit Climate + Within teams, good − Across teams, combative, lacking trust	

Job/Skills Match	**Motivation**	**Individual Needs and Values**
+ Good match between jobs and skills	*(Lowest-rated category)* − Average job satisfaction − Disempowered − Low morale − High frustration and anxiety	+ Work has significance, meaning − People lack control over jobs − Overworked − Lack balance between work and personal life − People feel undervalued

	Performance + Company making profit + Customer service improving − Individuals underutilized	

Note: + indicates positive comments; − indicates negative comments.

happen, moving forward and experimenting with different methods in their jobs. They were clear about the needed direction and felt it was relevant and acceptable. Interestingly, although questions relating to the vision and the mission were rated highly (3.63), those pertaining to the strategy for getting there were rated lowly (2.87).

Leadership (3.33) was perceived as committed and supportive. However, though highly enthusiastic, leadership was not seen as very participative or inclusive of people in decisions that affected them and their work.

There was an emerging *organizational culture* of risk taking and experimentation (3.06). Interestingly, while the old culture was beginning to melt away, there was confusion about what the new culture would look like. People were uncertain about the new rules of the game.

There was some tension with regard to *structure* (3.06). Support functions were not perceived as helpful or responsive, and more work needed to be done on clarifying interdepartmental roles and responsibilities. Although relationships *within* work units were good, relationships *across* work units were combative and distrusting.

Management practices received the highest rating of all the factors in the model (3.67). Managers in the organization were perceived as knowledgeable and entrepreneurial—important qualities during this early phase of change. But like the company's leaders, they lacked participative approaches to managing people.

Systems issues were mixed (3.16). Although people felt the sales, product, and technical training available was high quality, they lacked the time to attend. People needed better technology and information systems for responding to their customers. Technology was outdated and hampered people's ability to provide reliable and rapid customer service.

As for *work unit climate* (3.38), work units operated as teams. Within work units, people were cooperative and supportive of one another, but across work units, relationships were troubled.

Jobs were seen to match skills (3.27). The work done was seen as important and significant in moving the company forward.

Motivation and *individual needs and values* received the lowest ratings of all (2.92 and 2.93, respectively). As a result of the significant changes occurring, people felt less in control over their work lives, disempowered, and overworked, and they reported a lack of balance between work and personal life.

Even so, *performance* ratings (3.47) portrayed a company that was beginning to make a profit and improve customer relationships, even though people felt underutilized as individuals. Clearly, although performance was improving, people felt it could be even better if the issues regarding management's treatment of people could be addressed. A primary question emanating from the descriptive analysis was—since employee motivation was rated very low and performance only average at best—what aspects of the company's functioning were having the most impact on ratings of motivation and, ultimately, performance?

The Most Significant Drivers of Performance

We wanted to explore further the most significant areas affecting performance ratings. To do this, the results of the survey were statistically analyzed, using regression analysis of the summary factors in the diagnostic model. The twelve factors were generated using confirmatory factor analysis and were computed into twelve scales that were tested for their internal reliability. The resulting scales were analyzed further, and the performance and motivation factors were each regressed on the remaining factors. Figures 2.3 and 2.4 illustrate the factors that influenced performance and motivation ratings most significantly. The arrows show the strongest causal effects.

Perhaps the most interesting finding in this comparative regression analysis was that what accounted for a more motivated workforce had little or no relationship to what predicted higher performance ratings. On the one hand, people who rated their motivation as higher reported a better match between job and skills, improved state-of-the-art technology to do their work, and a greater balance between work life and home life. Overall performance ratings, on the other hand, were more influenced by the clarity of purpose in the vision and a clear strategy for attaining the vision, along with a culture of risk taking and experimentation and the ability of managers to manage their work units participatively.

Obviously there are good reasons for improving all areas that receive low ratings. However, this analysis shows that in this financial services organization in 1993, the greatest improvements to

Figure 2.3. A Financial Services Organization:
1993 Stepwise Regression Results of Performance.

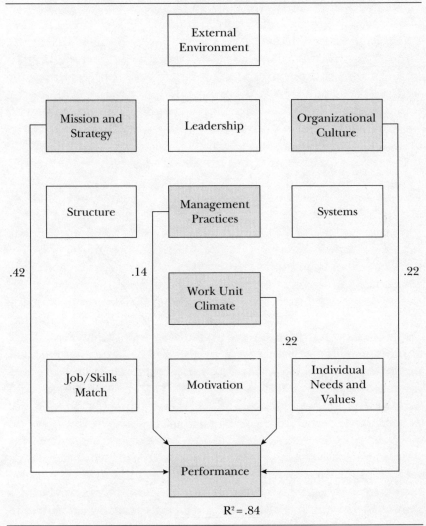

Note: p < .01. Numbers astride the arrows represent unstandardized coefficients.

**Figure 2.4. A Financial Services Organization:
1993 Stepwise Regression Results of Motivation.**

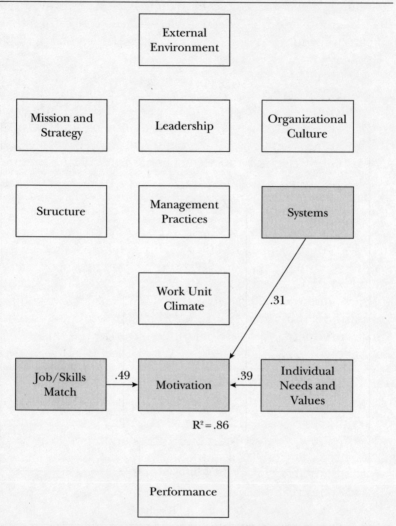

Note: p < .01. Numbers astride the arrows represent unstandardized coefficients.

performance ratings were likely to be gained by concentrating on the factors of mission and strategy, organizational culture, management practices, and work unit climate, while improvements in people's motivation had more to do with the factors of job/skills match, individual needs and values, and systems.

Action Planning Efforts

The results of the survey were reported in full in a special report distributed to all employees, and large-scale meetings were held to discuss the results further. This was done primarily to open up lines of communication between management and employees and to address significant issues affecting people's morale and motivation. Communication of the survey results in full, immediately following data gathering, helped rebuild trust that had eroded during the early stages of change.

Subsequently divisions within the company began profiling their own ratings against the company results overall. Divisional results were incorporated into the business planning process for the following year, and the strides that were made in focusing the entire company on the customer were reflected in the company's key business initiatives. A stronger market presence, expansion efforts, products and services designed to meet customers' needs, and efforts at greater efficiency all became a part of the next year's work. A major initiative to revamp the management information systems, upgrade technology, and reduce the paperwork that got in the way of employee-customer interactions was attacked with great diligence. The organization sought out "success stories"— capturing on video people who were "doing the right things" and distributing these tapes to help clarify what was appropriate behavior. It was an active year, and as it closed, the question was, "So? After another year, have we made a difference?"

Measuring Progress the Second Time

A comparison of results from the 1993 and 1994 organizational surveys enabled us to pinpoint the areas where the greatest gains were made, areas that continued to challenge the organization, and areas where it had lost some ground. On balance, the trends resulting from our two survey assessments indicated that the organization had made significant progress in its efforts at transformational change (see Figure 2.5).

What Was Going Well

Employees continued to report positive results in *performance* (3.32). They continued to value their customers highly and to provide high-quality customer service in addition to maintaining profitability. With regard to the *job/skills match,* people continued to see their work as relevant to the vision and their skills, knowledge, and abilities as fitting their jobs (3.34).

The biggest improvements occurred in the area of *mission and strategy* (3.45), specifically through the business planning efforts. Since 1993, the path toward success had been much clearer, more measurable and achievable. People were much clearer about what they needed to do to be successful, and they reported significant contributions to the success of the company.

What Was Not Going Well

Even with these positive gains, employees reported that they were not taking as much action or making as many needed changes as they could. *Motivation* was rated at 2.90. During 1994, people had perceived less active support of the change effort on the part of *leadership* (3.15) as well as on the part of their own *managers* (3.43). Paradoxically, although people perceived their managers to be more enthusiastic and excited about work in 1994, they rated them lower in 1994 in terms of delegating, encouraging new approaches, seeking and acting on customer feedback, communicating what and why change was needed, soliciting employees' opinions before decisions were made, and encouraging employee participation in planning changes.

With regard to *systems* (2.84), although people were providing high-quality customer service, they felt less adequate in their ability to introduce new products and services, due to insufficient time and lack of full knowledge of the products offered. Although product and technical training was offered, people still had no time to attend the needed training. As a result, employee morale was somewhat lower in 1994, and people were feeling less in control of changes that affected them.

**Figure 2.5. A Financial Services Organization:
Comparison of 1993 to 1994, Through the Lens of the Model.**

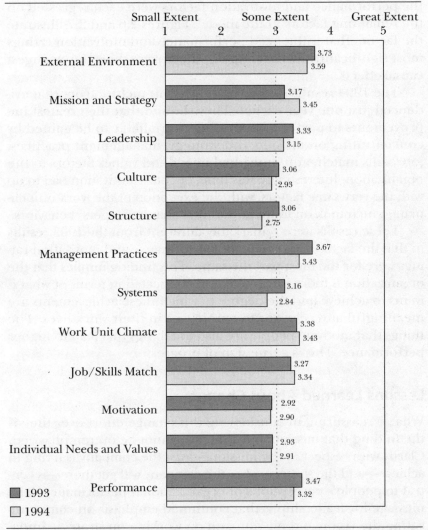

The 1994 results were analyzed further to examine the factors that influenced ratings of performance and motivation. As in 1993, the performance and motivation factors were each regressed on the remaining factors in the model. Figures 2.6 and 2.7 illustrate the factors that influenced performance and motivation ratings most significantly in 1994. Again, the arrows show the strongest causal effects.

The 1994 results suggested a different picture from that evidenced just one year earlier. They showed that the greatest improvements to performance ratings were likely to be gained by concentrating on mission and strategy, management practices, job/skills match, and individual needs and values factors in the organization. Interestingly, this time, people's motivation had to do with the very same factors, with the exception of the work unit climate, which took on more importance than managers' behaviors.

These results were remarkably different from the 1993 results in that the factors that predicted performance and motivation ratings were for the most part the same. This finding implies that the organization is more integrated and connected in terms of what it wants to achieve and the degree to which these achievements are meaningful and relevant to employees in their work lives. The things that motivate people are also the things that lead to higher performance. This is a true sign of progress.

Lessons Learned About Change

What is reassuring in considering this change effort over time is the finding that mission and strategy cannot be overemphasized. Clarity with respect to the mission—*what* the company is trying to achieve—and the strategy—*how* the company will get there—is central to people's perceptions of organizational performance. The message for leadership is that continued emphasis on communicating the vision and mission and on working on strategic initiatives that are in line with the vision and mission are fundamental activities if change is to be successful.

This financial services company is fundamentally a different organization from what it was a year ago; it is stronger, more customer focused and customer responsive. The issues that it faces year after year continue to change depending on where it focuses

**Figure 2.6. A Financial Services Organization:
1994 Stepwise Regression Results of Performance.**

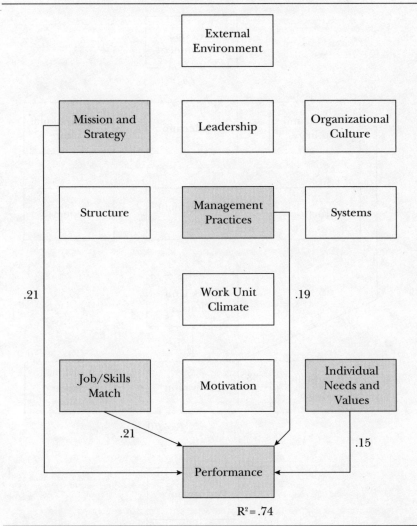

Note: p < .01. Numbers astride the arrows represent unstandardized coefficients.

**Figure 2.7. A Financial Services Organization:
1994 Stepwise Regression Results of Motivation.**

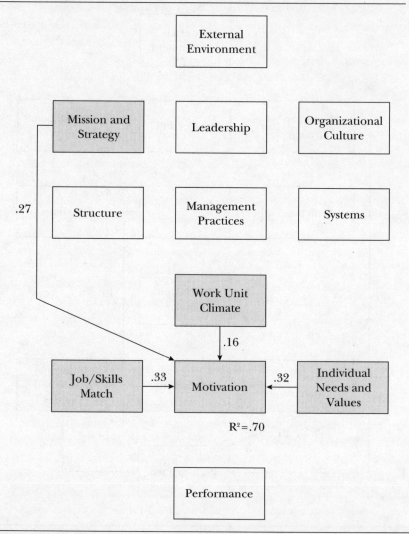

Note: $p < .01$. Numbers astride the arrows represent unstandardized coefficients.

its efforts. It is not surprising, for example, that after the initial attention company leaders put on communicating the vision and the importance of change, they began to focus more on external issues facing the company. However, employees are asking for a renewed commitment from senior management as to the importance of change, as well as an opportunity to be recognized for their successes and to be more included in carving out the future steps needed.

Recommendations for Effective Use of Surveys in an Organizational Change Effort

Our experience in using surveys as tools for organizational change has helped us identify several important principles and recommendations.

   1.   *Remember, you only get what you measure, and (the corollary) if you don't want to know, don't ask.* The data generated from any survey process are only as good or as bad, as general or as specific, as the questions asked. A survey designer needs to be sure that the items used cover the appropriate range of issues in the organization. One way to ensure that the items do cover the right issues is to conduct an organizational diagnosis—based on interviews, focus groups, and an examination of company documents—before constructing the survey. The use of a framework such as the Burke-Litwin diagnostic model can also be very helpful in guiding item development and content. Additionally, one needs to make sure that the level of information obtained will be useful for identifying target areas for change and planning follow-up strategies. Although in some instances an item may seem very interesting, if the responses do not provide data that are useful or meaningful, it should probably not be included.
   2.   *The process of designing, implementing, administering, and reporting back the data from an organizational survey is as important, if not more important, than the actual results that are generated.* In other words, a survey is a process, not an event. How the survey process is conducted may be more important than the content of the specific questions asked. Moreover, a survey should be a means to some end, not an end in itself. Since surveys also function as vehicles for

communicating to people which cultural and organizational issues are most important, their initiation and implementation alone can serve as powerful tools for communicating key messages (for example, questions about mission can convey important points senior management may want to make about that mission) and for initiating and facilitating change. Additionally, when employees are involved in the total process—including survey construction (through focus groups and pilot testing), data collection (through completing the survey instrument), and problem solving and action planning (through sessions based on the data feedback)—they are ultimately being invited to help shape the future state of the organization. Thus, surveys can be used by organizational development, industrial and organizational psychology, human resource development, and Total Quality Management practitioners to stimulate and catalyze all kinds of organizational transitions.

3. *Surveys represent a particularly powerful method for examining specific relationships between perceived behaviors in the workplace and employee attitudes and perceptions.* Through the use of statistical procedures, clear linkages among critical variables can be identified as targets for interventions. Customized models of how a given organization functions and where its strengths and limitations lie can be generated and used for development efforts. In other words, while most consultants have their own organizational models that guide their recommendations, without data from those who work in any given organization, they do not have the necessary information to determine which *paths* (or relationships) are actually the most important for change in that given context. A survey can provide specific information regarding these relationships, particularly when it is based on a model or framework of organizational performance and change.

4. *Do not ask the questions unless there is a willingness to share the results with all those who are surveyed.* As a rule, people want to be involved in their organizations, and by soliciting their thoughts and opinions, one is stimulating their interest and investment. This is clearly a good thing. Failure to take action on the issues and problems identified from a survey, however, is one sure way to cause people to avoid, if not resist, a similar process in the future. Why should people invest in their own or in others' improvement if the issues they raise will not be taken seriously by those in a position

to make change happen? Thus, a clear plan and commitment to action must be made publicly by key senior managers.

Another way to alienate the people surveyed is simply to avoid the data feedback stage altogether. Under most circumstances, it is far worse to conduct a survey and completely ignore the results (for example, because the scores are low and morale is already a problem) than to share openly and honestly with employees the concerns raised by the data. Although anxiety is created by almost every type of assessment process, including organizationwide surveys, more anxiety is produced when the results seem just to disappear into the hierarchy. As one organizational member put it, "While telling us the truth may hurt, it is better than keeping us in the dark. Besides, no communication sends the message that there is something to hide."

At first if results are not shared, people will just question the usefulness of the process, but their attitude can quickly move from one of skepticism and irritation to one of fear and alienation. Clearly, if one plans to conduct a survey and use the data effectively and efficiently (and bear the associated process costs), the results must be (1) shared with everyone involved through both general and local (for example, work group or departmental) communication methods and (2) actions must be planned and ultimately implemented based on the issues identified for improved organizational performance.

Conclusion

This is the era of feedback. More and more organizations are going through the process of surveying staff on a continuous basis. Organizational surveys are becoming annual events with the results being scrutinized in very much the same way as the company annual report. Integrating survey results into the business planning process can only make for better managed organizations.

References
Burke, W. W. (1994a). Diagnostic models for organization development. In A. Howard & Associates (Eds.), *Diagnosis for organizational change* (Society for Industrial and Organizational Psychology, Professional Practice Series, pp. 53–84). New York: Guilford Press.

Burke, W. W. (1994b). *Organization development: A process of learning and changing* (2nd ed.). Reading, MA: Addison-Wesley.

Burke, W. W., & Jackson, P. (1991). Making the SmithKline Beecham merger work. *Human Resources Management, 30,* 69–87.

Burke, W. W., & Litwin, G. H. (1989). A causal model of organizational performance. In *The 1989 annual: Developing human resources* (pp. 277–288). San Diego, CA: University Associates.

Burke, W. W., & Litwin, G. H. (1992). A causal model of organizational performance and change. *Journal of Management, 18*(3), 523–545.

Burns, J. M. (1978). *Leadership.* New York: HarperCollins.

Church, A. H., Margiloff, A., & Coruzzi, C. A. (1995). Using surveys for change: An applied example in a pharmaceuticals organization. *Leadership and Organization Development Journal, 16*(4), 3–11.

Hackman J. R., & Oldham, G. R. (1980). *Work redesign.* Reading, MA: Addison-Wesley.

Katz, D., & Kahn, R. L. (1978). *The social psychology of organizations* (2nd ed.). New York: Wiley.

Nadler, D. A., & Tushman, M. L. (1977). A diagnostic model for organization behavior. In J. R. Hackman, E. E. Lawler III, & L. W. Porter (Eds.), *Perspectives on behavior in organizations* (pp. 85–100). New York: McGraw-Hill.

Spendolini, M. J. (1992). *The benchmarking book.* New York: AMACOM.

Tichy, N. M. (1983). *Managing strategic change: Technical, political, and cultural dynamics.* New York: Wiley.

CHAPTER 3

The Role of Surveys in Transforming Culture
Data, Knowledge, and Action

David B. Wagner
Janet L. Spencer

We understand that some readers may expect this chapter to provide a cookbook approach to the use of surveys as a way to change organizational culture. But we have no simple answers and no magic formulas—for two reasons. First, changing an organization's culture is a formidable and complex task, one that requires long-term commitment from everyone within the company, starting with the CEO and the senior management team. Second, we believe that surveys should be only one part of a total toolkit of interventions. The use of that toolkit should be driven by a well-articulated business rationale for changing the organization's culture and guided by an integrated change agenda that is based on a systemic view of organizations.

What this chapter does offer is a discussion of the issues you are likely to face as you consider how to augment your cultural change efforts with appropriately designed and implemented survey processes. It also offers some examples of how other companies have effectively used surveys in their own ongoing struggles to change their organizational cultures.

After defining and reviewing organizational culture, we discuss how cultural change can be facilitated through surveys and survey feedback processes. We describe in detail how each step of a well-developed survey process—designing the survey, conducting it, reporting the results, and creating a cultural metric (or measurement system)—can support and enhance changing an organization's culture.

A Definition of Organizational Culture

Entire books have been written discussing various ways of defining and studying organizational culture. Our purpose here is not to engage in a debate about the various perspectives; instead, we will simply state our working definition of culture and proceed. We follow Schein's definition (1992) of the culture of a group: "a pattern of shared basic assumptions that the group learned as it solved its problems of external adaptation and internal integration, that has worked well enough to be considered valid and, therefore, to be taught to new members as the correct way to perceive, think, and feel in relation to those problems" (p. 12). Schein also says that these assumptions "come to be taken for granted" because they solve the group's problems "repeatedly and reliably" (p. 6). Moreover, because these assumptions operate unconsciously and automatically, culture is often a difficult concept for organizational members to understand, measure, and change.

Some common themes and understandings can be identified from this definition of culture.

- An organization's culture will be more (or less) effective to the degree that it supports the organization's mission and strategy, is consistent with or aligned with the other components of the organizational system (formal and informal organization, work processes, and people), and helps the organization to anticipate and adapt to environmental change.
- An organization's culture provides a sense of meaning for people, particularly when they are confronted with ambiguity or competing alternatives for action. The successes of the organization reinforce its specific cultural characteristics; over time, the behavioral patterns and the deeper values, beliefs, and underlying assumptions become unquestioned and implicit standard operating procedures.
- Culture serves as an integrating perspective for the social system and a sense of identity for that system's members. Because

of this characteristic of culture, changing an organization's culture may also involve changing the way individuals view their own identities. This is yet another reason why culture is so difficult to change.

- Often there are identifiable subcultures within an organization. For example, the research and development function may have many cultural attributes similar to the attributes of the corporate culture, but it may also have attributes that are unique and quite distinct from those of other business units or functions.
- The strength of a culture is associated with member stability. Over time, the collective success of an organization's responses leads to greater member stability, which in turn reinforces the development of members' automatic responses and assumptions about how to respond to situations, which in turn leads to an ever stronger culture. This ongoing reinforcement can present a paradox; we believe that the strength of an organization's culture can block the organization's ability to adapt to a changing environment.

Culture as the Soft Side of Business

In our work, we see a growing awareness among senior executives of the necessity to focus on and understand organizational culture. Historically, there has been a reluctance and even resistance on the part of management to focusing on culture. A number of reasons have contributed to that resistance: the "soft" side of the business is much more difficult to measure than the "hard" side, and the causal link between the soft and hard sides is not always clear. As a result, the soft side is often not accepted as a valid topic of discussion for managers. However, there is a growing recognition among corporate leaders that managing the soft organizational issues such as culture is very difficult—that the soft stuff is the hard stuff. In interviews that researchers conducted with CEOs regarding large-scale organizational change efforts, these top executives often spoke of the cultural and human aspects of change. As one CEO put it, "A lot of people act as though 'when in doubt, change the organization.' I believe that nine out of ten reorganizations are a total waste of time. It's much more difficult to change the way people think. We took the attitude, 'We'll get to the reorganization later.' We wanted a total change in mindset, orientation and thinking" (Nadler, Shaw, Walton, & Associates, 1994, p. 258).

There has also been an increasing awareness among progressive companies and their leaders that their people are a key to organizational competitiveness; thus, cultural change is a way to harness this people component. Another CEO says, "Values to me are like buoys in the channel of commerce. In other words, one is changing directions and testing and making strategic decisions all the time, but if one doesn't have values to guide one, there is a disorientation. So deciding early on, even before you start fooling around with your strategy, what you believe in and what's the company all about, is important" (Nadler, Shaw, Walton, & Associates, 1994, p. 258).

Link Between Organizational Culture and Performance

There is increasing evidence of a link between an organization's culture (how work gets done) and its business (what actually gets done). Corporate culture can, in fact, significantly affect performance within a firm and in turn the firm's long-term financial viability. In studies conducted by Kotter and Heskett (1992), firms that emphasized all key managerial constituents (customers, stockholders, and employees) and leadership from managers at all levels outperformed by a huge margin firms that did not have these cultural traits.

Strong cultures provide stability and predictability for their members, as they supply people with clear direction, ground rules for behavior, and ideas about how to respond or make the most appropriate decisions in ambiguous situations.

One classic example of organizational culture influencing decisions is Johnson & Johnson's dilemma following the discovery of poisoned Tylenol on store shelves. On the one hand was the threat of more deaths if it should turn out that there were additional bottles of tainted Tylenol in the stores; on the other hand was the enormous cost to the company of removing all Tylenol from the stores. Ultimately, the Johnson & Johnson "Credo," a set of well-articulated corporate values, clearly and quickly drove the company to decide to pull Tylenol from the shelves. As it turned out, the decision had a tremendous negative short-term impact on the company financially, but the company's actions created a very positive impact in the minds of its customers and the public in general.

Another example of a company's strong culture guiding its decision process involves Intel's release of its Pentium computer chip in late 1994. In early testing, the company realized there was a small probability that an integral part of the chip—the floating-point unit—would not always perform reliably. While the company was quite open about the problem, it thought that consumer re-actions would be minimal, and at first, it simply denied that the problem was a serious one. That initial response relied on the company's engineering perspective; it emphasized the statistically small chance that a customer would ever encounter the problem. When that view did not satisfy customers, the company explained that most people did not actually need "enhanced accuracy." Next, the company established a product return policy that required people first to justify their need for a new chip before it would be replaced. These actions, while consistent with the company's engineering culture of emphasizing rational thought and probabilities, did little to instill trust and confidence in Intel in the eyes of the consumer. Only weeks later, when public criticism became overwhelming, did the company reverse its original decision and allow any consumer to obtain a replacement chip with no questions asked.

As the Intel example illustrates, a strong culture can also work against a company. When the environment changes or market expectations shift, the culturally dominant response of the organization may no longer be appropriate. The danger of a strong culture is that the organization may become so confident in its own success that it does not focus externally on critical changes in the environment, it refuses to see the need for change, or it does not have the flexibility or internal capacity to change. It is not the strength of the culture per se that prevents change; rather, it is the inherent lack of *adaptive* characteristics in the culture that prevents the organization from changing (Collins & Porras, 1994; Kotter & Heskett, 1992).

Why Change an Organization's Culture?

Changes in the external environment frequently require a business to adapt in order to ensure its future success. As a result, an organization must often shift its strategy, adopt new technologies, redesign or reengineer its work processes, restructure to better serve its target markets, and so on. Major discontinuous change frequently requires changes in the organization's culture as well. The implication is that the old culture may no longer be consistent with, or align with, the organization's new strategy, structure, work processes, and the like.

Many now believe that strategic organizational changes require accompanying changes in the culture if they are to be sustained: "In the final analysis, change sticks when it becomes the way we do things around here, when it seeps into the bloodstream of the corporate body. Until new behaviors are rooted in social norms and shared values, they are subject to degradation as soon as the pressure for change is removed" (Kotter, 1995, p. 67).

We would add one very important caveat to these concepts about the need for cultural change. Organizational culture should only be changed in the context and purpose of organizational performance. A few years ago, the CEO of a Fortune 100 company raised the question with us of how to change his company's culture. When probed about specific symptoms and performance problems, he could not identify any. When asked directly why he wanted to change the organization's culture, he replied, "I want to make it different, make it a more comfortable place to work." Our advice: if you do not have a compelling business reason to change your organization's culture, don't try!

How Surveys Can Contribute to Cultural Change

At many points during a survey process, there are opportunities to define and shape the desired organizational culture. While survey data and the feedback process are obvious tools for cultural change, each step in the survey process is also an opportunity. Listed below are some common survey process steps, followed by a discussion of the ways to best leverage each step to facilitate cultural change. Where applicable, we also provide examples.

• *Designing a survey.* This entails translating, or operationalizing, the desired culture into questionnaire items applicable to the survey goal, the respondents, and the context of the intervention. During the design process, it is important to be aware that the desired culture will (and should) include both new and old cultural elements, which can be seen as past and future strengths of the organization.

- *Conducting a survey.* This is the process of collecting the data. Thinking about the survey as both a measurement tool *and* a vehicle for communication can lead to innovative approaches.
- *Reporting survey results.* The manner in which the data are reported and the design of the feedback process as an intervention can be powerful tools for shaping the desired culture.
- *Creating a cultural metric.* Often what gets measured is what is viewed as important. A cultural metric, defined as a common measure or set of measures that is incorporated into management's organizational measurement system, is a way of assessing how the organization's culture is changing and how effectively the culture is aligned with the other components of the organization. Creating a common metric builds a baseline for comparing progress over time, and making it a routine topic of organizational performance sends a message that cultural change is important.

Designing a Survey to Drive Cultural Change

Designing a survey, the first step in the survey process, offers opportunities to link the desired culture and the business strategy, facilitate cultural change, and initiate interventions that redefine the existing culture.

Survey Design to Link Culture and Business

Linking the concept of culture to the strategy of the company helps organizational members understand that there is a solid business rationale for the cultural change effort. People need very persuasive and very clear reasons if they are to understand why many of their underlying assumptions about their organization are no longer valid. It is also important to keep a balance between change and continuity with the past—the links between the desired culture and the core competencies of the organization should be made explicit (Collins & Porras, 1994).

Survey processes can reinforce the culture–business connection, particularly when they are part of a coherent organizational performance system. For example, AT&T uses three broad classes of performance categories, each explicitly tied to business strategy: economic value added, customer value added, and people value added. The categories are a useful framework for linking strategy to multidimensional performance metrics associated with core processes and subsystems. By explicitly linking the desired culture of the organization to performance measures, AT&T avoids treating culture simply as a buzzword and increases the probability that it will be considered an important construct demanding management attention.

At another level, using the organization's mission, vision, strategy, and/or values as starting points in the development of survey items will shape the type of opinions you poll on issues critical to running the business. This technique can help you ensure that respondents make the connection between the business and their organizational culture. Therefore, a critical step prior to developing surveys to support cultural change is to ensure that the organization's purpose and direction (mission, vision, strategy, and values) have been clearly defined and articulated. (Examples of how to develop a shared organizational purpose are beyond the scope of this chapter; however, interested readers may turn to organizational development books that include descriptions or case examples, such as Senge, Kleiner, Roberts, Ross, & Smith, 1994, or Block, 1987.)

Design of Survey Items for Cultural Change

Several methods can be used to generate potential topics for survey items that will facilitate cultural change. On one end of the continuum are approaches that focus on identifying current problems or weaknesses in the culture, including behaviors, values, and underlying assumptions that are needed but are lacking or that exist but are inconsistent with the desired culture. A theoretical perspective consistent with this approach is the *action research model* (Schein, 1980). The goal is to specify the aspects of the culture that need to stop or change, determine the root causes of these problems, and focus interventions to address the root causes.

On the other end of the continuum are approaches that focus on the current strengths and possibilities of the culture that will be required for the organization to be successful in the future. One theoretical perspective consistent with this approach is *appreciative inquiry* (Cooperrider & Srivastva, 1987), a method for discovering, understanding, and fostering the best of "what is" in an organization to help ignite the collective imagination of "what might be." This approach is particularly useful in cultural change, where continuity with the past can help facilitate change (Salipante, 1992).

It is critical for survey designers to acknowledge at the outset that the identity of the process sponsor is key. We strongly believe that for long-term cultural change to occur, senior management, and in particular the CEO, must take ownership of the cultural change process. It cannot be delegated; if it is, the cultural change effort simply will not be sustained. At the same time, while the senior team and a broad sample of key people within the organization should be responsible for defining the organization's values and behavioral exemplars, we recommend that an industrial-organizational professional with strong survey research experience be responsible for developing, pilot-testing, and revising the potential survey items to create a final survey.

Because each organization has idiosyncratic cultural characteristics that are a meaningful part of its identity, we believe that generic survey items are often not as useful as those designed specifically for the organization and context at hand. Cultural change survey items tap into more than do the typical employee opinion survey items related to job and company satisfaction, supervision, intention to stay, or job characteristics. They probe issues of leadership, management systems, work processes, and the like as these issues relate to specific organizational strategies, values, and culture. Therefore, we do not recommend the use of generic surveys as intervention tools for cultural change. Further, the normative information that generic surveys can generate should not be an expected outcome of most cultural surveys. In fact, using normative data for cultural change may be detrimental because it focuses the organization's members on normative comparisons when they should be focusing on the difference between the organization's current state and its desired future state.

Survey Design as Intervention

As we mentioned earlier, many potential cultural change benefits are associated with the design and implementation of the various steps of the survey process. At many points, there are opportunities to define and shape the new culture and to demonstrate new behaviors or ways of doing things, demonstrations that effectively model aspects of the culture you are trying to build. At the same time, even during the survey planning and development stage, potential downsides must be considered. Misjudgments along the way can jeopardize not only the survey but also the desired outcome of the cultural change intervention itself.

The survey designer's careful consideration of sensitive issues and dynamics cannot be emphasized enough. Special attention to leverage points for cultural change, appropriate uses of surveys, the important link between culture and business strategy, and the process used to discover relevant survey topics, as well as to the writing of the survey items themselves, is an important element of the survey design phase. A survey process that is well-planned from the outset will go a long way toward enhancing your potential for success in the end.

Conducting the Survey

It is important to recognize from the outset that the actual administration of a survey operates as an intervention, affecting people's perceptions not only of the survey itself but also of the change effort in general. Every action—from the determination of who will be involved in designing the survey to how the results will be formatted—sends messages to employees about the importance of the survey, the topics it attempts to measure, and to some degree, the change process itself.

Survey Process as Communication Vehicle

Prior to conducting a survey, those responsible for leading the effort must recognize and be sensitive to the fact that the mere introduction of a survey raises anxiety for many. The level of anxiety will depend upon the type of survey employed (360-degree, intergroup, organizational, and so on) and the organization's degree of experience and sophistication with such surveys. Typical questions people immediately ask include "Why are we doing this?" "How will the results be used?" and "Will I be identified—either as a respondent or as the person responsible for the ratings?" As Champy (1995) rightfully points out, "Measurement means evaluation; judgments must be made. But, none of us likes to be judged; many don't even like to judge. . . . People want to shield themselves from judgment, deflect it, share it as widely as possible, muddle it with bureaucratic process, anything to avoid standing in the glare of a clear, unequivocal measurement of their worth" (p. 124).

The way in which these and similar questions are addressed and people's previous experiences can either enhance or detract from the success of the survey (in terms of rate of response, validity of data, and utility of results) and from the success of the overall cultural change effort. Many companies wisely invest heavily in developing mechanisms for telling employees, before the survey is launched, why a survey is being conducted, what its link is to the business strategy, and how the results will contribute to mobilizing the change effort. A carefully and strategically planned survey communication strategy provides opportunities not only to answer questions and alleviate concerns but also to deliver vital messages to a wide audience of employees.

Executives are learning more and more that effective communication is the cornerstone for any successful change effort. As social and psychological contracts between employees and employers change and the ties that keep people working for a company become more tenuous, there is a growing need for authentic communication—honest concrete exchanges of information between management and employees that encourage listening, responding, confronting, asserting, and disputing (Champy, 1995). This communication need places an increasing burden on senior management to model desired behaviors and to set and live up to the highest performance standards.

The communication of the survey process must be championed by top management: senior executives should be involved in every possible phase of communication. Indeed, each aspect of the actual survey—from the accompanying cover letter to the development of survey topics (if not the actual items) to the thank-you at the end—should have top managers' visible signatures.

Qualitative Data Collection Methods
Qualitative data can often be a valuable supplement to the survey process, allowing a better understanding of the quantitative results. The use of write-in questions, focus groups, and interviews are

three qualitative data collection methods that are used extensively in survey processes to add flesh to the bones of numeric information. Each of these methods is potentially labor intensive, and the utility of such methods may appear to diminish when one is considering conducting a large sample or census survey. However, the many benefits to collecting qualitative data can often outweigh the costs involved.

Focus groups and interviews are two methods of collecting information that can supplement quantitative survey information. Typically, these methods are used early on in the survey design process to identify the content areas the survey should cover. However, there are also situations in which focus groups and/or interviews can yield valuable information during the data collection phase.

Write-in or open-ended questions often provide a means of capturing valuable thoughts that are triggered in the respondent as he or she completes the survey. Survey items typically have a fixed-response format. This means they can probe only one specified dimension of the respondent's perspective. Giving respondents the opportunity to express themselves also in their own words allows them to articulate assumptions, values, or biases that may lie behind their one-dimensional ratings; it serves to capture much richer perspectives. Write-in comments often reveal a wealth of in-depth information on key issues that would be missed if the survey used only rating-scale questions. Answering write-in questions may also provide an opportunity for respondents to air feelings, concerns, or questions that are most salient at that time, and therefore the process can often also act as a venting, or cathartic, mechanism.

The potential downside of write-in questions often boils down to cost: In order to be adequately analyzed, responses to each write-in question must be content coded by the issues represented. Depending on the size of the survey, this can be a very time-consuming and relatively expensive task compared to analyzing the quantitative ratings, even when only random samples of written responses are coded.

Survey Methods and Cultural Change

The selection of methods and materials used to conduct the survey often provides opportunities to reinforce the changing culture.

From simple choices like a logo for the survey and the colors and format of a paper-and-pencil questionnaire to more complicated options like survey distribution and collection methods (whether to use computerized or telephone surveys, for example), possibilities exist to use approaches that are consistent with and help to motivate change toward the desired culture.

For example, a company formed by the merger of a U.S. company with a company based in a different country was trying to build a new culture characterized, in part, by greater awareness of the company's new global identity and its emphasis on the use of superior technology. In the past, each of the original companies had employed traditional survey methods that involved distribution and collection of paper-and-pencil surveys via company mail. The newly merged organization developed a survey process to communicate and instill its guiding principles as well as to perform important tracking of data on employees' perceptions of the changing culture. The first administration of the new survey combined paper-and-pencil and telephone survey methods to collect responses. The paper-and-pencil surveys were translated into multiple languages and distributed to all participants outside the United States while the telephone survey process was implemented within the United States and encouraged as an option for participants who preferred that technology to the more traditional paper-and-pencil route. This multiple-method process attempted to address and reinforce such aspects of the desired culture as becoming paperless and being more sensitive to the needs and expectations of employees from varied cultures.

Reporting Survey Results

While every step in the survey process requires careful attention and consideration, the process of reporting the results is perhaps most important in determining a survey's effectiveness as a cultural change tool. A brilliantly designed, well-communicated, and creatively administered survey may yield vital data, but the process that is used to understand and act on the results is what turns data into actionable information. More explicitly, the dynamic can be thought of as shown Figure 3.1.

The point is that there is a process by which survey results must be digested before action can be taken or even planned. In our

Figure 3.1. Turning Data into Action.

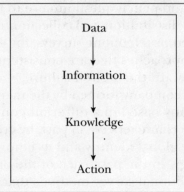

experience, we have found that the success of this process is largely driven by sufficient investment in the design of the reporting phase and is very much related to the success of the survey overall—a carefully planned and well-executed reporting process can, we believe, result in true learning and mobilize effective cultural change.

Types of Surveys and Reporting Processes

While there are any number of possible methods for reporting survey results, the method chosen will depend heavily on the type of survey—the key topics or substance of the survey should drive the mode of feedback and thereby the mechanisms for cultural change.

For example, results from a large-scale cultural survey are often best reported to a large group of senior executives then worked on in smaller groups—typically as part of a larger change-oriented agenda at a company off-site meeting. This approach helps ensure commonality of understanding regarding the findings, opportunities to discuss the implications, and time to begin the initial planning for change in the larger context of organizational issues. Often action plans for changing the culture are begun in the small-group discussions, communicated to the entire group, and used as a basis for going forward in more detail and depth in subsequent regional, divisional, or departmental meetings.

The design of the feedback session is a critical intervention in and of itself and should involve key stakeholders such as the CEO and members of the senior team (see the earlier discussion of survey design for more on the importance of sponsorship and involvement). Several firms have used cultural surveys as one aspect of their overall change agenda and have planned matters so that the availability of survey results coincides with an opportunity to engage senior leadership in the type of off-site meeting mentioned above. We often recommend that planning for such a feedback meeting begin at the same time the survey items are developed. Parallel development tracks help ensure a strong connection between the type of data collected and the process used to work them.

Conversely, results from an individually oriented behavioral change survey (such as a 360-degree survey administered to direct reports, peers, bosses, and possibly even internal and external customers) are often best reported directly to that individual, sometimes in a small-group setting. Many consulting organizations structure the delivery of the feedback to coincide with personal development sessions that take place over the course of several days—the Center for Creative Leadership's Benchmarks feedback process is a good example of such an approach. One session outcome that is critical to a cultural change effort is obviously an individual's development of action plans that promote his or her accountability for change in the direction of the desired culture. Such action plans are often enhanced and better adhered to when produced and monitored by individuals' managers in collaboration with a formal feedback coach.

Reporting Methods and Cultural Change

Methods and materials used in reporting survey data can in and of themselves reinforce cultural change when they are different from what has been used in the past but are consistent with the desired culture. For example, many organizations have recently been experimenting with *automatic response systems*. In these systems, members of a large audience use personal electronic keypads to indicate their reactions to a question posed by the presenter. The computerized process tabulates and displays survey results immediately, vastly enhancing the interactive component of a large meeting. One CEO used this method during an organizational assessment involving 180 of his most senior managers from around the world and received high marks from participants in postmeeting assessments. His willingness to respond in real time to difficult issues and to engage in an open question-and-answer format was a clear example that the culture was changing in that organization and was widely applauded.

Another reporting method that can assist in cultural change is the use of the *double loop* (Argyris, 1994) focus group. In part due to an acknowledgment of the need for continual communication between management and organizational members, this method is gaining acceptance in some organizations as a process by which data can be simultaneously reported and collected. In this method, a facilitator (preferably a trained member of the senior team) reports survey findings to a group of employees and asks them to discuss both the data and the reasons and underlying assumptions that might lie behind the data.

"Double loop learning" is a process that "turns the question back on the questioner. It asks what the media would call follow-ups. . . . My favorite example [of single loop learning] is a thermostat which measures ambient temperature against a standard setting and turns the heat source on or off accordingly . . . [whereas] double loop learning would wonder whether the current setting was actually the most effective temperature at which to keep the room and, if so, whether the present heat source was the most effective means of achieving it" (Argyris, 1994, p. 78). According to Argyris, without double loop probing, the learning that results from data collection is one-dimensional and does not explore all the fundamental issues at the core of an organization's dynamics.

One firm that has recently adopted this approach to survey reporting has found that the impact on its overall cultural change process has been successful beyond its expectations. While people are eager to view the results of the survey, they are doubly eager to engage with members of senior management (who were initially trained and who have become well versed in conducting these sessions) in probing discussions on the dynamics that shape both their culture and the way their organization functions. The people perhaps most affected by the use of this reporting method have been the senior leaders themselves, who have received tremendous recognition from employees for their new efforts to engage in such discussions and who have learned firsthand much more about their own organization and what it will take to change it.

Importance of Trained Facilitation

Our last note on the reporting process concerns the training of people who will both deliver and work with the results. Adequate training is absolutely vital to the success of this phase. Although professionally trained internal or external consultants can be employed, should time and resources allow, it is often best to train a cadre of line managers—senior executives who have significant credibility and are seen in the organization as thought leaders. Involving these individuals in the release of survey results not only signals the importance of such information but also provides people with access to the thoughts and reactions of those deemed to be key players.

Creating a Cultural Metric

Propelled by the movement away from command-and-control management, the sweeping influence of total quality, and other pervasive changes in the management of organizations, the value of measurement is increasingly being emphasized in organizations today. The mantra "You get what you measure" is being chanted in most corporate hallways, and we find that management measurement these days includes not only financial, or results-oriented, metrics but soft metrics as well.

We define the term *metric* as *the set of key measures used by the organization to assess performance related to achieving its vision, strategy, values, and desired culture.* As discussed earlier, many companies are adopting an approach that associates multidimensional performance metrics with strategy and core processes. The balanced scorecard has caught on as a way of "[providing] executives with a comprehensive framework that translates a company's strategic objectives into a coherent set of performance measures" (Kaplan & Norton, 1993, p. 134). Often this framework incorporates and balances both internal (for example, safety) and external (for example, competitive pricing) information as well as softer measures of internal functioning (for example, employee empowerment). With the growing acceptance of this type of framework comes an increasing need to develop measurement systems for such softer processes as cultural change.

Monitoring Cultural Trends over Time

It should be noted that processes to measure culture do not, or should not, look like many traditional employee opinion benchmark survey processes of the past. Oftentimes those processes involved the administration of a static survey at regular intervals for the purpose of measuring either the change from the time of previous administration or the absolute difference between one organization and another. While there is undoubtedly some value in this approach, it is much more important in these times of rapid and escalating change to compare where you are to where you want to be. For that reason, using identical survey items or even the same survey process over a period of time is probably not a wise idea. If firms want to develop a means to track progress over time toward desired standards and goals, we advocate striking a balance between old and new items and processes. On the one hand, the value in using the old is that a direct comparison can be made and progress in an absolute sense can be empirically measured. In addition, mistakes that might have been made in the previous administration of the survey can be rectified, and the process therefore improved. On the other hand, the danger exists that you may be asking questions that are no longer important, missing more relevant information, and/or not capitalizing on opportunities to contribute to the change process with the use of new methods consistent with the desired culture.

Changing the Way in Which Results Are Managed

In line with the need to update the content and the process of a survey, it is important to pay close attention to how survey results are managed within the measurement system and to focus on increasing the impact of the results over time. For example, surveys may initially be incorporated into an integrated change agenda as a way to effectively raise awareness and mobilize early change efforts. Over time, the purpose may evolve—for example, from using a 360-degree feedback process for developing managers to using the process to recognize and promote cultural role models—as the organization becomes more accustomed to and fluent in the use of culturally relevant data. The need some organizations feel for absolute confidentiality (in the sense that even positive results are not shared) may diminish in favor of open acknowledgment and recognition of positive change. This shift may continue to the point where there is increasing emphasis on accountability for results, both positive and negative. Obviously this progression in the way the data are managed is dependent on a number of factors, but it is important to consider what the optimal objective should be for any cultural measures and then to strive for that objective.

Implications

Survey processes designed to support cultural change efforts are becoming ever more sophisticated and complex, and this development has implications for both those who conduct surveys and those who work with the results.

First, those responsible for designing and administering surveys need to be grounded in the strategy and operations of the business as well as in the fundamentals of survey research and organizational development. As we have stressed, the success of any change process and its related surveys is dependent on the explicit link to business needs. This means that the burden is on survey designers and statisticians to have an intimate (preferably first-hand) knowledge of corporate and industry matters.

Second, senior executives need to appreciate the interrelationship between the soft and the hard sides of the business and also understand the importance of metrics in driving change. Making data-based decisions using relevant and current-to-the-minute information is a managerial requirement in today's turbulent environment, and surveys can play a vital role in that process.

Last, all who are involved in the cultural change process need to view surveys as tools to stimulate interactive dialogue within the organization regarding the gap between what is and what might be. This is a critical change from the more traditional use of surveys as a means of benchmarking against the past or other companies. This new perspective implies that ongoing reciprocal communication between management and employees is not only possible but necessary to effect lasting changes in the organization's culture.

Conclusion

There are several critical issues involved in implementing survey processes that drive cultural change efforts. The most important points to remember are the following:

- Changing an organization's culture depends on long-term investment from all, starting with the sponsorship of the CEO and his or her leadership team.
- Surveys should be only a part of a total toolkit of interventions driven by a well-articulated business rationale for changing the organization's culture.
- Both survey data and survey processes provide opportunities to change culture.
- The process of reporting the results is perhaps the part of the survey that has the most potential as a cultural change tool.
- There is a growing need to develop management measurement systems for softer processes such as cultural change as companies increasingly focus on measuring multiple aspects of their performance.
- A cultural change process may involve various types of surveys and the distribution of multiple surveys over a period of time. It is important to consider developing an integrated plan to coordinate and leverage the various survey processes.

References

Argyris, C. (1994). Good communication that blocks learning. *Harvard Business Review, 72*(5), 77–85.

Block, P. (1987). *The empowered manager: Positive political skills at work.* San Francisco: Jossey-Bass.

Champy, J. (1995). *Reengineering management.* New York: HarperCollins.

Collins, J. C., & Porras, J. I. (1994). *Built to last: Successful habits of visionary companies.* New York: HarperCollins.

Cooperrider, D. L., & Srivastva, S. (1987). Appreciative inquiry in organizational life. In R. W. Woodman & W. A. Pasmore (Eds.), *Research in organizational change and development* (Vol. 1, pp. 129–169). Greenwich, CT: JAI Press.

Kaplan, R. S., & Norton, D. P. (1993). Putting the balanced scorecard to work. *Harvard Business Review, 71*(5), 134–147.

Kotter, J. P. (1995). Leading change: Why transformation efforts fail. *Harvard Business Review, 73*(2), 59–67.

Kotter, J. P., & Heskett, J. L. (1992). *Corporate culture and performance.* New York: Free Press.

Nadler, D. A., Shaw, R. B., Walton, A. E., & Associates. (1994). *Discontinuous change: Leading organizational transformation.* San Francisco: Jossey-Bass.

Salipante, P., Jr. (1992). Providing continuity in change: The role of tradition in long-term adaptation. In S. Srivastva, R. E. Fry, & Associates, *Executive and organizational continuity: Managing the paradoxes of stability and change* (pp. 132–167). San Francisco: Jossey-Bass.

Schein, E. H. (1980). *Organizational psychology* (3rd ed.). Upper Saddle River, NJ: Prentice Hall.

Schein, E. H. (1992). *Organizational culture and leadership* (2nd ed.). San Francisco: Jossey-Bass.

Senge, P. M., Kleiner, A., Roberts, C., Ross, R. B., & Smith, B. J. (1994). *The fifth discipline fieldbook: Strategies and tools for building a learning organization.* New York: Doubleday.

CHAPTER 4

Driving Change Through Surveys
Aligning Employees, Customers, and Other Key Stakeholders

William A. Schiemann

This chapter will show how organizational surveys can be a primary tool to drive change through the linkage of all members of an organization to other key organizational stakeholders. I discuss the following premises:

1. Competitive advantage requires rapid sustainable well-managed change.
2. To manage rapid change, an organization must create alignment between its strategy and its key stakeholders.
3. Competitive alignment requires timely, precise information from key stakeholders so that strategy, tactics, and resource deployment can be adjusted at frequent intervals.
4. Alignment also requires the integration of information from different sources.
5. Organizational surveys can be a rich source of information and even a primary indicator of current and future success in financial and marketplace performance.

The remainder of the chapter is devoted to supporting these premises and discussing research and practice that link organizational surveys to financial, marketplace, and other key stakeholder outcomes.

Competitive Advantage Requires
Rapid, Sustainable, Well-Managed Change

Globalization, industry integration, never-ending changes in customer expectations, durability of workforce skills, and changing societal norms all require an organization to have the ability to create a dynamic, rapidly adapting workforce. However, recent research (Schiemann, 1992) suggests that nearly one-half of major change efforts are falling short of expectations, as reported by managers and executives in a sample of over 100 of the Fortune 500 firms. Table 4.1 identifies the six largest barriers to successful change indicated by these managers.

"Employees' resistance to doing things in new ways" is the number one factor cited by nearly three-quarters of the managers surveyed as their biggest barrier to change. Resistance was reported not only in the depths of the organization but, notably, at the top as well. This finding is consistent with the view of David Kearns, the former CEO of Xerox. Reflecting on that company's turnaround from the brink of extinction, Kearns noted that senior management in many ways offered the greatest resistance to change (Kearns & Nadler, 1992).

The second largest barrier to change was "inappropriate culture to support change," cited by two-thirds of the survey respondents. In my interviews with many senior managers, also, most have said they have difficulty describing the future culture they need to support change and trouble securing agreement on the characteristics of their current culture. Based on the research my colleagues and I have conducted over the past decade, it appears that even those who presume they know their cultures are often substantially off the mark. Some top leaders, like Jack Welch at GE or Larry Bossidy at AlliedSignal, leave no doubt what type of culture they expect, but it is unclear whether these cultures have staying power beyond the career of a single dominant leader.

The remaining four barriers listed in Table 4.1 (poor communication, incomplete follow-through, inability to agree on strategy, and insufficient change skills) also relate strongly to culture, and all are symptomatic of cultural gaps. It is also interesting that all six of the barriers relate to people and that people issues are frequently reported to be the issues least well understood in organizations.

Table 4.1. Six Largest Barriers to Change.

Barrier	% of Companies Reporting ($n = 102$)
Employees' resistance to doing things in new ways	74
Inappropriate culture to support change	65
Poor communication of purpose/plan for change	45
Incomplete follow-through to change initiative	42
Lack of management agreement on business strategy	39
Insufficient skills to support change	39

Source: Schiemann, 1992, pp. 53–54. Used by permission.

This lack of understanding can, in part, be attributed to inadequate measurement of people and culture. While information on financial, product, and operations standards is readily available to management in most organizations, information on cultural and behavioral standards is frequently limited, nonexistent, or available only in forms almost impossible to use for decision making. While many organizations are talking about desired cultures, few have operative values, attitudes, and behaviors that enhance their products and services to meet or exceed customer expectations or other stakeholder needs more effectively than the competition's offerings. Ill-defined standards and inadequate information result in a lack of clear priorities, poor decisions, conflict, and low-value-added outputs.

To Manage Rapid Change, an Organization Must Create Alignment Between Its Strategy and Its Key Stakeholders

Historically, most organizations have focused primarily on shareholders and have used their own internal operating standards as their primary indicators of strategic success. One study (Lingle & Schiemann, 1996) found that organizations with an agreed-upon set of balanced measures—most frequently measures that targeted customers and employees in addition to shareholders and internal operations—outperformed their counterparts who relied only on the two traditional strategic measurement areas. Lingle and I applied the label *measurement-managed* to firms that regularly reviewed measures for three or more stakeholders (employees, customers, shareholders, suppliers, communities, and regulatory agencies, among others). These firms were more often leaders in their industries, had higher financial performances, and had dramatically higher rates of success with major change efforts. These measurement-managed firms reported success rates with change that exceeded 90 percent.

Some industry leaders have been using balanced sets of measures for some time. For many years, Johnson & Johnson has defined four key stakeholders in its vision statement—customers, employees, community, and shareholders—and has launched different measurement systems over the years to capture its performance in each targeted stakeholder area.

AT&T, for example, uses measures called EVA, CVA, and PVA—economic value added, customer value added, and people value added—to drive the company and each business unit (Ferling, 1993). Some companies, again like AT&T, have focused most heavily on shareholders, customers, and employees as the three crucial stakeholder groups that must be satisfied if the organization is to grow and prosper. Gaps in meeting the expectations of these key constituencies are seen to reduce the likelihood of competitive success.

An organization succeeds through its ability to effectively manage (that is, meet or exceed the expectations of) these constituencies and to align its strategy and its infrastructure with stakeholder expectations. The infrastructure includes the essential processes used to produce products and services, formal organizational and job structures, systems (for example, technological and human), capabilities, and culture, including the values that drive or inhibit individual behaviors. Based on early open-system theories by Katz and Kahn (1978), more recent work by Gale (1994), and the host of recent articles and books on quality and customer service, Figure 4.1 presents an integrated view of the linkages among shareholders, customers, employees, and the various elements of the organizational infrastructure.

Figure 4.1. Strategic Alignment for Peak Performance.

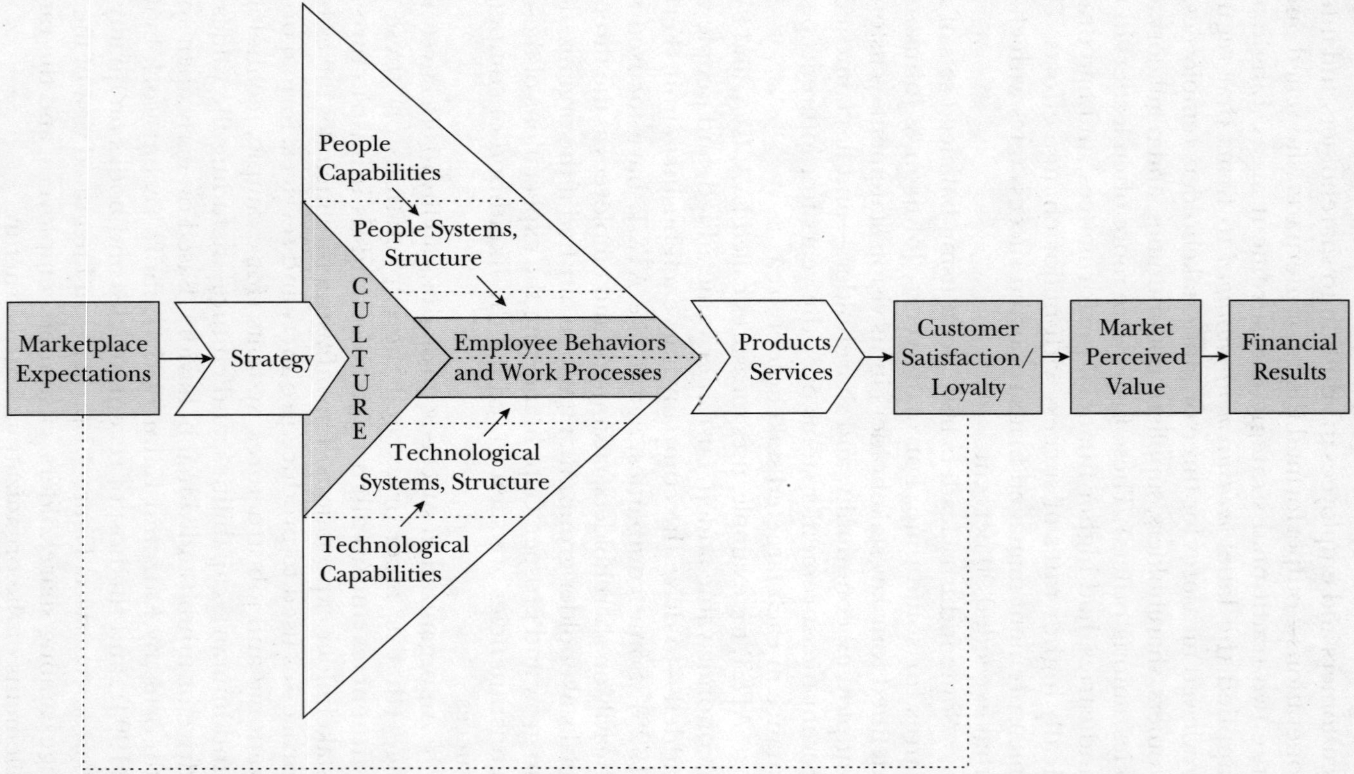

Marketplace Expectations → Strategy

CULTURE

People Capabilities

People Systems, Structure

Employee Behaviors and Work Processes

Technological Systems, Structure

Technological Capabilities

Products/ Services → Customer Satisfaction/ Loyalty → Market Perceived Value → Financial Results

As the figure illustrates, financial results are a function of attaining a strong competitive market position, which in turn is dependent on achieving high market perceived value for the products and services offered by the organization (Gale, 1994), where *market perceived value* is defined as the perceived quality of products and services relative to their price and compared to competitive alternatives. It is important to obtain these judgments from both customers and noncustomers in the marketplace.

Customer satisfaction is one very important element in achieving high market perceived value. It is dependent on delivering products and services that meet or exceed customer expectations, and this result requires employees who are highly motivated, skilled, and focused to perform the essential behaviors required to produce and support the products and services offered. Employee behaviors must be aligned with the important business processes and technology to efficiently and effectively produce products and services. The organization's shared values (an element of the cultural triangle in Figure 4.1) will either inhibit or facilitate the needed behaviors.

This organizational infrastructure should be propelled by a business strategy based on customers' expectations within the targeted marketplace. The business strategy sets the playing field by defining the primary markets and all core competencies required for success. Both the strategy and the infrastructure must be regularly reviewed and realigned to reflect dynamic changes in marketplace expectations.

For the sake of simplicity, this Figure 4.1 does not show the various regulatory and community stakeholders that also either inhibit or facilitate the delivery of high-quality products and services. For example, one pharmaceutical company has been thwarted from releasing its major product in the United States due to regulatory barriers connected with the Food and Drug Administration. The company has been debilitated owing to its inability to produce and deliver in one of its major worldwide markets, resulting in the loss of market share to other competitors, the loss of distribution channels that have made commitments elsewhere, and dramatic downsizing and malaise in the company's remaining workforce.

What has become clear is that constituencies including customers, employees, communities, regulatory agencies, and others are interlinked with an organization in various ways and create different levels of influence and performance requirements. The organization will exceed or fall short of its competitors to the extent that it can align its internal organizations with its key constituencies. Successful change requires obtaining rapid high-quality information from these groups. Unfortunately, research suggests that most organizations lack high-quality well-integrated information from these different stakeholders (Lingle & Schiemann, 1994).

Competitive Alignment Requires Timely, Precise Information from Key Stakeholders So That Strategy, Tactics, and Resource Deployment Can Be Adjusted at Frequent Intervals

Organizations that will survive in the next decade will have the ability to adapt continuously and to make required changes in strategic and tactical thinking. In the competitive milieu, interventions that are chosen to drive change must be honed to utilize scarce resources more efficiently. Shaping these interventions will require rapid intelligence systems that enable the organization to redirect resources and refocus continuously. For example, on-line market and customer data already enable retailers to change prices daily and to make adjustments in response to local competition, buyer demographics, and economics. Financial markets often require information updates by the minute. With increasing dependence on computer-controlled manufacturing processes that affect entire operations rather than single lines or batches, data on operational breakdowns must be deliverable within minutes to save huge operational costs.

While substantial work has been done in developing organizations' financial, market, and operating information systems, their people systems lag in accuracy, speed, and perceived criticality. Many executives still do not understand how to use people information for business decisions, and even when they do use it, the data are often not timely or are subject to much debate and interpretation. In the recent interviews Lingle and I held with senior executives, they said that the alignment of the workforce with the business strategy continues to be the number one issue for many of them (Lingle & Schiemann, 1996). The availability of information on critical people dimensions, coupled with meaningful education on how this information can be deployed strategically, will constitute a distinct breakthrough for many firms in the next three to five years. Those that have already made this breakthrough are significantly ahead of the pack.

While people issues are mentioned frequently by top executives as the area that most causes them to lose sleep at night, few have the type of information that enables them to understand these stakeholders. Their uncertainty regarding the state of their workforce causes anxiety. Individuals are more disposed to action when, rather than experiencing anxiety, they have information in their hands that they believe (information credibility), understand (information clarity), and see as relevant to their goals (information relevance).

In one study that I conducted of presidents and vice presidents in twenty-three companies regarding their views of employee information, almost every executive reaffirmed the importance of obtaining top-level information on workforce performance, satisfaction, commitment, capabilities, and understanding of strategy. However, most also leveled criticisms at the *relevance* of much of their workforce information. They also lamented the *lack of speed* with which they got employee data. Most of these executives live in a world of frequent information updates, yet most were lucky if they saw top-level employee information (for example, on employee satisfaction, values, and capabilities) biennially. Some received such feedback more often, but it was rarely linked to other key business objectives or to data from other stakeholders. Finally, a significant number of these executives were concerned about the *credibility* of the information they did get, often wrestling with the meaning of company satisfaction indices or measures of empowerment from surveys of organizational members. Few found the information easily accessible, and fewer still saw performance data as unbiased. My interviews indicated that executives have a need to find measures that are broadly reflective of their workforces and that are predictive of success in satisfying their other crucial stakeholders, most frequently shareholders and customers.

Alignment Also Requires the Integration of Information from Different Sources

Organizations face some significant problems when they must integrate information from different sources (employees, customers, suppliers, communities, and regulatory groups) in order to achieve alignment.

• Data from these different sources historically have been guarded by different functions, such as human resources, marketing, and finance. These guardians have been reluctant to share information that is part of their turf. After all, information has given them power and has been their unique way of adding value to the organization. Sharing information opens them to a variety of risks—loss of ownership, control, and power—that they would prefer to avoid.

• Different research traditions have been employed (for example, by market researchers versus organizational psychologists), using different scaling methods (for example, Likert scales versus semantic differentials), different tools (for example, questionnaires versus interviews), and different analysis techniques (for example, cross tabulation versus conjoint analysis versus cluster analysis versus factor analysis) that make data from the different traditions difficult, if not impossible, to compare. Industrial psychologists, for instance, have frequently gathered employee belief and satisfaction data using a 5-point Likert scale in questionnaires administered in a work setting. In contrast, pollsters and communications researchers such as Daniel Yankelovich have frequently used 4-point scales (no neutral or average response allowed) in telephone interviews of shareholders or customers to assess their beliefs and attitudes. Moreover, market researchers have often used 7- or 10-point scales to assess importance or satisfaction. Market researchers also frequently use so-called trade-off formats to learn what importance customers place on different product and service attributes. In sum, it quickly becomes difficult to make linkages across the various stakeholders.

• Data from different sources have been deployed in very different ways and used at different levels of the decision-making process in organizations. Data gathered for assessing the values, satisfaction, and commitment of the workforce often have their own set of follow-up and action processes so that users, usually top and middle management, can develop initiatives from the data and implement changes that focus on improving employee satisfaction and workforce productivity. The processes often involve the entire organization and require commitment from the entire senior management team. In contrast, data gathered by market researchers usually involve a narrower set of decision makers and are frequently used by fewer implementers within the organization.

• Data from different sources carry historical baggage affecting their credibility, importance, and strategic relevance. Unfortunately, while data are indeed value-free, user's perceptions of them are not. Often, data on people and culture have been considered "soft." In my practice, I find that many senior managers who have come from "hard" backgrounds in engineering, finance, or operations look askance at perceptual data, although most enlightened managers realize that each person is driven by his or her own perceptions, not someone else's "reality."

There continues to be a tension between hard and soft data in people's perceptions but also a growing awareness that some of the traditionally soft measures are valid representations of stakeholders' beliefs, which in turn drive behaviors such as employees' turnover, customers' brand switching, and shareholders' stock sales. The true challenge is getting these measures onto the strategic table as important metrics to guide the enterprise or prevent it from derailing. Some of the linkage work I describe later has helped increase managers' awareness that many soft measures are excellent predictors of important environmental, customer, market, and financial outcomes.

Organizational Surveys Can Be a Rich Source of Information and Even a Key Indicator of Current and Future Success in Financial and Marketplace Performance

One of the most effective ways of integrating organizational surveys with measures from other stakeholders is through the balanced scorecard or strategic performance gauge concepts alluded to earlier. These concepts, discussed by Kaplan and Norton (1992) and Lingle and Schiemann (1994, 1996), suggest that an organization needs a set of top-level strategic measures to guide its strategy implementation and provide a surveillance system of indicators that show how well the strategy is being executed. These measures must be tied closely to the stakeholders—shareholders, customers, employees, regulatory agencies, and so on—whose satisfaction and support will determine the success of the organization. This level of metrics then becomes an important bridge between employees and other stakeholders.

Furthermore, strategic performance gauges are the best indicator of what the business strategy really is, because in essence, the way in which strategy is measured becomes the way in which it operates. The old adage applies here, "What isn't measured doesn't get managed."

Strategic performance gauges, however, represent a number of different outcome levels. Financial measures are always an end result of how well the organization is doing in the marketplace. It is high customer satisfaction and perceived value that lead to loyal customers who increase their purchases and frequently refer new customers, thereby increasing market share. If this customer satisfaction is coupled with efficient production, the financial numbers are likely to be strong. Employees are major contributors to both satisfied customers and effective, efficient production.

Beyond being a major influence on customer and financial indicators, employees also contribute to their communities, work safely and ethically, and comply with regulatory requirements to a greater or lesser extent. These contributory behaviors influence most environmental performance gauges (for example, degrees of success in supporting Community Chest drives, meeting EPA standards, and meeting OSHA goals and compliance standards). In many instances, employees can be looked upon as the primary stakeholder group that influences all other major stakeholder groups. As problems arise with employees in the short run, surely problems will follow with other stakeholders and ultimately with financial success in the long run.

The model provided in Figure 4.1 shows the relationships among the key elements of an organization and its key inputs and outputs. Figure 4.2 shows how each of the major stakeholder groups relates to the dynamics of an organization. While it is impossible to discuss all the linkages in this model in this chapter, it should be evident that employees affect all of the other stakeholder groups. Therefore, it should be possible to develop metrics relating to employees that can also be linked to other stakeholders and to the strategic performance gauges associated with them.

As Figure 4.2 illustrates, employees have a unique vantage point on products and services, critical work processes, organizational culture, required capabilities, effectiveness of people systems (for example, reward and recognition programs and performance improvement programs), the business strategy and its implementation, customer expectations, and actions related to environmental requirements (such as regulatory compliance or commitments to the local community).

What most organizations have not done is to (1) identify the crucial people requirements that arise when employees are viewed as stakeholders with their own set of needs and expectations and (2) specify information that can be garnered from employees relating to the organizations' other key stakeholder objectives. Organizational surveys can serve both these needs.

With regard to the first need, most organizations wish to achieve a highly satisfied and motivated workforce that causes minimal disruptions to production (due to absence, turnover, illness, and the like), provides high-quality output, and grows and develops over time to increase the organization's overall capabilities. Quite a few of the factors important to these objectives can be tracked using organizational surveys (these factors are discussed in numerous other publications and will not be addressed here). With regard to the second need, employee perceptions can be linked to a wide array of metrics for other stakeholder groups. These are discussed in the next sections.

Linking Employees and Shareholders

Although the direct link between employees and shareholders may appear tenuous, employees are often in a tug of war with management over the allocation of earnings to shareholders versus the reinvestment of earnings in the business in order to provide a

Figure 4.2. Measuring the Dynamic Organization with Strategic Performance Gauges.

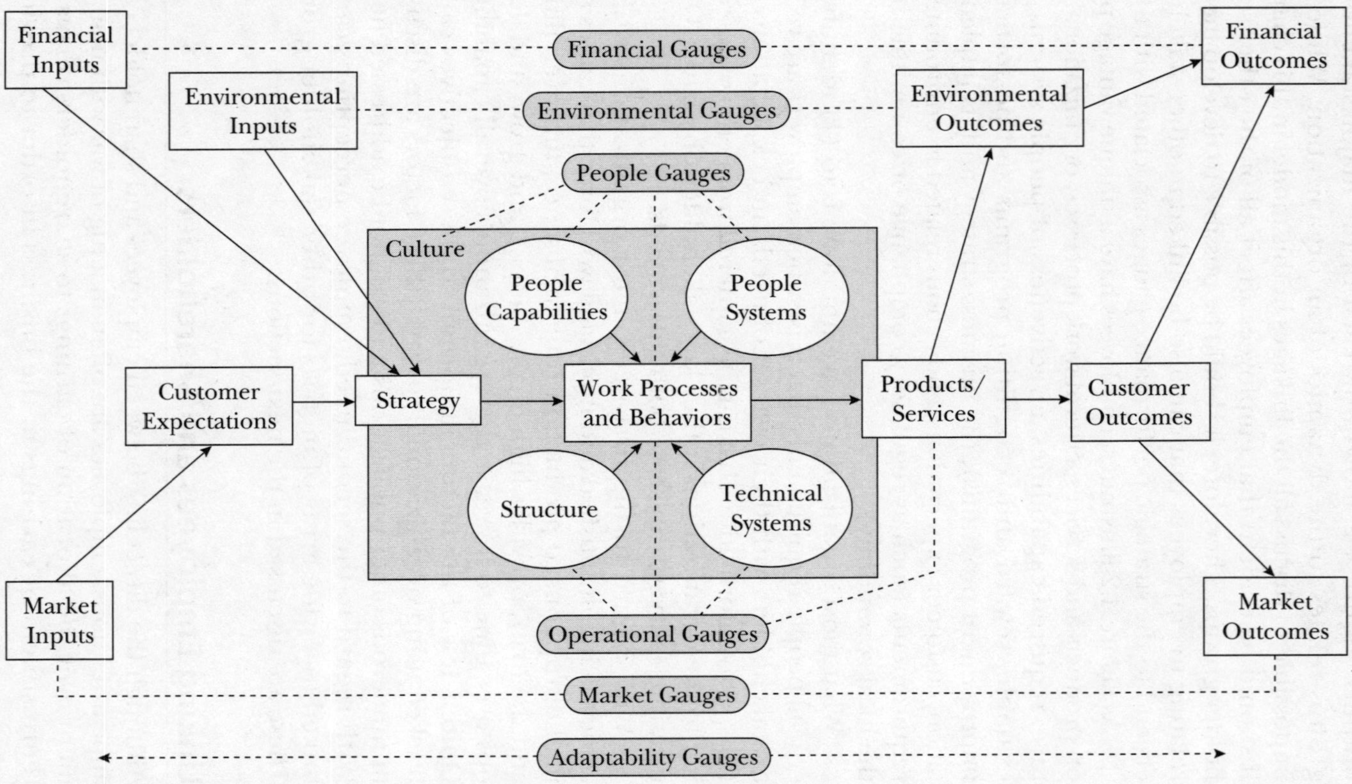

reduced workload through a higher headcount, productivity-enhancing technologies, and employee training. In ever increasing numbers, employees are also shareholders themselves, holding or receiving stock from the company. Employee stock ownership has produced stronger organizational performance in some cases (Leech, 1992), but usually this linkage is limited because the value of the shares owned by each employee is small relative to the value he or she obtains as an employee, which includes compensation, bonuses, benefits, and other value derived from the employee role.

While it may be argued that everything an employee does relates to financial performance, Table 4.2 lists some of the employee dimensions that most directly relate to financial performance, based on practice and theory.

The linkage between employees and shareholders is most direct in cost-reducing or productivity-enhancing activities. Employee dimensions that measure motivation and commitment, capability to serve the customer by producing quality products and services, clarity of goals, and incentives for performance utilize the basic tenets of motivation and goal-setting theory to predict individual and team performance. Other things being equal, the higher these performance dimensions, the higher productivity and earnings will be. Furthermore, higher commitment levels to the enterprise and greater job satisfaction (Lee, 1988; Lee & Mowday, 1987) will usually result in lower costs due to lower turnover and absenteeism.

Measures that uncover evidence of a high-performance culture by assessing productive attitudes can also be useful. For example, one leading-edge auto plant uses attitudes toward productivity, teamwork, and performance as important hiring criteria that predict an individual's success in working as a member of a high-performance team.

Other helpful attitudinal questions ask about perceptions of management support for quality improvement, shortcuts in quality that are being taken in the interest of higher output, and decisions that are made about cost reduction, waste, and bureaucracy. These perceptions are often good indicators of productivity gaps and helpful diagnostics that show where to address problems.

Many surveys fail to ask direct questions about productivity, such as questions about the six most important barriers to improved productivity or about continuous improvement activities,

Table 4.2. Employee Dimensions That Link to Shareholders.

Dimension	Extent to Which:
Continuous improvement/learning orientation	There is an orientation toward continuous improvement and learning at the individual and unit level.
Cost/waste reduction	There is a focus on cutting unnecessary costs.
Customer orientation	Employees and management have a commitment to serving customers well.
Enterprise commitment	Employees see a commitment to serving shareholders well.
Goal clarity	Organizational/unit goals are clear.
Motivation	Employees demonstrate high energy to perform well.
Performance orientation	Performance is highly valued over tenure or other criteria.
Product and service quality	Products/services meet or exceed standards.
Productivity, including efficiency and effectiveness	Organization/unit delivers the right products with the least cost.
Rewards, incentives	Rewards are linked to performance.
Supervisory capability	Supervisors have strong technical and interpersonal skills.
Top management/ leadership capability	Management is accessible, fair, and competent.

Note: Dimensions are listed in alphabetical order.

production norms, or actions being taken to increase quality output or reduce cost.

From my familiarity with many firms who have conducted linkage studies, I have found that one of the best predictors of financial and operating performance is employee rating of management capability, followed closely by employee perceptions of supervisory support and capability. *Over the years, I have come to believe that if I could measure only one dimension, it would be employee ratings of management.* Those ratings often account for the most variance in customer and financial performance.

Other dimensions that are usually good indicators of high levels of customer satisfaction and financial performance include employee perceptions of communication openness and effectiveness, rewards that are linked to performance, positive employee relations (usually best indicated by fair treatment, respect, and job security), and a culture of cooperation.

One of the hottest measures of financial performance in recent years is economic value added ("What's Your EVA?" 1993; McConville, 1994; Perkins, 1994). Little has been done to relate this indicator to employee measures, but workforce commitment, capabilities, and performance orientation would probably be good starting points. Firms with many units, such as AT&T or CSX Corporation, that are using EVA for all of these units (Ferling, 1993) are in an excellent position to determine which employee dimensions are the best indicators of EVA.

Other firms have also used organizational surveys to validate that certain financial practices such as maintaining adequate cash flow, making timely supplier payments, and engaging in ethical conduct are taking place.

Linking Employees and Customers

One of the most exciting areas of research and application is the relationship between market perceived value—the average value of goods and services perceived by current and potential customers—and market share, return on investment, and other key financial indicators. Brad Gale, in his recent work on market perceived value (1994), has demonstrated a clear relationship between market perceived value and customer loyalty, marketplace success, and financial performance. Value is determined by the perceived performance on key product attributes (for example, reliability, responsiveness, and professionalism of sales representatives) relative to the price of the product or service and relative to the competition. Therefore, when two or more firms produce the same product, the firm that delivers higher value on the key attributes will outperform the others. This is not a theoretical argument but one that has been demonstrated in a number of different industries over a wide range of products.

Employees and customers are similarly linked, since employees are a primary and in a service business perhaps the sole determinant of whether customer perceived value is high or low. Wiley (1994), for example, has demonstrated a relationship between employee and customer satisfaction that moves beyond the primitive gut feeling that happy employees yield happy customers. Summarizing the results of his linkage research, he identified a number of employee dimensions related to customer satisfaction: adequacy of resources for employees to do the work, fair treatment of employees, quality and customer focus, employee satisfaction with training for the current job, and recognition of employees, to mention a few.

Schneider and Bowen (1985) and Rafaeli (1989) discovered that employee job satisfaction can influence customers' perceptions of the quality of service, and Wiley (1994) found that employee retention is positively related to customers' satisfaction with the quality of service they receive. Given that employee turnover can be reasonably well predicted from employee survey items assessing intention to leave, a direct predictor of customer satisfaction could likely be established from those turnover intention data.

Brown and Mitchell (1993) investigated the relationship between employee perceptions of organizational obstacles and customer satisfaction and found a significant relationship between employee perceptions of co-workers, work environment, work materials, and information timeliness on the one hand and customer satisfaction on the other. Furthermore, Hauser, Simester, and Wernerfelt (1994) provided theory and mathematical formulas to demonstrate the importance of feedback to employees regarding their performance and perceived employee incentives in achieving high customer satisfaction. A summary of some of the most frequently cited employee measures used to predict customer satisfaction or other key customer outcomes is presented in Table 4.3.

Parasuraman, Berry, and Zeithaml, in a series of classic studies (Berry, Parasuraman, & Zeithaml, 1994; Parasuraman, Zeithaml, & Berry, 1985, 1988; Zeithaml, Berry, & Parasuraman, 1993), linked employee dimensions specifically to *customer service,* identifying five major service dimensions by which customers judge service quality. These studies were the basis for the SERVQUAL index, which measures these five dimensions. In subsequent work, based on theoretical relationships in the literature and on their empirical findings, Parasuraman, Berry, and Zeithaml identified a set of employee

Table 4.3. Employee Dimensions Reported to Predict Key Customer Outcomes.

Dimension	Extent to Which:
Adequacy of resources to serve the customer	There are adequate tools, people, and information to meet customer expectations.
Clear performance goals	Employees understand their performance goals.
Co-workers' capabilities	Co-workers have the necessary knowledge and skills to meet customer expectations.
Customer service orientation	Employees and management have a commitment to serving customers well.
Employee retention	There is actual employee turnover or intention to leave.
Fair treatment	There is consistent application of policies and procedures.
Information timeliness	Information is available when needed to meet customer expectations.
Job satisfaction	Employees are satisfied with the work itself.
Management support for customer service	Management takes actions that demonstrate its support of good customer service.
Performance feedback	Employees receive frequent performance feedback that enables them to improve their future performance.
Quality of products and services	Employees rate the quality of products and services delivered to customers.
Recognition/rewards	Employees are recognized and rewarded for their performance.
Role conflict	Employees feel torn between meeting the requirements of conflicting roles.
Training for current job	Employees feel they have sufficient training to perform well.

Note: The table contains a sample of the most frequently mentioned dimensions, listed in alphabetical order.

dimensions—including role conflict, lack of management commitment, and unclear performance goals, along with others—that lead to service performance gaps that affect the five service performance dimensions. Weitzel, Schwarzkopf, and Peach (1989), in fact, found that employee attitudes toward customer service were highly correlated with sales in a retail setting.

Thus, it is possible to measure the key customer service dimensions and their relationship to customer perceived value. Furthermore, it is possible to measure a sufficient number of key employee dimensions and link them to all or the most important of the five service quality dimensions that influence customer perceived value.

The five SERVQUAL dimensions are listed in Table 4.4 in order of importance across thirteen organizations, as reported by Berry, Parasuraman, and Zeithaml (1994). The distinct advantage of thinking in terms of the SERVQUAL measures is that they provide a generic set of categories for comparing any organizations using the same dimensions.

The disadvantage of SERVQUAL measures is that they do not capture product or service attributes and employee behaviors at the detailed transaction level that might be most meaningful to the customer and that would tell employees the specific nature of a

Table 4.4. SERVQUAL Customer-Defined Service Dimensions.

Dimension	Describes
Reliability	The ability to perform the promised service dependably and accurately
Responsiveness	The willingness to help customers and provide prompt service
Assurance	Employees are knowledgeable and courteous and are able to convey trust and confidence
Empathy	Caring, individualized attention is provided to customers
Tangibles	The appearance of physical facilities, equipment, personnel, and communication materials

Source: Adapted from Berry, Parasuraman, & Zeithaml, 1994.

performance gap. Furthermore, SERVQUAL global dimensions may not be contextually relevant to the respondent. A nice compromise is to use the SERVQUAL dimensions as a broad framework to represent the basic ways in which customers think about and evaluate any service and to develop specific behavioral survey items to assess the ways in which high or low ratings of a particular dimension are manifested within each service context, using the language of the customer.

The method of linking employees and shareholders and the method of linking employees and customers and their respective metrics are complementary and can be combined to set up employee metrics that correlate with customer satisfaction measures, which in turn relate to financial performance. This approach enables an organization to form linkages across stakeholder groups, from employees to customers to shareholders.

Frequently, survey questions do not provide adequate coverage of employee perceptions of product and service quality, service delivery processes, customer transaction relationships, customer expectations, and other market-related issues. Some organizations that measure customer service have taken the opposite road, using mostly customer-oriented items in their surveys of employees. However, these latter organizations often fail to capture some of the important "upstream" values, norms, capabilities, and leadership dimensions that are so crucial to achieving high service levels. Employees may be given the opportunity to endorse an item that asks if responsiveness to customers is rewarded but not be given the opportunity to assess the current level of training in responsiveness, the level of management coaching and feedback, and the degree to which high performance is rewarded. However, these later dimensions are often good predictors of customer satisfaction because they are key enablers.

Finally, I strongly suggest that organizations collect both customer and employee data within closely related periods so that data from the two sources can be analyzed for cause-and-effect relationships and so researchers can determine the extent to which employee values and capabilities and employee perceptions of human resource systems contribute to each of the customer-reported gaps.

In this process, it should be expected that customer reactions will lag employee behaviors and other internal processes. Customer satisfaction with service processes will be registered by the customer immediately, while customer satisfaction with product innovation, product warranty promises, and other attributes not immediately experienced may take months or years to register positively or negatively. Car buyers, for example, may not become dissatisfied with their purchase for several years—until that unexpected rattle shows up and cannot be fixed or until many service visits to the dealership for routine maintenance fail to meet expectations. Collecting data at meaningful time intervals facilitates the deployment of interventions that are highly focused yet holistic because they are based on a comprehensive look at the entire system and are not shotgun or knee-jerk reactions.

From a review of the literature and our own survey experience over the past years, my associates and I have developed an integrated list of product and service attributes that capture the key dimensions by which customers evaluate both products or services (see Table 4.5).

Table 4.5. Dimensions to Describe Products, Services, and/or Providers.

Dimension	Extent to Which:
Performance	The product or service does what it is designed to do.
Innovation	The products or services are viewed as leading edge, creative, or deploying the latest technology.
Professionalism	The product or service is delivered by employees in a manner deemed appropriate by customers (for example, employees are courteous, honest, and able to communicate clearly).
Responsiveness	Customer contact employees are quick to respond to inquiries and to resolve problems.
Features	The product or service offers special or unusual features beyond the basic deliverables.
Pricing	The cost of the product or service relative to other alternatives.
Image	The product, service, or supplier has a brand image that gives additional value to the customer.

Table 4.6 lists several dimensions that are not mentioned in Tables 4.2 or 4.3 but that I have found valuable in predicting important customer, financial, employee, and productivity outcomes. The employee dimensions in Tables 4.2, 4.3, and 4.6 and the customer dimensions in Table 4.5 are a good starting place for establishing the linkages described in Figures 4.1 and 4.2. This type of linkage research is already well under way in many leading firms and soon will become the norm.

Finally, note that caution should be exercised before assuming that a relationship predictive in one context will necessarily hold in another. Some relationships are fairly generalizable across settings (for example, one can predict the outcome of a union ratification vote from knowing employees' perceptions of fairness, supervisory quality, job security, trust, and communication (Getman, Goldberg, & Herman, 1976); however, the predictability of customer satisfaction should be tested carefully from setting to setting.

Table 4.6. Key Employee Dimensions.

Dimension	Extent to Which:
Commitment	Employees demonstrate commitment to the business and to serving their customers.
Communication	There is open two-way communication.
Employee empowerment	Employees are given the responsibility and authority to make decisions that influence their work and their customers.
Employee involvement	Employees are encouraged to participate in work and quality improvement efforts.
Innovation and creativity	Employees are encouraged to develop creative ideas, processes, or products.
Job demands	Work load is reasonable; employees can accomplish objectives in a quality manner.
Job security	Employees feel their jobs are secure.
Openness/trust	There is an environment in which ideas can be shared openly without fear of retribution.
Teamwork/ cooperation	Teamwork and cooperation are encouraged, supported, and rewarded.

Linking Employees and
Additional Stakeholders in the Environment

Employees also have a significant impact on a number of additional stakeholders who will vary depending on a firm's strategy, industry, geographical location, and other factors. For example, a number of prominent Fortune 100 firms, such as AT&T, Johnson & Johnson, DuPont, Hoffmann-LaRoche, Coca-Cola, Anheuser Busch, Sears, and most regional telecommunications and electric utilities have a strong orientation toward the communities in which they operate. Most of them believe that a strong relationship with the community will enhance their ability to execute their business strategies. For example, they may feel that they will receive better community support when difficult local, state, or federal regulations are under consideration, that their strong community image will create a feeling in the community of wanting to work for them, or that an image of being ethically, environmentally, and socially aware will make them less likely to be targets of activist efforts. A simple review of the *Exxon Valdez* oil spill and the way in which Exxon handled the situation demonstrates the potential problems that can arise when issues that affect communities are not addressed immediately and effectively.

Organizational surveys can be helpful in identifying the perceived values the firm espouses and the perceived values it practices. For example, a few years ago, I assessed the values in practice at a regional telephone company. It had crafted a set of values a number of years earlier that included environmental issues, and senior managers wished to see how well employees supported these values in philosophy and practice. They got a surprising response. Not only did the employees feel that the values were not being followed in practice, they also believed quite strongly that the management team did not support the values because important senior management actions and decisions had not demonstrated to employees that management was "willing to walk the talk." These employees drew upon many examples of management decisions that were inconsistent with the espoused values. A carefully crafted survey and follow-up focus groups were easily able to uncover such gaps.

Other organizations have used surveys of their members to assess attitudes and values that are predictive of critical outcomes relating to environment, community, and regulatory issues. For example, DuPont has an excellent reputation for safety. Its philosophy is that safety is not simply a set of practices to conduct in a given work setting but a whole way of thinking and living. That is why the company expects employees to think and practice safe behaviors at home as well as at work. At a typical DuPont plant, safety permeates the grounds, the buildings, and work practices and is reinforced through training, incentives, and information that demonstrate that only employees can prevent accidents and other OSHA violations. DuPont and others have used surveys to measure not only workforce perceptions of safety practices but also their beliefs in safety values, safety attitudes, and an awareness of important principles associated with safety.

In a context such as this, safety attitude indices can be created that predict accident levels, safety behaviors, and OSHA compliance. In fact, part of the reason for success in this context is the ability to measure enough about safety attitudes, beliefs, values, and behaviors to develop a clear empirical connection between them and a number of critical outcomes such as accidents.

Finally, yet another important use of organizational surveys is the assessment of ethics. Ethics violations are growing dramatically (recall, for example, news stories about Kidder Peabody's sales of derivatives or the savings and loan scandal), coupled with more whistle-blowing. Ethics issues may involve sexual harassment, information tampering, selection or termination of employees for inappropriate reasons, environmental cover-ups, and so forth. A number of leading firms have used organizational surveys to identify the extent to which employees believe that certain ethical values are being upheld in the organization.

Putting It All Together

A number of organizations now have balanced scorecards that include measures of different stakeholders, but few have put everything together, effectively integrating their employee measures with measures of the other stakeholders.

Johnson & Johnson is one far-sighted organization that has conducted a broad employee survey related to its credo—the vision statement that has guided the company over the past few decades.

The four tenets of the credo focus on commitments to the company's current and potential customers, its employees, the communities in which it operates, and its shareholders. A number of values and beliefs are espoused for each stakeholder group, and the practice of these values and beliefs is measured in the survey. Obviously, employees are in the best position to comment on values and beliefs related to them as a stakeholder group, but they also have a perspective on how they and the company, through company policies, honor their commitments to the other three groups of stakeholders. For example, a number of survey items relate to customer orientation and the related values that must exist and activities that must occur to serve customers well. Each stakeholder group has a similar set of supporting items. Johnson & Johnson has created over twenty indices that relate to different performance outcomes, and it provides feedback to local and senior managers on how well they are managing in the areas that ultimately influence their bottom line. Johnson & Johnson, along with some other companies, has identified indices that are highly predictive of overall company and business unit performance and are specific indicators of success.

Another company, a large service organization, divides its organizational survey into numerous indices that predict critical areas of workforce and organizational performance. One index, for example, has been used to predict quite accurately a union contract ratification vote. Other indices have been used to predict turnover, safety performance, achievement of unit productivity goals, customer satisfaction, and supervisory and managerial success. There was enormous elation among members of the managerial team when they realized that they could almost perfectly rank the performance of over fifty nearly identical business units by unit performance on a couple of key management and supervisory dimensions.

A health care firm uses six of its twenty or so indices to predict the performance of its 100-plus business units, which vary dramatically in size, product, and market. The company has invested heavily in a philosophy and vision that says that these units will be successful if they adhere to a particular vision and way of operating. It appears to work because managers who score highly on the six indices tend to outperform their counterparts in other business units. While the predictions are not perfect, they are clearly a major source of comparative information about how the units are operating, despite their being in very different businesses.

These examples provide a sense of what it is possible to measure and predict through the collection of meaningful employee perceptions. Much of these three companies' success can be attributed to their identifying a broad array of survey items, carefully honing them into meaningful indices, and then linking these indices to crucial business outcomes. This type of research and application raises organizational survey data to a new height with senior executives, who can then see a link between their people's management performance and important business outcomes. Not only do the data serve as a tool to evaluate the past on dimensions that may seem more relevant to employees interests than to business outcomes (lack of a business outcome emphasis is a frequent criticism of traditional employee attitude surveys), but they also begin to serve as useful predictors of future outcomes.

At another level of thinking, the employee dimensions described in this chapter become a way of understanding how the management of employees can have a significant effect on important business results. Managers who have been exposed to this type of thinking dig deeper into their organizational surveys, to understand which areas are strong and which are deficient on key indices so they can redirect resources toward the improvement of key outcomes. Improving "teamwork," say, or "communication" no longer is a nice or even an important thing to do because managers "think" it may influence quality, customer satisfaction, or cost reduction. Smart companies now know exactly what impacts such improvements have, and therefore they are more efficient in their deployment of resources to close performance gaps. Furthermore, they have an important metric with which they can determine whether the performance gap closes after the improvements have been implemented.

Conclusion

This is a very exciting time for organizational research relating to employee values, attitudes, and beliefs because business is entering a period in which there is top management interest in understanding the nature of the relationships between their employees (and, for that matter, their other labor suppliers, such as distributors, dealers, and contractors) and important financial, environmental, and marketplace indicators. For years, many progressive leaders have realized that people are organizations' most important asset, driving financial return through their impact on productivity, but the ability to justify this gut feeling and to identify specifically where and how this happens has until recently been only a dream.

As new databases spring up and organizations become willing to share some of their findings in this area, far greater gains in knowledge of how to use this kind of information effectively will emerge. But the call to action must be now, because much of the knowledge about how to develop linkages between employee dimensions and behaviors of other stakeholders and to use these linkages strategically is already within reach. Moreover, there is much to be learned within the context of each particular organization. Some general relationships may hold—job satisfaction as a predictor of turnover or accidents, for example—but other relationships may be unique to an organization, such as the relationship of a particular incentive system to customer satisfaction.

Furthermore, there are increasing opportunities to involve current professional associations in the creation of databases that can be shared among an association's membership. For example, a regional human resource planning association decided to create a database to identify how well human resource staffs serve their "customers." The association has created an integrated study among its membership to identify common reasons why some organizations receive high value assessments from their internal customers and others do not, with a focus on understanding the dimensions that make a difference. Studies like this one open up endless possibilities for helping particular organizational functions, like human resources, dramatically increase their learning and therefore their ability to make significant adjustments in their organizations that increase those organizations' perceived value to customers, thereby increasing their likelihood of future survival and success.

References

Berry, L. L., Parasuraman A., & Zeithaml, V. A. (1994). Improving service quality in America: Lessons learned. *Academy of Management Executive, 8*(2), 32–33.

Brown, K. A., & Mitchell, T. R. (1993). Organizational obstacles: Links with financial performance, customer satisfaction, and job satisfaction in a service environment. *Human Relations, 46*(6), 725–757.

Ferling, R. L. (1993). Quality in 3D: EVA, CVA, and employees. *Financial Executive, 9*(4), 51.

Gale, B. T. (1994). *Managing customer value.* New York: Free Press/Macmillan.

Getman, J. G., Goldberg, S. B., & Herman, J. B. (1976). *Union representation elections: Law and reality.* New York: Russell Sage Foundation.

Hauser, J. R., Simester, D. I., & Wernerfelt, B. (1994). Customer satisfaction incentives. *Marketing Science, 13*(4), 327–350.

Kaplan, R. S., & Norton, D. P. (1992). The balanced scorecard: Measures that drive performance. *Harvard Business Review, 70*(1), 71–79.

Katz, D., & Kahn, R. L. (1978). *The social psychology of organizations* (2nd ed.). New York: Wiley.

Kearns, D. T., & Nadler, D. A. (1992). *Prophets in the dark: How Xerox reinvented itself and beat back the Japanese.* New York: HarperCollins.

Lee, T. (1988). How job dissatisfaction leads to turnover. *Journal of Business and Psychology, 2,* 263–271.

Lee, T., & Mowday, R. M. (1987). Voluntarily leaving an organization: An empirical investigation of Steers and Mowday's model of turnover. *Academy of Management Journal, 30,* 721–734.

Leech, E. (1992). Employee ownership, incentives yield outstanding performance. *Bank Management, 68*(10), 60–64.

Lingle, J. H., & Schiemann, W. A. (1994). Is data scatter subverting your strategy? *Management Review, 83*(5), 53–58.

Lingle, J. H., & Schiemann, W. A. (1996). From balanced scorecard to strategic gauges: Is measurement worth it? *Management Review, 85*(3), 56–61.

McConville, D. J. (1994). All about EVA. *Industry Week, 243*(8), 55–58.

Parasuraman, A., Zeithaml, V. A., & Berry, L. L. (1995, Fall). A conceptual model of service quality and its implications for future research. *Journal of Marketing, 49,* 41–50.

Parasuraman, A., Zeithaml, V. A., & Berry, L. L. (1988, Spring). SERVQUAL: A multiple-item scale for measuring customer perceptions of service quality. *Journal of Retailing, 64,* 12–40.

Perkins, J. (1994). Economic value added: Meeting management's mission. *Accountants Journal, 73*(1), 41–42.

Rafaeli, A. (1989). When cashiers meet customers: An analysis of the role of supermarket cashiers. *Academy of Management Journal, 30,* 245–273.

Schiemann, W. A. (1992). Why change fails. *Across the Board, 29*(4), 53–54.

Schneider, B., & Bowen, D. E. (1985). Employee and customer perceptions of service in banks: Replication and extension. *Journal of Applied Psychology, 70,* 423–433.

Weitzel, W., Schwarzkopf, A. B., & Peach, E. B. (1989). The influence of employee perceptions of customer service on retail store sales. *Journal of Retailing, 65,* 27–39.

What's your EVA? (1993, September 20). *Fortune,* p. 44.

Wiley, J. (1994, April). Employee, customer and financial performance linkages: From research results to action plan. Workshop presented at the Ninth Annual Conference of the Society for Industrial and Organizational Psychology, Nashville, TN.

Zeithaml, V. A., Berry, L. L., & Parasuraman, A. (1993, Winter). The nature and determinants of customer expectations of service. *Journal of the Academy of Marketing Science, 21,* 1–12.

CHAPTER 5

Multisource (360-Degree) Feedback

Surveys for Individual and Organizational Development

David W. Bracken

Whether people like getting feedback or not, when they do get it, they want it to be accurate, specific, relevant, and timely. In the work setting, feedback is especially critical to improving both individual and organizational effectiveness, yet few people seem to be able to do it just right. Even when employees seek and solicit feedback, they are often frustrated in their attempts to find someone who is adept at giving it.

In the traditional work roles, where the supervisor ("boss") is expected to be a major source of feedback, more often than not we hear criticisms of that feedback on all of the criteria I have mentioned. It should not be surprising that performance appraisals come under constant criticism when the supervisor may be unable and/or unwilling to provide high-quality feedback. The prospects for improvement become bleaker as spans of control increase and the time-per-employee ratio decreases.

The search for new and improved sources of feedback has caused the research community to collaborate with organizations to examine alternative sources of feedback to the boss, primarily targeting peers and subordinates as the supplemental feedback providers (Borman, 1974). The meta-analysis reported by Harris and Schaubroeck (1988) on self-manager, self-peer, and peer-manager ratings cites studies going back to 1953! As early as 1978,

Morrison, McCall, and De Vries were able to review twenty-four commercial instruments developed for this purpose, although they also observed the general lack of theoretical and empirical bases for devising such instruments.

This chapter summarizes contemporary philosophy and practice in the collection of feedback from multiple sources, or *multisource feedback* (MSF). I also consider the possible uses of MSF and its maximal apparent potential, and I review critical methodological issues. The discussion is restricted to survey-based methods and does not include other potentially useful but more qualitative methods such as interviews and focus groups.

What Is Multisource Feedback?

As illustrated in Figure 5.1, multisource feedback draws upon existing research and practice in order to maximize the quality of feedback from managers, peers, and subordinates, and it expands the rater domain to include such other potentially valuable sources as team members, internal customers, and external customers. Feedback is collected systematically, simultaneously, and (often) anonymously from each relevant rating source to give ratees a 360-degree view of their behavior as it relates to successful job performance. (In addition to *360-degree feedback* and *multiple source feedback*, multisource feedback is sometimes also called *full-circle feedback*, and other labels are surely being created as I write.)

There are many variations of MSF, including versions in which only subordinates participate (upward feedback) or only peers (peer review) and so on. The combination of rating sources, which may include self-rating, will depend on such factors as the objectives of the process (for example, development versus appraisal), the nature of the job (for example, supervisory versus individual contributor), and the appropriateness of various feedback sources (for example, direct reports, peers, and/or customers). (The basis for determining rating sources is discussed further later in this chapter.)

Evolution

Various authors and consultants have laid claim to pioneering MSF going back twenty-five years or more, and the evolution of MSF can

Figure 5.1. Multisource Feedback Perspectives.

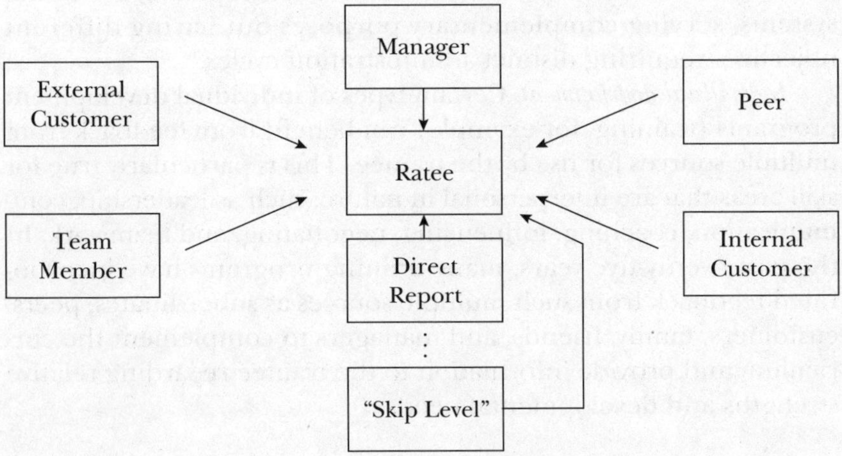

be traced to two primary methodological sources: organizational surveys and individual development processes.

Organizational surveys. Most surveys of organizational members have recognized the key role of the supervisor in determining employee satisfaction and commitment, and the content of survey instruments reflects this. Surveys often have a set of items along the lines of "My supervisor does X," describing some set of behaviors or skills. However, survey programs often underutilize the supervisory information they acquire by reporting it only at an aggregated level (department- or companywide, for example). When work group reports *are* provided, they often include data for all the survey items. In this latter case, the supervisor might be expected to address every issue identified in the survey items, including issues like pay and benefits, which may be beyond a supervisor's control. This kind of reporting inevitably leads to frustration and little action from the supervisory ranks, eventually dragging down the entire survey program.

Contemporary solutions to using organizational surveys for supervisory feedback will continue to use "My supervisor . . ." items, but will provide the supervisor with a report on only those items relevant to him or her, leaving the survey's culture and climate content for action at some higher level. We can expect organizational survey and MSF processes to evolve into separate, coexisting systems, serving complementary purposes but having different objectives requiring distinct administration cycles.

Individual development. Certain types of individual development programs (training, for example) can benefit from feedback from multiple sources for use by the trainee. This is particularly true for skill areas that are interpersonal in nature, such as leadership, communication, coaching, influencing, negotiating, and teamwork. In the past twenty-five years, many training programs have incorporated feedback from such multiple sources as subordinates, peers, customers, family, friends, and managers to complement the curriculum and provide information to the trainee regarding relative strengths and developmental needs.

Popularity

The increasing demand for MSF, often coming from organizational leaders, stems from several key sources.

Dissatisfaction with traditional performance appraisal. Organizations are constantly in search of the solution to the performance appraisal "problem" (Schneier, Beatty, & Baird, 1986), including such difficulties as nonstandard administration, lack of relevance and alignment, lack of performance differentiation, poor feedback, and demotivation. The MSF solution has promise for improving the quality and defensibility of performance appraisals (Bernardin & Beatty, 1984) and is expected to be routinely included as part of future appraisal systems (Murphy & Cleveland, 1995).

Participation and empowerment. Involving large segments of the employee body to provide feedback distributes the power of giving feedback; it no longer resides solely in the hands of the boss. Although empowerment often exists more in name than in practice in organizations, genuine empowerment of the sort MSF offers can be the foundation for successful organizations, which must respond effectively to rapidly changing external and internal demands.

Customer focus. Organizations are adopting the concept that employees should treat each other as "customers," even in the supervisor-subordinate relationship. Feedback from peers is also often positioned as "internal customer" feedback. Where appropriate, MSF also allows external customers to be directly involved in the feedback process; they can provide data potentially more actionable (that is, situation-specific, behavioral, and associated with a specific person) than that obtained from traditional customer satisfaction surveys.

Larger spans of control. With the flattening of organizational structures, the resulting larger spans of control have put supervisors in an even more difficult position than formerly when attempting to give quality feedback; they have less time to observe performance and less time to meet all the competing demands on them. However, positive organizational forces that might support the implementation of MSF include people's perceptions (and the reality) of fairness, an emphasis on skill development, and people's dissatisfaction with the change produced by traditional organizational surveys.

Typical Uses

MSF can be used for at least three major purposes in various combinations. Management's decision regarding MSF purposes, or goals, will have major implications for the design of the total process and will require up-front commitment and communication.

Individual development. Individual development is the major purpose of MSF, and individual development plans are based on an analysis of that feedback, typically performed by the ratees themselves. With proper guidance and resources, the ratee can be directed to training, developmental resources (such as books, videos, and coaching), and career planning. Proponents of the use of MSF exclusively for developmental purposes point to the following features, which when preserved can be expected to create acceptance of the need for behavioral change and the behavioral change itself:

- *Rater anonymity:* allowing raters to have anonymous input, owing to the belief that anonymous ratings are more honest and accurate. However, there is a question whether we can (or should) guarantee anonymity when MSF is used for administrative purposes.

- *Confidentiality:* allowing the results to remain the sole property of the ratee, who has no obligation to share the data with others and who knows there is no possibility that the results will become known to the organization.
- *Psychological safety:* allowing the ratee to "make sense" of the results and interpret them in a way that is consistent with his or her understanding of the context in which they were collected.
- *Self-awareness:* creating increased self-awareness through a process that begins with a self-assessment prior to receiving results and proceeds through an analysis of the results themselves. This process creates gaps between self-perceptions, feedback data, and desired states, gaps that should produce a desire and direction for behavioral change.

Administrative decision making. With appropriate design and usage considerations (discussed below), MSF can be used in making individual and organizational decisions, such as those required for performance appraisals and succession plans. Subordinates and peers are often in a better position than the boss to evaluate aspects of performance such as results and interpersonal behaviors (Murphy & Cleveland, 1995). When MSF has this decision-making purpose, the list of "owners" of the data will expand to include the ratee's manager and even the organization as personified by the human resource department.

Organizational development. MSF data can be aggregated to create a skill profile for the entire organization with implications for organizationwide interventions. When MSF has this purpose, other organizational benefits can include team building, increased communication, creation of a feedback-rich climate, increased customer contact, and improved morale. The very reversal of roles inherent in having subordinates rate the boss may serve to break down the barriers created by authority and traditional hierarchies (Murphy & Cleveland, 1995).

Appropriate Uses

The view that multisource feedback is the property of the individual for developmental purposes alone continues to receive support, but it may result in underutilization of the full potential of the process. Leaving feedback information solely in the hands of the ratee creates potentially serious implications for sustaining the process and realizing true behavioral change, due to the following factors:

- Ratees are not held accountable for follow-through and may lack motivation to change.
- Ratees see the feedback as supplemental information that is "nice to have" but tangential to their real work.
- Ratees see the feedback as an "event," happening only once or only at long intervals and lacking ongoing feedback or support.
- Raters may not see any evidence that their input is being used, and this may eventually reduce their motivation to participate and/or provide honest feedback.

The critics of the decision-making purpose imply (or even directly claim) that the very use of MSF for appraisal, for example, invalidates the data, due to the resulting motives of the raters (Farh, Cannella, & Bedeian, 1991). There certainly is strong evidence that the context for use has an influence on traditional supervisory ratings of supervisors (Longenecker, Sims, & Gioia, 1987) and even self-ratings (Farh & Werbel, 1985). Whether any of these effects can be circumvented through rater training remains unanswered.

Despite lingering doubts about the factors that can affect the validity of multirater processes, some I/O psychologists continue to support MSF's potential value when the process is coupled with a list of caveats (Bernardin, 1986; Bernardin & Beatty, 1987; Bracken, 1994; Dunnette, 1993; London & Beatty, 1993; Murphy & Cleveland, 1995). Possibly the greatest opportunity presented by MSF is for improvement of the performance appraisal process by supplementing it with multisource feedback. Murphy and Cleveland (1995), for example, state: "The almost universal reliance on the supervisor as the sole source of evaluation may make sense when considered from the perspective of the organizational power hierarchy, but it will not always make sense from the perspective of obtaining accurate evaluations" (p. 146).

Too many performance appraisal systems focus on the outputs (the ends) with insufficient emphasis on the process (the means). We all know of or have worked for people who accomplished their objectives using means that were inconsistent with company values but who moved on (and up) before the repercussions were felt. MSF can provide the organization with a method for identifying employees who do not support organizational values through their actions even though they do produce. This use of MSF, of course, assumes that the organization truly believes that the end does not justify any means of getting there.

Who Owns MSF Data?

The answer to this question has direct implications for the design of the process and its content. The issue is whether the process customer is the individual or the organization. Table 5.1 highlights the system components that are characteristic of the MSF process when the individual is the customer and when the organization is the customer. The distinctions are often not as clear-cut as suggested here. Even so, the planning and implementation of the system needs to consider the purpose and customer. The content of feedback items, for example, is likely to be quite different depending on the purpose and owner of the process, and there is with little likelihood of maintaining continuity when a process changes from developmental to administrative.

When it comes to data comparisons, the implications of purpose and customer affect both the rating process and the reporting of the data. Where the individual is the customer, what matter most are relative strengths and opportunities to improve, and everyone has the opportunity to select the areas where he or she can most benefit from improvement. The rater need think only of one person when completing the questionnaire, and supplying a list of top-ten and bottom-ten scores as part of the subsequent report is common. When the organization is the customer, it becomes more appropriate to ask the raters to make between-person comparisons, since the organization must make decisions between employees for the distribution of rewards such as pay and promotions. Both the organization and the ratee will want to know where the ratee stands in comparison to others *within the organization;* external norms are typically of little use.

**Table 5.1. Multisource Feedback Process,
Defined According to Customer.**

MSF System Component	Customer	
	Individual	Organization
Use	Skill development	Organizational development
	Self-awareness	Administration
Content	Job-specific	Organization-specific
	Skill-based	Values-based
	Standard	Custom
Participation	Voluntary	Required
Data comparisons	Ipsative (within person)	Normative (between persons)
Administration	As requested/ad hoc	As needed (for example, annual)

Murphy and Cleveland (1995) make one additional point about the importance of determining the purpose and customer. When the individual is the customer and the rater is making within-person comparisons, the actual observation and encoding of the information is based on this within-person purpose. Changing the basis of comparison from within-person to between-persons, especially after the observation and encoding process, may be confusing and reduce the accuracy of the feedback.

How Multisource Feedback Works: Steps in the Process

The successful MSF process will result from careful planning and consideration of lessons learned from such other related processes and systems as selection, performance management, leadership development, and use of organizational surveys. The following steps in implementing an MSF process are provided as core recommendations based on experience and research (although the opportunity and need remain to adapt and learn as we all gain more experience with this tool).

Communicating

All participants in the process need to have an understanding of the process and the expectations for themselves as raters and ratees. This understanding can include:

- *Purpose.* How will the feedback data be used? Who "owns" the feedback? If used for appraisal, how will it be integrated with other performance data?
- *Process.* How does it work? How will raters be nominated? Is participation voluntary or required? What is the timing?
- *Expectations.* Who should expect to be participating? Will ratees be expected to share results with raters? With their managers?

The communication phase should also establish a *contract with the process participants.* It is important not to overpromise where it will be difficult to deliver or to leave out significant pieces of information, such as who owns (that is, who will see) the data. This is management's first opportunity to emphasize the issue of *consistency* across all MSF users and to set expectations for important phases.

Establishing of Job Relevance

The beginning point for the step of establishing job relevance is for management to consider the implementation of MSF in the context of organizational mission, values, and strategies (London & Beatty, 1993). The MSF system needs to be designed to ensure that both its *content* and its *methods* support and in turn are reinforced by the organization's priorities.

Whether used for development or decision making, feedback content must capture important job competencies, if only to improve user acceptance (face validity) of the feedback. Some standard instruments used solely for developmental purposes rely on general competency models that can be applied to members of job families (such as managers, individual contributors, internal consultants, or salespeople). These instruments are typically comprehensive (and long) with some customization allowed, but they rely on the user and/or raters to determine the aspects of the competency model that are most important for the ratee's job.

When MSF is used for decision making, particularly in performance appraisals, the demands for establishing job relevance become more important and are coupled with the demand to make the instrument more focused (that is, shorter), due to the number of employees involved. The exact level of specificity needed for a job-relevant instrument is a question that requires careful consideration. For example, can one instrument (or portion thereof) be applied universally across an organization regardless of position? I call this instrument a *values-based competency model.* It describes, in behavioral terms, the expected behaviors for all employees in such areas as ethics, integrity, teamwork, diversity, respect for the individual, customer focus, continuous improvement, risk taking, empowerment, and so on.

Designing the Questionnaire

Standard multirater instruments can be very useful for employee development applications. Since these tools are often used on a targeted population and/or on a long cycle (two years or more between administrations), most organizations are willing to invest in their use. Standard instruments often include normative data and developmental prescriptions as well, enhancing their value to the individual and the organization. (A comprehensive review of multirater instruments has been completed by Van Velsor and Leslie, 1991, and is an excellent source for those searching this market.)

A majority of the organizations using or planning to use MSF for decision-making purposes are creating custom instruments (Ewen, 1995; Timmreck & Bracken, 1995). The typical objectives in choosing full customization are to simultaneously increase job relevance and minimize length. The typical custom instrument will be no more than fifty items long, possibly with different versions for different rater groups, such as subordinates, peers, and customers (Timmreck & Bracken, 1995).

Questionnaire items should be written in behavioral terms that minimize rater subjectivity and judgment, rather than in broad trait terms. The following are examples:

Broad trait statement   This person believes in empowerment.

Behavioral statement   This person has direct reports make decisions in their areas of responsibility.

Other verbs beside *believes* that require inference beyond observation are *knows, understands,* and *values.* Every effort should be made to minimize or eliminate their use in MSF content, even though they are commonly found in organizational values statements.

Despite arguments regarding response sets and the need for negatively phrased items, I also believe that items should be phrased in positive terms, describing the desired behavior as a model (that is, items should describe what to do, not what not to do). This practice also helps considerably in the processing, reporting, and interpretation of the results (discussed below).

Since the instruments most typically used for MSF have a format of multiple-choice items, a major consideration is the *response scale* used to rate behaviors. A review of thirty instruments currently used by major organizations in an "upward feedback" consortium (Timmreck & Bracken, 1995) produced the list of different scales shown in Table 5.2, presented in descending order from most used to least used.

All response scales are *not* created equal, and the choice of scale alone can affect the distribution of responses. Bracken and Paul (1993) report that *frequency scales* and *satisfaction scales* applied to the same item stems produce very different results, and they conclude that frequency scales are not recommended for MSF applications.

Importance scales are a feature of many standard instruments because they are consistent with the need to allow users to determine the aspects of the competency model most relevant to their jobs as perceived by their raters. Sometimes importance ratings are given at the dimension rather than the item level. The use of importance scales is much less prevalent in custom instruments, reflecting the equal (high) importance of all competencies on these particular instruments and reinforced by the need to keep the instruments short and user-friendly. In the survey of thirty instruments used in an upward feedback consortium, only two included importance ratings (Timmreck & Bracken, 1995), and these were standard "off-the-shelf" instruments.

Write-in questions can be a valuable source of information for ratees as they interpret their results and create action plans. The most common format for write-ins places them at the end of the instrument, possibly asking for comments on what the ratee should "stop doing," "start doing," and "continue doing." In my experi-

Table 5.2. Response Scales for Upward Feedback.

Scale	Number of Responses	Top Anchor	Bottom Anchor
Extent	4, 5, 7	To a great extent	To little extent
Agreement	5, 7	Strongly agree	Strongly disagree
Satisfaction	5, 6	Very satisfied	Very dissatisfied
Effectiveness	5	Extremely	Not at all
Expectation	5	Does not meet	Far exceeds
Truth	4	True	False
Strength	3	Strong	Development area
Forced choice	3	[Behavioral]	[Behavioral]
Frequency	5	Always	Never

ence, formats that ask the respondent to illustrate each rating with a behavioral example may overburden both the respondent (lowering response rates and quality) and the consumer of the information. If this burden reduces the probability that the rater will complete the questionnaire, then any benefit the write-in might have is lost. Also note that analyzing write-in comments is typically the most costly part of data processing.

Decisions about the length, format, and use of write-ins must be weighed in the light of their impact on the quality of the information, their effect on response rates, and their associated cost. Compared to response rates for organizational surveys, response rates for MSF questionnaires are of greater importance due to the small groups typically surveyed (four to five people), with a typical requirement for at least three responses before data can be reported (Timmreck & Bracken, 1995).

Establishing Instrument Reliability and Validity

An important part of establishing the reliability and validity of the instrument is to conduct a *pretest* with a sample of users to determine clarity of instructions, readability, relevance, and user reactions. Ideally, enough pretests, or a pilot study, can be conducted to begin the collection of data that can be applied to a determination of the instrument's psychometric properties (such as factor structures, internal consistency, and response distributions).

Reliability is the sine qua non of validity, and the MSF process presents some interesting questions about reliability. We might reasonably assume, for example, that raters from a common perspective (peers, for example) given equal (and sufficient) opportunity to observe should show some interrater agreement and that having a sufficient number of raters should produce a better evaluation than could any single-person rating. However, what makes a "sufficient number" is arguable, and some MSF systems allow as few as two raters to generate the data (Timmreck & Bracken, 1995). It may also be unreasonable to expect or require that raters from different perspectives should agree. In fact, the very rationale for MSF is based on the uniqueness of each perspective, each potentially providing an independent view of performance (Bernardin & Beatty, 1987). The meta-analysis results reported by Harris and Schaubroeck (1988) of moderate agreement between self-peer and self-supervisor ratings and higher agreement between peers and supervisors seems to support sufficient reliability, especially since the highest agreement was between the "external" sources (peers and supervisors).

In addition, Murphy and Cleveland (1995) point out that differences between actual and rated performance do not necessarily reflect measurement error. The rating process is strongly influenced by organizational forces that actually discourage accurate rating! Raters can be expected to use the rating process to communicate multiple messages to the ratee and the organization, and these messages can be expected to differ further depending on the rater's perspective.

Definitions of reliability based on test-retest measurements should also be used cautiously due to the developmental objective of the feedback, with the direct implication that behavior (and its resulting assessments) is expected to change, perhaps immediately.

Administration

Survey administration requires decisions about the technology to use, the importance of real and perceived anonymity, the means of identifying the correct ratee, and rater training.

Technologies. While paper-and-pencil administration remains by far the most prevalent administration method for MSF (and for organizational surveys as well) (Kennedy & Bracken, 1995), the availability of such alternative technologies as on-line, diskette, telephone, and fax surveys is giving practitioners more experience with and exposure to these newer methods. (These technologies are also examined in Chapters Eight and Nine.)

Kennedy and Bracken (1995) come to the conclusion that paper-and-pencil remains the preferred technology. A recent anecdote I encountered suggests one reason for this. A supervisor with only one direct report received feedback from three "subordinates." The processor was able to locate the actual survey forms, and it turned out that all three surveys had the same responses and were in the same handwriting. A situation that could have jeopardized the credibility of the entire process was diffused and addressed due to the processor's ability to access the actual questionnaires. Until we know more about technologies' effects on responses, implementers of MSF systems are strongly encouraged to either (1) pick one technology for use throughout the system and/or (2) conduct the necessary research to demonstrate that different technologies are not systematically producing different rating patterns. User reaction should also be considered and evaluated when multiple or novel technologies are being used to ensure that the raters are able to use the tools properly and are sufficiently motivated to produce quality feedback.

Anonymity. One of the factors that leads Kennedy and Bracken (1995) to recommend paper-and-pencil administration is the problem with perceived and/or actual anonymity with on-line and telephone surveys. (The question whether raters *should be* anonymous is addressed below.) Perceptions of anonymity do seem to affect ratings, with ratings being higher when respondents are not anonymous (Antonioni, 1994).

Logistics. The challenge of correctly pairing the rater and ratee is a major logistical problem in large-scale companywide MSF processes. The process often begins with "nomination" of the raters by the ratee, with a recommended approval by the ratee's manager or a human resource representative. If the nominations are then loaded into a master database (spreadsheet), some useful options are available, including the detection of people who have been nominated so many times that they cannot be expected to complete so many assessments in a quality manner.

A critical information requirement is the indication on the questionnaire of who is being rated. Having the rater or even the ratee fill in this information is the most risky solution due to the inevitable errors. A preferred solution is to have the name preprinted by the survey vendor, ideally with a scannable code (for paper-and-pencil surveys) to allow for rapid data capture.

When an MSF survey uses a rater nomination process, one other possibility is to print all the ratees assigned to a given rater on a single form. This method requires that the rater read a competency (behavior) statement and rate all the targets at the same time, in effect comparing the ratees in the process. Besides reducing the number of forms required to be read and completed, the comparison of ratees could be expected to help solve the typical MSF problem of results highly skewed toward the high end of the scale with little differentiation between ratees. In addition, this process would seem to be consistent with the MSF purpose of aiding in decision making that involves a between-persons comparison.

Rater training. The considerations in methods for administering surveys are covered elsewhere in this book (see Chapters Six and Eight). In the case of MSF processes, an additional consideration is the need for rater training, particularly in systems where the results are to be used for decision making (Bernardin & Beatty, 1984). Many organizations are realizing benefits from training raters on the basics of completing the forms accurately, supplemented with training on the rating process itself.

Processing and Reporting

While accuracy in data capture and reporting is desirable for all surveys, the demand for accuracy in MSF systems is especially high due to the small group sizes and the possible impact of errors on the overall results. This demand is accentuated if the information is to be used for decision-making purposes.

Calculations. Special care needs to be taken when negatively phrased items are used, to ensure that the scoring is indeed reversed. A record must be kept showing whether the raw data were reversed or a scoring algorithm was used. This whole problem can be bypassed by avoiding negatively phrased items altogether, as recommended earlier.

Another practice used by some consultants is an Olympic scoring process that omits the highest and lowest scores from the calculation of the mean. The inference is that these extreme ratings are somehow inaccurate. However, extreme ratings may actually be the most accurate, coming from raters with the most interaction and information on the ratee. The Olympic practice is not defensible in MSF surveys and is considered by some users (including this author) to be improper since it systematically excludes the input of a potentially large percentage of raters who have a right to expect that their feedback will be used. To compound the problem, raters could be expected to learn through experience not to give high or low ratings for fear that their input would be arbitrarily discarded.

Reports. Another challenge in MSF processes lies in supporting all the ratees who must correctly interpret and use the information provided to them. This support begins with the provision of a report in a format that is easily read and interpreted. A pretest of formats can be useful in detecting confusing forms of reporting.

Using the Results

The final link in the process requires that the results be used properly and fully. This step begins with providing support to the ratees, but proper and maximum value of the information will also depend on how the data are used by the ratees' managers, the raters, and the organization as a whole.

Ratee training. It is (I hope) obvious that it is insufficient to give a data report to the ratee and expect that things such as accurate interpretation and behavioral change will simply happen. The support given to ratees in using and acting on their data can take many forms. The *low-touch*, or minimal, approach is to provide, along with the each data report, a workbook that prescribes a process for interpreting the report and creating a standard action plan. Expecting a workbook to suffice, however, requires a great leap of faith, and the organization can expect variable results.

A *medium-touch* solution is to integrate the workbook into a workshop. In this scenario, ratees are required to attend a group session where they learn how to use the workbook to create an action plan. Time is usually provided for analysis, and some small-group discussions can also be structured. If the ratees are expected to discuss their results with their raters and/or manager later, some time can be dedicated to helping them prepare for that event. The immediate benefits of the workshop include answering questions, dedicating time to work on the results, and ensuring that ratees are doing their analysis properly.

The *high-touch* approach provides each ratee with individual coaching and counseling, perhaps in a one-on-one session with a trained counselor. Some organizations will provide this service through prearranged telephone sessions.

Ratee reactions. It is worth noting the impact that MSF will have on many participants. Receiving this kind of information is often a unique experience and can be a positive reinforcement for some and an unpleasant revelation for others. The organization should anticipate this fact and provide resources for ratees who require support and guidance. The organization should also expect denial from persons receiving unanticipated negative feedback, and should craft solutions that will encourage ratees to be more open to and accepting of their feedback.

Fairness. One of the substantial benefits of an MSF process lies in its promise for reducing bias through the involvement of raters from varied perspectives and, hypothetically, diverse backgrounds. There are data to support negligible effects due to gender and race of raters and ratees in multirater systems (Bracken & Paul, 1993). Ewen (1995) reports substantially greater acceptance and per-ceived fairness with performance appraisal processes that include MSF from participants, regardless of age, race, or gender.

Creating action pans. Whether the MSF is used for development or decision making, the ratee might be expected to create a per-sonal development plan based on his or her analysis, lead or facil-itate a meeting with his or her raters, and have a discussion with his or her manager. Incorporating the action plan in the personal development portion of the performance appraisal is a construc-tive use of this output.

Manager training. Some MSF processes do not require the ratee to share the results with his or her manager, but without such a requirement, personal development should not be expected to occur for many participants. Whether the manager sees the actual report or just the ratee's analysis and/or action plan, the manager should be a partner in the action planning process since resources of some kind (training, time, coaching) are usually required. Managers will benefit from training that (1) defines their role in the MSF process, (2) ensures proper data usage, (3) describes proper use of the feedback data, and (4) defines relevant policies and procedures.

Ties to performance appraisal. The process of using development plans as part of a performance appraisal was described above. A more direct use of feedback occurs when the results themselves are acknowledged in the performance appraisal process. This integration of feedback into appraisals is facilitated when the feedback report and the appraisal form use the same dimensions. The risk is that managers may overuse the feedback data and abdicate their responsibility for making necessary judgments beyond the feedback scores. It is critical that managers consistently and properly use the feedback in the appraisal process, and this should be a major component of the manager training.

Feedback to raters. Requiring that supervisors meet with their raters (direct reports) to review the results from upward feedback and the ensuing action plans is a critical step in ensuring that (1) the feedback is fully and properly understood, (2) the raters agree that the ratee has identified development plans that fit the feedback, and (3) the raters feel that their input has been received and used, thereby increasing the likelihood that they will participate in such surveys in the future. Meeting with peer raters also seems desirable but often presents major logistical problems.

Should we (can we) guarantee anonymity? In a practice perhaps derived from their organizational survey roots, practitioners have gone to great lengths to ensure that rater input will be anonymous. The assumption is that anonymity leads to honesty and prevents retribution. However, supervisors being rated by subordinates quickly note that supervisors are not anonymous when they provide feedback during appraisals. Supervisors also prefer knowing the source of their ratings (Antonioni, 1994).

I would argue that raters providing input to administrative

decisions should be held accountable for the quality of their feedback. Raters who are gaming the system or arbitrarily answering questions (for example, giving random responses or choosing only one response alternative) should be dealt with, including having their input removed when detected. In some systems, raters are given feedback about their performance as raters! This obviously requires that the rater can be identified by the organization, and the ramifications for anonymity need careful consideration.

Monitoring and Evaluating

As an MSF system rolls out and evolves, it is important to create systems for monitoring the process and determining outcomes. Some benchmarking of best practices can be useful, including participation in consortia of multirater users.

System abusers. It is probably inevitable that some raters and ratees will act in ways inconsistent with the spirit of the MSF process. One example of rater abuse of the MSF process is the submission of multiple surveys by one person. (Multiple submissions are also a problem with on-line, telephone, and fax surveys unless a personal identification number [PIN] is used, a practice that may appear to compromise anonymity.) Another abuse is sandbagging someone with low ratings to "get back" at him or her. This can be detected through algorithms that detect unusual response patterns.

Ratees can abuse the system as well, as did the person who filled out all the forms himself instead of distributing them to raters. More subtle attempts to influence raters are not uncommon. At the point of feedback, stories abound regarding ratees' attempts to discover who gave them particular ratings and/or to threaten raters with dire consequences if "this happens again." One solution to the abuser problem is to create a comments and observations clearinghouse, perhaps in the form of an MSF resource person in the human resource function.

Detecting behavioral change and other outcomes. One of the keys to sustaining a successful MSF process will undoubtedly lie in the organization's ability to attribute behavioral change and other positive outcomes to MSF participation. Here are some potential problems that can undermine the strategy of tracking individual results over time to detect changes and trends in behavior:

- The use of items and/or response scales that cannot detect true behavioral change
- Insufficient time between measures to allow for change to occur
- The changing expectations of raters who "raise the bar"
- Any changes to the instrument and/or process that might affect measurement

Despite these challenges, Hazucha, Hezlett, and Schneider (1993) report that participant skills do increase after feedback, and that people's skill development is related to their later advancement. Behavioral change for low to moderate performers appears to be more attainable than change for more skilled managers (Atwater, Roush, & Fischthal, 1995; Smither et al., 1995), suggesting the need to segment the population before coming to general conclusions regarding ability to detect subsequent changes in behavior.

Other measures used to evaluate the effectiveness of an MSF process include response rates, timely implementation, participation rates, perceived behavioral changes, process evaluation ratings, rater training effectiveness, ratee training effectiveness, and ratee adherence to policy and practice guidelines (such as timeliness, selection of raters, feedback to raters, and meeting with the manager) (Timmreck & Bracken, 1995).

Other Issues in Implementing a Multisource Feedback Process

Many of the considerations in implementing MSF processes are parallel or identical to those that confront the implementers of organizational survey programs. Each kind of program is designed to create change at some level (individual, team, and/or organizational), and creating change often surfaces significant barriers.

Organizational Readiness

Before implementing an MSF process, the organization should undergo a self-assessment of its readiness. Whether intended for development or appraisal, a large-scale implementation might fail for a number of reasons not directly related to the system itself. Readiness factors include the following:

Trust. Employees must have a basic level of trust that the promises made prior to, during, and after the administration of an MSF survey will be honored. Trust is an explicit requirement in every phase of the process. Bernardin, Cardy, and Carlyle (1982), for example, reported that raters with high trust provided ratings with less leniency compared to raters low in trust, regardless of the purpose of the ratings.

Management commitment. Along with being trusted, management also must be committed to the process. Signs of commitment often surface in the amount of investment management is willing to make at every stage, including investment in professional design, on-site (on company time) administration, professional or quality data processing, and support for ratees in the form of counselors, workshops, and training resources.

Stability. Introduction of an MSF process during a major upheaval, such as downsizing, can create the perception that the data are being used for hidden purposes. It is also likely that implementation under such conditions will receive inadequate attention and resources.

Feedback climate. Implementation of an MSF process in a climate that is averse to feedback may require both the rater and ratee to use skills with which they are not familiar. Some organizations are known for military-like cultures where upward feedback in particular has been discouraged or even punished.

Long-term focus. Organizations managed with a focus on short-term results will grow impatient with the time needed to realize the potential benefits of the process. Management must have realistic expectations regarding the short-term costs and the long-term benefits.

International Implementations

An MSF process implemented in countries other than the United States may encounter specific barriers to success at almost every stage. The following are some areas to be considered:

Competency models. The organization should not assume that the competency model applies universally as a descriptor of success in all cultures.

Translations. Great care needs to be taken with any translation to ensure that it continues to reflect the original intent. The use of simple language in the original English version certainly helps.

Feedback climate. Some cultures do not encourage the giving of feedback, especially to such power figures as supervisors. (Although there is some anecdotal evidence that cultures such as the Japanese culture, in which upward feedback has not been supported, are seeing the MSF process as a means to create the kind of feedback climate that will be necessary to compete in a global marketplace.)

Regulations. Formal regulations regarding the transportation and transmission of data across national borders need to be researched. Some cultures also have less formal but no less intense desires to keep the process within their borders.

Cost. Overseas costs can be higher for many procedures and items that support the MSF process. One example of a need for which higher costs might be incurred is data entry and processing services.

Multisource Feedback and Organizational Surveys Compared

On the one hand, I/O psychologists have learned a great deal from organizational surveys that can be applied to the implementation of a successful MSF process regarding item writing, response scales, response rate determinants, instruction writing, logistics, data processing, and reporting. On the other hand, organizational survey experts have learned that MSF systems have many important and difficult demands above and beyond those of the typical survey of organizational members.

Increased emphasis on measurement. The measurement characteristics (reliability and validity) of an organizational survey are often taken for granted, probably due in part to the view of surveys as only "discussion starters" or "prioritizers" for action planning. Multirater systems typically place more emphasis on the establishment of good measurement characteristics that provide valid information and can detect changes in behavior over time.

More reports on smaller groups. One major demand of the MSF process is a cost-effective, timely solution for generating a large number of reports. Many processing systems designed for organizational survey processing are inadequate for this purpose. Database management systems that interface with other processing and reporting software systems (for example, graphics, word processing, and spreadsheet programs) are being designed specifically for MSF systems with large databases.

Increased demands for accurate data processing. Given small group sizes and the possible use of the results for decision making, every step in an MSF process should be designed to create accurate information and to detect the instances where errors do occur. When groups may be as small as two or three respondents, inaccurate or missing data have major implications.

Support for a large number of users (ratees). Whereas the typical survey of organizational members has a relatively small number of people who directly access the data, a multirater process may have hundreds or thousands of people receiving data reports virtually simultaneously. This situation puts extreme demands on the report for clarity and simplicity. The organization must also be prepared to enable the ratees to properly interpret and use the results, ideally following up with some mechanism to ensure that result use is indeed happening as intended.

Conclusion

My observations and conclusions about the use of multisource feedback sum up some final practical points.

Is MSF a fad? If we define a *fad* as "a practice or interest followed for a time with exaggerated zeal" (*Merriam-Webster's Collegiate Dictionary,* 10th ed.), we will probably find that MSF will indeed be a fad in some organizations. Those organizations that are simply unable to sustain the process due to lack of planning, execution, and follow-through will lose their investment and some credibility. Of more concern are the cases where exaggerated zeal translates into actual harm to individuals and the organization as a whole due to hasty implementation and bad decisions made on bad information or to improper use of the information.

Regardless of the purpose, an MSF system should be designed to gener-

ate valid, reliable data. We often fall into the trap of believing that we are freed from researching and validating our systems if they are used only for developmental purposes. However, the implications for success and for the resources used at both the individual and organizational levels are very significant no matter what the purpose. The major threats to validity can probably be sorted into two large categories: lack of relevance and lack of consistency. *Relevance* requires that each ratee be evaluated on important skills and behaviors consistent with job and organizational expectations, with the evaluations provided by knowledgeable sources. *Consistency* requires that methods for collecting and using the information do not create real or perceived unfairness in the ratings. We unfortunately still do not know much about the different effects on ratings of the various methods and procedures available to us as practitioners of multirater systems.

MSF systems used for development and decision making can coexist but should be kept separate. This is partially a logistical issue due to the demands on MSF systems used for decision making across the organization. Just as important, this separation helps focus the ownership and use of the information for all parties involved, an important part of setting expectations for all participants.

Until more research is available, try to control for possible effects due to method. Where feasible, strive for consistency in every aspect of the process (lack of consistency is one of the notable threats to validity discussed above). Do not mix developmental and appraisal systems. Use the same technologies (for example, paper-and-pencil, on-line, or telephone surveys) throughout the organization, use rater training for everyone, and so on. Whether these factors (and others) actually affect ratings will someday be more apparent than they are now.

A performance management process that includes MSF will be more effective and fairer than one that does not. User (rater and ratee alike) acceptance of performance management will be greater with increased participation (Ewen, 1995), and the quality of the feedback will be enhanced with added perspectives. This result requires management's full consideration of all the factors that define a "good" MSF system and, especially, those factors that if ignored or violated can threaten the validity of the information and the resulting decisions.

References

Antonioni, D. (1994). The effects of feedback accountability on upward appraisal ratings. *Personnel Psychology, 47,* 349–356.

Atwater, L., Roush, P., & Fischthal, A. (1995). The influence of upward feedback on self- and follower ratings of leadership. *Personnel Psychology, 48,* 35–59.

Bernardin, H. J. (1986). Subordinate appraisal: A valuable source of information about managers. *Human Resource Management, 25,* 421–439.

Bernardin, H. J., & Beatty, R. W. (1984). *Performance appraisal: Assessing human behavior at work.* Boston: Kent.

Bernardin, H. J., & Beatty, R. W. (1987, Summer). Can subordinate appraisals enhance managerial productivity? *Sloan Management Review,* pp. 63–73.

Bernardin, H. J., Cardy, R. L., & Carlyle, J. J. (1982). Cognitive complexity and appraisal effectiveness: Back to the drawing board? *Journal of Applied Psychology, 67,* 151–160.

Borman, W. C. (1974). The rating of individuals in organizations: An alternative approach. *Organization Behavior and Human Performance, 12,* 105–124.

Bracken, D. W. (1994). Straight talk about multirater feedback. *Training and Development, 48,* 44–51.

Bracken, D. W., & Paul, K. B. (1993, May). *The effects of scale type and demographics on upward feedback.* Paper presented at the Eighth Annual Conference of the Society for Industrial and Organizational Psychology, San Francisco.

Dunnette, M. D. (1993). My hammer or your hammer? *Human Resource Management, 32,* 373–384.

Ewen, A. (1995, June). *Diversity fair assessment.* Paper presented at the American Society for Training and Development International Conference and Exposition, Dallas, TX.

Farh, J. L., Cannella, A. A., Jr., & Bedeian, A. G. (1991). Peer ratings: The impact of purpose on rating quality and user acceptance. *Group and Organization Studies, 16,* 367–386.

Farh, J. L., & Werbel, J. D. (1985). The effects of purpose of the appraisal and expectation of validation on the quality of self-appraisals. *Journal of Applied Psychology, 71,* 527–529.

Harris, M. M., & Schaubroeck, J. (1988). A meta-analysis of self-manager, self-peer, and peer-manager ratings. *Personnel Psychology, 41,* 43–62.

Hazucha, J. F., Hezlett, S. A., & Schneider, R. J. (1993). The impact of 360-degree feedback on management skills development. *Human Resource Management, 32,* 325–351.

Kennedy, J. K., Jr., & Bracken, D. W. (1995, June). *Employee survey administration: Evaluating the technologies.* Paper presented at the American

Society for Training and Development International Conference and Exposition, Dallas, TX.

London, M., & Beatty, R. W. (1993). 360-degree feedback as a competitive advantage. *Human Resource Management, 32,* 353–372.

Longenecker, C. O., Sims, H. P., & Gioia, D. A. (1987). Behind the mask: The politics of performance appraisal. *Academy of Management Executive, 1,* 183–193.

Morrison, A. M., McCall, M. W., Jr., & De Vries, D. L. (1978). *Feedback to managers: A comprehensive review of twenty-four instruments.* Greensboro, NC: Center for Creative Leadership.

Murphy, K. R., & Cleveland, J. N. (1995). *Understanding performance appraisal.* Newbury Park, CA: Sage.

Schneier, C. E., Beatty, R. W., & Baird, L. S. (1986). How to construct a successful performance appraisal system. *Training and Development Journal, 40,* 38–42.

Smither, J. W., London, M., Vasilopoulos, N. L., Reilly, R. R., Millsap, R. E., & Salvemini, N. (1995). An examination of the effects of an upward feedback program over time. *Personnel Psychology, 48,* 1–34.

Timmreck, C. W., & Bracken, D. W. (1995, May). *Upward feedback in the trenches: Challenges and realities.* Paper presented as part of the Upward Feedback symposium at the Tenth Annual Conference of the Society for Industrial and Organizational Psychology, Orlando, FL.

Van Velsor, E., & Leslie, J. B. (1991). *Feedback to managers: Vol. 2. A review and comparison of sixteen multirater feedback instruments.* Greensboro, NC: Center for Creative Leadership.

The Survey Process

Part Two takes a close look at *how* an organizational survey is done. It covers the nuts and bolts of professional practice, from the early design issues to later actions and follow-through.

In Chapter Six, Allen Kraut guides the reader through the planning and conduct of the typical phases of a survey. The key decisions that need to be made at each step are considered, along with the pros and cons of alternative choices. Issues to be decided include who to survey and whether to use a sample or a census of the population. How to determine an appropriate sample size is explained, along with basic do's and don'ts for writing good questions. Kraut reminds us that an organizational survey is essentially a problem-solving process, with many steps, which may extend as long as a full year. At each step, the guideposts for better decisions are the strategic purposes for which the survey is being done. Keeping the survey objectives in mind helps us make the right decisions at the many choice points we face along the way.

Vital to setting the course of an organizational survey is the initial set of conversations with top management. David Nadler devotes Chapter Seven to revealing how such conversations might realistically go. After noting the role of surveys in energizing and directing organizational behavior, he lays out a likely exchange of questions and answers between a survey director and a top executive. Drawing on his extensive academic and consulting experience, Nadler describes the ideal dialogue under three different conditions: when the primary survey purpose is organizational assessment, organizational change, and individual or team change. In each case, these chats with top management are critical to setting up appropriate management expectations. Through a series of suggested answers to executives' questions, Nadler shows how we can help position executives to do their part at various stages in order to make the survey successful.

Dealing with the data gathered by organizational surveys is a formidable job, one detailed in Chapter Eight by William Macey. He shares with us his expertise about the task of collecting the data and the selection of methods to do so. The processing and analyzing of the data may seem mundane, but in fact, they are operations requiring great skill and a true appreciation of all the things that can go wrong. Macey notes that some of the most important actions are taken before a survey is ever put together, such as preparing the organizational codes that allow data to be reported back to specific units. After collection, data must go through editing and "cleaning" to ensure that they are correct and trustworthy. Macey also describes the special considerations that govern the collection and analysis of write-in comments. Inevitably, there are conflicts among some data management choices we must make, and Macey's writing helps us think through these conflicts.

Although most surveys are still conducted by some form of paper-and-pencil administration, alternative survey methods are available and proliferating. In Chapter Nine, Karl Kuhnert and Dan McCauley review the most popular of these methods: telephone, fax, computer, and electronic mail. Each is described along with its impact on perceptions of confidentiality and its flexibility, time and logistic requirements, ease of use, and cost determinants. Kuhnert and McCauley also warn us against selecting any method for its distinctiveness or for its mere availability. As much as the merits of the technology, they tell us, we need to consider the organizational climate and needs. Their review gives us an insight into the technologies likely to be more widely used in the coming years.

John Hinrichs describes the steps necessary after data are collected to turn them into meaningful action. In Chapter Ten, he tells that we must go through the work of understanding the data, prioritizing the issues, planning our intended actions, and finally implementing and following through on those intentions. The feedback and action planning part of the organizational survey is described in detail. Hinrichs also reviews options for giving feedback of results to employees and explains why having managers hold feedback meetings is likely to be the most effective choice. He gives clear and systematic guidelines for running a feedback meeting and for training managers to be capable meeting leaders. Also provided are the criteria for creating effective action plans and ideas on how to communicate these plans to employees. A key point stressed by Hinrichs is the importance of holding management accountable for taking action.

CHAPTER 6

Planning and Conducting the Survey
Keeping Strategic Purpose in Mind

Allen I. Kraut

It is tempting to think (or wish) that there is one best way to do a survey, but in fact there are many good ways to do a survey. This chapter will illustrate how the "right" way, to be truly effective, depends on the strategic purposes a particular survey serves. I aim to present the nuts and bolts of planning and conducting an opinion survey in an organization and to show how the survey's purposes will guide practitioners' actions.

During the course of the typical survey process, many specific decisions must be made about the survey's scope and administration. These may range from seemingly obvious issues, such as who will be surveyed and what questions will be asked, to more subtle ones, such as who will see what data afterward or how the appearance and fact of data confidentiality can be ensured. In every case, survey directors can make sounder choices if they are fully in touch with the strategic purposes of the survey.

This chapter lays out the different phases of a typical survey: planning and design, administration, data analysis, feedback and interpretation, action planning and follow-through. Then the key decisions and work accomplished in each stage are discussed. But first, we need to review the purposes typically served by organizational surveys.

Why Do a Survey?

The reasons for doing surveys are not always voiced publicly or frankly. Sometimes, executives have a very clear idea of what they want to accomplish. On other occasions, they can be surprisingly inarticulate, opining that surveys seem like "a good thing to do" or that they "can give us useful information" or simply that "other companies do them."

As I detailed in the Introduction, organizational surveys are done primarily for two reasons: *assessment* and/or *change*. Organizations want to evaluate people's thoughts and feelings about certain issues and/or promote new ways of working and behaving. Under these twin umbrellas of assessment and change, a number of more specific reasons for doing surveys can be summed up.

- *To pinpoint areas of concern.* A common desire is to "see how things are going," that is, to do an assessment in the organization. This type of evaluation may be aimed at particular issues, units, or demographic groups.
- *To observe long-term trends.* A closely related issue is to keep tabs on relevant issues and significant groups over time. To some executives, such surveys are analogous to an annual physical examination.
- *To monitor program impacts.* Getting reactions to earlier change is a legitimate purpose of organizational surveys. Such changes can include reorganizations, reductions in force, relocations, and the introduction of new personnel practices.
- *To gain input to future decisions.* Some organizations use surveys to gather data such as employee preferences that will influence future management decisions in areas like benefit plans or training programs.
- *To add a communications channel.* As organizations grow larger or more widespread, management often expresses the need for communication systems that supplement the already existing ones. The opinion survey can play that communication system role.
- *To conduct organizational behavior research.* Surveys can be used for research to understand and influence behaviors like

absenteeism, turnover, accidents, pro-union activities, and work accidents.

- *To monitor organizational change and improvement.* Surveys can evolve into a way of life that encourages organizational improvement through self-assessment and the use of the resulting data to stimulate and guide desirable changes.
- *To communicate symbolically.* A major strategic purpose of the organizational survey is symbolic communication, sending a message. The survey can signal the interests of the firm's leaders and be a powerful educational tool, especially for cultural change and for new initiatives.

As we can see, surveys are done for different reasons. In a profound sense, such reasons form the strategic purposes behind any survey, and these purposes will guide many later operational decisions. It is also worth noting that a particular survey will sometimes try to achieve several different purposes, which can overlap or even conflict with one another.

Survey Phases

The timeline in Figure 6.1 shows the different phases of a typical survey: planning and design, administration, data analysis, feedback and interpretation, action planning and follow-through.

As shown, the time from start to finish for a first-time survey can cover a full year. With greater experience and resources, and/or less attention to some phases, this span may be shortened. A year may seem quite long until you look at all the steps required for the complete successful survey process. Many of the critical details are not always visible to the casual observer. The longest single phase is the planning and design, which includes the development of the questionnaire itself. The feedback and action-taking phases are also part of the total one-year period. Some of the phases may overlap with one another. For example, work on data analyses may start before survey administration is completed.

The time it seems to take to do a survey is often mistakenly based on how long it takes to write the survey, administer it, and compile results. This, indeed, may be only a matter of months or

Figure 6.1. Sample Timeline for an Organizational Survey.

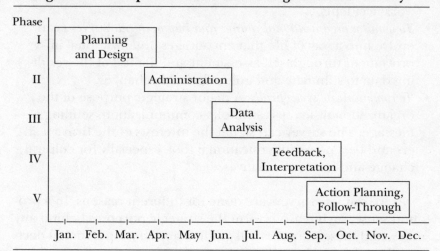

even weeks. But it omits the planning and design of the total process, and it ignores the follow-on time used for feedback and taking action. The total time for an effective survey process includes all the phases shown in Figure 6.1.

(My discussion here assumes either a paper-and-pencil survey or a more advanced technology already in place. Installing a new technology, such as on-line computer administration, introduces special considerations, which are discussed along with advantages and disadvantages in Chapters Eight and Nine.)

Planning and Design

Now we turn our attention to the key issues that are typically handled at each survey stage, starting with the planning and design, the initial phase. Many of the issues dealt with in the beginning are in preparation for what will actually take place in later stages of the process. But as Covey (1989) has noted, success often requires that one "begin with the end in mind" (p. 97).

Each phase of a successful organizational survey demands that the true purpose(s) or outcomes of the survey be remembered as choices are faced. Few choices are correct in the abstract. Mostly, a choice is right or wrong only in terms of accomplishing the overall purpose of the survey.

Steering Committee

An organizational device that can be very helpful to the success of a survey is the *steering committee*. Such a group (which might also be called the advisory board or survey committee) is made up of a half dozen representatives of key units or functions and acts as a sounding board, or group of advisers, at all stages of the survey. The advisers' role can range from suggesting topic areas to reviewing draft questionnaires, results of data analysis, and potential areas for action (for a detailed example, see Kraut, 1992).

Because a survey involves many choices, a steering committee can be of enormous help. Committee members may sometimes be proxies for other management groups and can be a great asset in developing understanding and commitment to the survey throughout the organization.

Sponsor's Expectations

A significant portion of the planning and design stage should be spent articulating the purposes of the survey and the ends to be achieved. Survey sponsors and survey researchers should share common clearly articulated understandings of why the survey is being done. These should be written out and shared with those involved in the survey planning (and with many others, as I discuss later).

As Nadler details in the next chapter, participation in a meaningful dialogue about the intent of a survey is a good way to understand management's hopes or aspirations for the process. In fact, this conversation should make clear who is truly the client for the project. Such a dialogue is often an opportunity for executives and survey researchers to educate one another as well. The survey researcher can communicate what the different types of surveys entail, the resources and commitments that will be required, and how they may affect the organization. The sponsors (that is, the managers wanting the survey) can describe their aims, assumptions, experiences, and hopes. Together, the two parties can expand their sense of the survey's potential and work out mutually clear understandings and expectations.

Whom to Survey?

One of the first decisions concerns who should be surveyed. In some organizations, an "employee" opinion survey may exclude all managers or all higher-level managers. Who, exactly, should be included? The best decision on this issue is not always straightforward. As a general rule, we should survey those people whose opinions and perceptions are needed to accomplish our purpose. Not everyone in an organization should be included in every survey. In some cases, participants may be only nonmanagement employees and, at other times, only managers. In most cases, both groups or some sample of both of them will be participants.

Inclusion of any group adds a benefit beyond just receiving that group's data. Having people take part in a survey gives us not only their comments but also their involvement. If we want people to use and act on survey findings, we should consider the impact of including them in the survey. Conversely, we should carefully consider the impact of excluding them. Do we make some statement when they are left out? In general, if segments of an organization are expected to act on survey data, they ought to be numbered among the survey participants.

What about top executives? All organizations need to face this decision. In some companies, survey sponsors may feel they do not want to "bother" the top executives, or they may feel the survey is inappropriate for these executives (but it may not be). In most cases, there are important gains in education and ownership to be made by having top executives take part as fully as possible.

When executive data can be grouped with other high-level inputs from the same or related units, the reports invariably get a lot of attention from the executives themselves as do the comparisons with the results from other levels. The differences revealed are often strong motivators for executives to get a deeper understanding of the feelings behind the data. I believe a stronger involvement is fostered by encouraging executives to take part whenever possible. In any case, they should be part of the decision as to whether they participate.

Sample or Census?

A question related to whom to survey is whether to sample one or more groups or to take a census of the entire population of interest. In large organizations, this question may have major cost implications. A sample, involving fewer people, means less cost at almost every stage of the survey. But cost should not be the only issue of concern.

If the survey's purpose requires each unit to act on the data, then a census is often mandated in order to obtain full data for each unit. Partial data often prompt concerns about the accuracy or usefulness of the findings for smaller units. Where data are to be reported for lower-level units, such as employees reporting to first-level supervisors or second-level managers, the small unit size may preclude getting a sample that anyone would regard as reliable.

Conversely, if all that is needed is an organizationwide estimate of how employees feel about a topic such as the various employee benefit plans, it may be redundant to sample all the people in the organization. If the data are not to be reported to or used by lower-level units, a sample should be considered.

If the survey purpose is to launch a change in the organization's way of life, it may be worthwhile to have every member of the firm take part, as a way of making it clear to all that this is a change and to educate them on the change. Subsequently, to track the actual changes in major units, it may be sufficient to take samples of the organization.

Samples can be some fraction of the entire organizational population or samples of units. In the latter case, a follow-up survey may sample some fraction of all the units. For example, a nationwide firm might sample 25 percent of all units in each region or district every three months, thus surveying all units over a year. Along the way, the firm would get a reading on the survey topics every quarter.

How Big a Sample?

The issue of determining sample size is both technical and political. The technical aspects of the determination, which revolve around the sample size needed to reach certain levels of precision, are a bit more arcane but sometimes easier to resolve.

Based on well-known aspects of sampling theory (for fuller discussions, see Kish, 1965; Warwick & Lininger, 1975), three considerations dictate the size of the sample required to satisfy a particular situation.

Margin of Error

Margin of error refers to how close we expect our reported value to be to the true value for the population of interest. The reported value is usually expressed as being within a certain margin of error (such as "plus or minus 5 percentage points"), which is sometimes also referred to as a *confidence interval.* The greater the precision required, the larger the sample must be. (Naturally, the precision may depend on the criticality of the use to which the data will be put.) The sample size needed to be accurate to plus or minus 3 points is much larger than that needed to be accurate to plus or minus 5 points. In a population of 5,000, a sample of 880 people is needed for the former and only 357 for the latter (at a 95 percent level of confidence).

Level of Confidence

The concept of *level of confidence* refers to how certain we want to be that our sample findings are correct (within the margin of error). We may be content to know that the odds of our findings not being a chance result are nine out of ten (a 90 percent confidence level). If we want to be 99 percent certain, we will need a much larger sample. Most researchers, for most purposes, try to achieve a 95 percent level of confidence.

Occurrence of Characteristic

A somewhat more technical consideration is the frequency with which the measured variable or characteristic occurs in the population. For statistical reasons that do not need to be detailed here, at a given confidence level and margin of error, a 90 percent/10 percent split (say, in favorable versus unfavorable responses) is easier to detect than a 50 percent/50 percent split. Thus, we would need a somewhat larger sample if the attitude or view being measured is evenly split in the sample than we would if only a small fraction of the sample reported it. (If the split cannot be estimated in advance, a conservative approach would be to estimate a 50/50 split.)

Population Size

The three considerations just described can give very exact requirements for the size of the sample. Of course, the assumption underlying this discussion is that the survey will use simple random sampling of the population. If survey designers get into stratified sampling, or sampling of units, a more complex logic comes into play. (See Babbie, 1992, for a clear discussion of more sophisticated treatments.) However, even for simple random sampling, you must first know the size of the population in the unit (firm, division, or branch office) where the survey is being done. The larger the unit, the larger the *number* of people needed in a sample to reach a specified level of precision, even though the *proportion* may become smaller. Table 6.1 contains some examples of required sample sizes.

This information in Table 6.1 assumes a 100 percent response rate from those sampled. If only half responded, a much bigger sample would have to be invited. Of course, this discussion also assumes that there is no systematic difference between respondents and nonrespondents. All the factors under discussion here form a strong reason to stimulate a high response rate, as discussed below. Note, however, that the required sample size increases very slowly for larger units. Accurate data for very large organizations can be provided with proportionately very small samples. Most people, then, are surprised to see that they need relatively large fractions of small units to be equally accurate. This is illustrated in Table 6.1. For the same level of precision, a unit of 50,000 people requires a sample of 381, or 0.8 percent of the total, while a unit of 5,000 requires 357 people, or 3.7 percent of the total. However, a much smaller unit of 500 people would need a sample of 217, or over 43 percent of the total!

Finally, in the case of smaller units, it may be politically unwise to sample only part of a unit, despite the relative accuracy of the data acquired. The sampling approach may generate much concern and speculation on why and how only certain people were chosen to take part. In such cases, it may be more sensible to include all unit members in a survey for strategic rather than statistical purposes.

Stratification and Weighting

There may be some occasions when stratified sampling is needed. That is, the researcher consciously chooses from various known

Table 6.1. Determining Sample Size from Various Populations.

Population Size	Required Sample	As % of Population
50,000	381	0.8
25,000	378	1.5
10,000	370	3.7
5,000	357	7.1
2,500	333	13.3
1,000	285	28.5
500	217	43.4
250	152	60.8
200	132	66.0
100	80	80.0
50	44	88.0
25	24	96.0

Note: These sample sizes assume a confidence level of 95 percent, a margin of error of 5 points (plus or minus), and a 50/50 split in the characteristic being measured.

Source: Adapted from Rea & Parker, 1992.

groups, using different sample fractions for each. For example, in a study of diversity, women or particular ethnic groups may be a small part of the total organization and may need to be oversampled to get meaningful findings. Or when divisional units are sampled, small units may have a higher proportion of their members take part than would large units.

In general, it is useful to sample enough people from each group to reach the same confidence level and confidence interval for each group. This requires sampling *relatively* more people from smaller groups. For example, in one study, my colleagues and I sampled all of an organization's small number of African American employees and only a small fraction of the majority who were white employees.

Occasionally such fractions are merged to give an estimate for the total organization. In combining these data, it is important to adjust, or weight, the data from each group to avoid distorting the data for the totals. (This process is detailed in Chapter Eight.) In the example just given, African Americans represented 5 percent of the organization but fully half of the total sample. Where their attitudes were different from the whites', merely combining the results arithmetically, without weighting, would have misrepresented the total organization.

Unions

In some firms, union-management relationships are generally positive, and surveys are just another occasion for cooperation. Generally, unions expect to have input on the survey questionnaire and certainly to receive copies of the findings. Where surveys have not been done before, the content and the conduct of the surveys become another set of issues for the union and the management to work out.

In companies whose relationships with unions are not felicitous, a careful strategy must be charted. If organizational change is the strategy, there may be powerful reasons to get the union involved. However, such issues as cutbacks, downsizing, or negotiations on economic or other issues subject to collective bargaining are very touchy. Indeed, it may already be obvious to you that doing a survey for the first time during a period of union organizing activity could be seen as an unfair labor practice (this is also discussed in Chapter Fifteen). However, if other surveys have been done, and this one is on a previously established schedule, it probably would be seen as business as usual and would not be a problem.

Unions might reasonably be expected to want survey data on issues like pay and benefits, among others. To avoid this possibility, some companies have omitted such items from the surveys going to union members.

Questionnaire Development

The development of the survey questionnaire itself is a major part of the planning and design phase of the survey process and poses some critical choices.

Topics to Cover

Nowhere is a survey's purpose more vividly demonstrated than in the content of the questions asked. The choice of topics to cover must begin with a clear understanding of the survey's intended purpose. This is not always as simple as it may seem.

If you are doing a sample survey to gain perceptions of, say, employee medical benefits coverage or reaction to a change in such coverage, the focus should be very straightforward. Even so, such questions may be only part of a larger questionnaire covering other issues relevant to the same sample of people. Sometimes, it may be desirable to include sensitive questions in a larger survey to avoid highlighting them.

Some survey researchers hold an often unvoiced assumption that all surveys of organizational members should cover a minimum set of common topics like satisfaction with pay, promotion, work, management, and the company. However, when a survey is intended to foster organizational change and development, such assumptions are not only unsupportable, they can be counterproductive. Excellent surveys fully supporting strategic purposes can and do omit some so-called standard topics.

Example of Topics Chosen for a Survey

A petrochemical company recently went through a "missioning and visioning" experience to implement and live by a "quality-driven" motif. Top management asked for a survey that could be done periodically to reinforce and measure progress. The successful result was a questionnaire that covered the eleven tenets ("guiding principles") of the vision.

- Quality process
- Excellence in health, safety, and environmental performance
- Community involvement
- Customer satisfaction
- Integrity
- People orientation
- Teamwork
- Performance recognition
- Open communications
- Rewarding and enjoyable work
- Innovation

The survey had no items concerning pay or benefits. All the questions about management asked specifically how managers behaved or supported the desired new behaviors. Because the survey was done as a census, results could be reviewed with each unit in a clear effort to support the new culture.

Interviews with Management

Dialogues with top management are an important means of clarifying the survey's purpose and potential and developing real commitment to the survey. An initial interview should ask executives what they would like to achieve as well as asking about their past experiences, hopes, and concerns. This interview can also be the time to share information about what may be needed to make executives' goals happen and perhaps even about other uses of surveys. Such meetings can be followed with reviews of draft questionnaires and executive involvement in other critical steps in the process.

A mutual understanding achieved at this time will also focus top management on their role in the process. This role may mean taking actions like announcing the survey, discussing it and advocating support of it at employee meetings, signing critical correspondence, and even taking part in the kick-off activities at the start of survey administration.

Use of Focus Groups

Part of the process of developing good surveys includes talking with samples of the people who will take part as respondents and with the unit managers who are often the eventual users of the data. These conversations can help define the issues that are of greatest concern to the respondents, and they often provide the slang or idioms that people typically use to discuss these issues among themselves.

The focus group method is often used for this stage. Typically, eight to twelve people are brought together for a two-hour meeting. They are told this is an early stage of the survey process and, after proper assurances of confidentiality, are given questions that draw on their ideas and perceptions.

Lower-level employees might be asked, "What do you like about working here, and what don't you like?" If the survey is to be focused on organizational effectiveness, they might be asked, "What are the things that help you and your colleagues to do a better job, and what are the things that hinder you?" Unit managers might be asked, "What kind of survey topics and data would help you manage better?"

To facilitate the meeting, the survey researcher may use process skills like those employed in brainstorming sessions. Focus sessions are often tape-recorded so important ideas and phrases can be captured for later use.

Use of Off-the-Shelf or Customized Questions

A perennial, and difficult, issue is whether to use previously prepared questions or to develop new customized items. The correct answer is, "It depends!" If the survey is a general assessment of morale, you could use many of the Mayflower Group items (see Chapter Eleven) or mimic surveys that colleagues in other companies might share.

In 1969, Robinson, Athanasiou, and Head compiled a volume showing the large variety of instruments existing at that time. However, much of that material cannot be used without permission. The reader is also urged to read Chapter Fifteen for a discussion of plagiarism and other issues related to using others' questionnaires.

Consequently, if you are involved in an organizational change, it is almost always better to create new items that cater exactly to your firm's interests. This may be the only way to get the right items. It is also a wonderful opportunity to ask executives what they would like to find out. While executives' wording may not be used exactly in the questions, their involvement in developing the survey will build understanding and commitment to using the results.

In those cases where previous surveys have been done, using the same items in subsequent surveys may yield useful trend data. In start-up surveys, consultants often prefer to have a substantial number of items come from their own libraries. This approach can shorten development time, supply items with a track record of successful prior use, and make possible normative data comparisons with other organizations. Normative data comparisons are a mixed bag, however. While initially interesting, they may detract from the organization's focusing on its own issues. However, one advantage of having prior data available is that they may demonstrate psychometric aspects of the survey questions, such as their reliability.

Existing data may also show the relationships among different questions and the extent to which they can be combined into meaningful indices of the various content domains in a questionnaire. Thus, the JDI (Job Descriptive Index) (Smith, Kendall, & Hulin, 1969) covers five domains, and the MJSQ (Minnesota Job Satisfaction Questionnaire) (Weiss, Dawis, England, & Lofquist, 1967) while scorable for twenty facets generally yields two overall scores (for intrinsic and extrinsic satisfaction).

Writing Good Questions

Several volumes have been written about composing good items (see, for example, Rea & Parker, 1992; Babbie, 1992). Here is a summary of do's and don'ts that are sound guidelines for writing good items.

Do

- Use simple words
- Make items short
- Use unambiguous terms
- Use familiar language

Don't

- Use double-barreled items
- Use double-negative items
- Use strange or exotic terms
- Use words that are indefinite in time or imprecise
- Ask about issues outside the respondent's experience
- Ask "loaded" questions
- Ask overdemanding questions
- Use overlapping alternatives

As Dillman (1978) notes, at times some of these guidelines may conflict with one another. Writing questions well, we are reminded, means to keep in mind the particular survey population and purpose and also the other parts of the survey questionnaire.

Survey items most commonly have five response alternatives symmetrically arranged around a neutral point (for example, the alternatives might read: "very satisfied," "satisfied," "neither satisfied nor dissatisfied," "dissatisfied," and "very dissatisfied"). Seven-point items are also often used.

Some executives (and a few researchers, too) favor 4- or 6-point scales, taking out the middle response. They want to force people to answer positively or negatively and not sit on the fence. Unfortunately, this may only push people to answer in a way they do not really feel and thus provide misleading data. For most items, responses in the middle category can be very revealing, as when they show a lack of knowledge or sentiment that was expected to be present. For items like pay questions, normally answered with unfavorable ratings, middle answers may be relatively favorable. And for some questions, "don't know" or "no opinion" is a justifiable response and should be offered as an option.

Informal research suggests that the proportion of positive to negative answers remains the same when scales have 4 or 6 points. That is, if respondents who would have marked the middle category on a 5-point question have to answer a similar question as a 4-point item, they will split in the same positive-negative proportion as those who would have chosen positive or negative answers in the first place.

Although many items in organizational surveys are typically written with evaluative responses (such as "very good" or "very satisfied"), it is far easier to write many items with descriptive responses (such as "describes my situation very well"). In particular, the use of agree/disagree responses makes item writing much easier. It is instructive that virtually all the recently written Mayflower Group items (see Chapter Eleven) use an agree/disagree format.

Open-ended items can provide very illuminating answers in people's own words and give powerful examples to explain the percentage statistics on closed-ended questions. Experience suggests the most useful answers do not come from broad questions like "What do you like about working here?" Instead, the most value comes from focused items like "What advice would you give your CEO on how to improve the performance of this company?" However, open-ended items are more time consuming and expensive to process and analyze.

Use of Demographics
Many surveys include demographic questions, asking respondents for data on their age, sex, education, length of service, job cate-

gory, work unit, and so on. Such information can be very useful but also bears a risk.

If demographic data are actually used to analyze or report responses, they can be quite valuable. It may be helpful to compare how new and experienced employees feel about some issues or to see if men see some issues differently than do women. In reality, because of workload or lack of expertise or management support, such analyses are often not done, even when the demographic data have been collected. When these data are not used, the survey is burdened with unneeded items. More important, such items often make respondents anxious about their anonymity. Given low trust levels or unfamiliarity with the survey process, demographic questions raise respondents' concern. I believe such items should not be asked at all unless a strong case can be made for using each one.

Of course, if the purpose of the survey is to look at issues by unit or to make units responsible for acting on the data, we must develop and use codes that identify questionnaires from each unit (see Chapter Eight for more on this point).

If demographic questions are asked, they should appear at the end of the survey. (Questions about organizational codes are one major exception to this guideline.) Although this practice is violated in some surveys, most survey professionals prefer to place demographic issues at the end for two reasons, both of which recognize the fact that respondents are free to omit their answers. First, the respondents get into the subject matter of the survey more quickly and presumably will answer the subject matter questions because the topic is interesting. Second, if the demographic questions are at the beginning, the respondent who does not want to answer them may decide not to answer the following subject matter questions either. Moreover, putting demographic items at the front of the questionnaire, just after confidentiality is usually promised, is bound to raise participants' eyebrows.

Writing Instructions

The first page of every survey should have a brief set of instructions on how to complete the questionnaire. Instructions may include "obvious" issues like answering all questions as frankly and completely as possible, recognizing that there are no right or wrong answers, and selecting the responses that come closest to the way one feels. They may also include an illustration of the correct or incorrect way to complete an answer sheet if one is used.

Choosing the Number of Items

In general, a survey should be long enough to get the needed data without feeling onerous to the respondent. The trend in survey size seems to be toward shorter and more focused questionnaires. Most surveys seem to be between fifty and one hundred items, but some are much longer, over two hundred items in some cases. However, I know of one large company that annually polls all employees with a thirty-two-item survey that uses agree/disagree responses and is printed on one page!

Pretesting

It is hard to overstate the importance of pretesting a questionnaire after a draft version is readied. This step is critical to see if the instructions are understood, if the questions make sense, and if the survey leaves people feeling that it is a worthwhile effort. A pretest should be administered to a few dozen people who resemble the actual participants and under conditions like those that will actually exist. A convenience sample (rather than a representative one) is adequate for this purpose.

After the pretest participants have answered the questionnaire, it should be reviewed with them, starting with the introduction and going through every question to see if the items were clear, responses reasonable, and the flow of questions sensible. Misunderstandings have to be explored, and participants should be asked for suggestions. A group setting works well for pretest reviews. This entire procedure may need to be repeated if successive drafts are prepared.

Survey Administration

The administration of a survey can be a complex undertaking. It is also key to the success of the survey and involves a number of decisions and actions that will vary according to the particular situation.

Group or Individual?

One of the biggest choice points for the popular pencil-and-paper survey is whether to administer it on a group or individual basis. A survey can be given to a large group of people convened in an auditorium, classroom, or cafeteria so that they all take the survey at the same time. In contrast, a survey can be given to individuals. For example, surveys can be mailed to individuals for them to complete and return at their convenience. Surveys done by telephone or computer, by their very nature, are almost always individually administered.

To some extent, the choice of survey administration mode depends on an organization's survey maturity. Closely related to this experience factor is the degree of comfort that participants have with surveys and their use. A big part of this comfort is the level of trust felt by respondents toward the organization and its use of sensitive data. In general, greater experience and trust are needed for successful administration of a first-time survey on an individual rather than a group basis because the respondent is likely to feel more exposed and subject to a loss of anonymity. If people have been through prior surveys and feel they can depend on assurances from their company, they are more likely to extend this trust to an individual form of survey administration.

Group administration is often a good choice for first-time surveys (assuming paper-and-pencil questionnaires). It allows much greater control over the process and immediate feedback on participation levels. Group administration maximizes participation rates and minimizes collusion in responses. More important, it permits a clear and consistent communication of the process to all management and participants. This can be both a wonderful opportunity to communicate the survey's purpose and a greater workload for survey administrators. If well done, group administration can build survey maturity and trust.

The location and nature of a particular workforce sometimes dictate the choice of group or individual administration. Doing a survey by groups is easiest when most people work in one or a few large locations and is most suitable for people who are new to surveys or who otherwise need considerable explanation or encouragement to take part. Widely scattered workforces or those who come into central sites only rarely may be attractive candidates for individual administration. Group administrations can still be done with such people but require a lot of effort.

Example of Survey Administration

A company with a few hundred branch locations embarked on an annual survey program of all employees, with unit feedback planned for each branch location. An administrator was appointed at each branch several weeks in advance of the group survey administrations and given a brief checklist with instructions on how to communicate, schedule, and prepare for the survey session, conduct it, and return the completed surveys (and get makeup questionnaires filled out by absentees). The clear list of actions and timetable were created centrally and given to every location administrator, along with telephone numbers to use to ask for clarification.

Top management recognized the need to show support and commitment to this new program and to encourage the use of the data for organizational improvement. The CEO spoke via a videotape shown at all locations at the start of each survey administration, thanking employees and promising appropriate action after the survey and feedback were concluded. These latter actions were also dramatized during the six-minute videotape. As testimony to the success of these efforts, the participation rate was over 98 percent!

The details for a group administration can be significant, requiring both staffing and preparation. At a minimum, the details include having or preparing

- Appropriate times and places
- Bulletin board notices and posters about the survey
- Desk space and pencils to complete questionnaires
- Arrangements for getting the surveys to the administration
- Trained administrators
- A standardized introduction to the respondents and readiness to answer questions
- An explanation of what codes, if any, must be entered by respondents

- A schedule of which employees attend at which times and ways to give enough them advance notice
- A means of keeping track of how many people come from each unit and a readiness to call managers if people do not show up as expected

Symbolic messages must be considered, too. For example, group administrations often cut into work time or are scheduled before or after normal hours, when overtime pay may be incurred. Although the survey cost is raised by this scheduling, so is people's understanding that management thinks the survey is an important work activity. A mailing of surveys to the workplace can have a similar impact if instructions make it legitimate for individuals to do the survey during work hours. Conversely, a mailing to the home that does not encourage completion during work hours is likely to be resented for seeming to exploit people's personal time or for seeming not really important in management's eyes.

Another point of sensitivity may be the treatment of second-shift employees, who typically get things second. To make a point, they might be surveyed the evening before the day when the first-shift people complete their surveys. A similar logic might suggest starting a survey administration in branch offices before moving on to the headquarters location.

Confidentiality

In addition, administrators must address people's potential concerns about confidentiality. Steps to be taken with paper-and-pencil surveys may include such actions as scheduling managers to complete the surveys in sessions other than the ones their employees attend. Completed questionnaires should be dropped in a "post-box" or otherwise handled so that specific individuals cannot be matched to specific forms.

Questionnaire surveys done on a sample basis are typically administered individually. Modes of data collection other than paper-and-pencil surveys, such as computer surveys, are also almost always individually administered. While the method may be identical for all persons, each one takes part at a different place and time. This demands a reasonable amount of respondent trust and comfort with the process, or response rates and truthfulness of responses may suffer. Indeed, as mentioned earlier, most companies using telephone or computer administration have previously used paper-and-pencil surveys and have built up some employee confidence in the survey process. (The reasons to choose various methods are covered in following chapters. Also see Rea & Parker, 1992.)

Suffice it to say that all methods of administration must address, at a minimum, certain common issues for participants. These include

- Why was I chosen?
- What will be done with the data?
- How will this affect me?

Participants in organizational surveys must understand the procedure and their role in it and be motivated to take part with a proper understanding of the likely consequences. (See Kahn & Cannell, 1957, for a discussion of how these points apply to individual interviews in survey research.)

Detailed Planning

If you have not done a survey before, it is hard to imagine the amount of detailed planning needed for a survey to be conducted without disaster. Dillman (1978) provides a good, if somewhat overzealous, catalogue of the manifold steps for telephone and mail surveys. For mailed surveys, for example, he lists experience- and research-based recommendations that cover such minutiae as the color and type size for letters and other printed matter, the need for survey booklets to fit into the envelopes to be used, the need for preaddressed return envelopes to fit into the materials sent out, the use of postcards and other reminders to raise response rates, the methods by which labels with up-to-date correct addresses get attached to envelopes, the need to determine how envelopes will be stuffed to be sent and how they will be opened upon return, and the arrangements for bulk and individual mailings.

All these considerations and many more must be taken into account in putting together a realistic survey schedule. Every step, from the typing of a draft through pretesting and revision to management approval and booklet printing and binding must be put in the best order. Some administrators use Gantt charts or PERT charts (Emory & Cooper, 1991) for scheduling, making the process reminiscent of the preparation and details for a space launch.

Wishful thinking in place of realism can get survey users into trouble. In one survey using an effective internal mail system, it was hoped that two weeks would be ample time for surveys to go out and be returned. In reality, it was more than twice that time before the survey "window" could be closed. Figure 6.2 shows the cumulative return rates and reveals that only after a mailing of reminder postcards and thirty elapsed workdays did the return rate approach a ceiling (Kraut & Berger-Gross, 1979). In the absence of clear data about timelines, it is prudent to estimate conservatively.

Figure 6.2. Sample Study Cumulative Return Rates.

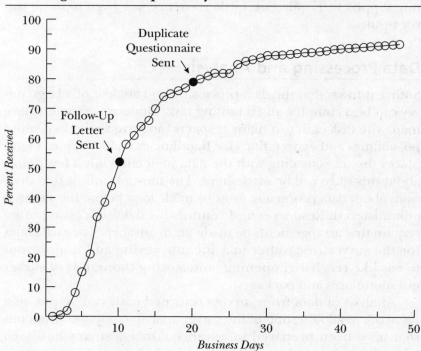

Response Rates

A major reason for good survey communication and administration is to get a high response rate. Not all people invited to take part in a survey will actually respond, but when *most* do not, it is hard to have confidence in the results. The response rate is an especially sensitive issue in a sample survey, where conclusions are based on only a fraction of the population. Respondents may be more or less favorable than nonrespondents, and managers are likely to feel data are distorted and unreliable when response rates are low.

What is a satisfactory response rate? Most companies with successful survey programs regularly get response rates of 80 percent or better. In my experience, management confidence in the results slips sharply when fewer than 65 percent of those invited take part. Low response rates invariably denote problems with the survey process, including employee attitudes toward surveys and management. In one organization undergoing downsizing and with a history of strained union-management relationships, the response rate slipped to 17 percent. Little credence was given to these survey results.

Data Processing and Analysis

Suffice it to say that the data processing and analysis of a large survey can be a complex and daunting task. Modern computers have made the task easier in many respects but have also raised more possibilities and expectations for handling data. In Chapter Eight, Macey discusses dealing with the data in detail. Only a few points about this stage will be made here. The most obvious is that decisions about data processing must be made long before the survey is administered. Resources and vendors for data processing often require that arrangements be made far in advance. Essential issues for the survey researcher may include vexing and nonobvious needs like receiving, opening, and storing thousands of survey questionnaires and packages!

Analysis of data from surveys returned early can be put on a fast track to allow testing of the survey analysis computer programs that have been prepared in advance. Once a survey has been administered, people usually have a high degree of interest and urgency in seeing the processed results. If prior or corollary data (like customer satisfaction or business performance data) are to be used in the analysis, they should be obtained ahead of time.

Feedback and Reporting

Like analysis phase planning, the plan for the feedback and reporting of the results should be worked out and agreed upon during the planning and design phase. Where possible, all parties should know in advance who will get what information and in what order.

Hinrichs discusses much of the specifics of feedback in Chapter Ten. In addition, I would note that the anticipated degree and type of feedback are crucial pieces of information for shaping the questionnaire itself. Most notably, if survey data are seen as forming a platform for future discussions of issues and problems, then there is less demand on the questionnaire itself to cover every imaginable facet of each issue the survey addresses.

The extent of detail produced by a questionnaire ties to a common complaint of managers who get survey reports, a complaint sometimes voiced as, "What did they mean?" or, "Why did they answer that way?"—often delivered as a criticism of the survey. Underneath this complaint is a tacit assumption (or is it a hope?) that the survey data will explain everything, with no further dialogue needed. In fact, the label of "feedback" may be misleading. It implies that management will report back to the respondents. But this stage can be seen more accurately as a chance for respondents to feed back more data to management and explain their earlier answers. Dialogues are often needed to move forward in prioritizing problems and developing solutions to them. Nadler (1977) lays out several models, suggesting that the organizational level and participants in the talks will depend on the type of issues to be discussed, and these considerations will in turn dictate the flow of the data feedback.

Systemwide issues need to be dealt with at an organization's higher levels and suggest the use of a *waterfall* method of feedback, starting at the top. A *bubble-up* order of feedback, starting at the bottom, is suggested when local issues are the focus, and intergroup meetings or ad hoc groups can be the place for feedback on issues that involve several different units.

To enable the users to get the data they need, the planned reports should include appropriate tabulations and show results for relevant groups. Also, the delivery system for these reports must ensure that users get any training they need to understand and use the data. Further, the survey director should anticipate some anxiety and defensiveness from managers who are getting their units' results, and he or she should be prepared to deal with these feelings.

When a survey is based on a sample and no reporting back of results through the normal management chain is planned, respondents should be told in advance that this is the case. Two other methods of reporting are to send participants a summary of the survey results and to publish the findings to all employees, through a company publication.

Action Planning and Follow-Through

An invariable effect of doing a survey is to raise the expectations of those you poll. People taking part will expect something to be done with the results. Management would be foolish to sponsor a survey if it is not willing to do something in response or to explain why it will not take action. The underlying message of nonresponsive behavior, intended or not, comes across to employees as, "We heard you, but we don't really care what you say."

Experienced survey researchers will agree that follow-on action is the most problematic part of organizational surveys. Quite often, no meaningful action takes place, and when it does, it may be invisible to respondents or seem unconnected to the survey itself. Therefore, not only must action be taken, it must be *communicated* that the action is part of the survey process. Some methods of communication are labeling changes as related to survey results, making suitable bulletin board and house organ pronouncements, and having executives and managers talk about the changes.

A straightforward way of checking on perceived progress after a survey, used by many firms, is to add some questions on this topic to later surveys. For example, one company used the following items with the following results:

Statement	Agree *(percent)*	Neither *(percent)*	Disagree *(percent)*
Results of the last [Company X] survey were communicated to me.	73	11	16
Completing this survey is a useful way to provide input for tracking progress in achieving [Company X's] Vision and Values.	61	26	13
I have seen actions taken as a result of the last [Company X] employee survey.	34	33	33

(The results shown here are typical, and one can easily understand how a reviewing executive might be disappointed in them. In this particular case, the data varied by unit, perhaps because some units had done better jobs than others on feedback and follow-through, and reviews with both types of units could be expected to reveal what kinds of actions lead to the perception of progress among organizational members.)

The key to making something worthwhile happen from a survey is to get the understanding and commitment of top management in the very beginning of the survey process. The key executives need to get involved in the data and their meaning. Members of top management must be role models in dealing with the survey findings. They need to express clear expectations for lower-level managers to take appropriate actions, and they must follow up with the managers on a regular basis.

Conclusion

The full survey process is essentially a problem-solving process. Survey findings help define areas that deserve attention and stimulate the generation of various potential solutions. The actions chosen and, it is to be hoped, implemented are informed by the survey data, and their impact can be measured by later surveys.

The touchstone for critical decisions rests in the strategic purposes underlying the survey. Unless survey designers are clear at the beginning about the real goals of the organizational survey and keep them in mind over the course of the survey process, their decision making will often be flawed. The successful survey is based on keeping in mind what you set out to achieve.

References

Babbie, E. (1992). *The practice of social research* (6th ed.). Belmont, CA: Wadsworth.

Covey, S. R. (1989). *The 7 habits of highly effective people.* New York: Simon & Schuster.

Dillman, D. A. (1978). *Mail and telephone surveys: The total design method.* New York: Wiley.

Emory, C. W., & Cooper, D. R. (1991). *Business research methods* (4th ed.). Belmont, CA: Wadsworth.

Kahn, R. L., & Cannell, C. F. (1957). *The dynamics of interviewing: Theory, technique, and cases.* New York: Wiley.

Kish, L. (1965). *The Survey Sample.* New York: Wiley.

Kraut, A. I. (1992). Organizational research on work and family issues. In S. Zedeck (Ed.), *Work, families, and organizations* (pp. 208–235). San Francisco: Jossey-Bass.

Kraut, A. I., & Berger-Gross, V. (1979, September). *A note on the rate of questionnaire returns.* Personnel Research Department, IBM Corporation.

Nadler, D. A. (1977). *Feedback and organization development: Using data-based methods.* Reading, MA: Addison-Wesley.

Rea, L. M., & Parker, R. A. (1992). *Designing and conducting survey research: A comprehensive guide.* San Francisco: Jossey-Bass.

Robinson, J. P., Athanasiou, R., & Head, K. B. (1969). *Measures of occupational attitudes and occupational characteristics.* Ann Arbor: Institute for Social Research, University of Michigan.

Smith, P. C., Kendall, L. M., & Hulin, C. L. (1969). *The measurement of satisfaction in work and retirement.* Skokie, IL: Rand McNally.

Warwick, D. P., & Lininger, C. A. (1975). *The sample survey: Theory and practice.* New York: McGraw-Hill.

Weiss, D. J., Dawis, R. V., England, G. W., & Lofquist, L. H. (1967). *Manual for the Minnesota satisfaction questionnaire.* Minneapolis: Industrial Relations Center, University of Minnesota.

CHAPTER 7

Setting Expectations and Reporting Results
Conversations with Top Management

David A. Nadler

A central challenge for the CEO of any complex organization is to master the leverage points for change. Perhaps the most common complaint of a CEO in his or her first year in office is a feeling of relative powerlessness in getting the entire enterprise to change. As one new CEO commented, "I found myself on the bridge, moving the controls but finding out that these controls were not connected to anything down below!"

As the CEO grows into the job, he or she learns that there are limited tools at his or her disposal. These include staffing, rewards, organizational structure, and other similar devices. One of the most important tools, however, is measurement. Measurement sends a message about what is more and less important. It enables observation from afar and allows comparisons. Measurement facilitates the assessment of individuals and the allocation of rewards. It is therefore not surprising to hear, "What we view is what we do." Those things that are measured are those things that people pay more attention to and act on.

The past few years have witnessed a major shift in the philosophy of organizational measurement. For decades, measurement was virtually dominated by retrospective financial indicators. Financial and managerial accounting-based metrics were accepted as the primary (and in some cases the only) basis for assessing performance. Stimulated by concepts of Total Quality Management and some forward-thinking management experts, a change occurred in the late 1980s and early 1990s. The concept of stakeholder-based measurement and the "balanced scorecard" (Kaplan & Norton, 1992, 1993) began to get attention. The idea is that the performance of an enterprise can best be understood as a set of measures that reflect how well the organization meets the needs of its various stakeholders. The primary stakeholders are seen as customers, employees, and owners (shareholders); although other stakeholders such as communities, suppliers, partners, and the like are also considered in many cases. In a growing number of companies, leaders have articulated the concept of a "three-legged stool" of measures covering customers, employees, and owners. The customer measures have included traditional indicators such as market share but also newer measures such as customer satisfaction and customer value added (Eisman, 1995; Ferling, 1993). Owner-based measures have similarly included traditional measures of financial performance but also such new concepts as economic value added (EVA), market value added (MVA), and total shareholder return (TSR) (Birchard, 1991; Stewart, 1991).

It is in this new environment of measurement that the whole question of organizational surveys needs to be considered. For many years, surveys of organizational members were seen as a tool to be used by the human resource function primarily for the measurement of satisfaction, or "morale," and for the assessment of such human resource matters as compensation and appraisal. As such, surveys were viewed as a functional activity, conducted at a distance from the senior management and not involving the CEO and the senior team. Then, in the enterprise committed to stakeholder measurement, organizational surveys become an important component in one of the three legs of measurement. Understanding and dealing with survey results has now become part of the work of the CEO.

A second factor has contributed to the change in the role of surveys. The technological, economic, and competitive turmoil of recent years has brought the whole subject of organizational change to the attention of CEOs. Basic changes in the environment have created a change imperative that company after company has had to face (Nadler, Shaw, Walton, & Associates, 1994). In response to this imperative, we have seen many companies engage in CEO-led change initiatives to fundamentally reshape the nature of the enterprise. There are numerous chronicles of such change in companies such as GE, Xerox, AT&T, Motorola, and Corning.

In these cases and others, the CEO personally developed an architecture for the change and led the transition. The CEO had a *change agenda,* which typically included a variety of activities related to strategy, organizational structure, management style, organizational culture, cost reduction, productivity, and so on. At the core of the change agenda, however, was an intention, indeed a requirement, to change the behavior of a large number of individuals within the organization—their behavior toward the customer, toward the product, toward the work, and toward each other. As one CEO said, "We need to have a hundred thousand people act differently, every day!"

It is this challenge of behavioral change that has brought surveys to the attention of senior management. Surveys are a means to measure people's perceived changes in behavior and the resultant changes in their attitudes. Survey feedback can also be a potent tool for behavioral change. In a typical organization in the midst of change, many individuals are convinced of the need for change and will confirm that others need to change their behavior but are unaware of the changes that they personally need to make. Human beings are notably poor observers of their own behavior. Survey data can perform a significant function in helping people understand how their own behavior needs to change and in assisting them in planning and assessing that behavioral change.

So the combination of stakeholder-based measurement and the change imperative has put the organizational survey on the table in front of the CEO and the senior team. The survey is no longer a functional tool, the use of which is delegated to staff groups. The survey is a tool for top management to use to assess the organization and its members and to bring about change. In light of this new role for the survey, the role of the CEO in the survey process is critical.

This chapter is intended to address some of the questions that

CEOs raise as they confront the new reality of organizational surveys. Before dealing with those questions, I review some key assumptions about measurement, surveys, and behavior. Second, I provide a way of thinking about the different types of surveys that are conducted within organizations. Using the resulting typology, I then identify the types of questions typically raised by senior management when a survey (or survey process) is proposed and talk about the responses to those questions. Finally, I address some selected issues that practitioners face when doing survey work.

Assumptions About Measurement and Surveys

The fundamental reasons for conducting an organizational survey are assessment and change. Even where data are collected primarily for assessment, the ultimate purpose is to determine possible actions either to deal with a problem or to bring about improvement. Therefore, it is important to understand how measurement and feedback influence behavior and bring about change. There are three specific questions to be answered: How does measurement itself influence behavior? How does feedback of information influence behavior? What is the pattern of response that people have to unfavorable feedback?

How does measurement itself influence behavior? The underlying theory of why measurement brings about behavioral change has been discussed elsewhere (Nadler, 1977). In brief, the act of collecting data, combined with people's perceptions about the accuracy of the measures and the extent to which the data will be used by individuals and groups with power within the system, creates expectations that the data collection will have consequences that will affect important outcomes for individuals. Once something is measured, then it can be observed, assessed, rewarded, or sanctioned. Thus, the mere act of data collection generates energy around those activities that are being measured.

Energy leads to behavior, but that behavior can be either productive or counterproductive. In this instance, productive behavior would be action to positively affect the performance or activity being measured. Counterproductive behavior would be action to invalidate the measures, make measurement difficult, or convey misleading data. The direction of the behavior, productive or counterproductive, is determined by the perceptions people have of how the data will be used. These perceptions are in turn determined by the perceived contract that people have with those collecting and using the data and by people's past experience with the power group's use of data.

How does feedback of information influence behavior? Feedback is the act of reporting data for the purpose of bringing about change. Data can be reported back to those who generated them, and/ or they can be reported back to others who have an interest in the responses, such as senior management. Data feedback influences behavior in two ways. First, feedback serves an energizing function, as it disconfirms previously held ideas or creates expectancies of either internal or external rewards. Second, feedback serves a directing function through cuing people about errors and showing them where learning is needed (see Table 7.1).

What is the pattern of response that people have to unfavorable feedback? Obviously, feedback that includes positive responses or good news is inherently different psychologically for the receiver from unfavorable feedback. My observation, based on years of facilitating feedback sessions, is that people go through a series of responses to unfavorable feedback that resembles the series of the typical psychological responses to death or other losses (Kübler-Ross, 1970).

The first response to unfavorable feedback is denial. The recipient questions the validity of the feedback and looks for reasons to deny the existence or veracity of the data. At a certain point, the recipient accepts that the data are real and valid, and then he or she moves to the second stage, anger. In this stage, the recipient expresses anger toward those who supplied the data. They clearly do not understand, are wrong or misguided. The problem lies with those who responded to the survey, not the receiver of the data. At some point, the recipient concludes that the negative responses cannot be blamed on the those who supplied the data, and he or she moves to the next stage, which is flight—specifically, fleeing away from the data. In this stage, the recipient accepts that the data are valid, accepts that they are not the result of misguided, misinformed, or malicious individuals, but avoids personal responsibility by looking for other causes for the unfavorable feedback, such

**Table 7.1. How Feedback Affects Group
and Individual Performance.**

Feedback Function	Mechanism	How the Mechanism Works
Motivating	Disconfirmation	Feedback motivates behavior by providing information that reveals inconsistent perceptions.
Motivating	Internal creation of reward expectancies	Feedback motivates behavior by setting up expectations that actions will generate data, expectations that generate positive feelings.
Motivating	External creation of reward expectancies	Feedback motivates behavior by setting up expectations that actions will lead to the generation of data, which in turn will lead to the attainment of other valued rewards from the environment.
Directing	Cuing	Feedback calls attention to error that can be corrected through known and established routines of behavior.
Directing	Learning	Feedback calls attention to errors for which corrective behavior has not yet been identified and must be discovered.

as the larger environment, larger organizational actions, or other factors. In the extreme, flight involves complete withdrawal from the data. If the recipient can work through this stage, the next stage is acceptance, where the individual comes to understand that the data are valid about him or her and his or her responsibility. Only after acceptance can the individual move to the next stage, which is to use the data for finding problems, for understanding the real problems of which the data are symptomatic. After problem finding, the individual can engage in problem solving.

This description suggests a process that is more linear than in reality it is. In practice, people move back and forth among the various stages. However, there seems to be some regularity in responses. It is natural for people to go through denial, anger, and flight. It also is difficult for a person to begin problem finding and problem solving until he or she has gotten to the point of acceptance.

While feedback processes are discussed further later on, it is worthwhile to note here how we might deal with these responses. A first step is to make people aware of the sequence of responses and help them understand that these are natural and human responses to unfavorable information but that action, growth, and learning do not occur if a person gets stuck in any one phase. Raising the responses to consciousness gives people a language system for talking about their feelings, and that in itself helps people work the feelings through. A second step is to push people through the stages through pointed inquiry. When a person is in denial, the question to ask is, "Is there anything in the data that is valid, or is everything invalid?" When a person is angry, the question is, "Is all of this feedback due to someone else, or is there anything here that you feel responsible for?" When a person is in flight, the question is, "Is all of this feedback due to outside forces beyond your control, or is any of this related to your own actions?" Finally, when a person is in acceptance, which sometimes leads to inaction, the question is, "Is there anything noted in this feedback that can be changed or that can be done better?"

The broad implication of this set of concepts related to measurement and feedback is that the whole process of planning data collection and feedback, of contracting with people who will be involved, of determining measures, and of structuring and implementing the feedback process is critical. I will come back to this issue when discussing the questions CEOs raise. First, however, the next section defines the scope of survey work in organizations.

Types of Organizational Surveys

By *organizational surveys*, I mean all questionnaire or survey activities aimed at eliciting the responses of organizational members. Organizations survey their employees for a whole host of reasons, and the instruments cover a wide content range. I have observed, however, that there are three primary classes of surveys that account for most of the survey activity that goes on. In addition, there are numerous specialized or targeted surveys, although this chapter focuses less on these. The three basic types are summarized in Table 7.2.

The most common form of survey is the instrument designed for *organizational assessment.* This survey, frequently called the employee opinion survey, is designed to measure and assess the state of the human assets of the enterprise. It is also designed as a general measure of organizational health and functioning. As such, it is designed to identify and help diagnosis problems and assess progress over time. This assessment survey is usually administered on a periodic basis throughout the organization, either through sampling or universal participation. It typically has a broad scope of content, including measures of motivation and satisfaction as well as a whole set of questions designed to elicit perceptions of how the organization functions.

The feedback process for the organizational assessment survey usually involves some organizationwide reporting back of results through meetings, written presentations, summaries in house organs, videotaped presentations, and so on. In addition, data may be presented to senior management, to unit management, or to teams chartered to investigate specific issues or concerns. The focus of the feedback is understanding the state of the organization.

There are a number of critical issues in the design and implementation of the organizational assessment survey. Survey results have more power if they can be presented through a model or conceptual framework (Lawler, Nadler, & Cammann, 1980) rather than as a plain data readout. Also, because data are often viewed at a distance from the actual phenomena being measured, the reliability, validity, and consistency of the measures are important. Finally, the impact of the data collection and feedback, consistent with the model of measurement and behavior presented earlier (see Table 7.1), will be determined by people's perceptions of whether the data will have an impact on rewards or not. In those organizations where survey data are linked to bonuses, people obviously pay much more attention to the data.

The second class of survey is aimed at *organizational change and improvement.* This type of survey is a part of the kinds of change initiatives discussed above. As part of the planning, implementing, or tracking of a change agenda or a specific part of it, the survey is

Table 7.2. Basic Survey Types.

Type of Survey	Primary Purpose	Data Collected	Feedback Process	Critical Issues
Organizational assessment	Measurement of the state of human assets and organizational health; identification and diagnosis of problems	Organizationwide broad measures of motivation, satisfaction, and perceptions of organizational functioning	Organizationwide reporting, unit-level sessions, and issue-focused teams; aimed at understanding and organizational problem solving	Assessment model Reliability, validity, and consistency of measures Linkage to rewards over time
Organizational change/ improvement	Support of a change agenda; stimulus, catalyst, guide, and assessment of change	Measures focused on a specific issue or on a specific part or level of the organization, linked to issues of the change agenda	Sessions with senior management, change planning teams, and relevant units; aimed at understanding and action	Linkage to change agenda Intensive feedback, problem solving, and action planning required
Individual/team behavioral change	Diagnosis and change of individual and team functioning	Measures of perceptions of behavior of individual leaders and/or teams	Individual and team feedback sessions; focused on problem finding and contracting for action	Focus on actionable issues Behavioral orientation Feedback process design and facilitation

used as a tool for communicating, for stimulating activity, for diagnosing problems, and for tracking progress. Compared to the broad organizational assessment questionnaire, the organizational change and improvement survey will be more narrowly focused. As a result, it will collect in-depth data about a relatively smaller set of variables such as quality, management style, values, or other similar topics. Depending upon the state of the change initiative, the survey may focus on a particular part of the organization, specific units, or specific levels of the hierarchy.

The feedback from this survey is directed toward senior management and/or those who engaged in the planning or management of the change, such as special teams, task forces, or planning groups. The feedback is aimed at informing the planners and sponsors of change. It is critical for these surveys to be linked to the change agenda, and the feedback process must enable intensive feedback, problem finding, problem solving, and action planning.

The third class of survey is even more focused and is aimed at collecting and feeding back data to *individual leaders and teams* about their own patterns of activity and behavior. The individual leader/team survey is also focused on change but on the individual and group level rather than the organizational level. The primary purpose is the diagnosis of problems and the catalyzing of change for the individual leader and his or her team. Data collected usually involve perceptions of the behavior of individual leaders and/or teams. The focus is on behavior and on issues that are actionable by those who are receiving the data.

In this type of survey, the feedback process is an absolutely central and critical element. Feedback occurs through individual (one-on-one) and team feedback sessions, with a heavy emphasis on problem finding and contracting for action. The critical features of this type of survey are the focus on actionable issues, the orientation toward observable behavior, and the design and facilitation of the feedback process.

In addition to these three types of surveys, there are many other specialized applications of survey methods in organizations. Surveys may focus on peer relations, on response to a specific action (such as downsizing), on change readiness, on values, or other topics.

Questions from Senior Management

The discussion so far has been intended to provide some background and context for the core focus of this chapter—the conversations with top management in general, and the CEO specifically, about proposed survey activities.

Many organizations have long histories of using surveys as important tools to understand and manage the enterprise. However, there are also many companies where the survey activity has been peripheral to senior management and where senior managers have taken the role of spectators rather than participants in the survey process. When a survey (any of the three types) is proposed, there is a set of questions that senior managers typically raise. I might add that even if these questions are not raised, they frequently are on the minds of executives. It therefore might make sense for the feedback specialist or consultant to raise and answer these questions in any situation. For ease of reading, in the following discussion I describe the questions as being raised by the enterprise CEO (designated here by "he" although the CEO could be a he or a she), even though they could easily be raised by the CEOs of operating units or by other members of the top management team. The questions typically are as follows:

1. *Why do it?* As with any proposed action, the immediate question raised by the CEO is, "Why do it?" He wants to understand the rationale, what the company stands to gain from this activity, what are the costs, and what are the benefits. Specifically, he wants to know what investment is required to do the survey right. More than money, he typically is concerned with the required investment of time, both his time and the time of other senior managers. Finally, he will want to understand the risks.

2. *How do I position it?* The CEO recognizes that when a survey is introduced, it is in itself a message to the organization. He is concerned about what that message might be or how it might be interpreted. Specifically, he may ask: "How do I describe this to the organization?" "Are we doing this because we are concerned, afraid, or worried about how people feel?" "How can we position this so that people will see it as an act of strength rather than an act of weakness?" For the CEO who has never participated actively

in a survey process, there is the added challenge of demonstrating personal commitment to a process he has never personally experienced. He wonders, "How can I answer questions about this without sounding ignorant?"

3. *What will be measured?* The CEO seeks to understand the value of the data he will be seeing, and this leads to a set of questions about what will be measured. He wants to know what will be asked in order to make sure that the important questions are asked, that the potentially inflammatory questions are avoided, and that he will have control over what is included in the survey. He also wants to understand what kinds of data will be coming back to him, including what types of comparisons.

4. *What data will be reported back to people?* A major concern of the CEO is feedback and, specifically, what data will be reported back to which individuals and/or groups of people in the organization. He is concerned about the risks of showing data to people, particularly negative data.

5. *What is the process that will be used to feed back data?* A related question the CEO will have is exactly how people will see the survey information: "To what degree do people see all versus some of the data?" "How much time will this take?" The CEO wants to understand fully what the data will be like, what the sequence is for reporting data, and what the degree of control is over what data will be seen by whom.

6. *What is the process for problem solving and action planning?* The CEO is often interested in how the data will actually be used to solve problems or take action as opposed to simply reporting back problems and concerns. A related question is, "How can we ensure that the data will be used to improve the organization rather than to support and reinforce negativism?" CEOs often want to understand how the problem solving will be done. "How much time will all of this take?"

7. *What's my role?* Ultimately, the CEO gets to one of the questions that is perhaps most important for him. He asks what his role will be. He wonders what will be expected of him, what the personal risks are, how he keeps himself and others from being defensive in the face of negative information, and what he needs to do and/or avoid doing.

Answering the CEO's Questions

There are many different approaches to answering the questions of the CEO. To give the reader a feeling for the conversations that occur, I provide samples of the responses that I and my colleagues find ourselves giving to CEOs when we hear these questions. The answers differ for each type of survey (organizational assessment, organizational change, and individual/team behavioral change). Therefore, for each survey type, I provide a set of practical answers in the form of a script, that is, the exact words I would use with a CEO or senior executive. This format will necessitate some repetition, but I feel it is worthwhile to provide extra clarity. The script shows the CEO's question in italics, as before. The answers that follow each question are spoken by the internal or external consultant. Table 7.3 summarizes the content of the responses, organized by type of survey.

The Organizational Assessment Survey

The organizational assessment survey is probably the easiest survey to discuss with the CEO. Compared to the other types, this survey occurs at the greatest psychological distance from the CEO. Recently, the concept of the balanced scorecard and/or stakeholder measurement has gotten broad exposure and acceptance, so the resistance to this survey is generally low. Following are the seven CEO questions and potential consultant answers when an organizational assessment survey is being discussed.

1. *Why do it?* "You measure all kinds of things here in your company already. What you measure is important because it sends a signal about what you believe is important. The kinds of data that you collect focus your attention and everyone's energy on different issues. If all you do is collect financial information, for example, you send a message that the financials are all that are important, and you end up spending your time, individually and with your team, focusing on the financial data and issues. Collecting data about the organization and the people in the organization sends a message that you feel these issues are important. That

Table 7.3. Answering Top Management Questions.

Question	Organizational Assessment	Organizational Change/ Improvement	Individual/Team Behavioral Change
1. Why do it?	It is critical to track organizational health as you would track other indicators of the enterprise's performance.	An effective change process benefits from a survey—as a catalyst, as a form of instruction and communication, and as a means for tracking and assessment.	Surveys can bring about change in individual leadership and team behavior.
2. How do I position it?	This is the third leg of the stool in measuring performance of the enterprise.	We are committed to change, and therefore we need to measure how well we're doing.	Surveys and the feedback process are an important tool for all of us to improve our effectiveness. Change in individual behavior is necessary to change the organization.
3. What will be measured?	Employee perceptions and affective responses, including satisfaction, motivation, and perception of organizational functioning.	Specific issues related to the content of the change initiatives (will vary according to situation).	Individual leadership practices, observable behaviors. Team practices, observable patterns of behavior.

4. What data will be reported back to people?	Analyses of data for the entire organization, for major units, for different levels, and around specific high-priority issues; organized by a conceptual model.	Data reflecting areas of progress and areas that need more attention.	Individual and team behavior linked to a model of action and outcomes.
5. What is the process that will be used to feed back data?	Reporting of data analogous to other measures. Periodic reviews at multiple levels of the organization.	Primary focus is on the group's responsibility for planning and managing the change, including the senior team. Feedback is aimed at planners and sponsors of change—focusing on their responsibility for managing the change.	Individual sessions with facilitators and facilitated team feedback sessions.
6. What is the process for problem solving and action planning?	Action planning is focused on specific issues, driven by the data and by organizational performance.	Planning teams analyze data and determine actions—part of a plan-do-check-act cycle.	Action planning is an integral part of the one-on-one and team feedback session.
7. What's my role?	Customer for the data. Champion of stakeholder measurement.	Architect of the change. Champion of change. Customer for those planning and managing the change.	Champion of the process. First user. Model of desired participation. Articulator of experiences.

motivates people and enables you and your team to spend time on those issues."

2. *How do I position it?* "You position the organizational survey as a natural extension of your belief that the company needs to measure, display, track, and act on data about all of its major stakeholders—customers, people employed in the organization, and owners. You tell your people that you feel it is important to the health and continued success of the organization for senior management to have a set of valid measures about customers and people in the organization, measures that are leading indicators of performance, as opposed to having just retrospective financial information.

"You signal to them that you really are serious when you talk about the values of the company or how people are so important by making a commitment to measure, on a continual basis, the state of the human assets, not just the physical assets. You commit to use these data in understanding and guiding the company, and to make this information available to all employees so that they, too, can participate in understanding where you are in diagnosing problems and in working to solve problems and engage in continuous improvement."

3. *What will be measured?* "We will be measuring a whole range of perceptions and employee attitudes related to many different elements of the organization. By perceptions, I mean that we will be measuring how people see things, or what they perceive. What we measure will include perceptions of how the organization functions, of what is rewarded, of the way that managers act toward people, and so forth. By attitudes, I include how people feel about what they perceive, whether they feel good or not, whether they are satisfied or not, whether they are motivated or not. We will measure many different factors based on a model or framework that will help us understand what the driving or causal factors are as opposed to those that are results or outcomes."

4. *What data will be reported back to people?* "We will give people a very full and complete picture of how the organization is functioning and how people feel about it. We will show them data for the enterprise as a whole, data about their own particular function or unit, and relevant breakdowns, such as level differences. We will include comparisons with other leading organizations so people

will have a frame of reference and comparisons to data collected here in the past. We may also focus on data relating to a specific issue that is of importance to people throughout the company. We will organize the data around a road map or model so people can understand what causes what."

5.   *What is the process that will be used to feed back data?* "We will cascade the data feedback, beginning with you and your immediate team. We will hold a meeting of the senior management or use one of the regular senior management meetings to review the data and to discuss them. Each unit of the organization will then have feedback sessions to review the company data and the data relevant to their own piece of the business. Within each unit, different approaches might be used to report the data, based on the priorities of the local unit leadership. Ultimately we would see the reporting of this data to be a regular event."

6.   *What is the process for problem solving and action planning?* "In the feedback sessions we've already spoken about, we will start the process of problem analysis and action planning. Similarly, this work will be done within the individual units. However, we probably will need to set up some specific teams or make some functional assignments to work with the data and explore specific issues that emerge from the data."

7.   *What's my role?* "You need to support the effort in general, make time for the feedback sessions, and participate actively in those sessions. You should take the lead in chartering any specific problem-solving or action-planning work. If recommendations come out of this work, then you should be a champion of action. Perhaps most important, you should start talking about and referring to the survey just as you talk about comparable financial and/or customer results. If people perceive that you view the organizational survey as a relevant and important measure of the organization's performance and that you are intimately familiar with the results, then they too will use the survey as a constructive tool."

The Organizational Change/Improvement Survey

The targeted survey for organizational change and/or improvement is in many ways a narrower version of the organizational assessment survey. The content of the survey will vary depending upon the content of the change. The CEO may have initiated a new strategy, a new organizational structure, new processes, a changed culture, a different management style, or new values. Typically, the change agenda of the CEO includes several of these elements. The broad intent of the survey is to assess perceived progress in each of the content areas of the change and the perceived impact on the organization as a whole.

When talking with the CEO about this type of survey, the consultant or feedback specialist will use many responses similar to those for the organizational assessment survey. The following dialogue, therefore, focuses on the answers that are specifically different for this type of survey.

1. *Why do it?* "You've put a lot of time and effort into all of the change initiatives. It is now time to do some assessment, to see how well you're doing, and to find out how the people in the organization perceive this activity. It's valuable to do an assessment for several reasons. First, the measurement itself will serve as a reminder and reinforcer of what you're trying to accomplish. Second, it will be a catalyst, to get people reenergized around the change. Third, it should give you a sense of how people are perceiving your efforts and initiatives. It's dangerous for you to continue to plan and implement changes without knowing the impact of those actions you've already taken. The survey is not the only way of finding that out, but it is one important way of collecting a lot of data from a lot of people quickly."

2. *How do I position it?* "Position the survey and the change as part of a plan-do-check-act cycle [Deming, 1986]. Let people know that you are interested in their views of the change process and initiatives and that you recognize the need to measure how well things are progressing. Use the survey as a means to demonstrate your commitment to the change. You believe it is necessary to change, you are committed to the change, and therefore you feel it is critical to measure the impact of the change. You plan to use the data to modify your approach, so this is a means for people throughout the organization to provide input to you and your team."

3. *What will be measured?* "There are several things to measure here. First, you need to determine whether people perceive and

recognize the actions that you are taking. Second, you need to include some general measures of organizational effectiveness so that you can see if there is any relationship between the change activities and the effectiveness of the enterprise. Third, you need to get people to assess the change initiatives in terms of whether they are the right actions, whether they are being implemented effectively, and whether they are having any impact. In addition, you probably should provide space for some open-ended comments so that people can respond to the general question of change and its assessment, even if we don't know exactly the right general questions to ask. While you want to get a broad set of perceptions, you probably can do this through a sampling of various units, groups, and levels rather than surveying everyone in the organization."

4. *What data will be reported back to people?* "We should provide people with a summary of the results. It is not critical to give people a readout on every question being asked. We should analyze the data, review the findings with you and with others who are critical to planning and implementing the changes, and then decide what data would be useful to feed back to the organization at large."

5. *What is the process that will be used to feed back data?* "After we've reviewed the data together and determined what the data mean, we can use a variety of feedback processes. We should do some form of general feedback, either through large meetings or through other forms of communication (videotape, print, and the like). This would be a means to provide a 'report card' on the change, reflecting the input of a sample of people. We should hold in-depth sessions with the specific individuals, groups, or teams charged with planning and managing the change."

6. *What is the process for problem solving and action planning?* "The focus for problem solving and action planning should be you, your immediate leadership team, and others who have major leadership roles in the change. You need to combine these data with other data available to you and with your own observations and judgments to determine what should be done. The survey data are important but just one of a number of sources of input."

7. *What's my role?* "You should support this assessment, but others may be the primary sponsors (the 'transition managers' or

'change leaders'). You should display a strong interest in the data and actively participate in the problem solving, as appropriate. You should set a tone of inquiry and learning, rather than blame or defensiveness. You can model the use of the survey to learn, to assess, and then to modify actions in response to that learning."

The Individual/Team Behavioral Change Survey

The survey aimed at individual and team behavior is in many ways radically different from the other two types. Since the focus is on the individual leader and his team, the CEO has two separate roles. On the one hand, the CEO is the champion and advocate for this process of behavioral change. On the other hand, the CEO is an individual participant in the survey process. In my view, one role cannot happen without the other. Specifically, the CEO must personally participate and must make the nature and content of that participation public if he is to be a credible champion of the data feedback process. The CEO's questions, therefore, have to do with both his own personal participation and the broad survey feedback initiative that will affect others.

1. *Why do it?* "For some time now, you've been talking about the need for change and how that requires everyone to reflect on and change his or her own behavior. We believe that one of the most powerful tools available for behavioral change is the survey and the survey feedback process. While you might (and perhaps should) have individuals do in-depth work on their own behavior with some form of internal or external resource, the survey provides you with an opportunity to get to a lot of people quickly and repeatedly.

"As you know, people are notoriously ineffective observers of their own behavior. They see the need for others to change, but they frequently don't have accurate perceptions of their own behavior and its impact on others. The survey is a means for people to get a picture of how their actions are perceived, the impact that their actions have, and how their behavior lines up with the direction of change that you have articulated."

2. *How do I position it?* "This should be seen as part of a larger process to improve the organization and to enhance the quality of

leadership. In the positioning, we think it is critical that you let people know that you and your direct team will be participating in this and that you will go first. You won't be asking them to do anything that you haven't already done. It is also important to position this survey process as primarily developmental. While it can be thought of as an 'upward appraisal,' the focus is on learning and growth rather than on evaluation."

3.   *What will be measured?* "Two things will be the focus of the measurement. First, each leader will be 'rated' by others who will fill out a questionnaire that elicits their perceptions of how the leader behaves in terms of observable, concrete leadership practices. The questions will ask people, 'To what extent do you see this individual doing the following things?' So the survey will be a measure of frequency of action rather than an evaluation of goodness or badness. Second, each person will be asked to answer similar questions about the team of which he/she is a member. The focus, again, will be on perceptions of team behavior. In addition, there will be some measures of team effectiveness."

4.   *What data will be reported back to people?* "Each individual leader and team will get a feedback report containing a profile of that leader's and that team's data. Therefore, each individual leader will be getting a report that summarizes how others have perceived him or her. This report will be organized around the same leadership model that guided the questions the survey will ask. We recommend that you make it clear that each individual will be expected to share his or her data with the individuals who have provided them.

5.   *What is the process that will be used to feed back data?* "We recommend strongly that each individual be required to hold a feedback session with those who have provided the data input. These people are usually the members of the team that the individual leads. Typically, we hold a one-on-one session with the individual leader first, so that he or she can see the data, understand what they mean, do some initial problem finding and problem solving, and plan the approach to the feedback meeting. Following that, we recommend a feedback meeting with the team, to review the data and use them for problem solving and action planning. Subsequent follow-up sessions might also be held to continue the problem solving and action planning.

"Over time, we see this becoming a regular part of the management process. Once a year (or every eighteen months to two years), leaders would repeat the data collection and feedback process. I can't stress enough how important these sessions are. Research and experience indicates that most of the value of this process comes from the feedback meeting. Those people who receive data but don't hold feedback sessions show much less change and improvement over time when compared to those who do."

6. *What is the process for problem solving and action planning?* "The individual session and the team feedback meeting are the key elements of the problem-solving and action-planning process. Since the data are very specific and people may feel defensive, it frequently is useful to have some form of third-party resource, either an internal or external facilitator, who can help structure the meeting, moderate defensiveness, and promote productive inquiry and effective problem solving.

"In these sessions, we also find it is frequently useful to have the team talk about the leader for a while with the leader out of the room. This frees up the group members to share individual data, find points of consensus, and develop a shared group perspective on the data without the individual risks inherent in proposing ideas and testing consensus in the presence of the leader."

7. *What's my role?* "You have two roles here. As with other surveys, you need to be a champion, advocate, and leader. In this type of activity, it is essential that you lead by example. You need to do this first (or, at least, right after any initial pilots). You need to model active and nondefensive responses to the data. You need to conduct yourself well in your feedback meeting, take the data seriously, and demonstrate real change as a consequence.

"In addition, you can help to legitimize and support the process by actively talking about your participation, sharing some of the 'good news' and 'bad news' that you received, and talking about your specific actions and the personal goals that you have set as a result of this. By doing so, you make it legitimate and acceptable for others to actively participate in the same process."

Other Issues in Organizational Surveys

Throughout the discussions about a survey with senior managers, many other issues will come up. This section briefly discusses some of these issues. The experiences I and my colleagues have had with surveys have led us to points of view that we can advocate in our work with senior managers.

Models of Behavior and Organization

There are two different approaches to building organizational surveys. The first approach is empirical. The issues that might be surveyed are identified, and an instrument is built to collect data on the relevant variables. Ideally, pilot work is done to verify the basic reliability and validity of the survey items and scales to the extent possible.

The second approach is theory driven. A conceptual model of organizations and/or behavior is used to build the survey. Again, to the extent that new items and scales are used, a pilot is done to assess and tune the instrument. It is our view that the theory-driven approach provides a number of distinct advantages. The primary advantage is that it provides the analyst and the ultimate users of the data (in feedback sessions, for example) a road map that helps them interpret the data.

We find that people in organizations in general, and executives specifically, do not find great value in an empirical data dump. They want to understand what the data mean, what the leverage points or drivers are, and what the outcomes are. They find it much more useful to have a framework that helps them understand the data and helps them turn data into information, information into knowledge, and ultimately knowledge into action. The only downside to model-based feedback is the necessity to invest in education and communication about the model before people can employ it to understand and use the data. (An in-depth discussion of models for assessment can be found in Lawler, Nadler, and Cammann, 1980, and Howard, 1994.)

Feedback Formats

The way in which data are displayed partly determines executives' receptivity. While executives may have great tolerance for complexity in financial information, they are typically impatient with great masses of numbers. The question is one of familiarity; they have learned to understand the format and syntax of financial and operating reports.

In light of this, our approach is to format feedback data in a manner as simple, straightforward, and user-friendly as possible. We use graphics liberally and avoid dense pages of numbers. The purpose of the feedback report is to provide meaning, with enough backup information to enable analysis and discovery but not necessarily the complete reporting that one would do for scientific data analysis.

Comparisons and Norms

At the senior executive level especially, people search for meaning in feedback data by looking for comparisons. Without a frame of reference, they do not know if a 5.4 on a 7-point scale or a 60 percent favorable response is good or bad. They need relevant comparisons. The standard approach is to provide some form of comparison group, standards, or norms. These comparison points can be tremendously helpful to people in understanding what data mean, and they also correct for some of the inherent response biases built into questions. Some survey organizations, such as International Survey Research, in Chicago, purport to go further and build specialized norms beyond the broad group of companies they survey. Senior managers in particular are very concerned about the composition of the comparisons. They want to be sure that comparative data are indeed comparable. Providing senior people with comparative data from lower-level administrations in firms of different sizes, in different industries, and perhaps in different geographical or transnational distribution is not very helpful and often counterproductive.

Multisource (360-Degree) Feedback

More and more, organizations are finding it useful in the individual/ team survey to collect data from a variety of different sources. The reality of today's organizations, where lateral relations are critical and people work in matrices, teams, and temporary structures that cut across boundaries and levels, makes the traditional hierarchy-based approach to data collection less relevant and less informative.

Current multisource surveys on behalf of an individual typically include data from the individual's subordinates, data from the individual's own manager, data from colleagues and peers outside of the person's work group and at different levels, and finally, data from self-rating. The full picture provided by this broad landscape of information can be powerful and informative. Both the consistencies and inconsistencies among the different sources can be sources of learning and insight. This approach does raise questions of feedback formats and feedback meetings, which become more difficult and more complex than in traditional feedback, but these issues are manageable. At the executive level, the multisource approach has great attraction since executives seem to recognize that some of the most valuable data about their own behavior come from peers.

Use of Data for Assessment, Appraisal, and Rewards

Perhaps one of the most problematic survey issues facing executives today is whether to use survey data for assessment, appraisal, and rewards, and if so, how to go about it. There are two sides to this argument. On one hand, the traditional view of survey data is that their use is primarily developmental—to help individuals, teams, and organizations to learn and thus grow or improve. Under this view, survey data are never used as the basis for appraisal and reward because of the potential for defensive behavior, manipulation of data (to enhance personal or organizational outcomes), or unwillingness to share problematic data. Many survey programs in the past, therefore, have tended to operate under the guideline that each person's individual data are his or her own property; that no one is required to disclose his or her survey data, at least not upward in the organization; and that survey data will not be a basis for performance evaluation or rewards.

On the other hand, some would argue that if the development of the human side of the organization is to be seen as an important area and a priority, then survey data should—in fact, must—be considered as input for appraisals and rewards. Without this linkage, the organizational survey lacks teeth, and a message is sent that the organizational and human data are clearly less valid and less important than the "hard" data about financial performance or even the data about customer satisfaction.

This debate remains unresolved in many companies, but the

trend appears to be in the direction of using survey data for making appraisals and rewards. In practice, I recommend that this use be implemented in phases. There first needs to be an understanding of the nature of the data, the meaning of the measures, and the nature of the feedback process. Once there is familiarity, understanding, and acceptance of the validity of the data, then it can start to be linked to the evaluation and reward process.

The Integrated Feedback System

Finally, as the organizational survey becomes recognized as an important measurement system and tool, organizations will need to rationalize their survey efforts. They will need to think of the various surveys, including assessment surveys, change surveys, surveys connected with training programs, individual/team behavioral surveys, and special surveys as parts of a system with related elements.

In practice, many organizations have fragmented survey activities. Part of the value of a survey is that it introduces a language system for the topics it covers and a way of thinking about people, organizations, and leadership. However, if inconsistent and/or conflicting language systems are introduced because survey efforts are fragmented, then the potential impact of any survey is underleveraged. We are finding great power is created when an organization builds a set of survey tools based on common conceptual models, using common language, and sending the same messages in a range of different settings. Much as organizations have integrated managerial and financial accounting systems, the integrated organizational survey system can provide coherence to the enterprise as it faces the human issues of organization. This coherence increases the value of the survey as a tool for the leadership of the enterprise.

Conclusion

This chapter has focused on some of the issues that senior managers face when considering the decision to use surveys as an organizational measurement and improvement tool. A very promising outcome of the organizational turmoil of the late 1980s and early 1990s is the emergence of a much more balanced and sophisticated view of the enterprise and its stakeholders. A balanced view of stakeholders leads senior management to the conclusion that regular and consistent measurement of the perceptions and attitudes of employees is a requirement for effective leadership. The survey has come to the executive table and has become recognized as a potentially powerful tool. Surveys have become senior management work.

References

Birchard, B. (1994, October). Mastering the new metrics. *CFO, 10,* 30–38.

Deming, W. E. (1986). *Out of the crisis.* Cambridge, MA: MIT Center for Advanced Engineering Study.

Eisman, R. (1995, January). Eyes on the prize. *Incentive, 169,* 43–47.

Ferling, R. L. (1993). Quality in 3D: EVA, CVA, and employees. *Financial Executive, 9*(4), 51.

Howard, A. (1994). *Diagnosis for organizational change: Methods and models.* New York: Guilford Press.

Kaplan, R. S., & Norton, D. P. (1992). The balanced scorecard: Measures that drive performance. *Harvard Business Review, 70*(1), 71–79.

Kaplan, R. S., & Norton, D. P. (1993). Putting the balanced scorecard to work. *Harvard Business Review, 71*(5), 134–147.

Kübler-Ross, E. (1970). *On death and dying.* New York: Macmillan.

Lawler, E. E. III, Nadler, D. A., & Cammann, C. (1980). *Organizational assessment: Perspectives on the measurement of organizational behavior and the quality of work life.* New York: Wiley.

Nadler, D. A. (1977). *Feedback and organization development: Using data-based methods.* Reading, MA: Addison-Wesley.

Nadler, D. A., Shaw, R. B., Walton, A. E., & Associates. (1994). *Discontinuous change: Leading organizational transformation.* San Francisco: Jossey-Bass.

Stewart, G. B. III (1991). *Quest for value.* New York: HarperBusiness.

CHAPTER 8

Dealing with the Data
Collection, Processing, and Analysis

William H. Macey

This chapter is about data management. It is written from the perspective of the individual who gathers survey responses, analyzes the resulting data, and subsequently prepares reports for the internal or external client.

Despite the significant time and costs normally associated with these activities, little literature is available regarding conventional practices. Therefore, what follows is a framework for understanding the decisions associated with data management and their implications for the survey process. Importantly, much of this chapter is not prescriptive; the different methods practitioners use frequently conflict both in assumptions and outcomes. Therefore, my aim is to present the major issues in data management and discuss the alternative strategies.

The chapter is organized around seven phases of data-handling activity.

- *Administrative planning.*
- *Survey administration and data capture:* the process of gathering responses from survey participants, including the administration of survey documents and forms, the interviewing of respondents to gather their opinions, and any other activity with the purpose of collecting survey data.

- *Data receipt:* the collection of completed surveys (via mail, overnight delivery, direct wire transfer, and so on) prior to processing.
- *Data entry and editing:* the activities associated with the conversion of survey responses into some usable form. These activities might be confined to a data entry process but may also include data editing and "cleaning" activities meant to ensure that captured data accurately represent survey responses.
- *Data analysis and reporting:* the aggregation and summarizing of information using descriptive statistics and the presentation of the results in a form useful to the consumer or sponsor of the survey research, including preparation of graphical summaries and statistical analyses.
- *Capturing, transcribing, and reporting verbatim comments:* the recording of the responses to the open-ended questions often used to supplement traditional Likert-style ratings. Issues of confidentiality and data reduction must be addressed.
- *Data storage:* the retention of the results for future use.

Administrative Planning

Administrative planning in this context refers to the implementation of systems for data receipt, management, and reporting. Most challenges associated with data management can be avoided through the proper implementation of administrative and quality control systems. While the effort associated with the design and implementation of such systems is not trivial, the value of survey information, the cost of errors and lost data, and similar concerns mandate appropriate attention to detail.

Organizational Coding Strategies

It is particularly important to determine survey reporting needs prior to survey administration. Commonly, survey results are reported for organizational groups (for example, departments, plants, locations, facilities, and the like) rather than or in addition to the organization as a whole. However, data can be reported at group level only to the extent that preestablished coding allows for group identification.

Group membership is conventionally identified by assigning

alphanumeric codes to groups and then providing the coding structure to survey respondents, who use the codes to self-report their group membership. Aside from concerns about protecting respondent anonymity, any alphanumeric method of uniquely identifying groups is sufficient for this purpose.

Survey reporting requirements frequently call for the *roll-up* of survey data in a manner parallel to the organizational structure. For example, it is common to aggregate data across groups within larger units for reporting purposes. This pattern may be repeated from the smallest through the largest subunits within the organization. A properly designed survey coding structure can facilitate the roll-up of survey data.

This structure is best arrived at through the concatenation of separate codes defining organizational levels. For example, assume a six-digit code, as shown in Figure 8.1. The first two digits might be used to identify all possible organizational groups at the first level (divisions within the organization, for example), the second two digits might identify units within divisions, and so on. The final organizational coding structure is the concatenated set of all group codes.

The organizational coding structure should also be designed to accommodate the combination of subgroups if the return rate for one or more subgroups falls below the minimum number required to maintain confidentiality of responses. Often, this can be accomplished by combining smaller groups within larger ones. However, again, such groups must first be uniquely identified within the coding structure.

Survey Administration and Data Capture

Survey content constrains the strategies that can be used to capture data. Some survey questions are not amenable to data capture with specific technologies. For example, fewer methods are available for capturing verbatim comments as opposed to numeric survey responses. Additional criteria relevant to determining data capture strategy are

- Cost
- Accuracy
- Time
- Administrative flexibility
- Survey response rate

Figure 8.1. Sample Organizational Coding Structure.

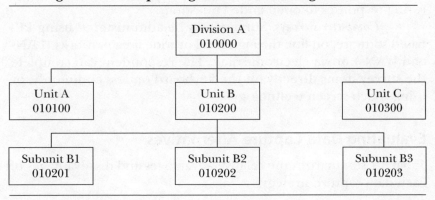

I consider each of these criteria in the subsequent discussion of alternative data-handling strategies.

Choosing a Data Capture Method

Whether a respondent circles a number on a survey document, shades a "bubble" on an optically scannable form, presses a button on a telephone keypad, or verbally answers the questions of a telephone interviewer, the individual responses must be captured. The more viable alternatives for data capture include the following:

- *Paper-and-pencil survey.* The most common data capture method remains administration of the paper-and-pencil survey. This method has many variants (for example, circling the selected response option, writing the response, and shading circles on an optical scannable form). Verbatim comments are often captured on paper as well.
- *Telephone survey.* In this method, the respondent dials a telephone number and is prompted by a prerecorded voice to enter his or her survey responses using the telephone keypad. Often, the respondent is given the survey in written form along with dialing and completion instructions. In this variation, the respondent can have the option of listening to each survey question in full or entering a response any time after the narrator starts the item. Available technology allows for the recording of chosen options and time

and date stamping of each call. Options are also available for capturing responses to open-ended questions.

• *Computer surveys.* Surveys may be administered using PC-based software, on-line through local or wide area networks (LANs and WANs) or via electronic mail. The respondent can complete the survey items directly on the keyboard or, less commonly, by using touch-screen technology.

Evaluating Data Capture Alternatives

Table 8.1 summarizes the relative advantages and disadvantages of each data capture strategy.

• *Cost.* Data capture is often one of the costly components of the overall survey budget. Costs can include computer programming, data processing, typesetting and layout, key entry, scanning, and so on. Moreover, the trade-offs associated with each strategy are often compensatory. For example, although development of survey forms and printing costs may be higher for scannable than nonscannable forms, data entry costs for scannable forms may be lower. Importantly, many of the costs associated with particular technologies are hidden costs (productive job time lost, for example) and therefore not easily identified and incorporated into the evaluation of alternatives.

For large samples, optical scanning is typically the most economical method of data capture. For smaller samples (say, 1,000 or less), overall data capture cost is lowest when key entry methods are used. However, even this general conclusion must be considered in light of other parameters such as survey length and format.

• *Accuracy.* Complete accuracy is often assumed by persons interpreting survey results. However, even though the process of ensuring data quality appears easy to accomplish, practitioners invest considerable effort in identifying and correcting errors that originate with respondents or are introduced within the system (key punch errors, for example).

• *Timeliness.* The time required to administer surveys and record responses is significant in nearly all survey applications. Other factors can be significant as well. The time required for survey form layout and printing can be considerable, particularly when surveys are long, when forms are intended for optical scanning, when

Table 8.1. Comparison of Alternative Data Capture Strategies.

	Paper-and-Pencil	Telephone	Computer
Cost	Typically lowest overall cost.	Programming and telephone line charges can be high. Key entry costs are eliminated.	Programming costs can be extensive. Total cost also depends upon method of data aggregation (that is, on-line surveys versus disk collection).
Accuracy	Constrained by key entry accuracy; higher levels of accuracy can be obtained with optical scanning.	Error rates are determined by respondents. Medium offers limited opportunities to provide feedback to respondents without significantly increasing the time needed to complete the survey.	Allows for sophisticated editing and verification at the point of data entry.
Timeliness	Printing time can be significant as can key entry of responses; scannable documents provide efficient data entry.	Provides almost instant turn-around. However, lead time for developing a survey and contracting for telephone carrier access can be significant.	Upfront programming can be lengthy; data collection can occur quickly.
Administrative flexibility	Most flexible until surveys are printed.	Flexibility can be programmed, but changes are difficult.	Can be highly flexible and even adaptive to respondent needs.
Survey response rate	Depends upon administrative method (mail versus group settings).	May be as high or higher than paper methods.	Most significant issue can be access to computer terminals or PCs.

translations to foreign languages are required, or when there are multiple versions of the survey to be used with different organizational units. Importantly, there are significant trade-offs by choice of technology. For example, on the one hand, traditional paper-based survey technology requires relatively little effort for layout and printing yet its choice can have a significant impact on data entry time. Telephone response technology, on the other hand, can require significant up-front activity yet can completely bypass the need for subsequent data entry.

The relative advantages of a particular method will depend considerably on survey length and the number of survey respondents. Telephone response technology, for example, is generally limited to administering shorter surveys (eighty questions or less) yet can provide nearly instantaneous availability of data following administration, regardless of sample size. Optical scanning provides for very fast data capture, although verification is still needed in most cases.

• *Administrative flexibility.* Survey projects rarely unfold as planned. Last-minute changes in survey content are common, but because plans and expectations have often been communicated to and by management, the pressure to meet original commitments can be strong. Some survey administration methods offer greater flexibility than others. In general, the more technologically advanced methods of data capture offer less rather than more flexibility.

• *Survey response rate.* Maximizing survey response rate is a pressing issue in virtually all settings. Organizations have experimented with a variety of strategies ranging from the ubiquitous reminder card to contests staged to reward employees in organizational units with the highest return rate. These practices are an implicit acknowledgment of the concern for *nonresponse bias* and its unknown impact on the interpretation of survey results.

It is widely accepted that the most effective practice for ensuring high return rates is to administer paper-based surveys to groups in captive settings (for example, the so-called cafeteria-style survey administration). I am aware of only anecdotal evidence supporting this conclusion. Furthermore, organizational differences may account for much of the difference between application results, making method comparisons difficult. Additionally, factors other than administration method (including item ordering) can influence return rates (Roberson & Sundstrom, 1990) and complexity (Martin & McConnell, 1970).

Data Receipt

The period of time from the start to the end of survey administration can be referred to as the *data receipt window* or *data administration window*. The size of the window reflects the method of survey administration, the time required to distribute surveys, and the practical demands on the time and availability of survey respondents.

The size of the window has significant implications for survey return rate. Consider the typical scenario in which surveys are mailed to employees at their work addresses. A letter of introduction accompanies each survey, requesting that the employee return the survey by a specific date, which might be two to three weeks after the mailing date. A preaddressed postage-paid envelope is enclosed for the employee's convenience. One week to ten days later, each employee receives a reminder card, again emphasizing the importance of completing the survey and requesting that he or she complete and return the survey at his or her earliest possible convenience.

Experience with this administration strategy indicates that a significant number of surveys will not be returned until the published due date or several days after it. Furthermore, these late returns can be expected regardless of the size of the window. Consequently, it is common to publish one deadline but plan for an extension of seven to ten days to allow for procrastination, mail delays, and the like.

Low response rates are often cited by research sponsors as a reason to discount survey results, particularly in situations where the results paint an unfavorable picture of the current organizational state of affairs. This resistance is perhaps of greatest concern to the practitioner who views the survey as part of a larger organizational development strategy.

Tracking Survey Returns

At times, lagging survey returns can signal other more significant issues than a general resistance to the survey (for example, a very low return rate in a specific department or organizational unit might signify a problem in distribution or local management's resistance to an intervention effort). To proactively identify these areas of concern, practitioners often find it useful to establish tracking systems that allow them to monitor daily return rates. Essentially these systems provide early warning signals that alert the survey sponsor to the need to take corrective action while appropriate intervention is still feasible.

The need for intervention to ensure adequate return rates is inversely proportional to the number of surveys returned from units with the fewest employees and for which descriptive statistics must be reported. Some minimal number of respondents is typically preestablished as the baseline below which survey results will not be reported. Thus, lack of response could limit the number of units for which results can be reported.

Administrative Controls

A minimal administrative control is a log of the number of surveys returned by organizational unit and date. A log permits a direct count of data received; however, in certain situations, it may be insufficient. For example, when 360-degree feedback survey data are being collected, it is often important to track the return rate by respondent type (for example, how many peers or subordinates of a particular manager have responded). Clearly, this places an administrative burden on the survey administrator as more detailed response information must be tracked.

Tracking survey returns is also a significant issue when conducting large-scale surveys where data must be shipped from multiple locations to a single processing site. The problems associated with regular mail deliveries have been highlighted in the nationwide press. Given the value of survey information, the extra expense associated with the delivery services that offer shipment tracking is not significant. It is also worthwhile to implement systems that regularly confirm data receipt to the shipping party.

Reporting Early Returns

In some settings, practitioners develop formal feedback mechanisms to encourage survey return. For example, some organizations post daily survey return statistics in public areas. Where return rates fall below expectations, interventions can be useful. Also, when organizational conditions such as dramatically increased work load are suspected as the cause of a low return rate, it is not uncommon to announce the extension of the due date. Other, more extreme measures might include a repeat mailing of surveys where evidence suggests lost mail or other administrative problems.

Of course, interventions such as these are not unobtrusive, and may even inadvertently affect survey results. The early publication of survey return statistics can be interpreted by some employees as an indication that anonymity has been compromised. It is particularly inappropriate to provide early feedback of actual survey results. One can imagine the reaction of employees whose manager inappropriately comments on the lack of favorable results while survey administration is still in progress! Another negative effect of early feedback is that preliminary values may differ from final results, again affecting the credibility of the project.

The concern for maximizing return rate generally reflects two specific issues. The first issue is the external validity and generalizability of survey results. At best, nonresponse presents particularly unattractive problems for the weighting of survey results and, in the extreme, can lead to uninterpretable outcomes altogether. The second issue, as noted earlier, is the impact of low response rates on the credibility of the survey process.

Differences in Early Versus Late Returns

Despite best intentions, it is often necessary to extend a data receipt deadline, owing to low response rates, mailing delays, and so forth. In practice, all data, whether received earlier or later, are aggregated into one common data set for purposes of analysis. However, although it appears sensible and appropriate to do this— in that all the surveys represent the same population—the practitioner should be aware that extending a data receipt window may influence response favorability in an unknown direction, not merely raise the return rate.

Multiple-Wave Designs

Multiple-wave administration periods may be used in large survey projects, typically as a result of different agendas and business needs within individual units. In this paradigm, different organizational units are surveyed at different times, although perhaps in close succession. This multiple-wave administration pattern poses a challenge for data analysis and interpretation. An obvious concern is the appropriateness of comparing units surveyed at different times and perhaps under different conditions, since intervening events may significantly influence survey outcomes. This can become a particular problem when data are to be aggregated differently depending on date of survey. Administratively, the most direct method of proactively addressing these problems is to use a coding structure that explicitly identifies the survey window as part of the organizational coding.

Data Entry and Editing (Fixed-Response)

Opinion surveys in organizations include questions of essentially two types, distinguished by whether responses are selected from a fixed set of alternatives (requiring a numeric rating, for example) or are unrestricted (written responses to an open-ended question, for example). Both types must be captured in a form that permits data reduction, analysis, and reporting.

While telephone and computerized survey administration strategies offer direct output of results, other forms of data collection require a separate data entry stage. The available options include key entry, optical mark scanning, and optical character recognition (OCR).

Key Entry

Key entry is perhaps the most traditional and familiar form of data entry. It is cost effective in most situations, and support for it is, for practical purposes, universally available. Moreover, for some time, PC-based software packages have been available that mimic the operation of dedicated software and hardware data entry platforms.

Typically, double key entry methods are employed, where two different key entry operators independently enter the same survey data. In this paradigm, the second operator is responsible for verifying discrepancies between the second and first entries. Accuracy of double key entry rates are typically guaranteed by service providers to be in excess of 99 percent and in practice often exceed this rate.

Importantly, a survey's print format significantly affects data entry costs and quality (error rate). For example, experienced survey professionals often print record position information directly on the survey form as a work aid for the key entry operators. In contrast, forms printed so as to compact as many items on one page as possible increase the likelihood of key entry error as well as key entry cost. In general, both accuracy and cost are negatively affected by form designs that require any form of mental calculation simultaneously with key entry.

Optical Mark Scanning

This methodology has been available for more than two decades and is commonly—although not uniquely—associated with surveys of large scope. The advantages often attributed to this method include cost savings, processing time savings, and accuracy. The cost savings come from the minimal labor costs associated with the strategy. The time savings come from modern optical scanning equipment, which scans thousands of forms per hour, thereby also providing rapid availability of survey results.

Importantly, the accuracy of form scanning is suggested by data-processing vendors as far exceeding that of key entry strategies. However, it should be noted that individual practitioners have experienced widely varying degrees of success in implementing technology using scanners; accuracy also depends considerably on the care with which forms are completed, on whether the scanning can read ink as well as pencil marks, and on the software used in conjunction with specific hardware.

One disadvantage associated with the optical scanning method is the testlike appearance of the survey form, presumably a feature negatively perceived by survey respondents. Yet another perceived disadvantage is the inconvenience associated with the requirement of using No. 2 pencils—a criticism quite common in environments where administrative paperwork is unusual. Finally, the belief that seemingly greater care must be taken to preserve scannable documents from physical damage is cited as an obstacle in those work environments where surveys are completed on company time.

Optical mark scanning presents several significant challenges for the data entry process. First, survey respondents often choose to ignore the instructions for completing the forms. The classic example is the respondent who chooses to use a pen rather than a No. 2 pencil, resulting in marks that may not be scanned consistently. Second, some respondents indicate that they find optical mark forms more difficult and time consuming to complete than other kinds. As the lost-labor cost associated with the time respondents spend completing surveys during work hours is one of the more significant costs of the process, perceptions of form difficulty can be a significant issue.

Optical Character Recognition

OCR technology has only recently been regarded as a method of data entry. Currently, both software and hardware platforms exist for capturing hand-printed responses directly from survey documents. With this technology, digitized images of the survey responses are captured that can then be directly interpreted by software, and where ambiguous, edited by equipment operators. This technology circumvents the disadvantages of the optical mark form; the survey form can have a more conventional appearance and be generally less sensitive to relatively minor variances in printing specifications. Moreover, for this method, PC software is available that can be used with inexpensive facsimile machines.

Identifying Respondent Errors

Respondent errors are inescapable. They can be the result of poor form design, inadequate attention to survey administration procedures, or carelessness and/or lack of motivation on the part of respondents. Most often, however, they result from faulty assumptions on the part of both the survey professional and the survey respondent. On the one hand, the survey professional assumes that respondents will follow clear instructions. On the other hand, the respondent assumes that those responsible for the survey process will closely examine each survey form returned and adjust to any modifications or special conditions encountered.

For example, consider the survey respondent who is unsure

how to respond to an item and therefore places a mark midway between two alternatives. The respondent is oblivious to the dilemma facing the key entry operator, who must have some rule or protocol for determining what should be entered. The more typical forms of respondent error are the following:

• *Multiple marked items.* The respondent marks one survey item, changes his or her mind, and marks another without erasing the first. Alternatively, the respondent may simply be unable to decide among multiple alternatives and may mark several. Incomplete erasures are a variant of this respondent error.

• *Cross marked items.* The respondent circles a group of response alternatives down the length of the page rather than circling each response alternative individually. Some practitioners regard such data as invalid; however, this assumption may not be warranted, presuming they have the ability to infer the motivation of the respondent.

• *Changes to survey items.* The respondent edits the item on the survey to reflect the content he or she wishes to address and then answers the edited item. Such changes may not be detected if a scannable form is used and the response column is marked according to instructions. Of course, problems of this sort should be minimized with adequate pretesting of the survey.

• *Middle marks.* The respondent decides that none of the response options fits his or her liking and then creates a response option of his or her own choosing by, for example, deliberately circling two response options.

• *Mismarked responses.* The respondent erroneously marks a response alternative other than that intended. Clearly, this type of error can generally neither be recognized nor corrected without some form of intervention and feedback from the survey respondent. Because problems such as these are undetectable, particular care should be taken during item writing to minimize their likelihood of occurrence.

• *Misaligned responses.* The respondent marks the intended response but for the wrong item. For example, the respondent might respond to the seventy-fifth question in the space provided for the answer to the seventy-sixth question. After this initial error, the subsequent responses will all be off by one. This is particularly common with survey forms printed in compact form or in small print. This error pattern is particularly problematic in that any correction requires a strong inference as to the source and intention of the survey respondent. It may be noted that this error is more likely when respondents use separate answer sheets and survey booklets.

Problems such as these can and should be anticipated and appropriate instructions provided to minimize their occurrence. Of course, each problematic case requires a judgment on the part of the key operator. Minimally, the survey professional should anticipate these common problems and provide decision rules about rectifying them for the key entry operators. For example, key entry operators should receive explicit instructions as to what constitutes an "invalid" response and what key symbol is to be used to represent that response. Technologies for capturing data that can detect errors as they occur and provide immediate feedback to the respondent can automatically control these sources of respondent error, thereby reducing the need for expensive data editing.

Data Cleaning

Data cleaning refers to the systematic analysis of responses to identify entry, coding, or respondent errors. The practitioner examines response distributions to determine whether patterns fall within expected boundaries. For example, the survey researcher might cross-tabulate gender and organizational level demographic variables. It would be uncommon to find a higher proportion of female than male executives in this cross-tabulation; therefore, such a result might signal the presence of errors.

Clearly, data cleaning can be accomplished only with some understanding of the organization surveyed. However, even decisions regarding what appear to be obvious errors can be problematic. Consider, for example, possible answers to two demographic questions: the first requests identification of the respondent's organizational group (Division A or Division B, for example), the second identification of the respondent's geographical region (East, Midwest, or Pacific, for example). If a combination of responses arises that is organizationally impossible (Division A–Midwest, for example, when Division A has no presence in the Midwest), a decision must be made whether it is best to recode one of the two responses (which would involve making an assumption about which demographic question was more likely to be answered correctly and which incorrectly) or to recode both responses as missing. However, it also should be recognized that such apparently wrong combinations may not be mismarked responses. A respondent from Division A may be on temporary assignment in the Midwest.

Both data editing and data cleaning require general rules for exception handling. These rules should be codified and followed rigorously. Experience plays a significant role here. There is much to be gained from maintaining records of decisions made that fall outside the scope of the exception-handling rules. In time, a knowledge base of effective data management practices can be compiled and used to both prevent and resolve future challenges to data integrity. At a minimum, it is necessary to maintain records of changes made to data records, particularly where recoding of survey responses is required. (Smith, Budzeika, Edwards, Johnson, & Bearse, 1986, offer a more detailed discussion of the issues regarding data integrity.)

Reducing Errors Through Effective Survey Design

The preceding discussion clearly points to the need for effective survey design. Here are some general design principles for paper-based surveys.

- *Format survey items so as to minimize cross-page scanning (eye movement).* This can often be best accomplished by printing the survey items in multiple columns per page.
- *Clearly mark response alternatives on the page.* Column spacing of response alternatives should be sufficient so that respondents can easily distinguish the areas to be marked. Where possible, areas to be marked (for example, shaded or checkmarked) should be identified with mnemonic representations of the appropriate alternatives (*SD* for "strongly disagree," for example). Column shading can be useful to distinguish response alternatives from one another.
- *If more than one response scale is used, clearly mark any shifts or changes.* Some practitioners use statements such as "Note Change in Response Scale," printed in bold letters or otherwise formatted to draw respondents' attention.

- *Present response scale definitions and other instructions so respondents can read them without rotating the page.*
- *Provide instructions that show sample markings.*

Additional principles apply for telephone and computer surveys.

- *Repeat response alternatives for each survey item.*
- *Allow electronic scrolling through survey responses.* Scrolling gives respondents the opportunity to review and modify their responses, much as they are able to on a paper-based survey.
- *Use technology that allows continual feedback on the response alternatives selected.* Often this feedback indicates the response alternative chosen by the respondent and requests verification of that choice. This can be overdone, however; continual feedback can become irritating to respondents, and it also increases administration time, which can in turn negatively affect response rate.

Pretesting

Following the survey design recommendations listed above does not reduce the need for adequate pretesting of any survey. Most, if not all, survey problems can be anticipated through adequate pretesting and pretest respondent debriefing. It is particularly critical to evaluate the assumptions inherent in the data administration strategy. Issues to consider include survey respondents' expectations in terms of time, setting, and so forth. Pretesting conditions should be reasonably similar to those of actual survey administration; small pilot studies therefore serve as the most effective pretesting device.

Data Analysis and Reporting

Because the consumer of survey research is typically faced with overwhelming amounts of data, parsimony is the guiding virtue in reporting results. At the extreme, survey results may be reported in terms of a single summary statistic (for example, average score across items). However, more typically, results are reported by item and by some smaller number of dimensions, indices, or factors.

The most typical survey summary statistic is category percentage by response option. In this method of reporting, survey results are summarized as the percentage of individuals who responded "strongly agree," "agree," and so forth. Most common is to report survey results recoded into categories of favorable, neutral, and unfavorable response. Thus, the total percentage of respondents indicating either "very satisfied" or "satisfied" to a survey item would be considered the percentage of favorable response. (Of course, if not all items are easily recoded, it may indicate the need for item revision.)

Less frequently, means are reported. This method is considerably more common when reporting 360-degree and upward feedback data than when displaying organizational opinion survey data. In large part, the difference in strategy reflects a concern for preserving anonymity; reporting percentages by response alternative or reporting measures of dispersion can raise questions about sources of discrepant ratings.

Standard deviations may also be reported. However, while increasing numbers of employees are being exposed to statistical concepts through quality training, many do not possess the knowledge necessary for interpreting statistical measures of dispersion. Thus, when reporting measures of dispersion is deemed necessary, some practitioners elect to report the interquartile range.

Topic Scores

It is typical to aggregate data across items to calculate topic scores. For example, data for all items addressing issues of "senior management leadership" might be summarized by a dimension score (mean, percentage of favorable responses, and so forth), calculated by aggregating individual responses for each item within a topic. The topics themselves are often rationally derived, although confirmatory factor analysis strategies can be used to affirm assignment of items to topics. Topics may also be determined through use of exploratory factor analysis. Regardless of the strategy for determining which items belong to which topic, items are typically unitweighted (simply added together) in the calculation of topic scores.

Minimum Reporting Requirements

The concern for anonymity in reporting survey results is ubiquitous. Survey respondents are typically told that results will only be reported for groups of some minimum size. This minimum varies considerably in practice, depending on the nature of survey content, the purpose of the survey (in particular, whether it is an upward or a 360-degree feedback survey as opposed to an employee opinion survey), and the degree of people's trust in management and the survey process. A typical minimum group size for reporting employee opinion survey results is seven; the minimum for reporting 360-degree or upward feedback survey results is often as low as three.

The minimum reporting size is often different for fixed (that is, numeric) response data and written responses to open-ended questions, reflecting the heightened degree of concern for anonymity in reporting written comments even though they are presented typed (not handwritten) in the survey report. For comments, the minimum reporting size for employee opinion survey results is typically in the range of twenty to fifty respondents.

The characteristically smaller minimum reporting size for upward or 360-degree feedback results in part reflects practical considerations; many managers would not receive upward feedback if the minimum reporting size were set at five to seven respondents. One strategy used by some practitioners is to report only measures of central tendency when reporting size is less than five; measures of dispersion, including responses by category, are reported only when the reporting size is five or greater.

The minimum reporting size is often communicated in advance to employees as part of the assurance of anonymity. When return rates are not as high as expected, managers often request exceptions to the rule. Rather than compromise the integrity of the process by granting such exceptions, many practitioners aggregate employee opinion data by combining data from different groups when they are part of a larger organizational unit. Some practitioners choose to report the results for the larger group only and provide a combined report for the smaller group. Others report only combined results for both groups.

Nonresponse and Missing Data

Conventionally, missing data are ignored for the purposes of data analysis and reporting. Category percentages, for example, are calculated using the number of valid responses as a baseline. This method is most likely a matter of convenience, as imputation methods for compensating for nonresponse are available in the literature (see, for example, Platek, Singh, & Tremblay, 1978). Lower and upper confidence limits for sample proportions are easily calculated by assuming that all nonrespondents agree (or disagree) with the specific question (for related discussion, see Cochran, 1963, and Viswesvaran, Barrick, & Ones, 1993).

The decision to adjust (or not adjust) for nonresponse error is a critical one to the extent that nonrespondents are systematically different from respondents, thereby affecting the generalizability of survey findings. When the characteristics of nonrespondents are known, it is at least possible to identify the extent to which respondents and nonrespondents differ. Their similarity supports the choice of nonadjustment. However, in most instances, it is not possible to identify nonrespondents other than by group membership, making such analyses impossible. Similarly, methods for adjustment requiring substitution based on factors other than unit membership are not viable.

A respondent's decision not to answer can be differentiated from his or her determination that an item is not personally relevant when a "not applicable" response option is available. Nonetheless, "not applicable" responses are characteristically treated in the same way as missing data. However, making a distinction is important in cases where imputation procedures are used to estimate missing values.

Weighting Procedures

When surveying large employee populations, it is common to sample employees by organizational unit. To meet desired levels of sampling precision, it is common to sample units disproportionately, in relation to size. As a result of this over- and undersampling, weighting is often considered desirable.

Consider a simple organization with a total of 1,000 employees. Employees are assigned to one of two divisions, or subgroups (A and B). Division A (850 employees) is considerably larger than Division B (150 employees). To report results for each division with a minimum precision of plus or minus 5 percent (95 percent confidence level), as is desirable (see Chapter Six), the required sample sizes are 265 and 108 respectively. For simplicity, a 100 percent return is assumed. Clearly, however, the size of the respective samples is disproportionate relative to the divisions' relative sizes within the organization. Thus, while Division B is 15 percent of the organizational total, it represents 29 percent of the sample. Consequently, if Division B results are significantly more or less favorable than Division A results, the results tabulated for the organization as a whole will be disproportionately weighted to reflect Division B results.

In these cases, weights are calculated to reflect the differential probability that cases have been selected within subgroups. The weight to be given to all cases within a particular subgroup is computed as follows:

$$W = W1/W2$$

Where

$W1$ = (size of subgroup divided by population size)
$W2$ = (number in subgroup sampled divided by number in population sampled)

In the context of the present example, the weight for Division A is 1.196—that is, $(850/1,000)/(265/373)$—and the weight for Division B is 0.518—that is, $(150/1,000)/(108/373)$. The reader may wish to verify that when these weights are multiplied by the actual sample sizes (265 and 108, respectively), the weighted samples will be in exact proportion to the employee percentages represented by the divisions.

While the arithmetic to calculate weights is uncomplicated, significant issues in the application of weighting procedures should not be ignored. Of particular significance is the issue of adjustment for nonresponse (Bailar, Bailey, & Corby, 1978).

Adjustment for Rounding Error

During survey feedback meetings, it is common for individuals to question the fact that when all category percentages (as reported) are added together, the total is not necessarily 100 percent. This is, of course, due to rounding error. Some practitioners address this concern by "adjusting" percentages to force them to equal 100 percent, thereby obviating the concern. Two different strategies are commonly used to make this adjustment. The first strategy is to modify the middle, or "neutral," category. In the second strategy, the difference between each category percentage and its rounded value (to the next whole number) is calculated. The category with the largest difference is then adjusted. While there are many who believe strongly that such adjustments are valuable, I do not concur; it is sufficient to include a note saying that responses may not total 100 percent due to rounding error.

Use and Misuse of Statistical Significance Testing

Differences among organizational units are often of interest to management. As the question whether differences are "meaningful" often arises, some practitioners use common tests of statistical significance for guidance. These comparisons are appropriate when comparing samples. They are not appropriate when comparing data representing populations. Furthermore, tests of statistical significance are not particularly meaningful when samples are large; the practitioner will find it far more useful to evaluate impact in terms of utility (see, for example, Cascio, 1987).

Survey Report Design

Report content should reflect the needs of those using the survey information. Although needs may vary widely, the following principles apply in general:

- *Design the report for the intended audience.* Far too often, reports are formatted at the level of detail desired by the psychometrician.
- *Keep detail to a minimum.* Survey reports should make results clear. If more detail is required, produce additional reports as needed. Alternatively, detailed statistics can be printed in appendices if need be.
- *Reports or report sections should address one information requirement at a time.* For example, the identification of the most and the least favorable items deserves two reports, not one.

- *Proofreading is essential.* Minor yet obvious mistakes in reporting can be used as an excuse by management to disregard results and can directly affect credibility.

- *Provide space for note-taking.* Survey reports are generated for analysis and review. It makes sense to provide space for notes and comments.

- *Measures of dispersion should be clearly interpretable.* Consider the sophistication of the audience in determining the statistics to be represented.

- *Time is everything.* Regardless of what has been planned, those completing the survey want quick feedback. Responsiveness may be more important than visual appeal.

- *Support text with graphics.* Graphical representations of data convey results more easily than numbers alone. Conversely, however, graphical displays cannot be sufficient in themselves.

- *Keep copies of everything.* Whether data are electronically or otherwise stored, it is best to assume that whatever has been reported will be needed again.

Capturing, Transcribing, and Reporting Verbatim Comments

Managing narrative data or comments deserves separate comment because of issues unique to or particularly characteristic of this survey method.

Confidentiality

Survey respondents are characteristically assured anonymity. Typical instructions indicate that responses to open-ended questions will be typed and reported only for larger groups. Even with these safeguards, strict reporting of verbatim responses challenges the promise of anonymity. Therefore, it is common practice to "sanitize" written comments by removing references to proper names, administrative titles, and so on. The reader will recognize that this can at best be only partially successful; the author of a comment can sometimes be known from the context and the detail provided (see Chapter Fifteen for a general discussion of the ethical issues involved in maintaining anonymity).

Communication with the client regarding expectations for reporting comments is essential, and the following issues should be discussed in advance of data capture:

- *Implied promises of anonymity to respondents.*
- *Maintenance of original survey records and schedule for destruction.*
- *Editing for offensive and vulgar comments.* The client should be informed that such comments are likely to be received. Vulgarity is often, although not universally, edited from written comments.
- *Editing for proper names and administrative titles.* Typically, all references to proper names and references to individuals by position title are removed.
- *References to illicit, illegal, or immoral activity.* On occasion, respondents make comments that can be interpreted as *accusations* of wrongful action. It is essential that protocols for reporting such comments and maintaining anonymity be established and agreed on prior to data capture.

From a practical standpoint, the task of sanitizing written comments is often left to those responsible for data entry. However, some form of administrative control or review is essential to ensure that efforts to sanitize comments are satisfactory.

Thematic Analysis

While illuminating, the volume of written comments can be overwhelming. The challenge of gaining understanding from written comments is even greater when the open-ended question is general (for example, "Is there anything else you would like to communicate to management?") rather than specific (for example, "What specific computer resources would help you do your job better?"). Therefore, it is common to organize written comments separately, by theme and/or affect. Three distinct strategies are employed for organizing comments.

- *Self-coding.* The respondent receives a list of categories or areas for comment. Often, the categories are derived from thematic analyses of survey data collected on previous occasions.
- *Content coding by inductively defined categories.* Content coding is accomplished independently by judges who classify comments

according to the categories each represents. The categories are determined inductively from the comment pool to be coded and classified. This strategy requires that a taxonomy, or reporting structure, be developed prior to content coding.

- *Content coding by preestablished categories.* Often, open-ended questions are asked in an effort to clarify issues raised by previous surveys or to address specific topics, factors, or dimensions of interest to management. In these instances, it is common to classify comments by existing categories.

My experience is that the latter two strategies are most typical. More recently, some practitioners have found various computer programs useful in both deriving and classifying comments. Still, the process clearly is labor intensive; the labor hours required to categorize comments can equal or even surpass the time needed to type and enter those same comments.

Number of Categories

Obviously, value is gained only when the content coding sufficiently reduces the complexity of interpreting and understanding the comments. I find that a useful rule of thumb is to have fifteen to twenty categories, at a maximum.

Reporting Whole Comments Versus Parts of Comments

Consider this comment: "I really wish management would do something about pay. It's been three years since I last received a raise, and I've had four different supervisors in that time. If management expects me to continue working excessive overtime including Saturdays and Sundays, I should be compensated accordingly." This comment could be classified into multiple categories of interest (pay, performance management, working hours and conditions, and so on). On the one hand, reporting the entire comment may be essential to understanding the issue as expressed by the respondent. On the other hand, reporting the full comment separately under each category can increase the very complexity content coding was intended to reduce!

Frequency Distributions of Content Categories

In addition to reporting comments verbatim, it is often helpful to report a frequency distribution of comments by content category. Figure 8.2 exemplifies one such method of reporting results. This chart, in Pareto form, ranks the comment categories from most to least frequent. The percentages are calculated using the total number of comments as a baseline. However, it is also useful to report the total number of respondents providing comments. In fact, some practitioners prefer to use the number of respondents as the baseline for reporting percentages.

A cautionary note is appropriate here. Descriptive statistics can be deceptive, hiding the richness often evident in written comments. As results are disseminated within the organization, there is increasing risk that the original meaning and intent of the comments will be lost or misunderstood.

It is also important for data users to be aware that written comments are more often negative than positive. While the relative imbalance depends considerably on the choice of and the balance of the questions asked, the inexperienced reader of the comments may inaccurately generalize from the balance of comments that the state of the organization is much worse than is actually the case.

Reducing Complexity by Sampling

In large-scale surveys, it may be appropriate to *sample comments* for reporting. Representative reporting by category, particularly when complemented by frequency distributions for the entire set of comments, can be useful for reducing information overload.

A second sampling strategy utilized in some instances is to *sample cases,* recording and reporting all comments for selected cases. The reader may recognize that this method, while providing cost savings through reducing data entry costs, may be viewed by some as denying individuals the opportunity to express their opinions. Furthermore, sampling cases does not lend itself to full content analysis and subsequent reporting by comment frequency.

Capturing Comments in Multiple Languages

Survey research often crosses international as well as cultural and linguistic boundaries. Whereas precautions can be taken to ensure

**Figure 8.2. Example of Written Comment
Frequency Distribution (Pareto Chart).**

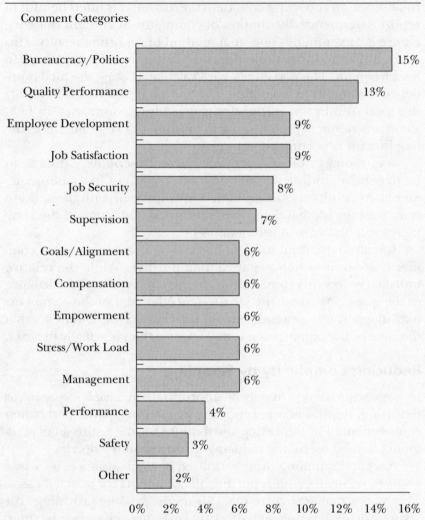

Comment Categories

Bureaucracy/Politics	15%
Quality Performance	13%
Employee Development	9%
Job Satisfaction	9%
Job Security	8%
Supervision	7%
Goals/Alignment	6%
Compensation	6%
Empowerment	6%
Stress/Work Load	6%
Management	6%
Performance	4%
Safety	3%
Other	2%

0%   2%   4%   6%   8%   10%   12%   14%   16%

Note: This example represents 591 comments, the total from 327 respondents.

the adequacy of a survey translation (for example, by independent retranslation), the aggregation of transcribed comments written in multiple languages presents unique problems, particularly in communities where multiple languages are spoken. It is my experience, for example, that anonymity can be compromised unless there is translation to a common language. It should also be recognized that translating comments has implications for both cost and accuracy.

Psychometric Considerations

As in other judgmental tasks, the reliability of content coding should be evaluated within the context of each specific application. One approach to assessing reliability is calculating and evaluating multirater agreement. However, the use of multiple raters (judges) to evaluate and categorize comments can add significant expense to the survey project. Therefore, it is common to evaluate reliability by drawing samples of comments categorized by multiple judges. The Kappa statistic as extended by Siegel and Castellan (1988) is an appropriate measure for determining agreement among multiple judges.

Data Storage

Smith, Budzeika, Edwards, Johnson, and Bearse (1986) emphasize the importance of maintaining accurate records of data coding as well as physically maintaining the data themselves. Although many individuals believe that electronically stored records are indestructible, there is a definite shelf life for media stored even under the best of conditions. More recent developments (for example, optical storage) show promise for greatly improved media life.

Provision should also be made for maintaining control of the original survey documents. Timetables should be established with management for the confidential destruction of the documents.

Conclusion

In managing data, the survey practitioner faces numerous decisions that affect the overall success of the survey project. In addition to attention to administrative detail, these decisions require significant professional judgment in situations where alternatives may appear equally attractive.

The practitioner should be aware that statistical and methodological rigor is not a substitute for common sense in data management. This was perhaps best put to me in the comments of a reviewer of a draft of this chapter, who stressed the need to work with the client to solicit input for better understanding of results and to emphasize simplicity in communicating those results in a manner that can be understood by the intended audience. I could not agree more and would only add that if "God is in the details," surely data management is a religious vocation.

References

Bailar, B. A., Bailey, L., & Corby, C. (1978). A comparison of some adjustment and weighting procedures for survey data. In N. K. Namboordiri (Ed.), *Survey sampling and measurement* (pp. 175–198). San Diego, CA: Academic Press.

Cascio, W. F. (1987). *Costing human resources: The financial impact of behavior in organizations.* Boston: PWS-Kent.

Cochran, W. G. (1963). *Sampling techniques.* New York: Wiley.

Martin, J. D., & McConnell, J. P. (1970). Mail questionnaire response induction: The effect of four variables on the response of a random sample to a difficult questionnaire. *Social Science Quarterly, 51,* 409–414.

Platek, R., Singh, M. P., & Tremblay, V. (1978). Adjustment for nonresponse in surveys. In N. K. Namboordiri (Ed.), *Survey sampling and measurement* (pp. 157–174). San Diego, CA: Academic Press.

Roberson, M. T., & Sundstrom, E. (1990). Questionnaire design, return rates, and response favorableness in an employee attitude questionnaire. *Journal of Applied Psychology, 75,* 354–357.

Siegel, S., & Castellan, N. J., Jr. (1988). *Nonparametric statistics for the behavioral sciences* (2nd ed.). New York: McGraw-Hill.

Smith, P. C., Budzeika, K. A., Edwards, N. A., Johnson, S. M., & Bearse, L. N. (1986). Guidelines for clean data: Detection of common mistakes. *Journal of Applied Psychology, 71,* 457–460.

Viswesvaran, C., Barrick, M. R., & Ones, D. S. (1993). How definitive are conclusions based on survey data: Estimating robustness to nonresponse. *Personnel Psychology, 46,* 551–567.

CHAPTER 9

Applying Alternative Survey Methods

Karl Kuhnert
Dan P. McCauley

Management revolutions come in all shapes and sizes, but all share a common history. First new technology emerges, followed by specific applications to fit that technology, and always much later comes an appreciation of the missed opportunities, the costs, and the benefits of the changes that resulted from the new technology. No different is today's "knowledge revolution" (Argyris, 1991; Senge, 1990), which is predicated on organizational commitment to rapid learning and to responsiveness to the requirements of customers in a global environment. The knowledge revolution is fueled by technology and is transforming business as we know it (Attewell, 1992; Carter, 1984; Foster & Flynn, 1984; Hiltz & Johnson, 1986).

Led by the personal computer (PC) and powerful telecommunications technology, this revolution has left virtually no organization unaffected by applications of electronic mail (e-mail), facsimile transmission (fax), teleconferences, and voice mail. For most of us, these technological applications have already become a part of everyday business life.

Management consultants who facilitate change for businesses and who must also be responsive to their clients' needs, have been quick to embrace new technology and apply it to organizational surveys. As a result, the organizational survey, which in the past was primarily a paper-and-pencil exercise, is now and perhaps forever changed by advancing technology. The computer, modem, telephone, and fax machine are now setting the standards for business communication.

This chapter examines survey methods in light of advancing technology. We make no claim to be exhaustive in our review of new survey methods, and we limit our review to those alternative survey methods for which we have direct experience. We do not review specific vendor products (for such a review, see Booth-Kewley, Rosenfeld, & Edwards, 1993). We do provide in the Appendix to this chapter, however, a partial list of vendors.

We have learned that not all survey methods are created equal and that it is wrong to separate the choice of survey method from the environment in which the method is applied (Kimberly & Evanisko, 1981). Our primary purpose is to distinguish among survey methods by evaluating the contexts in which employee opinion data are gathered. We feel strongly that the successful choice of survey method depends as much on factors such as organizational needs, survey ease of use, and the organizational climate for conducting surveys as on the merits of the technology itself. A second purpose is to review the costs and benefits of each survey method.

The chapter is organized into three sections. The first section reviews the four alternative survey methods of telephone, fax, personal computer, and e-mail. The next section reviews the critical issues in choosing among survey methods. We identify five issues: confidentiality, flexibility, time and logistical constraints, ease of use, and facilities and cost. The third section summarizes and previews alternative administrative methods the future may hold for conducting organizational surveys.

Four Alternative Survey Methods

For over four decades, organizational survey technology consisted of employees responding to questions presented in a paper-and-pencil format (Dunham & Smith, 1979; Golembiewski & Hilles, 1979; Kendall, 1986; Kuhnert, 1993; Seashore, 1987). Although the paper-and-pencil survey is still the most pervasive administration method, recent revolutions in computers and telecommunications have led to the emergence of alternative methods for administering the traditional organizational opinion survey. In this section,

we highlight four alternative survey methods: automated telephone, fax, personal computer, and electronic mail.

Automated Telephone Surveys

Telephone technology has been a mainstay of business communications for decades and represents one of the earliest alternatives
to traditional paper-and-pencil surveys. The initial applications of
telephone technology for conducting organizational opinion surveys involved the use of interviewers who contacted employees by
phone, simply asked a series of questions, and following presentation of a list of possible responses, recorded employee responses
for subsequent key entry.

Later versions of telephone surveys combine PC survey technology with personal interviewers. After contacting employees by
phone, interviewers, sitting in front of PC monitors, ask a series of
survey questions as presented on the monitor screen and immediately record employee responses via keyboard. In both applications,
the respondent can ask the interviewer for clarification and to
repeat questions and possible responses. In addition, the questions
presented to each employee can be tailored by the interviewer as
key information such as job level and position are obtained.

More recently, even telephone surveys have become computerized. In an automated telephone survey, question presentation
can now be entirely controlled by computer. More often now,
employees are given a telephone number to call, and a series of
prerecorded questions is presented. Employees respond to questions by pressing a number on the Touch-Tone number pad. As
with PC surveys, employees can back up and review previous questions and their responses and are instructed when a response is
"out of range." In addition, data are captured automatically.

Fax Surveys

In today's business environment, the fax machine has become as
common as the copier machine. Sending documents across the
state, the country, or the world has become as convenient as making a telephone call. With the aid of the fax machine, information
in document form can be transmitted and received in a matter of

minutes. Recently, organizational survey specialists have turned to this technology as a source for gathering employee opinion data ("Developers Send Clear OCR Messages on Fax Capacities," 1992; "Extending the Fax," 1992).

Fax surveys can be easily developed using software packages (see Appendix) that create a survey as a fax form. This form, similar to the traditional paper-and-pencil survey, presents questions or statements with associated response scales composed of boxes to check, circles to fill in, or numbers or text to circle. Outgoing fax surveys can be sent either by fax or mail or simply distributed by hand. Respondents fax completed surveys back to a central telephone number connected to a personal computer equipped with a fax board. As the survey comes in, the responses are automatically read and entered into a data set for subsequent analysis. In addition to converting marks and circles, some software packages are able to recognize handwriting and thus allow for the collection of an employee's comments. If segments of the survey population do not have access to a fax machine, their completed surveys can be mailed back to the central administration site to be either key entered or faxed to the central number by the survey administrator via any available fax machine.

PC Surveys

Once available only to large companies with sizable budgets and staffs of highly specialized technicians, computing technology is now accessible on the desktops of employees in companies of all sizes, even one-person offices (Booth-Kewley, Rosenfeld, & Edwards, 1993; Huttig, 1993; Koch, Dodd, & Fitzpatrick, 1990; Rosenfeld, Dotherty, Vicino, Kantor, & Greaves, 1989). As personal computer technology has become more and more powerful, it has also become increasingly inexpensive. Both these factors have led to the increased interest of survey professionals in adopting this technology for gathering opinion data.

Surveys administered via PCs can use either mainframe, diskette, or network systems. However, because of the rapid changeover occurring from mainframes to local area networks (LANs), we limit our discussion here to diskette and network systems. Numerous software products exist for PC surveys (see the Appendix). These products design a series of screens that present the survey questions to employees. The presentation of nonquestion information, such as statements from the survey sponsor, instructions, and descriptions of planned follow-up activities, is also possible. A respondent is usually presented with the questions one at a time and answers by pressing a numeric or letter key or by using a mouse to point and click on the icon that corresponds to the response that best represents his or her opinion. Error messages can be programmed to appear if an employee response is "out of range." The survey can also be programmed so that employees can review and change previous responses by pressing the appropriate keys.

PC surveys can be designed so that as the survey proceeds, the questions presented are dependent on previous responses (this technique is called *item branching*). For example, the employee who indicates that his job category is "service provider" can receive an additional set of questions asking about customer satisfaction issues. The employee who indicates that she has attended a training session on quality can be asked follow-up questions about training effectiveness. Conversely, if she indicates that she did not attend the quality training, the program skips the training follow-up questions.

As each employee completes the survey, the data are automatically stored. In the case of surveys on diskette, data are captured on individual floppy disks and then merged into a composite data set for analysis. Employee data collected through network-based surveys can be accumulated directly into a composite data set resident on the network. Some PC survey software has built-in capability to conduct basic data analysis. Other packages simply save the data in a form that can be imported into stand-alone statistical software.

E-Mail Surveys

Once used primarily in government and academic institutions, electronic mail systems are the latest addition to business communications. The merging of network mail systems and telecommunications has opened another avenue for information flow between remote locations. Once again, individual organizations are exploring how this burgeoning technology can be adopted for the purpose of conducting organizational opinion surveys.

Initial e-mail survey systems were fairly inflexible. Questionnaire forms were constructed and sent to the e-mail addresses of the employee population of interest. Recipients tabbed through the form and entered their responses. Item-branching features were not available within a given questionnaire form. Surveys were returned via the reply function. Like traditional paper-and-pencil data, information collected was key entered into a separate data set. Current e-mail survey systems are still evolving and greater flexibility and features such as automatic data entry, confidentiality safeguards, and item-branching capabilities are beginning to be built into the newer systems.

Choosing an Appropriate Survey Method

Choosing among the various survey methods is like trying on hats; while there are many colors and shapes to choose from only a few will really fit well and look good on your head. Choosing the best survey method for your organization requires a good fit among a number of important elements including confidentiality, flexibility, time and logistical constraints, ease of use, and facilities and cost. In the following sections, the four alternative survey methods are reviewed in relation to each of these elements (see also Table 9.1).

Confidentiality

The validity of the data gathered from employees is directly tied to their perception of trust toward the organization. Although there are many factors that lead to trust (McCauley & Kuhnert, 1992), perhaps the most important for conducting surveys is maintaining the confidentiality of employee responses.

Without truthful responses from employees, the data collected from surveys have little to no value for organizational decision makers. Employees, however, want to know whether it is safe to answer survey questions candidly, without fear of retribution or reprisal. Most surveys ask employees to respond about organizational matters such as work group trust and attitudes toward senior management. In some cases, organizations inquire about such sensitive and controversial matters as sexual harassment, employee honesty, and use of employee assistance facilities. When employee fears of company layoffs, downsizing, and possible mergers are added to

Table 9.1. Comparison of Survey Methods.

	Automated Telephone	Fax	PC	E-mail
Confidentiality	Perceptions of confidentiality are enhanced when individual initiates call.	There may be concerns related to linking of identification/phone number stamp.	Perceptions of confidentiality are enhanced when a central PC or set of PCs is used for administration.	Concerns center around linking of responses to e-mail addresses.
Flexibility	There is a lower level of tolerance for length, complex questions/responses, and open-ended questions. Item-branching capabilities are available.	Once faxed, flexibility is similar to paper-and-pencil survey.	There is greater flexibility for longer surveys, multiple question-and-response formats, open-ended items, and graphics. Complex item-branching capabilities are available.	Initial applications contain limited flexibility.
Time and logistics	Using external vendor technology, system can be running within a few weeks.	A short survey can be developed, distributed to limited population, and analyzed in a few days.	Requires more extensive development time. Central administration sites help control complexity.	Survey can be programmed within a week. Constructing extensive mail lists and integrating multiple e-mail systems can increase time requirements.
Ease of use	Responding becomes more difficult and frustrating with complex questions and long surveys. Providing a hard copy of survey for reference reduces frustration.	Completing survey is similar to completing paper-and-pencil survey.	Because survey may be administered to employees not familiar with PCs, detailed instructions may be necessary.	Because survey may be administered to employees not familiar with PCs and e-mail, instructions may be necessary.
Facilities and cost	Costs include specialized vendor techology and phone charges.	Costs include a PC equipped with fax board and phone charges.	Costs include software and additional hardware, if necessary.	Main cost is software.

the situation, it is easy to understand why ensuring confidentiality is so important. When designing a survey, the survey specialist needs to ensure that employees can answer truthfully. Moreover, introducing new technology to employees in turbulent times may in itself create additional fears, especially if past technological advancements have resulted in lost jobs.

Many alternative survey methods have designed sophisticated safeguards such as data encryption and removal of identification "footprints," to increase the actual level of employee anonymity. Unfortunately, none of the alternative methods can guarantee respondent confidentiality, but some methods may invoke greater perceived levels of confidentiality than others.

Automated Telephone Surveys

Perceptions of confidentiality in automated telephone surveys vary, depending on how the call is initiated. If the call is made by the computer to either the employee's home or business location, employee confidentiality concerns tend to be quite high: "If they know my number, they know me and how I'm responding." Employees seem to be less worried that they may be identified when they are given a central survey number to call and the call can be placed from any phone at any time.

Fax Surveys

In fax surveys, concerns about confidentiality center around the perception that returning a survey through a particular fax machine identifies the respondent. Most fax machines are programmed to include an identification stamp, including the phone number of origin, when a document is sent, and many employees are familiar with this feature. If the members of a small group (or a single individual) are the only ones to return surveys from a fax machine at a particular location, they may feel that their confidentiality has been compromised.

PC Surveys

For surveys on diskette, employee perception of confidentiality may be enhanced when a single diskette is used for a large number of employees. In addition, the diskette containing the programmed survey can be passed around, and individuals can take the survey on any available PC. Employee confidentiality concerns may also be relieved if a central PC or set of PCs is reserved for survey administration. Employees are likely to feel that they are less likely to be identified under these circumstances than they are if they complete the survey on their individual PCs or on a separate diskette.

For surveys on a network, employee concerns about confidentiality seem to be greater when the employee must access the survey from his or her own PC. The employee perceives that the connection from the PC to the network will identify him or her as the respondent. Although safeguards exist that will remove electronic footprints from an employee's returned survey, perceived confidentiality may again be enhanced when a central PC or set of PCs is used for survey administration.

E-Mail Surveys

Confidentiality concerns with e-mail surveys center around the linking of an employee's e-mail address with his or her responses. E-mail surveys are usually distributed to employees through a central mail list. Even though current e-mail survey systems are able to remove any resulting footprints from a submitted survey, some employees remain suspicious.

Flexibility

Organizations, if they are to succeed, must adapt to a complex business environment. In order to cope with changing business demands, surveys have become more flexible in the amount and type of data gathered and in the way these data are presented to respondents.

Automated Telephone Surveys

Although flexibility can be programmed into automated telephone survey systems, the tolerance level of people taking telephone surveys may limit the scope of certain features. In our experience, individuals tend to tolerate a lower number of questions on the telephone as opposed to other forms of questionnaires. Therefore, telephone surveys typically do not exceed forty questions. Although open-ended questions can be posed, people have difficulty responding without a moment of reflection and often opt not to respond to these question. Also, people have difficulty comprehending and responding to a detailed oral question followed by multiple response options. Although people taking automated telephone surveys can have the questions repeated to them, we find they often get frustrated. For this reason, organizations often distribute the questionnaire in paper form to employees, so that when an employee calls in, he or she can refer to the questions on paper and have prepared responses ready to read for open-ended questions. As in PC surveys, complex item branching is possible; however, this feature is complicated when the telephone survey is accompanied by a paper version. Again, questions can be targeted to particular subgroups based on employee response to particular questions.

Fax Surveys

Fax surveys are comparable to paper-and-pencil surveys in terms of flexibility. Once the fax is transmitted to the participant, the experience of completing the questionnaire is the same. Fax surveys can be lengthy; a survey of a hundred questions would not pose a problem. As already described, current software can also handle open-ended questions. However, also as in paper-and-pencil surveys, item-branching techniques are not transparent. To answer questions targeted to particular subgroups, employees must follow specific instructions, for example, "If you are a service provider, skip to Question 33."

PC Surveys

PC surveys offer a great deal of flexibility to survey designers. Questionnaires can be as long as respondents can tolerate. In fact, some evidence suggests that individuals completing questionnaires on computer monitors perceive time to pass by more quickly (Lukin, Dowd, Plake, & Kraft, 1985) than do individuals completing other kinds of surveys. Responses to open-ended questions can easily be saved as part of the data file. As discussed above, one of the most attractive features of PC surveys is item branching. Questions can be targeted to employee subgroups defined by job category, location, years of service, participation in company programs, or any other variable of interest to the organization. PC surveys may also have options for making the questionnaire more appealing to the respondent, such as changes in screen color or font and the inclusion of graphics.

E-Mail Surveys

E-mail surveys are still evolving in terms of the features available to the survey specialist. Although there are no program limitations to length, typical applications of e-mail surveys tend to be less than eighty questions. Like PC surveys, e-mail surveys can pose an organization's open-ended questions to employees, and the information can be easily saved and translated into a format for subsequent analysis. Item-branching features are not fully developed, but we expect that will change soon. In current versions of e-mail surveys, employees either tab through the survey or jump from question to question using a mouse.

Time and Logistical Constraints

The popularity of alternative survey methods is due to the quick feedback they offer on changes occurring both inside and outside the corporation. Time stresses resulting from geographical dispersion and shortened planning, development, and delivery cycles plus increased environmental volatility have drastically reduced acceptable reaction time (Keen, 1991). These time stresses are driving business not only to just-in-time inventory but to just-in-time everything, including organizational surveys. The demand for quick turnaround of survey results has never been greater.

The time it takes to survey employees and analyze the data can be dramatically reduced by alternative surveys. All the alternative methods reduce the need for separate key entry of the data, which reduces coding errors as well as saving time. Most often data are in a form that allows for immediate processing of the results.

The differences among the methods have less to do with the speed offered by their technologies and more to do with the logistics of survey administration. This is especially true if access to the technology required is not available to everyone or if the supporting infrastructure for the technology does not currently exist in the organization.

The logistics of survey administration, regardless of the survey method, are seldom straightforward. Factors to consider include sample size, choice of administration sites, timing of the survey, employee familiarity with the technology underlying the survey, and the existing technology infrastructure. These issues become even more complex when employees are geographically dispersed and operate on different daily schedules. While alternative surveys alleviate some administrative burdens, unfortunately they create others. The discussion below underscores some of the logistical burdens characteristic of alternative survey methods.

Automated Telephone Surveys

To create an automated telephone survey system, most organizations utilize an outside vendor that has the technology and expertise available to get the survey up and running within a few weeks. Most automated telephone surveys use an 800-number. The number must be communicated in some manner to survey respondents, and this is done in a variety of ways. Often a postcard with the survey phone number is sent to individuals at the office or at home. Access to a phone does not present a problem for most employees.

Fax Surveys

Administering a survey via fax is one of the most attractive alternatives for organizations interested in getting answers to a brief questionnaire in a relatively short period of time. With software currently available, a fax survey of a few dozen questions can be constructed and distributed in a couple of days once survey content is finalized. No special survey forms are needed; questionnaires can be printed on a common laser printer. The obvious requirement for distributing a fax survey is that the survey takers be accessible via a fax machine.

Since a single fax machine usually services each location or department, fax surveys are typically designed for small populations that are geographically dispersed. A typical example is a survey sent to eighty sales directors who manage separate sales territories from eighty different offices. Upon receipt of the survey, each sales manager completes it and faxes it back to the central administration site. As the fax comes in, the data are automatically read into a data set, eliminating a separate data entry phase. Data analysis can begin whenever an acceptable return rate is achieved, theoretically the same day that surveys are distributed. However, the realities of employee availability—travel schedules, sick days, and multiple responsibilities—will usually require a longer administration window.

PC Surveys

The development of a PC survey is potentially more time intensive than development of other surveys. One of the appeals of conducting a PC survey is the item-branching capability that enables survey specialists to target particular questions to specific populations with a "single" survey. However, this added complexity can greatly increase the instrument development phase. By making the choice of subsequent items contingent upon previous responses, PC surveys can target employees who share a common experience, such as attendance at a training program, across their different departments, regions, or groups. Before one of these "single" surveys with different questions for different employees is distributed, it is necessary to pretest it to ensure that the complicated item branching functions as intended. The amount of time needed for this additional pretesting will increase with survey complexity.

A small organization is likely to have a fairly uniform type of PC. Large organizations, however, are more likely to have an extensive variety of PCs in the field. Moreover, organizations do not convert their entire information systems overnight. Thus, in addition to pretesting a survey's item-branching features, it is also necessary to pretest the survey on the range of PCs that will be used for its administration, including PCs with different monitors, disk drives, keyboards, operating systems, and so on. Organizations that have attempted PC surveys are often amazed at the differences they find in hardware and software across locations. For this reason, many have opted for central administration sites, where the type of PC used can be controlled.

The time required to install a PC survey system is dictated by the supporting technology infrastructure. If an organization's infrastructure is loosely coordinated or undersupported, the development time for installing a PC system can be extensive.

E-Mail Surveys

Like fax surveys, e-mail surveys can also be constructed in a relatively short period of time. Once the survey is constructed, it is merged with a mail list, if available, and distributed to the target population. Additional development time is necessary when the mail list must be created. As with PC surveys, differences in technology need to be considered when designing the survey. In this case, differences in electronic mail systems will be of particular importance. Obviously, all employees in the target population must have e-mail addresses in order to participate. A few organizations have set up "voter booths" that allow employees who do not have access to e-mail to participate. Data entry may occur automatically as participants return their surveys. Again, as with PC surveys, the duration of the survey development phase will be determined by the sophistication of the organization's existing technology.

Ease of Use

Historically, successful technological applications have had one thing in common: they have been user friendly. Whether the application was microwave ovens, VCRs, or personal computers, all were easy to use before they gained widespread public acceptance. The same is true for alternative survey methods: if they are to succeed, they must be easy to use. Fundamentally, successful organizational surveys facilitate communication between people. Therefore, people need to feel comfortable enough with the survey technology that they will communicate their opinions through it. Below, each alternative method is evaluated in terms of its ease of use.

Automated Telephone Surveys

Negotiating one's way through an automated telephone survey is quite a different experience from taking other types of surveys. As described earlier, questions are read to the respondent by a pre-recorded voice, and the person responds by pressing the number on his or her Touch-Tone pad that corresponds with his or her preferred opinion. Questions and response options can be repeated, and previous responses can be reviewed and changed. However, remembering a complex oral question or a long series of response options can be difficult and often leads to frustration. To improve ease of use, many organizations provide employees with a backup, a paper copy of the survey.

Fax Surveys

To the respondent, a fax survey is one of easiest of all the alternative survey methods. Filling it out is identical to filling out a paper-and-pencil survey, and returning it involves simply typing in a phone number and pressing a single button. Fax surveys are usually sent to individuals who are quite familiar with operating a fax machine.

PC Surveys

An individual taking a PC survey is presented with a series of screens containing either information or a request that the participant respond to a question by pressing the key that corresponds to his or her opinion. Because PC surveys are often administered to employee populations who do not use PCs in their everyday work, this task can be difficult for some respondents. Detailed instructions are usually necessary at the beginning of the survey and on each screen.

Typically, participants use a limited number of keys to respond to items (for example, number keys, arrow keys, the Enter key, and so on). An employee who wants to review a previous item can do so by pressing a particular key (for example, the Esc key). After the review, the employee must return through the survey to where he or she left off. If the questionnaire is long, people may get frustrated and confused when they go back through many items. To alleviate this, PC surveys are often organized so that once a person completes a section, he or she cannot return to it; however, this, too, may frustrate some people. Recent survey developments include a list of items (a menu) that serves as a guide, helping participants negotiate through the survey. People also find it helpful if they know which question number they are on and how many additional questions remain.

E-Mail Surveys

Taking an e-mail survey is similar to taking a PC survey. The respondent is presented with a series of questions and either tabs down or uses a mouse to reach the area in which he or she will record a response by pressing a limited set of keys (number keys, arrow keys, and so on). The respondent can scroll back through the questionnaire to review previous responses. Once the survey is complete, the respondent simply uses the reply function to return the survey.

Facilities and Costs

The most important and least documented and discussed aspect of alternative surveys is their total cost. One of the major reasons for this situation is that costs associated with software, hardware, and vendor expertise continue to fluctuate dramatically from year to year. The identical software program that sold for $2,000 dollars several years ago costs $250 dollars today. Because we expect the price of technological applications to continue to rise and fall dramatically, we find it impossible to estimate costs with any confidence. What we can do, however, is identify the source of the costs for each alternative survey method.

Automated Telephone Surveys

Although an organization may look to external consultants for assistance with each of the alternative methods of survey administration, a specialized vendor is almost always used for an automated telephone survey, and the vendor represents the main design charges. Additional cost is incurred when there are long-distance telephone charges. The length of the survey as well as the geographical dispersion of the participants will obviously increase these expenses.

Fax Surveys

The costs associated with conducting a fax survey include providing a PC equipped with a fax board that serves as the central administration point for both survey distribution and survey receipt. The central PC also needs to be equipped with special software that designs the outgoing survey and allows incoming surveys to be read into a data set. Companies that administer surveys via fax do so because fax machines already exist at the participating sites and extra hardware expenses are usually not incurred. Additional costs may include long-distance phone charges for both out-going and incoming surveys.

PC Surveys

Specialized software is also needed for the design of a PC survey. Other costs associated with this method include the diskettes required for administration as well as diskette duplication expenses. In addition, some software products are priced based on the number of field (that is, individual) disks that are be duplicated. The price of network software, however, is usually all inclusive. There are obvious hardware expenses associated with conducting a PC survey, although additional costs are only incurred when an organization must rent hardware if the necessary PCs either do not exist or are not available for survey administration. Costs will obviously be greater for organizations with less developed technology infrastructure. In addition, costs will increase when external expertise is required to develop that infrastructure.

E-Mail Surveys

The main cost of administering an e-mail survey is associated with the software necessary to develop and distribute the questionnaire. Costs will vary depending on whether an e-mail system is already in place and whether or not it is integrated across locations.

Conclusion

Changing technology is driving the next generation of organizational surveys. In this chapter, we have reviewed the major alternatives to the paper-and-pencil survey: fax, PC, automated telephone, and e-mail surveys. The choice of survey method to use depends on the particular circumstances under which it is administered. Five issues that should be considered when deciding which survey method to use are confidentiality, flexibility, time and logistical constraints, ease of use, and facilities and cost. A full understanding of these issues in relation to each organization's particular context will allow survey designers to extract the most value from their survey endeavor.

Perhaps the most critical error a survey specialist can make is to choose a method based solely on the availability of existing technology in the organization. We hear managers saying, "We have fax machines in every district office so let's use that method." The problem is that this decision is made without considering the nature of the fax format (flexibility) and without considering whether employees will feel comfortable answering truthfully on the fax survey (confidentiality). If the survey format is inappropriate or the perceived confidentiality is low, the value of the information received from the data will be compromised.

Another related error is to choose a method based exclusively on the latest technology. We can imagine a manager choosing a PC survey system and saying, "Let's build it, and they will come." Unfortunately, the creation of a PC survey takes a lot of time and requires considerable expertise. The system is very costly to implement. It is not reasonable to expect a survey "field of dreams"; there must be full appreciation of the costs and benefits involved.

This is not to underestimate the role that PCs will play in the future of surveys. We believe PCs linked with powerful telecommunications technology, such as the Internet or the World Wide Web, present a compelling vision of the future for organizational surveys. One of the most exciting aspects of the next generation of surveys will be the unlimited ways to display information, both in the survey itself and in feedback of results. Indeed, many organizations currently use PCs to deliver survey reports featuring stylish typography, colorful graphics, push-button interactivity, and even sound and video. The organizational survey of tomorrow will certainly look different from any survey conducted previously.

Unfortunately, choosing the best survey method for an organization requires more than deciding on the technology alone. Despite all the technological wizardry and glitz in alternative survey methods, a good survey hinges on the honesty of survey respondents. The truth is, an organizational survey is no better than the information practitioners collect from employees. As always, the success of a survey is determined after data are collected. A successful follow-up strategy includes the use of focus groups or quality action teams to examine the data to further refine the issues as well as to generate recommendations. Ultimately, success results from taking specific action to address employee concerns. Applying alternative survey methods does not on its own guarantee the success of a survey program. Unfortunately, gathering data via fax or PC does not increase the likelihood that action will be taken. Recognizing that the opinion survey is a political instrument that has consequences in people's lives and dealing with it as such is as relevant today as it was for the first paper-and-pencil survey over forty years ago.

Living in today's knowledge revolution means that all of us must work faster and smarter to keep pace with the competition. Alternative survey technologies will become only more popular in the years to come. Only a deep understanding of survey technology and how it can be used can give us the undistorted insight into this survey era that we need to rise to its greatest challenge.

Appendix: Partial List of Vendors of Alternative Survey Products

Currently, there are many survey products available to consumers. Our list is not inclusive; we list only products with which we are personally familiar.

Automated Telephone Survey Products

Sawtooth Technologies
1007 Church Street, Suite 402
Evanston, IL 60201
(708) 866–0870

Fax Survey Products

Cardiff Software, Inc.
6351 Yarrow Drive, Suite E
Carlsbad, CA 92009
(619) 931–4530

PC Survey Products

Acumen International
3950 Civic Center Drive, Suite 310N
San Rafael, CA 94903
(415) 492–9190

Anderson-Bell Corp.
P.O. Box 5160
Arvada, CO 80006
(303) 940–0595

Bruce Bell & Associates, Inc.
425 Main Street, Suite 10
P.O. Box 400
Canon City, CO 81212
(800) 359–7738

Conway Information Systems
1115 Blanshard Street
Victoria, BC Canada V8W 2H7
(604) 382–3262

Creative Research System
140 Vista View, Suite 100
Petaluma, CA 94952
(707) 765–1001

Cybernetic Solutions Co.
3479 West 7480 South
Salt Lake City, UT 84084
(800) 359–3386

Raosoft, Inc.
6645 N.E. Windermere Road
Seattle, WA 98115
(206) 525–4025

Sawtooth Technologies
1007 Church Street, Suite 402
Evanston, IL 60201
(708) 866–0870

Scantron
1616 South Amphlett Boulevard, Suite 205
San Mateo, CA 94402
(415) 525–3825

Statpac, Inc.
3814 Lyndale Avenue South
Minneapolis, MN 55409
(612) 822–8252

StatSoft
2300 East 41st Street
Tulsa, OK 74104
(918) 749–1119

Westchester Distribution Systems
P.O. Box 324
Scarsdale, NY 10583
(914) 723–5230

E-Mail Survey Products

Survey Tracker
Training Technologies, Inc.
11449 Lebanon Road
Cincinnati, OH 45241
(513) 769–4121

References

Argyris, C. (1991). Teaching smart people how to learn. *Harvard Business Review, 69*(3), 99–109.

Attewell, P. (1992). Technology diffusion and organizational learning: The case of business computing. *Organization Science, 3*(1), 1–19.

Booth-Kewley, S., Rosenfeld, P., & Edwards, J. E. (1993). Computer-administered surveys in organizational setting: Alternatives, advantages, and applications. In P. Rosenfeld, J. E. Edwards, & M. D. Thomas (Eds.), *Improving organizational surveys: New directions, methods, and applications* (pp. 73–99). Newbury Park, CA: Sage.

Carter, N. M. (1984). Computerization as a predominant technology: Its influence on the structure of newspaper organizations. *Academy of Management Review, 27*, 247–270.

Developers send clear OCR messages on fax capacities: Windows ware enables PCs to "read" faxes in background (optical character recognition). (1992, December 14). *Computer Reseller News,* p. 71.

Dunham, R. B., & Smith, F. J. (1979). *Organizational surveys.* Glenview, IL: Scott, Foresman.

Extending the fax (automated facsimile software packages). (1992, December 8). *PC Magazine,* p. 310.

Foster, L. W., & Flynn, D. M. (1984). Management information technology: Its effects on organizational form and function. *MIS Quarterly, 8*(4), 229–235.

Golembiewski, R. T., & Hilles, R. J. (1979). *Toward the responsive organization: The theory and practice of survey/feedback.* Salt Lake City, UT: Brighton.

Hiltz, S. R., & Johnson, K. (1986). User satisfaction and computer-mediated communication systems. *Management Science, 36,* 739–764.

Huttig, J. W. (1993, January). This is your survey: This is your survey on PCs. Any questions? *PC Today,* pp. 20–23.

Keen, P. (1991). *Shaping the future: Business design through information technology.* Boston: Harvard Business School Press.

Kendall, S. (1986). *Employee attitude surveys.* New York: Modern Business Reports.

Kimberly, J., & Evanisko, M. (1981). Organizational innovation: The influence of individual, organizational, and contextual factors on hospital adoption of technological and administrative innovations. *Academy of Management Journal, 124,* 689–713.

Koch, W. R., Dodd, B. G., & Fitzpatrick, S. J. (1990). Computerized adaptive measurements of attitudes. *Measurement and Evaluation in Counseling and Development, 23,* 20–30.

Kuhnert, K. W. (1993). Survey/feedback as art and science. In R. T. Golembiewski (Ed.), *Handbook of organizational consulting* (pp. 459–465). New York: Dekker.

Lukin, M. E., Dowd, E. T., Plake, B. S., & Kraft, R. G. (1985). Comparing computerized versus traditional psychological assessment. *Computers in Human Behavior, 1,* 49–58.

McCauley, D. P., & Kuhnert, K. W. (1992). Trust in management: The importance of supervisory support and professional development. *Public Administration Quarterly, 16,* 265–284.

Rosenfeld, P., Dotherty, L. M., Vicino, S. M., Kantor, J., & Greaves, J. (1989). Attitude assessment in organizations: Testing three microcomputer-based survey systems. *Journal of Psychology, 116,* 145–154.

Seashore, S. E. (1987). Surveys in organizations. In J. W. Lorsch (Ed.), *Handbook of organizational behavior* (pp. 140–154). Upper Saddle River, NJ: Prentice Hall.

Senge, P. M. (1990). *The fifth discipline: The art and practice of the learning organization.* New York: Doubleday/Currency.

CHAPTER 10

Feedback, Action Planning, and Follow-Through

John R. Hinrichs

The chapters up to this point have dealt with important measurement topics in conducting an effective organizational survey—design, implementation, data processing, and analysis. These topics are important unto themselves and perhaps sufficient where there is little real concern about any follow-up impact upon the respondents providing the information. But in the kinds of surveys with which this book deals, there is usually

- A strong involvement of employees and employee interest in the ongoing internal operation of the business
- A continuing need for communications to flow in all directions—up, down, horizontally—in order to support ongoing operations
- A situation in which the mere process of collecting data can raise expectations that something will be done with the findings
- A situation in which the survey is not a one-shot measurement but part of an ongoing program in which surveys are used repeatedly to monitor employee attitudes and commitment
- An intention to use the survey data as a catalyst for change and a tool for organizational development
- A desire to support teams and autonomous work groups as self-governing systems within the context of broader organizational entities

Under these conditions, measurement is only one leg of a three-legged stool. And, as any farmer knows, a one-legged or even two-legged stool is not very useful for milking a cow!

Today, the organization that really wants to milk full return from its survey investment needs to add the other two supporting legs to its process. One of these supports is the reporting back of survey results to the individuals who provided the data, in order to be sure that the results are properly understood and specific explanatory examples are identified. The other necessary support is involving employees in planning, and taking actions to deal with any issues that the data have raised. These are the issues we shall address in this chapter.

Figure 10.1 illustrates a model for using surveys in organizational development. A fully productive survey includes five key steps. So far this book has dealt with only step 1—*measuring and assessing*. We still need to devote considerable effort and time to *understanding* what the survey is really telling us (step 2); working with the groups of employees most directly involved and *prioritizing* the issues that are most important (step 3); *planning* what to do to correct any critical problems and deciding who will be accountable for implementing these solutions (step 4); and finally, *implementing* and following-through to be sure that the action plans have been carried out (step 5).

Figure 10.1. Steps in Survey Utilization.

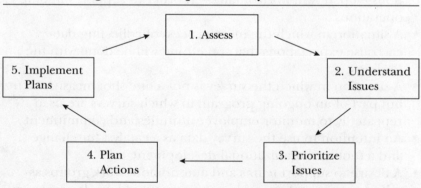

Readers will recognize the close similarity of this model to the more general problem-solving strategies used widely in organizations today. To the extent feasible and appropriate to the issues that emerge, the productive survey process includes the active involvement and participation of employees in each of these problem-solving steps on the "back end" of the survey. Too often, in years past, these steps have received little more than lip service in many organizations conducting surveys, and many surveys have yielded relatively limited bottom-line payoff. Fortunately, the situation is changing dramatically today, and these critical steps of feedback, action taking, and follow-through are being built into the survey practices of more and more companies as they adopt this powerful tool for aligning their workforces behind their business strategies.

Why Give Survey Feedback?

There are two basic reasons why feeding back data about survey results is important for organizational change. First, feedback and discussion help clarify issues, arouse awareness, generate feelings, and make the members of a unit open to new ideas and plans. Second, once members of the organization have been motivated to become involved around the data, the feedback points out needs, suggests desirable outcomes, and energizes employees to search for paths to attain those outcomes.

The importance of employee feedback has been highlighted by a number of authors (Alderfer & Ferriss, 1972; Dodd & Pesci, 1977; Klein, Kraut, & Wolfson, 1971; Mann, 1957; Miles, Hornstein, Callahan, Calder, & Schiavo, 1969). In a study conducted by a large manufacturing company (Alper & Klein, 1970), employees' attitudes about management and the survey process in locations where survey feedback was conducted were compared with reactions of employees where no feedback was given. Eighty-four percent of the employees in locations with no feedback felt the survey results would not be utilized well; only 11 percent of those who received feedback felt this way (p. 55). There were similar differences in employees' evaluations of management and other aspects of the survey process.

There are a number of reasons why such feedback is important.

- As any good teacher knows, feedback is one of the essential prerequisites for learning. The same is true for organizational learning.
- Feeding back survey data to employees gives them an opportunity to validate the quantitative results, explain any ambiguities in the data, provide specific examples about why the results came out the way they did, and prioritize the most important issues to be resolved.
- Feedback is a symbol of the organization's regard for employees and its desire to involve them fully in understanding and using the survey results. Failure to share survey data breeds rumors, resentments, ungrounded guesses, and expectations of the worst.
- A good feedback session (particularly if the process cascades down through the organization, as I shall discuss in more detail shortly), provides a model for all organizational levels of how survey results should be used and how change should be undertaken.
- The process of feedback can be a catalyst for involvement, building relevance, shared understanding, and ownership for each individual.
- The conclusions coming out of a feedback session are a basis for goal setting. Feedback of survey data initiates a logical transition into a broad-based action-taking phase for relevant organizational change and workforce involvement.

Theory and Research

Today, the concept of feedback is a much used one. It originally flowed out of a 1940s concept for machine systems, articulated by Norbert Wiener (1950) as "cybernetics." A thermostat is a simple example of a machine system that uses feedback.

Kenneth Berrien (1968) later articulated a comprehensive theory of social systems and an explication of where feedback fits into that theory. His discussion deals with "maintenance" and "signal" inputs to any social system, inputs through which changes are initiated (p. 25). Outputs are registered as "formal achievement" and "group need satisfaction" (p. 117). Berrien's concepts are relevant to the survey feedback process. The organization's commitment of resources to support a full-scope survey-involvement-action process—its investment of time, money, training, and facilities—is essential as a maintenance input to the system. Without it, few tangible results can be expected. The set of survey data itself can be thought of as a signal input to the system and thus a catalyst to energize and direct people.

Berrien's model suggests that two distinct outputs can be expected from a survey feedback process. The first, formal achievement, is registered in the action plans that are generated and the initiatives that are actually implemented. The second output consists of need satisfaction of employees—their commitment and alignment with the objectives of the enterprise. This social system framework is important because

- It clarifies the prerequisites for a successful feedback process: adequate organizational support and relevant survey data injected in a constructive and catalytic manner.
- It emphasizes that multiple outputs may (and should) be expected from a well-designed and implemented survey feedback process: constructive actions taken and enhanced employee attitudes and commitment.

Years ago, at the University of Michigan, Daniel Katz and Robert Kahn (Katz & Kahn, 1978) dealt extensively with the role of survey feedback in organizational change. They drew heavily on the early work of Floyd Mann, a colleague of Rensis Likert at the Survey Research Center (Mann, 1957). Mann outlined three basic requirements for productive feedback of survey data (p. 162):

1. Systematically collecting information about how an organizational system is operating.
2. Reporting this information back to the system. Today, team or department would probably be the most relevant organizational unit, each dealing with the findings at its own level.
3. Using the information for the organization to make adjustments in its operations.

These three umbrella requisites are as relevant today as they were forty years ago when developed by Floyd Mann.

Katz and Kahn elaborate five additional factors that they believe are important for effective survey feedback:

1. Individual team members need to be permitted—encouraged—to participate fully in the interpretation and analysis of the findings.
2. The information that is fed back has to be seen as relevant to the group working on it.
3. Groups participating in feedback sessions need to be given information about outcomes; they need knowledge of the results that the process attains.
4. Groups have to be supported with an atmosphere of cooperation, acceptance, and openness, with involvement of all members of the organizational entity.
5. The feedback process has to be organizationally legitimized. (One device for legitimating the process is to have feedback sessions take place in a cascading fashion, from top to bottom.)

David Nadler (1977) describes feedback in the context of data-based consulting as "the process of giving back data for the purpose of bringing about change" (p. 67). He outlines several dimensions on which collecting survey data and giving feedback affect how the data will be used. First of all, the organization's expectations in collecting data lay out some implied criteria about how the results should be used. Second, measurement generates energy because it enables and facilitates evaluation of what is going on in the organization. Finally, there are rewards associated with the process; in some organizations, explicit rewards exist in terms of compensation and evaluation tied to survey results, and in any survey, certainly implicit rewards (and punishments) exist in terms of recognition, both public and private, from superiors, peers, and others about the nature of positive and negative survey results. Managing these kinds of organizational sanctions and evaluations in a positive and constructive fashion is one of the key prerequisites for effective feedback sessions.

Critical Variables

Most frequently, the process of survey feedback, if done correctly, can have a positive impact on organizational effectiveness. But there is also the potential for great damage. If done poorly, a feedback session can arouse significant defensive behavior, misdirected efforts, and consequent decreased work group performance. Research and experience have identified some critical variables that can help prevent such negative outcomes (Dunham & Smith, 1979; Nadler, 1977).

To satisfy the strong expectations inevitably raised among employees as a result of a survey, it is important that the feedback process be visible and supported by high-level management. It needs to be very clear how the data will be collected and used. To some extent, satisfaction of expectations depends upon the original questionnaire design. If the survey questions are specific, relevant, and actionable, they will lead naturally to use of the data and to fulfilled expectations about positive outcomes.

It is also important that the survey and feedback system be benign. If there is any suggestion that data are being used punitively, the outcome is apt to be defensive behavior on the part of managers and/or employees. A helpful rule of thumb is to make it very clear that managers or units are not going to be castigated in any way for registering subpar survey results. However, it is acceptable to be critical of units that do not take the process seriously and do not make concerted efforts to deal with issues the survey raises. Cast the survey and feedback process in a constructive rather than a negative mode.

Finally, the outcomes of the feedback process need to be rewarding, and these outcomes will then lead to enhanced job satisfaction and motivation. Desired outcomes are greater effectiveness, recognition, and teamwork in aid of shared objectives. In the remainder of this chapter, I present some guidelines to support this view of the feedback process.

Feedback Variables

Survey data are used for a variety of purposes in organizations. Owing to this diversity, it is important to be sure just why data are being collected as one begins to plan how these data will be used. If there is ambiguity in the purposes, the odds are employees will be confused about what they are being asked to do, and the outcomes will be less than ideal. Is the survey intended primarily as an assessment of results achieved by the group, such as customer satisfaction or service quality; behavior of the individual group leader; internal group functioning and cooperation; group job satisfaction or morale; or something else? The proper expected role for employees in dealing with these different kinds of data vary widely, and employees need to be clear about what that role is.

Type of Survey

There are several dimensions along which most surveys may be categorized. In planning a feedback and action strategy, it will be useful to review the specific survey under consideration in terms of where it fits on the following dimensions.

Level

One dimension for categorizing surveys is the level or unit covered by the data. This level can range from individuals (as the subjects of data collected from peers and subordinates to generate personal feedback reports) to small groups (such as departments or teams) to total organizations. Typically, a specific and probably somewhat different feedback format will be optimal for surveys at each of these different levels. Nadler (1977) deals with these issues in some detail, outlining eight different survey models with varying approaches to data feedback.

Purpose

A second dimension for categorizing a survey is its purpose. Is it (1) to make assessments leading to administrative actions such as performance management, allocation of head-count or budgets, or product and marketing decisions or (2) to provide insight and data relevant to individual or organizational development.

Historically, most surveys at the organizational or team level have been designed to assess the degree of job satisfaction in the workforce and clarify how effectively the unit was operating. Today, however, organizational and team surveys are being used increasingly as catalysts for organizational development as well.

On the other hand, traditional surveys at the individual level—what are increasingly being referred to as *360-degree feedback* processes—originated primarily to provide information and insight that individual managers and executives could use for their personal development and growth. Today, however, these individual feedback surveys are being used increasingly as input to performance evaluations and management and, ultimately, in compensation and career decisions. Thus, depending upon the level of analysis (individual versus group), current trends for survey use seem to be moving in different directions.

That raises a potential problem! If the purposes of a survey become muddied, if it is not clear whether the survey focuses on measurement and/or administrative action or on personal and/or organizational development, then it will be difficult for the organization to have a clear focus when it comes to feedback and utilization of results. The two purposes are often in conflict. Where performance evaluation is the purpose, concern about negative assessments or sanctions will dominate the reactions and involvement of recipients of feedback data. Conversely, when the focus is on development, building acceptance of the data and constructive insights about behavior is the overriding issue. The defensiveness or resistance that often results after individuals receive evaluative feedback undermines the acceptance that is necessary when development is the objective. Conversely, the highly detailed and focused feedback necessary for learning and development often overlooks the performance- and outcome-focused feedback required for evaluation. Consequently, if there is lack of clarity about the purpose of a survey, there is apt to be confusion about the type of data that should be collected and used for feedback, and the feedback process is then apt to be ineffective.

The rest of this chapter deals primarily with information collected for use by departments or teams and by larger organizational systems and with the use of survey data for system development. Where there are mixed purposes or audiences for a survey, it is important to sort these out before attempting to hold a feedback or action session and to be sure that feedback receivers are clear about the uses to be made of the data.

Direction of Information Flow

The differentiating factor in the types of feedback for organizational surveys is primarily the direction of information flow. Some surveys generate primarily an *upward* flow of information about specific topics, designed to lead to administrative action—for example, market research information, assessment of employee reactions to various policies or practices, or data collected for specific administrative reasons. Typically, the decision making resides with senior management, and employee involvement in taking actions is not expected.

Other surveys generate primarily a *lateral* flow of information—for example, between suppliers and their customer or client groups, or among work teams where effective interdepartmental relations are important—and the data are used primarily for development of operating effectiveness. Here, the feedback process is critical to survey effectiveness. In yet other situations, the focus is primarily on a *downward* flow of information, and the act of asking for information through a survey is designed to communicate to participants awareness of such important issues as business strategy or company values or objectives.

Most of the surveys with which practitioners are dealing today have somewhat mixed directions of information flow. The point is that, as we design strategies to deal with survey results, it is important for us to be aware of the different purposes and information flows, as well as the potentially different survey frameworks, as we decide which issues to emphasize in structuring the feedback session. And the relevant framework needs to be communicated to employees as part of the data collection process and also in the introduction to the feedback session, to ensure that people's expectations are accurate and realistic and that follow-up feedback is appropriate to the purposes intended.

Feedback Vehicles

There are three ways in which survey results typically are fed back to employees.

1. Distributing a written (or video) summary of the results, either in the form of a feedback booklet or through a company newspaper or magazine
2. Presenting the overall survey results to employees in large "town hall" meetings
3. Conducting small departmental meetings in which results for an individual department are fed back directly to the employees in that department

Research and experience show that these strategies differ widely in the results they are able to achieve. The study described above (Alper & Klein, 1970, p. 56) found that 39 percent of employees in groups that received only written feedback felt that the survey results were well utilized, 57 percent felt this way in groups that attended a larger group (total plant) meeting, while 70 percent of those who participated in departmental feedback meetings felt results were well utilized. Thus, there was a clear impact on employee perceptions based upon the type of feedback session in which they participated.

Written feedback is clearly better than no feedback at all. It may be the only method available for informing some groups of the survey results (employees at remote locations, for example). Also, budget and scheduling constraints may dictate that this is the only feedback that can be supplied. If possible, however, written feedback should be supplemented with meetings that permit an open exchange of ideas and suggestions. When the survey results that are the focus of the discussion have been provided by the participants themselves, the potential for real understanding and action increases significantly.

Feedback Leaders

Assuming that feedback is given to intact departmental teams, another issue is determining who conducts the feedback sessions. Research by Klein, Kraut, and Wolfson (1971) suggests that generally feedback is most effective when line managers rather than staff personnel or outsiders conduct feedback sessions within their own areas of responsibility.

Sometimes, however, most frequently when survey results

reflect considerable employee dissatisfaction, it is just expecting too much to ask the manager to handle a survey feedback meeting. There may be such a climate of animosity or fear in the department that employees will not participate under any conditions. If the manager is a source of problems and employees are hostile, it will take a very secure person to face these issues constructively. In other instances, managers just may not have the skill and experience to conduct successful feedback meetings.

An alternative to having managers or team members feed back their own group's survey results is to appoint a cadre of feedback leaders from various departments throughout the organization or to engage outside consultants as feedback leaders. Such feedback leaders should be carefully selected. Experience suggests that they should have at least several years of experience and considerable familiarity with the operations of the organization and also intelligence, maturity, good verbal skills, and a positive attitude toward the survey process. Each feedback leader should be expected to conduct multiple feedback sessions.

Feedback Leader Training

Many managers in the organization may be uncomfortable with conducting feedback and action-planning meetings with their employees, especially if this is the first time the organization has conducted a survey. Managers who will be holding feedback sessions should be trained, so that they have the skills and confidence to be effective.

One reason for managers' discomfort with the feedback process is their anticipation of the range of issues to be covered and fear of becoming the focus of a free-for-all gripe session. Some managers may even have witnessed such conditions in past meetings. With training, however, managers can be taught specific techniques for avoiding such confrontations.

Good feedback training should prepare managers to perform the following tasks:

•   *Analyze the results for the work group.* Ideally, managers should receive their actual survey results in the training session and be given time to work with them and ask questions so that they can identify the most important issues embedded within the data.

• *Conduct effective feedback meetings.* Guidelines should be given for selecting the data to be presented, developing an agenda, and scheduling the meeting. Presentation and facilitation techniques should be demonstrated. Managers should have an opportunity to practice the skills they are learning.

• *Handle any roadblocks.* Managers should be made aware of the difficulties they may encounter in the feedback meeting and be given suggestions for dealing with them successfully. These problems include argumentative or shy employees, personality conflicts, and "zingers," that is, unexpected issues thrown out from left field. Feedback leaders' skill in getting around these roadblocks can make the difference between a successful and unsuccessful survey process.

• *Conduct action-planning meetings.* It is useful to show managers how to facilitate idea generation and evaluation with their departments, to provide managers with suggested ways to reach group consensus, and to explain to managers what is contained in a good action plan and what the administrative procedures are for tracking implementation.

• *Ensure follow-up.* Training should provide guidance to managers on how to keep employees' enthusiasm going.

Dodd and Pesci (1977) have shown that managers trained in these techniques, more often than untrained managers, were seen by meeting audiences as

• Understanding what employees were saying
• Taking notes on employee ideas
• Recapping the content of meeting discussions
• Making commitments to take actions
• Promising to report back on steps to be taken

Holding an Effective Survey Feedback Meeting

Where employee involvement must support survey utilization, feedback meetings should be scheduled as soon as possible after the departmental data are available and managers' feedback training is completed. Appropriate training will have both taught meeting behaviors and addressed administrative issues such as how the organization's composition or performance management systems operate or what reorganization strategies are already in place. The major considerations in scheduling feedback meetings are fivefold:

1. Participants should be notified of the meeting well in advance and a tentative agenda should be circulated.
2. If at all possible, participants should all be from the same work group and/or level so that they share common concerns and opinions and are able to deal with the data that they themselves submitted as part of the survey.
3. Groups should be held to a manageable size so that a free exchange of ideas is possible; somewhere around fifteen participants is ideal.
4. About two to three hours should be allowed for a typical survey feedback meeting.
5. The meeting room should be private and the meeting uninterrupted.

Meeting Guidelines

While there are many effective ways to feed back the results of a survey, experience has shown that the following guidelines will work well in most departmental situations.

If at all possible, individual managers should be responsible for feeding back the survey results to the employees in their departments. This arrangement gets managers and subordinates talking about work-related problems and working together to find ways to solve them. The intent is to create a team approach to problem solving.

Managers also need to share the survey results openly and work with employees to clarify issues and identify specifics by digging below superficial generalities for underlying causes. Managers have a responsibility to help the group develop actions and recommendations in response to the survey and then to follow through on agreed-upon actions and respond to recommendations. Finally, managers need to recognize the contributions of employees to the process.

Meeting Ground Rules

There are some time-tested meeting ground rules that can help groups achieve their feedback purposes. First of all, it is essential that individual survey responses remain confidential and anonymous. To support this need, results should be presented only for the total department (or work group), without breakdowns by demographic factors such as gender or length of service. Employees should be told that the purpose of the feedback session is to involve them in clarifying specific factors behind the trends revealed in the data. They should also be told that recommended and completed actions will be reviewed with higher management and that topics that cannot be addressed within the department will be referred to whomever will be able to take action. At the same time, employees should be made to feel responsible for constructive participation in the meeting process.

Ideally, as mentioned, feedback meetings should *cascade down* through an organization from the highest levels. This scheduling method allows departmental managers to experience the employee role in feedback meetings with their managers before having to conduct their own meetings. It also encourages senior managers to conduct their feedback meetings so as to provide good models for their subordinate managers. At senior management levels, often the first (and sometimes only) exposure to a "feedback meeting" is attendance at a *presentation* of systemwide results given by an HR professional or consultant. Such presentations are definitely *not* appropriate models for managers to follow in conducting department-level feedback because (1) the presenter is not responsible for taking action on the results and (2) the data in these systemwide results represent only marginally, if at all, the opinions of the audience. For these reasons, such presentations of systemwide data should not substitute for the models for conducting department-level feedback that senior managers should provide for the managers in their immediate team. The model meetings should deal with the *data for each senior manager's group,* not with results for the total organization.

After the feedback meetings have cascaded down through the organization, feedback summaries and action plans should then *trickle up* from departments to appropriate higher levels. These departmental summaries and plans can help senior management clarify the companywide issues identified by the survey and any overlooked issues will become apparent. Senior management can then address these issues strategically.

Preparing for and Conducting the Feedback Meeting

Typically, employees have a strong vested interest in the subject matter of a feedback meeting. If the manager has not done his or her homework to understand the issues, is not prepared to deal constructively with them, or gives the impression of being disinterested, employees are apt to turn off the process and also turn off the manager in other important aspects of the employee-manager relationship. Managers have to realize that holding a survey feedback meeting is a high-stakes activity, part of developing their personal managerial effectiveness.

Agenda Setting

Key to holding any effective meeting is preplanning to develop an agenda. Feedback leaders need to select the meeting topics and the order in which they will be presented carefully so that their presentation stimulates an open exchange of information and problem solving. Feedback leaders should resist the temptation to blindly follow the order in which questions were asked in the survey questionnaire and should instead structure the meeting around the most relevant themes and issues for the individual department.

Meeting Flow

A topical flow for a survey feedback meeting that has been found to work in many situations is as follows:

- *Introduction.* The feedback leader's introductory remarks should set a positive tone for the session, show that he or she is interested, review the objectives and ground rules, describe how the meeting will flow, and point out that the leader will ask questions and take notes on input. Any remaining questions that employees have about the meeting should be dealt with.

• *Lead topic and strengths.* To set a positive initial tone, it is usually a good idea to start with a survey topic with results that demonstrate a genuine interest in improvement and that are likely to generate good discussion about further improvements that can be made. It should then be possible to continue with less positive survey results as the discussion proceeds. Examples of lead topics might be efforts to improve communications, enhanced physical working facilities, or recognition of good performance.

• *Topics with mixed results.* Next, the leader should present topics that received somewhat mixed answers or contradictory answers on different survey questions. Here, it is important to probe for more clarity and to lead the group in arriving at consensus about the issues.

• *High-sensitivity topics and weaknesses.* Later in the session, it is appropriate for the group to tackle any areas that show weakness. By shifting to these areas only after positive discussions of less sensitive issues, the chances of having a more productive discussion are increased.

• *Concluding topic.* It is usually wise to save a topic for last that concludes the feedback on a positive note. Examples may be areas that show some long-term confidence such as pride in the company or teamwork in the department. This topic can be used to wind down in a positive way.

• *Summary.* Finally, the feedback leader should recap the major positive, neutral, and negative themes; identify and prioritize employee input on areas needing further investigation and follow-up; and either set a time for a follow-through action-planning meeting or move directly to action planning at this time.

Experience has shown that it is often necessary to schedule a separate subsequent meeting for action planning; frequently, it is just too much to handle both feedback and action in a single session. Also, if employees have time to digest the results of the feedback session before progressing to action, they are often able to develop good constructive ideas tailored to the specific issues identified in that session. To encourage this process, it may be useful for the meeting leader to solicit volunteers from the group who will research important background information around survey-identified issues. When this information is put on the table at the subsequent session, it can serve as a catalyst for the action discussion.

While this meeting outline is one that seems to work well in most situations, feedback leaders should adjust it to the uniqueness of each group and to the particular survey results. The major point for leaders to remember is to build an open exchange through ordering the topics in a logical and constructive flow. As in any meeting, it is important to use good presentation techniques. A sloppy or lackadaisical presentation just will not be very effective in interesting employees or getting them involved actively in generating understanding or in problem solving.

Follow-Through

The last but certainly not least important step in an effective survey process is to initiate and follow through on actions to deal with any problems or concerns raised by the survey. This step is the key to closing the loop on the survey and is where many surveys founder. While questionnaire results by themselves may generate considerable management and employee interest or concern, the survey is of limited value without action to correct problems and can create cynicism if the expectations it raises are not fulfilled.

An effective survey action strategy should follow the old commonsense management maxim, "Plan your work, then work your plan." For survey action taking, that translates into, "Decide what should be done to deal with the most important issues raised by the survey, then . . . do it! Make it happen!"

To keep the action process on track, it is important that everyone recognize its dual nature. Planning is necessary but not sufficient; the real key is implementing plans to yield results. The next two sections give some concrete guidelines.

Action Planning

The purpose of action planning is to build on specific insights from the feedback meeting and to clarify which are priority issues, to generate as many ideas as possible to address these issues, to evaluate and select the best ideas, and finally, to decide on the best approach for implementing the actions and determining who should be accountable.

Scheduling Action-Planning Meetings

As a general rule, action-planning meetings should be scheduled after all feedback meetings for the department have been held. Some additional time may be required for managers or employees to obtain information that will be important in generating and evaluating action ideas. There are at least four major considerations in scheduling action-planning meetings.

- To the maximum extent possible, an action-planning group should consist of the same employees who participated in the feedback meeting. This will ensure that everyone has a similar understanding of the major survey issues and shares any action priorities already agreed upon.
- In order not to bog down, the group should plan to address only one or two major issues in each meeting. If there are a lot of topics to be dealt with, a series of action meetings should be convened over a period of several weeks.
- Normally, about one to two hours is required for each meeting, but it is advisable to leave meeting times open-ended, so that it will never be necessary to cut off a really productive session.
- The meeting room must be private, and the meeting uninterrupted.

Conducting the Meeting

First, the group needs to define the problem to be addressed clearly and accurately. The groundwork for this definition should already have been done in the feedback session. It may be appropriate to have employees report on any background assignments that they agreed to complete.

Second, since the likelihood of finding a good solution to any problem increases with the number of possible alternatives, it is important for the group to generate as many ideas as possible before selecting the most acceptable ones. Brainstorming is one technique that is effective for this part of the action planning meeting. There are several steps to successful brainstorming. Generate as many action suggestions as possible without any restrictions on the flow of ideas. Do not evaluate any of the ideas until the group's suggestions run dry, no matter how "far out" an idea may seem initially. Get contributions from everyone. Let group members present their ideas without interruption. Encourage "piggybacking," that is, elaborating on or varying previous ideas.

Since the success of the survey feedback sessions depended upon reaching group consensus on priority issues, it is also important to reach group consensus on the actions to be taken in regard to those issues. This ensures that everybody's position is heard and understood, that the group explores disagreements rather than avoiding them, and that all group members will support the action decision once it is made. Meeting leaders should make sure that everyone contributes to the discussion and should ask for people's objections and the problems that people see with the preferred solution. It is often useful for meeting leaders to write each recommended action on a flip chart, showing all its steps. Finally, to ensure consensus, meeting leaders should ask, "Does everyone accept this plan?"

Often, there will be several solutions selected to address a problem area. Problems should be prioritized, and action plans made for high-priority items first. At the same time, there are likely to be important issues raised by the survey that are outside the group's control. These may be interdepartmental issues or senior management priorities. Even though resolution of these issues is beyond the group's direct control, recommendations to address them should still be developed, if possible. However, the group should be aware that the recommendations it develops may not be adopted. However, managers can also be encouraged to put a local "spin" on selected aspects of issues that are apparently beyond the group's control. The manager's aim is to help the group recognize that the department may have to live with the general condition but, at the same time, also to demonstrate leadership in doing what can be done at the local level. Compensation programs, working conditions, career opportunities, and so forth may be controlled primarily by organizationwide factors but also be addressable in some local aspect. If middle managers perceive lower-level managers to be "passing the buck" on issues that can be at least partially addressed at lower levels, rather than being sure that the problems they refer up the line are truly issues beyond their control, they can communicate such expectations back to their subordinate managers for implementation before communicating their own action plans and list of issues for higher-level action up the line.

During the action-planning meeting, action recommendations decided upon should be recorded (by the meeting leader or an employee assigned to that task). The following information should be included:

- *Objectives.* What will be accomplished by this action plan; what problem will be solved?
- *Resources.* What will be needed to achieve the objectives (personnel, materials, equipment, and so on)?
- *Implementation Steps.* What activities need to occur before the objectives can be achieved?
- *Responsibilities.* Who will be responsible for each of the implementation steps?
- *Timetable.* When will each step be accomplished? (Be specific and realistic about deadlines.)

Implementation

In the final analysis, the real measure of the effectiveness of any survey is what changes in the organization. While often there is an expectation that all the changes resulting from a survey will be initiated by senior management and will encompass the entire organization, in fact, it is the small actions, developed and implemented at the work group and departmental levels, that often add up to a more effective organization. So managers and their teams should be held accountable for planning and taking actions at the individual departmental or work group level, rather than being expected to simply kick the problem upstairs. At the same time, management needs to make sure that managers and teams have the authority and the resources they need to deal with the issues.

Trickle-Up Strategy

An action-reporting process should typically follow the trickle-up pattern that is essentially the reverse of the cascade down flow recommended for feeding back results. As I have described, problems revealed by the survey results for each department should be evaluated during the feedback meetings and action recommendations should be formulated at those meetings or at later planning meetings. Whenever possible, the recommendations should be implemented at the departmental level. However, when higher authority is required to deal with an action recommendation, that recommendation needs to be escalated upward. A tracking system should be implemented by the overall survey coordinator to ensure that all recommendations are addressed and that actions taken (or the reasons the recommendation cannot be implemented) are communicated back to the departments where they were initiated.

There is nothing in this action-taking strategy that says that all recommendations from the feedback and planning meetings have to be accepted. But the strategy does require that

- All recommendations must be resolved—either through implementation or through an explanation why they will not be adopted.
- The resolution of each recommendation must be communicated back to the originating department and shared with employees.

Resolving action recommendations may take anywhere from a few days to a year or more, depending on the nature of the problems. The important point is that all recommendations must be dealt with conscientiously and that some form of tracking and follow-up vehicle must ensure that this is done.

Communicating Actions Taken

It is not uncommon for a survey to result in many significant change actions, each one of which is visible only to a small fraction of the employee population. Thus, when the average employee is asked, "What happened as a result of the survey?" the sad but frequent answer is, "Nothing." The deck is now stacked against a successful follow-up survey in the future.

That does not have to be! Regular "to all employees" communications about actions taken as the implementation efforts unfold over the follow-up period will build people's credibility in and enhanced commitment to the survey process. This communication program should also include recognition and rewards for particularly effective contributions to the survey's success.

Monitoring Implementation

The only way for the survey process to have any positive effect is for the people who are accountable for action implementation to follow through on the plans that have been developed. Thus, the final task in a full survey process is to monitor the implementation of action plans for each department and to ensure follow-through on any commitments that have been made.

Ironically, experience has demonstrated that an overzealous human resource function can be one of the most common reasons a survey falls short of the high expectations originally set for it. In its desire to make the survey succeed, the HR function sometimes becomes overly embedded in the action stages of the survey process. Besides commonly having technical responsibility for designing and administering the survey, processing the data, and reporting results, HR may also find itself in the role of adviser to senior management about the quality of action that should be expected from subordinate managers. At the same time, HR may also be advising these same subordinate managers on the action quality they should deliver.

Once the overzealous HR professional crosses the line, in effect approving his or her own action plans, and the incestuous nature of this process becomes understood by subordinate management, then all the precious energy flowing into the action process can readily disappear into a bureaucratic black hole. Organizations in general, and HR personnel in particular, need to be sensitive to keeping line management—not HR—personally active in and accountable for the action process.

To help ensure this result, a cardinal rule for the HR function is to make sure that *only* line management, not HR, communicates or requests information having to do with interpretation of departmental survey results, action plan structure and content, any schedule for action plan reporting, and/or any follow-up on implementation and results attained from actions taken. Senior management must understand and reinforce this appropriate role for line managers.

Conclusion

In the final analysis, the most useful survey of organizational members will likely be the one that is viewed as a line management accountability, at all levels and at all stages of the process. There will be line management input into and ownership of the decision to survey, questionnaire topics, scheduling and administration procedures, and data analysis and reporting. The HR professional's role is to recommend direction, provide technical guidance, and lend process support but not to take on the direct content and action accountability held by line management. And this is nowhere more important than in the critical back-end survey stages of employee feedback and action taking.

References

Alderfer, C. P., & Ferriss, R. (1972). Understanding the impact of survey feedback. In H. A. Hornstein & W. Burke (Eds.), *The social technology of organization development* (pp. 234–243). La Jolla, CA: University Associates.

Alper, S. W., & Klein, S. M. (1970, November-December). Feedback following opinion surveys. *Personnel Administration,* pp. 54–56.

Berrien, F. K. (1968). *General and social systems.* New Brunswick, NJ: Rutgers University Press.

Dodd, W. E., & Pesci, M. L. (1977, June). Managing morale through survey feedback. *Business Horizons,* pp. 36–45.

Dunham, R. B., & Smith, F. J. (1979). *Organizational surveys: An internal assessment of organizational health.* Glenview, IL: Scott, Foresman.

Katz, D., & Kahn, R. L. (1978). *The social psychology of organizations* (2nd ed.). New York: Wiley.

Klein, S. L., Kraut, A. I., & Wolfson, A. D. (1971). Employee reactions to attitude survey feedback: A study of the impact of structure and process. *Administrative Science Quarterly, 16,* 497–513.

Mann, F. C. (1957). Studying and creating change: A means to understanding social organization. In C. M. Arensberg, S. Barkin, W. E. Chalmers, H. L. Wilensky, J. C. Wortly, & B. D. Dennis (Eds.), *Research in industrial human relations: A critical appraisal* (pp. 146–167). New York: HarperCollins.

Miles, M. B., Hornstein, H. A., Callahan, D. M., Calder, P. H., & Schiavo, R. S. (1969). The consequences of survey feedback: Theory and evaluation. In W. G. Bennis, K. D. Benne, & R. Chin (Eds.), *The planning of change* (2nd ed., pp. 457–468). Austin, TX: Holt, Rinehart & Winston.

Nadler, D. A. (1977). *Feedback and organization development: Using data-based methods*. Reading, MA: Addison-Wesley.

Wiener, N. (1950). *The human use of human beings: Cybernetics and society.* Boston: Houghton Mifflin.

PART 3

Special Applications

In this part, we cover some special topics of great interest to people doing organizational surveys. The common theme among these topics is that such surveys are currently widespread and have a substantial variety of possible applications.

In Chapter Eleven, Raymond Johnson describes the inner workings of the Mayflower Group, so named because its first meeting was held in the Mayflower Hotel in Washington D.C. This consortium of forty-two blue-chip firms obliges its member companies to use a common set of survey questions as a means of establishing and measuring matters related to their shared norms. As we learn of the history and progress of this group over the two decades it has been in place, Johnson also tells us about the committee structure needed for this group to work effectively, provides the actual questions used in common by Mayflower Group companies, and shows us the gradual evolution to include more questions that focus on the contemporary issues of quality and customer satisfaction. His discussion includes a thoughtful list of the advantages and disadvantages of such consortia.

Many companies with well-established survey programs are multinationals that use surveys overseas. Sarah Rassenfoss Johnson provides an overview in Chapter Twelve of the fascinating world of multinational surveys, concentrating on corporate-sponsored surveys. Special considerations include translations, collecting data in many dissimilar places, comparability of results, and the impact of cultural differences on the use (and even the acceptability) of organizational survey data. Johnson takes us through the manifold practical steps of preparing and administering a multinational survey.

She notes that these projects put a premium on building a world-wide team of people who understand and can work across very different cultural settings, and she describes ways to accomplish this team building. In addition, she summarizes much of the academic literature on cross-cultural differences that bears on organizational surveys.

The impact of employee satisfaction on bottom-line outcomes is increasingly a topic of interest and research. In Chapter Thirteen, Jack Wiley reviews prior studies and presents a new model of the relationships among key variables. Called the "linkage research model," it uses a broad set of findings to support its linking of leadership practices to employee results, to customer results, to business performance, and back to leadership practices. A case study shows how these linkages occur in a real company. The data indicate that true relationships must often be teased out, by a deep understanding of the particular situation and of the characteristics of the work being done. Overall, the findings support a belief that employee satisfaction is inexorably bound to customer satisfaction and, over the long term, to financial measures of business performance.

There is reason to believe that the largest user of organizational surveys is the federal government. In Chapter Fourteen, Marilyn Gowing and Anita Lancaster discuss the manifold use of surveys in the civilian and military sectors of the government, describing a wide array of surveys used by different agencies. It is noteworthy to see how many of these surveys affect policy decisions about particular workforces. The military seems to make surprisingly active use of such data. The reader will also be struck by the many commonalties with private industry practice. Many of these similar practices are deliberate, fueled by similar training among survey professionals and informal sharing among colleagues in governmental and industry settings. The authors conclude with a look at potential future directions for organizational surveys in the federal government.

This book concludes with an examination of ethical concerns that bear on organizational surveys. Marshall Sashkin and Erich Prien draw on their personal experience to explore these issues in Chapter Fifteen. They report two broad classes of ethical transgressions: those done in ignorance or error, by "blunderers," and those done in deliberate violation of clear norms, by "bounders." Sashkin and Prien point out how these misbehaviors can take place at every stage of a survey, from initiation of a survey contract to reporting and acting on the survey results. They present examples of unethical behaviors and give us a series of principles, or "Thou shalt not's," to guide our practice. Noting that survey professionals operate in many fuzzy areas and may often be tempted to stray, these authors make us more sensitive to potential danger zones and alert us to possible missteps.

CHAPTER 11

Life in the Consortium
The Mayflower Group
Raymond H. Johnson

Participating in a consortium of organizations with similar interests in organizational surveys of employees can leverage the value of each member organization's survey system. However, before an organization decides to join or form a survey consortium, it should evaluate the pros and cons of such an arrangement.

In this chapter, I describe life in a survey consortium based on my experience with the Mayflower Group—a survey consortium of forty-two blue-chip companies that was founded in 1971. As described in its bylaws, the Mayflower Group is an organization of large private-sector companies with survey professionals who administer high-quality organizational survey programs. Its vision is to provide norms, research, and education to foster the development of innovative, high-quality, timely survey programs relevant to the business needs of group member companies.

Ninety-three percent of the member companies in the Mayflower Group are included in *Fortune* magazine's list of most admired companies in America (Jacob, 1995). Twenty-five percent rank number one in their *Fortune* industry group. Today, the Mayflower member companies are 3M, Allstate Insurance, AT&T, Bank of America, Boeing, Carrier, Chase Manhattan, Chemical Bank, Citicorp, Corning, Dow Chemical, Duke Power, DuPont, Eastman Chemical, Eastman Kodak, Eli Lilly, Equitable, Ford Motor, General Electric, General Motors, GTE, Honeywell, IBM, Johnson & Johnson, Lockheed Martin, Merrill Lynch, MetLife, Microsoft, Nationwide Insurance, Pacific Gas and Electric, Procter & Gamble,

Prudential, Rockwell International, Shell Oil, Sears, Southland, State Farm Insurance, a telecommunications consortium (principally regional Bell telephone companies), Texas Instruments, Union Pacific Railroad, Unisys, and Xerox. Each company is represented by a principal representative and an alternative representative. Currently, sixteen of these companies have active international survey programs that together cover thirty-eight countries in the Asia-Pacific region, Europe, Latin America, and North America.

My point of view in this chapter is shaped by twenty years' experience in managing organizational surveys at Ford and serving as Ford's representative to the Mayflower Group in various leadership positions. I am a practitioner who has observed the development, operation, and growth of this consortium. Accordingly, the focus of this chapter is practical: it explains how things work in a consortium, describes the value of consortium norms and opportunities for information exchange, and lists some things to watch out for when joining or forming a consortium.

History and Evolution

The Mayflower Group was the brainchild of Richard Dunnington (IBM), Frank Smith (Sears), and John Stanek (University of Chicago), who invited a group of eighteen organizations with internal survey programs to a 1971 meeting in Washington, D.C. The group met at the Mayflower Hotel, which inspired the group's name. Fifteen charter members emerged from this meeting.

The Mayflower Group elected a governing board in 1972, adopted bylaws in 1973, and incorporated in 1976. The group's original objectives were to (1) develop "core" items that all members could ask in their surveys, (2) maintain norms against which member companies could compare their organizations, (3) exchange information on survey practices and other related topics, and (4) conduct research on attitude measurement. Over the years, Mayflower pursued these objectives by focusing its efforts in four principal areas: (1) organizational growth and structure, (2) item wording and research, (3) data confidentiality and sharing, and (4) mechanisms for exchanging ideas, presenting research, and sharing experiences.

Organizational Growth and Structure

Mayflower has pursued two competing interests. The group has always been interested in the open exchange of ideas and information among its members; this suggests keeping membership small and manageable. However, another interest is improving the quality of Mayflower norms and extending benefits of Mayflower membership to as many qualified companies as possible; this suggests expanding membership. The following review of the Mayflower Group's growth and structure explains how Mayflower has balanced these competing interests over the years.

Within two years of its founding with fifteen charter members in 1971, it had grown to nineteen members. Worried about the effects of becoming too large, Mayflower adopted a limit of twenty-five members and assigned each member to one of six "industry groups." Designation of industry groups allowed the membership access to industry group norms and allowed industry group members a voice regarding which member companies they would work with most closely. By 1976, membership had reached the limit of twenty-five, where it remained stable for several years. In 1978, the membership limit was raised to thirty-six, and each of the six industry groups was limited to six members to maintain balanced representation.

By 1979, membership had grown to thirty. In addition, a number of excellent companies that did not fit existing industry groups were inquiring about membership. The Mayflower board commissioned an ad hoc committee on growth and structure, and this committee raised the membership limit to forty by allocating four membership slots to "unusually attractive" companies that might not fit existing industry groups. This provision opened the door for some excellent companies that might otherwise have been rejected because they did not fit existing industry groups or because the industry group they did fit was full. The committee also put aside further discussion of growth until data submissions from current members improved (some were late, erroneous, or out of compliance with standard item wording). The rationale was that the group could make room for new members by asking noncontributing current members to leave.

Excellent companies could be rejected for membership if they did not fit one of the six industry groups or if they were not considered unusually attractive enough to fill one of the four extra slots. Concerned about the impact of this practice, in 1985 Mayflower dropped the requirement that new member companies must fit an existing industry group. Shortly after this policy change, Boeing, Merck, Procter & Gamble, and Johnson & Johnson were welcomed into membership. Membership expanded from thirty members in 1985 to forty-two in 1995—a growth rate of 40 percent in ten years.

Mayflower now has ten industry groups: aerospace, banking, computers/office equipment, diversified manufacturing, insurance, pharmaceuticals/cosmetics, retailing, telecommunications/electronics, utilities, and miscellaneous (the latter for new members only). All member companies are assigned to one of these industry groups, based on their primary business. Member companies have a say in where they are assigned, and there is now no limit on the number of companies within each industry group.

These industry groups are less important today than they were formerly because Mayflower members may now submit data coded by "kind of business," and they have access to norms based on kind-of-business breakouts. Kind-of-business coding allows conglomerate member companies to submit data from their distinctively different businesses (for example, Ford might submit data coded as either Ford Financial Services or Ford Automotive Operations data).

Item Wording and Research

In 1972, the group developed and adopted eighteen core items covering these twelve topics: amount of work, benefits, career and job security, co-workers, communication, financial rewards, interdepartmental relationships, nature of the work itself, management, physical surroundings, supervision, and training. In addition, the group developed a number of demographic questions covering such issues as the type of company and date of survey administration and the respondent's age, level of education, exempt/nonexempt status, geographical location, income, length of service, occupation, race, sex, and union/nonunion status. Contextual items identified unusual conditions in the organization when the survey was conducted (for example, union activities, reorganizations, layoffs, mergers and acquisitions, technology changes, top management changes, and organizational development or change programs).

The number of core items remained stable at eighteen from 1971 to 1980. Then a flurry of internal research activity occurred during the 1980s and early 1990s resulting in the addition of more items, bringing the total number of core items to thirty-four. In addition, usage of the original eighteen items was evaluated to determine whether any should be deleted from the core. One item, "People at the top of this organization are aware of problems at my level of the organization," was dropped due to low usage and to difficulty in interpreting what the item results meant. The seventeen other original core items (identified in the Appendix) were retained because the membership continued to find them useful.

Before a new item can be added to the core, it must undergo a rigorous research process that includes identification of the issue to be addressed, item development, pilot testing, and statistical analyses (for example, item analysis and factor analysis). The process ends with a membership vote on whether to adopt the new item as a core item. Typically, this process requires two or three years to complete.

During the period 1984 to 1994, the seventeen new items that survived this process and were added to the core addressed such content areas as

- Recognition
- Involvement in decision making
- Change management
- Productivity conditions
- Work quality
- Work load
- Physical working conditions
- Innovation
- Pride in company
- Quality (related to the Malcolm Baldrige National Quality Award criteria)

A complete list of the thirty-four Mayflower core items and their response scales appears in the Appendix. Each member is required to submit data on more than 50 percent of these core items (eighteen or more items) to retain its membership.

Through the process described, Mayflower evaluates its core items to ensure their relevance to current business issues while it maintains stability in its item database. In addition, Mayflower uses task forces to develop groups of items on topics of interest (for example, quality, empowerment, and diversity) with the intent of developing Mayflower norms for these areas in the future.

Data Confidentiality, Quality, and Sharing

Two operating principles make it possible for the Mayflower Group to function effectively. First, survey norms are shared among members without violating the anonymity of individual organizations and the confidentiality of the Mayflower norms. Because Mayflower respects the right of individual member companies to protect their proprietary survey data, Mayflower norms are not made public. Over the years, Mayflower has taken a number of actions to protect the confidentiality and quality of the data it receives while also pursuing its goal of sharing information among members.

In 1974, Mayflower developed guidelines for data submission and produced its first Mayflower norms. A university acted as Mayflower's first data-processing vendor. Each member submitted its company survey data identified by a company code to the vendor. Only the chairperson of Mayflower knew the company names associated with the company codes. This knowledge was necessary to monitor whether members were meeting requirements to submit data at least every two years.

A few years later, Mayflower changed to a commercial data-processing vendor, and the group agreed to have the vendor generate norm reports with data displayed for individual companies but without revealing company identities.

To improve the quality of data submissions, Mayflower published a detailed manual to help members understand and execute what was expected of them in submitting data. The Norms Committee started monitoring compliance with guidelines for data submission. The Norms Committee also started auditing questionnaires to ensure that core questions were worded correctly. All deviations in item wording were prohibited.

In 1985, the Norms Committee established the 70 percent rule, meaning that each member must submit data for at least 70 percent of the core items. At the time, this meant eighteen or more of the twenty-six core items. It was in 1994, after the core had grown as described earlier, that this minimum was changed to 50 percent or more of the thirty-four core items.

To improve the usefulness of the norms, the Norms Committee developed criteria for determining whether a company's data submission was representative of that company. The committee also developed two-year roll-up norms, in addition to regular annual norms. The rationale for this move was that because member companies must submit data at least every two years and, theoretically, in any given year, the number of companies could be half the total number of members, the roll-up would have the benefit of increasing the number of member companies in the norm base.

Another innovative approach by the Norms Committee to improving the quality and relevance of the database was to establish a "flex norm" procedure. Each member company submits a brief description of the organization(s) for which it is submitting data (for example, again consider Ford, which might submit descriptions for Ford Motor Credit Company and the Ford U.S. parent company). The Norms Committee consolidates these descriptions into a menu from which each member may select the company submissions it wants included in its customized (flexible) norms report. For example, a company may request flex norms for Baldrige award winners or for specific companies that it wishes to benchmark. The Norms Committee reviews each flex norms request to ensure that the identity of individual company data is protected. These flex norms supplement the industry group and kind-of-business norms that are produced routinely.

The Mayflower Group carefully monitors its data-processing vendor for quality, cost, and performance to deadlines. When problems arise, the group works with the vendor to improve its performance. In some cases where a pattern of recurring quality problems has occurred, Mayflower has selected a new vendor that could meet the group's complex data-processing needs.

Mayflower has adopted standards of ethical conduct to prohibit disclosure of Mayflower activities and data to nonmembers. These standards are important given the openness of sharing that members desire. Of course, such standards also raise the issue of what should and should not be shared with the external world. A special committee addressed that issue in 1989 and decided not to permit external presentations of Mayflower data. Instead, Mayflower agreed to sponsor research through external resources (university faculty) that would not identify Mayflower as the source of the data. Thus, it was possible to support Mayflower's goal of promoting research on attitude measurement while protecting the confidentiality of Mayflower data.

Exchanging Ideas

The sharing of survey experiences and research has been a vital part of Mayflower since its beginning. Most members consider sharing survey experience as important as getting access to national norms. Since 1974, member discussions of surveys and related activities have been a regular part of the Mayflower meetings that are scheduled twice a year. Gradually, this exchange of ideas has taken the form of structured roundtable discussions about a variety of topics, such as survey feedback, survey data display, use of survey data with senior management, and integrating survey systems with business objectives and strategy. Roundtable discussions frequently cover general human resource matters as well. Mayflower maintains a database of roundtable discussion topics so that members have easy access to who is doing what in these areas.

Networking with other Mayflower members has also been an integral and valuable part of the consortium. Strong relationships among members have resulted in ad hoc agreements to share survey items on special topics. Some members jointly develop specialized ad hoc norms on an informal basis. For example, representatives from three manufacturing companies arranged to share one another's data on overall employee satisfaction. Many members provide answers to one another's general human resource questions (or the member representatives provide referrals to other people in their organizations who can answer specific questions).

Presentations by members and guest speakers on survey and human resource matters are a regular part of Mayflower meetings. Example presentation topics include balance between work and family, human resource legislation, structure of the human resource

function, stress, productivity, linking survey data to business outcomes, and emerging issues that may affect the workplace in the
future.

Sometimes planned but often spontaneous discussions of hot
issues affecting member organizations have occurred. Examples of
these hot topics include downsizing, benefits rollbacks, quality,
mergers and acquisitions, and sexual harassment.

Benchmarking Survey Practices

To enhance learning about surveys among member companies,
three major benchmark studies of survey practices in Mayflower
companies have been conducted. The first was published in 1985
and was entitled *Survey Practices/Applications Manual* (SPAM). This
study involved extensive data collection through surveys and interviews of members. Experienced and new members used this document to learn quickly about one another's survey programs.

In 1991 and 1995, similar benchmarking studies were conducted and published for member use. Members are expected to
participate in these studies, and 100 percent have responded.
These studies provide specific quantitative information about
member companies' survey practices. Such benchmarking studies
make networking more efficient and provide a source of quick
answers to many questions asked by senior management in member companies. Individual companies are identified in these
benchmarking studies (in contrast to the anonymity procedures in
place for Mayflower norms) because benchmarking data from individual companies are less sensitive than survey results. Also, members participate openly in the benchmarking studies because they
know such information will be kept within the group. Mayflower
intends to continue to conduct benchmarking studies of survey
practices of its membership every three or four years, depending
on how rapidly and extensively members' survey systems change.

Evolutionary Shifts

Mayflower has developed significantly as an organization since its
founding in 1971. Membership has grown in number while maintaining quality (quality companies are defined as Fortune 500 firms

that meet their commitments to submit correct and timely data to the norms base and to participate actively in the group). Barriers that prevented recruitment of quality companies that did not fit into the existing industry group structure have been removed from the bylaws. The size, quality, and relevance of norms have improved dramatically. Mechanisms for sharing information about survey practices and experiences have become sophisticated and efficient.

In addition, subtle evolutionary shifts in the Mayflower Group's functioning have occurred, which may not be apparent from what has been described. Mayflower has struggled through the four stages of group development that most effective groups experience: forming, storming, norming, and performing (Tuckman, 1965). Successful groups move through these stages in sequence, addressing such issues as (1) How do I belong to this group? How do I fit in? (2) Who is in charge? Who controls the group? (3) What norms for group behavior will help us achieve our goals? (4) How can we maintain our closeness as a functioning group and avoid becoming arrogant or insular? In the early years, a particularly painful process was the storming phase, during which it seemed that members debated every issue exhaustively in a large group instead of relying on committee structures to do the work and present recommendations for approval by the total membership. As a result, decision making was not as efficient and effective as it is today. Stronger leadership by the board of governors combined with member frustration with the situation made the difference. Today, most issues are addressed by the board of governors or the appropriate standing committee, and when necessary, recommendations from these groups are approved quickly by the membership.

Mayflower committees now seem to get more done in less time, and Mayflower continues to address issues of quality, speed, value, and teamwork in its own functioning. In this regard, Mayflower mirrors the business issues that concern each of its member companies.

Over the years, Mayflower members have become increasingly open in sharing candid information with one another—as a result of the trust that develops among members in a stable group. When there is turnover of representatives from member companies, the board of governors provides a structured orientation to the new representatives to convey the group's procedures, behavioral norms, expectations, and benefits of membership. Informal social time together at the meetings also helps assimilate new representatives into the group.

Another shift involves Mayflower's increasing flexibility in the norms reports that it generates to meet member needs (flex norms reports, kind-of-business reports, and disk-based reports). Although flexibility in reporting norms has increased over the years, variability among companies on the wording of core questions has decreased. As already mentioned, auditing of member questionnaires for strict adherence to standard wording for Mayflower questions is conducted to ensure the quality of Mayflower norms.

Establishing and Maintaining a Consortium

This section explains how a consortium like the Mayflower Group is structured and how it functions to achieve its goals. Matters such as governance, committee structure, bylaws, and procedures for norms and membership are presented to clarify how they all work together to make the consortium successful.

Governance

The Mayflower Group Board of Governors provides leadership and is responsible for managing the day-to-day business of the Mayflower Group and for planning future directions consistent with the group's vision and bylaws. The board has full power to manage the property, affairs, business, and concerns of the organization.

The board of governors consists of seven members. Three are officers (the chairperson, vice chairperson, and secretary/treasurer). The vice chairperson chairs the Membership Committee. Four members chair standing committees (the Norms, Research, International, and Program Committees). Officers and committee chairs are elected to one-year terms by the membership at the annual fall meeting.

The board meets whenever necessary, typically three times a year (at the spring and fall meetings and within a few months after the election of the new board). Standing committees usually meet prior to general membership meetings to allow time for preparation before reporting status of committee activities and recommendations to the general membership. However, standing committees are free to meet at other times as warranted by their activities.

The real work of a consortium like the Mayflower Group is accomplished through its committee structure. It is important to know something about what these committees do.

Membership Committee

The Membership Committee recruits and screens new members, companies that will advance the vision and objectives of the Mayflower Group. The committee designs and administers the application process for membership, actively recruits and encourages select companies to apply for membership, reviews all applications for consistency with membership criteria and makes recommendations to the Mayflower Group, and provides candidate companies with feedback on their application.

The Membership Committee focuses its recruitment efforts on select large organizations that have a good corporate reputation, a quality survey system, and a good reputation in human resource practices.

Norms Committee

The Norms Committee establishes and maintains guidelines and procedures that promote the accuracy, integrity, and usefulness of the Mayflower database. The committee prepares and communicates to the membership formats for data submission, develops procedures to promote the accuracy and integrity of data submission, develops and maintains data-processing specifications for the Mayflower database, supervises the data-processing vendor, develops and maintains formats for Mayflower norms, supervises production of standard and flex norm reports in accordance with Mayflower requirements, prepares any special reports as authorized and in accordance with Mayflower bylaws, ensures security of the Mayflower database and protection of individual member data, and maintains historical data files.

Research Committee

The Research Committee proposes, facilitates, conducts, coordinates, and disseminates research in the measurement, feedback, and use of employee attitude data. The committee coordinates research to avoid duplication of research efforts, encourages presentations of research studies at Mayflower meetings (based on data from Mayflower or from individual companies), evaluates research proposals that require the use of the Mayflower database, consults with Mayflower members to facilitate survey research related to Mayflower interests such as development of new survey items, contracts and works with external professionals to perform research using Mayflower data, reviews Mayflower core questions periodically, conducts research on new items, and maintains documentation of research efforts.

Program Committee

The Program Committee develops and facilitates the agenda for Mayflower meetings. The committee provides members with opportunities to share and learn new developments in survey methodology and technology, develop a network of survey and human resource professionals, share and learn how companies use surveys to achieve business objectives, and keep current on new developments in survey practice and other human resource issues. The committee provides opportunities to share problems, experiences, and solutions related to survey practice and human resource issues. It also brings in outside resources to keep member companies informed of new developments in survey practice and human resource issues. In addition, the committee evaluates the effectiveness of each meeting and solicits ideas for future meetings.

International Committee

The International Committee supports and expands international use of organizational surveys. The committee initiates and coordinates the process that results in production and distribution of international norm reports. It maintains a library of Mayflower item translations and distributes translations to member companies on request. The International Committee encourages and supports formation of consortium groups similar to Mayflower in other countries.

Special Committees

In addition to the regular standing committees, the chairperson sometimes appoints ad hoc committees for special purposes. One example is the special task force appointed to develop a quality index related to the Baldrige award criteria. Similar task forces have been formed to develop measurement scales for empowerment and diversity.

All Mayflower members are encouraged to participate in at least one committee because committees accomplish much of the work of the Mayflower Group. The opportunity to participate on committees is available at the general membership meetings conducted twice a year.

Bylaws

As in any organization, rules exist within the Mayflower Group to ensure that quality standards are maintained. Mayflower's rules are contained in its bylaws. These bylaws are intended to be changed as necessary to support progress toward the Mayflower vision and to address emerging issues facing Mayflower and its members. The bylaws may be amended by a majority of members attending any properly called meeting. Because the Mayflower Group is incorporated as a nonprofit corporation in Delaware, the bylaws have been given careful legal review—a process recommended for any such consortium.

Mayflower bylaws address such matters as maximum size of the organization (now set at forty-five members), qualifications of members and conditions of membership, ethical standards of members, dues, number and kinds of meetings, governance and organizational structure, location of the group's books, and procedures for amending the bylaws.

What is expected of Mayflower members is explicit or implied in various sections of the bylaws. Members are expected to contribute to the health and effectiveness of the Mayflower Group by (1) conducting surveys using more than 50 percent of the thirty-four core items and submitting data on these items at least every two years and in compliance with norms procedures; (2) ensuring that the principal representative attends at least one Mayflower meeting per year; (3) participating actively in Mayflower committees; (4) paying annual membership dues (currently $1,000); (5) protecting Mayflower norms; and (6) conducting themselves in an ethical manner regarding the use of survey data, norms, publications, and other information shared among Mayflower member companies.

Norms Procedures

The Norms Committee provides each member company with a detailed procedure for submitting survey data to the Mayflower database. To ensure that deadlines are not missed, a calendar of key events much like the following is provided:

By January 31	Members submit international data (collected outside the U.S.) to the data-processing vendor.
By January 31	Members pay annual dues ($1,000).
By January 31	Vendor distributes U.S. norms reports.
March	Vendor distributes international norms reports.
April	Mayflower conducts spring meeting.
October	Mayflower conducts fall meeting (business meeting at which the new board is elected).
By November 1	Members submit requests for flex norms to the Norms Committee chairperson.
By November 1	Members submit current year's questionnaires to the Norms Committee chairperson for audit.
By November 30	Members submit U.S. data to processing vendor. Vendor performs validity checks on data to detect coding errors.
December or January	Board meets.

Membership Procedures

The ability of the Mayflower Group to meet its goals depends on the quality and commitment of its members. Mayflower uses a well-defined process for selecting new members, described below:

Step 1	Company completes and submits an application.
Step 2	The Membership Committee and board of governors evaluate the application based on established criteria for membership (quality of survey program, corporate reputation, and human resource function reputation).

Step 3   The Membership Committee invites a company representative for an interview (only if a company meets general membership criteria).

Step 4   The Membership Committee makes a recommendation to voting representatives (one vote per member company).

Step 5   Voting representatives review the application and listen to a presentation by a company representative.

Step 6   Voting representatives vote on the recommendation. Membership is approved if fewer than three members cast dissenting votes.

After passing step 6, the newly accepted company becomes a "conditional" member for two years. At the completion of the two years, if a conditional member company has met all membership requirements, it becomes a full member.

These six steps describe the process by which companies become members of Mayflower. In addition, the membership votes to accept or reject principal and alternate representatives from member companies. This is important because it allows existing members the opportunity to accept or reject individual representatives based on how they would fit in and contribute to the goals of the group. Rarely are new representatives rejected. As mentioned, for orientation, new representatives are invited to a breakfast meeting with the board of governors, at which the board discusses how Mayflower functions and mutual expectations.

If a member company fails to meet its obligations to Mayflower, it is placed on probation, and it may go through a recertification process. Typically, recertification is required of companies that have been on probation twice in five years or that have never gotten off probation once placed on it. The company is asked to make a presentation to the membership explaining why its membership should continue. The membership votes. If three or more oppose continued membership, the company is asked to leave the group. Rarely does noncompliance get to this stage. But the threat of the recertification process actually helps member companies maintain membership requirements by pointing out to their managements the consequence of noncompliance.

Most companies that leave the Mayflower Group do so because

organizational support for their survey programs has declined and they are no longer able to meet Mayflower membership requirements to submit data at least every two years. Typically, the company resigns with regret before being asked to leave through the recertification process.

Effective Use of Consortium Norms

One of the benefits of a consortium like the Mayflower Group is the availability of good norms against which a company can compare its survey results. Bracken (1992) identified a number of relevant criteria for evaluating the quality of a normative database. Does the database require that all contributing companies use the same wording and response scales without deviation? Are there strict rules for standardized item wording and response scales? How are company data represented in the database (by number of observations or by the preferred method of equal weighting by company)? Are data available by well-defined industry groups? How old are the data (data more than two years old may have limited usefulness)? Does the database provide information on the companies included? Is it possible to customize norms to meet a company's specific needs?

Mayflower norms meet these criteria, as Bracken acknowledges: "Membership requirements for Mayflower are stringent, but the Group takes great care to address many of the typical concerns about creating a high-quality data base" (1992, p. 53).

Bracken (1992) also suggests, however, that even quality norms may serve as distractions, giving a company's management a false sense of security when company results are the same as or better than the norm. There may be some truth to this, depending on the level of management involved. Many members of the Mayflower Group supply Mayflower norms only to their senior executives, not to lower levels of management, for good reasons. First, executive management needs good external norms because of its members' broader, external perspective, and indeed, one of the most common questions asked by senior executives is, "How do we compare with other major companies?" Executives who are responsible for the company, or large parts of it, want and need to know how their organization compares with other companies in the environment.

Second, lower-level management does not need external norms in order to benchmark performance. For these managers and supervisors, internal comparisons are available in the form of aggregations of larger groups above them in the company. In some cases, up to four or five such internal comparisons may be provided to assist interpretation. Adding yet another comparison, such as a Mayflower norm, only muddies the waters with information unneeded at this level.

How are Mayflower norms used by senior executives? This varies by organization. For example, one organization uses Mayflower norms for strategic goal setting; it has a stretch goal to be the best among Mayflower companies on overall employee satisfaction within ten years. This company moved 30 percent of the way toward its goal in two years. Another organization uses quartiles based on the Mayflower norms; its goal is to be among the top 25 percent in the Mayflower companies.

While many Mayflower organizations use the annual norms, based on all submissions to the database in a given year, others find it helpful to use the flex norms described above, the reports based on a subset of Mayflower companies (for example, all insurance companies, all manufacturing organizations regardless of industry type, or selected companies considered to be especially excellent). Procedures for Mayflower norms make it possible to create flex norms from a menu of data submissions while maintaining the confidentiality of individual company data.

Member companies with international operations like to compare their country norms against others' country norms and to view regional roll-ups of data for countries in Europe, the Asia-Pacific region, and Latin America. With the trend toward globalization, interest in these international norms is increasing—judging from the number and quality of international data submissions to the database.

Benefits of a Survey Consortium

The Mayflower Group provides a number of clear benefits to member companies. Among them are (1) annual availability of low-cost, high-quality national and international norms; (2) flexible norms to meet members' unique needs for comparative data; (3) access to benchmarking studies of survey practices in Mayflower member companies; (4) access to research on the development of valid and reliable survey questions measuring relevant business issues (for example, validation of Mayflower questions against business performance measures); (5) opportunities to establish a personal network of relationships with survey professionals in other companies; (6) opportunities twice a year to meet and learn about new survey developments; (7) opportunities to participate in forums on survey-related subjects; (8) opportunities to discuss other nonsurvey topics (for example, human resource issues, computer applications, or emerging issues); (9) access to a database of roundtable discussion topics that identify the activities in which member companies are engaged; and (10) internal leverage from being associated with companies recognized by *Fortune* magazine as among the most admired major companies in America.

Costs and Risks of a Survey Consortium

As with all good things, there are costs and risks associated with forming or joining such a consortium. Existing company survey systems may have to be modified to accommodate the requirements of the consortium. For example, Mayflower requires that members use exact item wording and response scales for its core questions. These may be different from the questions and response scales a member company has been using. Some of an individual company's questions and trend data may have to be scrapped to avoid redundancy with consortium items.

Another risk is that consortium questions may not change quickly enough to meet the evolving needs of member companies. Member companies may be required to use questions no longer of interest simply to maintain membership in the consortium.

An investment of time and money is required to attend consortium meetings and participate in the work of committees. The Mayflower Group is successful because of the active participation of its members in the work of the consortium. A risk is that some company representatives may not be able to commit enough time to consortium activities.

One further risk applies to forming a consortium. In its early days, especially during the storming phase, dysfunctional or ineffective meetings may be frustrating. Progress may be slow and time in short supply.

Alternatives to Joining a Consortium

Joining an existing consortium or forming a new one are not the only alternatives for companies wishing to access survey norms. For many organizations, neither of these approaches may be feasible. So what other alternatives can a company pursue?

One alternative is to purchase advice and normative data from consulting firms. A number of consulting firms provide these survey services. If you choose this path, consider asking the following questions before selecting a consulting firm, to ensure that your organization's needs will be met: What specific companies are included in the database (for each year and survey question)? You will need the answer to this question to understand what you are comparing against in the norm. Also, if a large company is mentioned, ask whether data from the entire company (versus a small division or office within the company) are included. Some consulting firms may be doing business in major companies and others in smaller companies and the industry concentrations may vary substantially. Ask about the stability of the norm base, that is, what companies have come and gone, for what reasons, and at what rate?

How much does it cost to access the consulting firm's norms? Are you obligated to contribute your organization's survey data to the consultant's database? Who owns the copyright to the survey questions for which consultant norms are available? Clarifying ownership and use of survey items is important because your company may decide later to disengage from the consultant but may want to continue using the norm questions.

Ask what quality control procedures are in place to prevent errors in reporting survey norms? Ask what scientific research has been conducted on the norm questions to provide evidence that the questions are reliable and valid? Ask what companies the consultant has worked for long term (five years or more) and identify references at these companies whom you can talk with regarding their level of satisfaction with the consultant's norms. Examine the items for which the consultant's norms are available. Evaluate whether these norms address the current issues in your organization. Ask whether the consulting firm has a network of clients that share ideas with one another. Most reputable consulting firms will welcome these questions because an educated consumer will appreciate the quality of their offerings and will be more likely to use their norms and services effectively.

Conclusion

In its third decade, the Mayflower Group continues to address issues and challenges to ensure the group's vitality and usefulness in the future. How can Mayflower stay current or ahead of member needs? What is the appropriate size of the group? How can Mayflower best help other survey consortia form? (Examples of consortia for whom Mayflower has played a mentoring role include a telecommunications consortium, described by Morris and Lo Verde, 1993, and the Australian Employee Survey Group.) How should Mayflower globalize and develop partnerships with other international survey groups like the Australian Employee Survey Group? How can meaningful research be conducted on the Mayflower database without breaching the confidentiality of member companies? How should Mayflower assist small companies who cannot join Mayflower? How can the content and process of meetings be improved to add value?

As a survey consortium, the Mayflower Group has met a corporate need during its first twenty-four years. It has grown and developed over the years and continues to attract and retain some of the nation's finest companies as members. Mayflower's ongoing challenge is to improve continuously its flexibility and its processes for adding value for its members in a rapidly changing and global environment.

Appendix: Mayflower Core Questions and Response Formats

Underscored words indicate permissible wording variations. An abbreviated response scale appears in parentheses after each question and a key to the scale abbreviations follows the list of core questions. Questions 1 through 17 are the seventeen original core questions still in use.

Core Questions

1. Overall, how good a job do you feel is being done by your immediate <u>manager/supervisor</u>? (VG/VP)
2. I like the kind of work I do. (SA/SD)
3. Considering everything, how satisfied are you with your job? (VS/VD)
4. My job makes good use of my skills and abilities. (SA/SD)
5. The people I work with cooperate to get the work done. (SA/SD)
6. How do you rate the amount of pay you get on your job? (VG/VP)
7. In comparison with people in similar jobs in other companies, I feel my pay is: (MH/ML)
8. How do you rate your total benefits program? (VG/VP)
9. How do you rate <u>the/this/your company (Company Name</u>) in providing job security for people like yourself? (VG/VP)
10. How satisfied are you with your opportunity to get a better job <u>in/at the/this/your company (Company Name</u>)? (VS/VD)
11. How satisfied are you with the information you receive from management on what's going on <u>in/at the/this/your company (Company Name</u>)? (VS/VD)
12. I have enough information to do my job well. (SA/SD)
13. Sufficient effort is made to get the opinions and thinking of people who work here. (SA/SD)
14. How satisfied are you with the training you received for your present job? (VS/VD)
15. I am given a real opportunity to improve my skills <u>in/at the/this/my company (Company Name</u>). (SA/SD)
16. Considering everything, how would you rate your overall satisfaction <u>in/at the/this/your company (Company Name</u>) at the present time? (VS/VD)
17. My work gives me a feeling of personal accomplishment. (SA/SD)
18. How satisfied are you with the recognition you receive for doing a good job? (VS/VD)
19. How satisfied are you with your involvement in decisions that affect your work? (VS/VD)

20. The/this/your company (Company Name) is making the changes necessary to compete effectively. (SA/SD)
21. Conditions in my job allow me to be about as productive as I could be. (SA/SD)
22. How would you rate the overall quality of work done in your work group? (VG/VP)
23. The amount of work I am expected to do on my job is: (FM/FL)
24. How satisfied are you with your physical working conditions? (VS/VD)
25. I feel encouraged to come up with new and better ways of doing things. (SA/SD)
26. How would you rate the/this/your company (Company Name) as a company to work for compared to other companies? (OB/OW)
27. [SENIOR MANAGEMENT (fill in your definition; you must have a definition either in the question or somewhere in the questionnaire)] shows by its actions that quality is a top priority in the/this/your company (Company Name). (SA/SD)
28. When choices have to be made, my (THE PERSON TO WHOM THE RESPONDENT REPORTS) usually places quality above other business objectives (production schedules, budget, etc.). (SA/SD)
29. My (SMALLEST WORK GROUP) has the resources (personnel, finances, etc.) necessary to do quality work. (SA/SD)
30. There is close cooperation among (SMALLEST WORK GROUPS) to achieve quality. (SA/SD)
31. I have the authority to make decisions that improve the quality of my work. (SA/SD)
32. I have received the training I need to do a quality job. (SA/SD)
33. The quality of (products AND/OR services) I provide my customers is an important part of how my performance is viewed. (SA/SD)
34. My (SMALLEST WORK GROUP) uses feedback from our internal customers [people inside the/this/our company (Company Name) who use our work OR products AND/OR services] to improve the quality of (our work OR products AND/OR services). (SA/SD)

Mayflower Response Scales

FM/FL
1. Far too much
2. Too much
3. About right
4. Too little
5. Far too little

MH/ML
1. Much higher
2. Higher
3. About the same
4. Slightly lower
5. Much lower

OB/OW
1. One of the best
2. Above average
3. Average
4. Below average
5. One of the worst

SA/SD
1. Strongly agree
2. Agree
3. Neither agree nor disagree
4. Disagree
5. Strongly disagree

VG/VP
1. Very good
2. Good
3. Fair
4. Poor
5. Very poor

VS/VD

1. Very satisfied
2. Satisfied
3. Neither satisfied nor dissatisfied
4. Dissatisfied
5. Very dissatisfied

References

Bracken, D. W. (1992). Benchmarking employee attitudes. *Training and Development Journal, 46*(6), 49–53.

Jacob, R. (1995, March 6). Corporate reputations. *Fortune,* pp. 54–94.

Morris, G. W., & Lo Verde, M. A. (1993). Consortium surveys. In P. Rosenfeld, J. E. Edwards, & M. D. Thomas (Eds.), *Improving organizational surveys: New directions, methods, and applications* (pp. 122–142). Newbury Park, CA: Sage.

Tuckman, B. W. (1965). Developmental sequence in small groups. *Psychological Bulletin, 63,* 384–399.

CHAPTER 12

The Multinational Opinion Survey

Sarah Rassenfoss Johnson

Multinational surveying is more than simply translating the home country survey into multiple languages and collecting the results. The multinational survey process must take into account the values, cultures, and issues of each of the countries involved.

Multinational surveying requires many of the same skills, and uses many of the same techniques described in the other chapters of this book. However, it also requires some unique skills and steps, such as cross-national team building and understanding of and sensitivity to cultural differences and issues.

In this chapter, I provide a brief background on the reasons for multinational surveying and the extent to which such surveys have expanded around the world. In discussing the practical considerations in administering such surveys, I cover only those issues unique to multinational surveys.

Value of the Multinational Survey

The value of the multinational survey is, for many companies, quite simply this: they operate in a global marketplace, designing, creating, and selling their products and services in many countries around the world. Half or more of their employees and revenue reside outside their home countries. A global or multinational approach to surveys is entirely consistent with the way in which these companies operate.

The proliferation of multinational corporations is astounding. Nearly 5 million Americans, or 5 percent of the business workforce, are employed by the affiliates of foreign firms in the United States. U.S. firms in turn employ over 6.5 million people in other countries around the world. In Mexico, more than half a million people work for affiliates of U.S. companies. By the end of the nineties, it has been estimated that one out of every six workers in the United Kingdom will be working for a Japanese company (Shenkar, 1995, p. 2). Given this level of global expansion, it would almost be surprising if a multinational company that surveys its employees did not conduct those surveys multinationally.

The primary value of organizational opinion surveys is for management to understand the similarity and diversity of opinions and perspectives that employees have about the company and the work they do. The multinational organizational opinion survey is really no different in concept than a multinational company's seeking out information about its customers in all the countries in which its products and services are sold.

Using Surveys Around the World

There is no concise history or timeline that describes the growth of survey use around the world. In my conversations with colleagues in multinational corporations, I have found that for many companies, expanding the opinion survey outside the home country occurred simultaneously with the initial survey in the home country or very soon thereafter.

In all, I have found three typical patterns in the spread of surveys in multinational companies. In the first, initial surveys were conducted in the home country and were then quickly followed by surveys in the other countries. This approach tends to be the most common and is a good way to work out survey details and gain some experience before tackling the greater complexities of surveying multinationally.

Other companies have jumped into multinational surveys from the start, including their worldwide employee population in the inaugural company survey. This second approach carries some risks to companies that are new to surveys but may work in a company that has a strong global focus, is expanding rapidly outside the home country, and implements other company initiatives in this fashion.

In the third pattern, surveys crop up independently of one another in various countries. These surveys may have little in common with each other since they are usually created to meet each country's special needs. It is very likely that expatriate managers with an interest in surveys have taken that interest with them as they have moved to new countries and that they have initiated a number of these independent surveys. Companies that typically allow operations outside the home country to function autonomously often allow these independent survey operations to continue without imposing controls. At other companies, there is an effort to standardize survey programs for greater corporate efficiency. In the latter cases, the home country headquarters will try to consolidate these homegrown processes into a common strategy and framework, while still allowing for country customization.

There is no single best approach for expanding surveys multinationally. The best approach for a company depends on its culture, its view of the multinational workforce, and the way in which it governs its operations.

Practical Considerations

In some respects, the multinational survey is no different from the domestic survey: the intent and purpose are the same, the issues addressed are often similar, and in many respects, the administration is the same. There are, however, complexities in administration and subtleties in interpretation that are unique.

Two General Approaches

Multinational surveys are typically conducted via one of two general processes. In the first, the *corporate-sponsored survey,* staff at corporate headquarters lead the development and administration of the survey, which uses a common methodology to survey all employees in all countries. These surveys may be either sample- or census-based, and countries may be surveyed either simultaneously or sequentially. In this model, the corporation or headquarters "owns" the process, while sharing planning, administration, and results with the countries.

In the second model, the *country-sponsored survey,* the countries or geographical regions are given flexibility to conduct their own surveys on their own timetables. Very often, the corporation provides guidelines or principles for survey administration (covering, for example, survey frequency, reporting guidelines, and core items). In this model, the countries "own" the process, and the corporation relies on the country to provide the survey data and insights into the findings to the corporation.

A company may choose to use either or both of these methods. For example, it may elect to run a multinational sample-based survey periodically to address issues of corporate interest, while the countries conduct their own surveys to address issues of local interest. Moreover, these two methods can be seen as the anchors at either end of a continuum that runs from total corporate control to total country control. Numerous variations along the continuum alter the roles of corporate headquarters and country staff. Corporate headquarters may administer a survey whose content is largely based on input from the countries, who then use the data in the manner they feel is best. Or countries may conduct their own surveys following a common format provided by corporate headquarters but allowing for significant local variation.

These two models clearly have implications for the type and amount of work that needs to be done by headquarters and country staffs. In the following sections, the unique administrative aspects of each model are briefly discussed, but greatest attention is paid to the corporate-sponsored survey, as this model is distinct in more ways from the common approaches to U.S. domestic surveys. Many of the specific issues discussed are applicable to most multinational surveys.

Administering a Country-Sponsored Survey

In essence, a country-sponsored survey is a domestic survey. As such, it follows the guidelines outlined in other chapters of this book, and all or most of the survey details are handled by local country staff. The keys to success, naturally, include the sponsorship and commitment of local management and the skill and experience of the local survey administrator. A skilled local administrator will be familiar with pertinent laws and language needs, can develop meaningful survey items, and will be able to establish the required vendor support within the country.

At the corporate headquarters level, it is important to establish and maintain a network of survey professionals across the countries, not only to assist in corporate learning about survey results around the world but also to be a support structure for those who conduct the surveys. The survey professionals in the resulting network can keep each other up to date on survey techniques, key issues, and surveying schedules.

Administering a Corporate-Sponsored Survey

Administering a multinational corporate-sponsored survey is an exercise in getting work done through others. Because the survey will be administered in multiple settings and in multiple languages throughout the world, the corporate coordinator will need to rely on the support of contacts in each country who will facilitate the process. A multinational team of advisers and administrators is essential. It is best to have one coordinator in each country in which the survey is to be administered. This establishes a local contact who is familiar with the language, laws, and customs.

The Global Survey Team
Creation of a global survey team should be the first task accomplished after deciding to conduct a corporate-sponsored multinational survey. Ideally, the members of the team from the different countries will have had some survey experience. This should not necessarily be a requirement, though, as many aspects of team members' duties and responsibilities may be learned via training. It is far more important that the leader of the team, the corporate coordinator, have significant knowledge of survey processes, which may be acquired through extensive experience with surveys or through academic training in a field such as industrial and organizational psychology. The corporate coordinator may also access the necessary survey experience by working with a survey consultant.

The team members should be thoroughly familiar with their

local organization, particularly its business structure and critical issues. They should have a good rapport with the local management team, and they should be viewed as credible and respected professionals. Team members must be well organized from an administrative standpoint, able to work effectively in a team environment, and interested in employee-company issues.

Communication with this team should begin early. Frequent crisp communications from the corporate coordinator to the team members can build team spirit and commitment to the project. Electronic mail (e-mail) is invaluable for such communications, although telephone conference calls and faxes can also be effective. Team members should clearly understand the purpose of the survey, and the expectations the company has of them must be explicit. Written summaries of meeting or conference call minutes and documentation of critical decisions, next steps, and dates (sent via fax or e-mail) can clarify expectations if they send consistent messages to all team members. Team members' commitment to the project is essential, since they not only assist in getting work done but also can promote the survey to senior managers and employees in their various countries. Because team members are operating at a great physical distance, the corporate coordinator must have complete trust in their ability to accomplish their tasks.

If at all possible, a face-to-face kickoff meeting with all global team members provides an excellent opportunity to build interest in the survey project and develop the network. The meeting allows the global team members to take part in the early planning stages and to make contributions to the content of the survey, administration dates, and many other administrative issues. Meeting personally helps build working relationships and personal accountability.

Sensitivity to a variety of national cultures and ways of doing business is needed not only in developing a survey instrument but also in creating and managing the global survey team. Working effectively across cultures is much more than simply applying the skills found to be most effective within the culture of one's own country. It also requires that the corporate coordinator and each team member can understand and cope with a variety of processes for communication and decision making (Smith, 1992). While a given survey may be viewed as multinational because many countries participate, if controlled too closely by the home country, it may reflect the values inherent in that country's culture, and these values may not be applicable outside that country.

For example, some team members (especially those from Latin countries) may not share the same sense of urgency in completing tasks as the coordinator; they may be more focused on building rapport and relationships (Kets de Vries, 1994). During group discussions, team members from Asian countries may not voice an opposing position to the group as a whole but will approach the coordinator and share their views after the discussion is over. Very often the language in which the business of the survey is discussed is not the first language for all the team members. This may make some of them hesitant to speak up in the group, or they may occasionally misunderstand what has been discussed or decided. A good coordinator must be aware of these differences, and ensure that each team member has had an opportunity to provide input in either a team or individual setting and that all decisions and directives are clearly understood.

It may be beneficial to have two levels of global team members: those at the country level and those at the regional level. A region might be a continental area (such as Latin America, Europe, or Asia) or a group of small countries within a specified geographical area (such as the Caribbean or Middle East). The regional team members, or coordinators, can relay communications to individual countries and also represent the countries' concerns to the global coordinator. They may also be in a better position than the corporate coordinator to deal with some geographically specific issues as they are familiar with local organizational structure, practices, and personnel. Significant issues, those that can have an impact at the parent company level, should still be handled by the corporate coordinator.

Training Global Team Members

The global team must, of course, be familiar with survey techniques, data analysis and interpretation, feedback, and action planning. The team members will serve as the front line of support in their own countries for developing many of these same skills in local employees, managers, and executives. The better people understand these issues, the more effectively the countries will be able to use the survey data.

Training the global team is, in essence, training the trainers. The necessary skills can be built in the global team in a variety of ways. The easiest way, of course, is to build a team from survey professionals, people who have been involved with surveys for a period of time and understand all that needs to be accomplished. This certainly is an effective method but may not be feasible if the company is new to surveys. Even for a team of experienced professionals, training is still needed to brief them on the specific processes used in the present survey.

An alternative method is to convene the global survey team in a central location for several days of training. This training should address the purpose and objective of the survey program, then review administration processes, the reading of reports, data analysis, holding feedback meetings, and creating action plans. Meeting planners should allow time during the meeting for social activities, such as dinners or lunches out, that build rapport among team members and create a team feeling.

If it is impractical to have all members of the global team travel to one location, the corporate coordinator can travel to them, or the regional team members can hold training sessions for the team members within their area.

Creating a Survey Schedule

All team members should provide input to the survey schedule. They are in the best position to estimate how long translations will take, note upcoming local holidays, decide whether local reviews of the survey are needed, and determine whether a suggested time frame is inappropriate because it coincides with local high work load periods. When team members have the opportunity to craft the schedule themselves, they will be more inclined to view it as reasonable and to do what they can to execute the survey within the defined time frame.

The time required to conduct a multinational survey varies by company. A good rule of thumb is to add about eight weeks to the time required to conduct a domestic survey. The extra time is required to develop the global survey team, translate survey instructions and items, and ship the materials overseas, among other tasks. Of course, the base time may be lengthened or shortened depending on the time required for internal survey reviews and vendor time to print the surveys, capture the data, and produce the reports (assuming the survey is done via paper and pencil).

Developing the Survey Instrument

It is not uncommon for a corporate-sponsored survey to focus on issues of corporate importance, irrespective of the countries represented. Such a list of corporate issues is a good starting point for survey development, and it is highly useful to collect global team members' input on the local interpretation of these corporate issues as well as their input on issues that are currently important in their country or region. Team members may derive this input from prior surveys, personal impressions, and/or from focus groups or interviews with local employees and managers.

Certainly, corporate issues may drive content, but survey developers must be careful not to focus content too closely on organizational behaviors or management theories that pertain to a single organizational culture. There is a growing body of evidence that suggests narrow cultural concepts do not transfer well to other cultures (Hofstede, 1980; Hoppe, 1993; Pennings, 1993; Randall, 1993; Riordan & Vandenberg, 1994). Here, the global team can serve as a filter of sorts. Team members can review the survey items and determine how the concepts that they represent may be interpreted in team members' countries. They can suggest whether an issue is important or not and even suggest how employees in their countries might respond to the item.

Developing the original survey items in English (or in any other language, for that matter) is fine, but be sure to write items in plain English, avoiding culturally based idioms. Keep concepts as simple as possible. Both of these recommendations will help survey developers create items that cross cultures conceptually and that can be effectively translated.

Depending on the survey strategy employed, there may be an opportunity for each country or region to add its own items to the base survey. When this opportunity exists, team members should provide copies of the extra items to the coordinator so that he or she can make sure the item is not redundant and is not contrary to the purpose of the survey. The ability to add local items offers countries a chance to get additional insights on their unique issues and may increase their willingness to participate.

The survey should include at least one opportunity for employees to add a written comment, even though written comments create a great deal of work in addition to offering valuable insights. Comments will need to be translated, either verbatim or in a summary format. Answers to demographic items, such as tenure, gender, and job function questions, can also add insights on the remaining data. However, some demographic terms commonly used in the United States have no meaning elsewhere. For example, the demographic categories of exempt and nonexempt employees refer to U.S. labor law and are not used elsewhere. Members of the global team should work with their local managements to determine if any local laws prohibit the use of certain demographic items.

Translating Survey Materials

Accurate translations of survey items are an absolutely essential component of multinational surveys. And more than just the survey instrument must be translated; translations of announcements or invitation letters, instructions, reminder notes, and in most cases, survey reports and feedback training materials will also be required.

Translation is a time-consuming and sometimes tedious task. Translators must do more than find equivalent words in their own language, for in many cases equivalents do not exist. Hofstede (1980), for example, states that in French there is no exact equivalent for the English word *achievement*. And in Japanese, there is no succinct expression for the English term *decision making*. Translators, therefore, must clearly understand the concept being conveyed in the question, even to the point of understanding how question results are to be used.

It is preferable to have the translations coordinated and checked by company employees in each country. These individuals are most familiar with company issues and the phrases and terms commonly used within the language of the company. In the event that an employee cannot be the translator, the next best option is to hire an outside professional and have the resulting translation carefully reviewed and edited by a local employee. The members of the global team will be invaluable in identifying translators and in checking the translation once it has been completed.

Some companies have found value in back-translation: once the survey is translated from the original language to another language, a second translator translates the survey back to the original language. This process enables survey developers to determine if the conceptual basis of the survey items is still intact after translation. The process of back-translation clearly adds time and money to the translation process; consequently, many companies are comfortable with a single translation done by a local employee familiar with the concepts covered in the survey.

A translation should be done for each country. While this may seem redundant, survey developers should keep in mind that European Spanish is not the same as Latin American Spanish nor is Canadian French the same as European French. Lack of local translations will cause employee confusion and misunderstanding of survey items. An inappropriate translation may even be viewed as an insult to a country's employees, because the company did not attend to their unique language usage. Multiple language options may be required in some countries. French and Flemish are both spoken in Belgium. Canadian law requires that surveys must be offered in both English and French.

Identifying Legal Concerns

While surveying employees is legal in the vast majority of countries, it is advisable to have the global team member in each country consult with his or her industrial relations adviser to determine restrictions or limitations. In many cases, all that need be done is to review the intent of the survey and the content of the instrument with representatives from the local unions or works councils. Companies that survey in organized labor environments may choose not to include certain survey items, such as those dealing with compensation, that may influence contract negotiations. The global team member can take the lead in accomplishing any necessary reviews. However, companies should keep in mind that unions or works councils may ask for a substantial period of time to complete their review and that the survey schedule should contain ample time for this contingency.

Selecting a Survey Vendor

Unless a company is self-sufficient when it comes to survey administration and processing, it will need to engage a survey consultant or vendor to handle some or all parts of the survey. While using local company vendors may make sense when countries are responsible for running their own surveys, the corporate-sponsored survey usually calls for a single central vendor. This vendor will be required to complete some difficult and complex tasks, not the least of which is printing survey materials in a multitude of languages. When reviewing vendors, companies should be sure they are capable of printing in multiple languages and have done so for other clients.

An alternative is to ask the global team to identify local printers, who can more easily create the materials in the local language. This alternative has some advantages, but its disadvantages include the difficulty of creating materials with a standardized look and of keeping multiple vendors in multiple locations to the same schedule.

Prior to going to press, materials should be reviewed by the appropriate members of the global team for typographical errors and other mistakes. After all, unless he or she is fluent in all the required languages, the corporate coordinator will not know whether there are zero or twenty mistakes in the materials.

Shipping Materials

An efficient way to distribute materials internationally is to bulk ship them to each member of the global team. Team members can then ensure that the materials are sent through the correct internal mail channels or that they receive correct postage for the country's mail system (which can be very difficult to calculate from overseas). The global team members can also arrange facilities for group administration, if that is appropriate. Once surveys have been completed, they can either be mailed directly back to a single central collection point or sent to the global team member for collection and bulk shipping back to the coordinating country.

The former alternative for returning completed surveys may produce greater feelings of anonymity on the part of respondents, since the corporate coordinator is much more likely than their global team member to be truly unknown to them. However, the disadvantages to this method include the difficulties of securing correct postage and the time the surveys might spend in transit. If the survey is being conducted electronically, it is most advantageous to ship materials from and send materials to the coordinating country directly.

Data Analysis and Interpretation

Regardless of whether the survey is census- or sample-based, data analysis and interpretation is a key step in putting the results of the survey to maximum use. From a technical perspective, analysis of data from many nations is really no different from the analysis of local survey data; the same statistical procedures may be used and the same assumptions hold. What does vary significantly is the way the results of the analysis are interpreted.

A good deal of research suggests that a country's culture can have a profound impact on such issues as people's interpretations of organizational events, people's preferences for a certain management style, and even whether certain organizational structures are likely to function successfully. Culture, therefore, will also influence people's responses to survey items that assess these issues. The basic theoretical framework in the area of international differences was developed by Geert Hofstede (1980), whose research is the most widely known and cited.

The Influence of Culture

Based on surveys of employees in a single organization around the world, Hofstede (1980) was able to identify four dimensions on which countries could be characterized: power distance, uncertainty avoidance, individualism, and masculinity. These dimensions describe such aspects of culture as a national population's response to inequality in power among its members (power distance), the way individuals in a country deal with dilemmas and unpredictable situations (uncertainty avoidance), the degree to which a country's citizens define themselves by the group or organization to which they belong (individualism and its corollary, collectivism), and the degree to which national populations differ in distinguishing roles and expectations for men and women (masculinity and its obverse, femininity).

Hofstede argued that since each country has a unique profile along these dimensions, any management theories or models created in that country carry with them "cultural baggage." This baggage influences the applicability of those theories across cultures with different profiles.

The results of Hofstede's initial study have proven to be quite durable and have been replicated in a variety of studies since (Hoppe, 1993; Huo & Randall, 1991; Randall, 1993). Subsequent research has provided additional support for Hofstede's argument that we cannot easily transfer organizational theories, or even work-related measures, across cultures. Riordan and Vandenberg (1994) administered the Organizational Based Self Esteem instrument and the Satisfaction with My Supervisor scale to a sample of Americans and Koreans. They found evidence to suggest that the Korean respondents used a different conceptual frame of reference when responding to the items. In this case, while each country's survey data may still be of value within that country, the different frames of reference people used in their responses make comparisons of the results across the two countries problematic and any conclusions drawn flawed.

Cultural differences can have a profound influence on preferences for organizational structure and functioning. Randazzo (1994) reports results for selected survey questions asked of Asian and European managers. While 90 percent of the European managers agreed with the statement, "In order to have efficient work relationships, it is often necessary to bypass the hierarchical line," only 47 percent of Asian managers agreed. In contrast, 53 percent of Asian managers felt, "It is important for a manager to have at hand precise answers to most of the questions that his subordinates may raise about their work," but only 10 percent of European managers agreed.

In a review of cross-cultural research on human resource issues, Hansen and Brooks (1994) discuss differences in motivation across cultures. While employees from the United States and India find similar rewards in work satisfaction, non-work-related activities, and work climate, the Americans were motivated by the job itself, and the Indians were motivated by a sense of self-esteem.

An article by Boyacilliger and Adler (1991) suggests that in collectivist cultures, organizational commitment is derived from ties with the managers, owners, and co-workers, whereas the commitment of employees in individualistic cultures (such as that found in the United States) may be due to the job itself or the compensation provided. As an illustration of this, Satow and Wang (1994) report that in China and Japan, managers felt higher confidence and made quicker decisions when the whole work group shared the responsibility and the decisions were based on consensus. In Japan, employee identification with the immediate work group of peers and manager is intense, and the collective commitment of the workforce and the importance of small groups is encouraged by Japanese companies.

As if taking country cultures into account does not provide enough complexity to data interpretation, those interpreting survey data must also be mindful of subcultures within a larger culture. Huo and Randall (1991) administered Hofstede's Value Survey Module in four Chinese-populated areas, Taiwan, Beijing, Hong Kong, and Wuhan and found strong subcultural differences between the areas. In some ways, the subcultural differences within China were stronger than those between China and other countries. Huo and Randall hypothesize that these differences are the products of long histories of political turmoil in some regions of China, and the varying degree of influence of political ideology in each region.

It has been argued that as businesses and economies become more global and barriers between countries are dismantled, there will be a convergence of national cultural differences and a multicultural culture will evolve (Webber, 1969). This argument has been made particularly for Europe, where the breaking down of barriers limiting the movement of workers, products, and services is creating a single European market. However, cultural differences in management style remain, and no general European style has yet emerged (Myers, Kakabadse, McMahon, & Spony, 1995). Hansen and Brooks (1994) reviewed numerous cross-cultural studies in human resources and also found no evidence of a global business culture that could cancel out the influence of country cultures.

Within-Country Analyses

So what does all this cultural research imply for analyzing multinational survey data? What it suggests is that country results are influenced to a great extent by culture. The influence may be so great as to make cross-country comparisons misleading and of limited value. Additionally, combining the results of many countries in a region into a composite will create a number that represents the average of that region. Combining the results of all countries in which the company has a presence will represent the average for the total company. While these numbers may provide useful profiles of average opinion around the world, an average, by definition, suppresses the unique qualities and subtleties in each country's results. A great deal of rich information will be lost.

Comparisons

The most useful comparisons to make are within-country comparisons. These may take the form of local company comparisons over time or within-country norming. The latter refers to comparing the local company's results to those of similar companies in that country. Norms for most countries are available through the relevant survey consultants or can be obtained through membership in survey consortia. Consortia have been created in Europe, Australia and New Zealand, and in the United States. Some of these consortia are able to provide not only data for the country in which they originate, but international norms for the other countries in which member companies do business.

Within-country norms are benchmarks for assessing the relative strength or weakness of a company's results. Tracking a company's results over time can show where there has been improvement or erosion in results. Analysis over time can also establish the typical pattern of results, identifying those issues or items that are usually highly rated and those that usually receive lower ratings. Such patterns discriminate between issues needing immediate attention and issues that are less urgent.

There is value in understanding the differences between countries. This information may guide organizational structure in a country, determine how and from whom information is communicated, and target effective motivators. Country management often finds it interesting to learn how the country compares with others, even if these comparisons are done on a blind, or anonymous, basis. However, it should be made clear to management that significant cultural and economic differences between countries may account for the differences in results.

Ownership

The issue of who "owns" survey data can be complex and is affected by a multinational company's degree of centralization or decentralization, the extent to which information is shared on a regular basis, and of course, organizational politics. Data can be owned on a number of levels. The most productive form of ownership occurs when the part of the organization that can have the greatest influence over an issue raised in the survey also has ownership of the related data. In some companies, countries may be seen as the owners of data on salary and benefits, as country management establishes the details of these programs within country laws. The corporate organization may be the most effective owner of data on more global issues, such as communication of company direction and strategy.

Although corporate headquarters is conducting the survey and thus could be seen as the overall owner of all the data, data can be well put to use when country results are shared with country management. Local managers can provide their own interpretations and implement local actions to address any issues that have arisen. The global team member for each country can work closely with country management to advise it on data interpretation and potential actions. The global team member can also serve as an information conduit to the corporate coordinator to keep him or her informed of actions being put into place.

Using Multinational Survey Data

Effective use of the data is what will make a survey program a success in any country. Data may be used most effectively when there is good advance planning, clear and user-friendly materials, and thorough training. Employee feedback meetings and action planning are critical components of any survey that is administered to most or all employees. When so many employees are involved in the survey, there is naturally interest not only in learning the overall outcome but also in learning how one's own group responded.

Of course, all reports, feedback materials, and feedback training materials must be translated into the local languages. Much of this work can be done during survey planning and administration.

Once the shell of the reports—instructions, column headings, and the like—has been translated, it is relatively simple to drop in the data.

However, it is a mistake to assume that this is enough and that those who receive a data report will know what to do with it. Even those who have been through a number of surveys will need a refresher periodically.

Feedback training is most effective after a report is in the hands of the manager or whomever has been designated as the receiver of the report. That way, the training can focus on how to read the report and can even delve a bit into interpreting the manager's own group data with the assistance of the trainer. For maximum understanding, feedback training should be conducted in the local language, preferably by one of the global team members.

While feedback in general is a critical component of any survey, the form that survey feedback and action planning takes needs to be slightly different in different countries. While employees in the United States or Canada may feel perfectly comfortable discussing or even debating survey results and identifying problems that need to be addressed, employees in Asian countries may find a meeting that focuses on publicly critiquing the company, management, and the team distressing and uncomfortable. Employees in all of these countries will be interested in learning of the results of the survey and making suggestions for improvement, but the way in which they receive feedback and make suggestions will need to vary by culture if the process is to be effective.

Alternatives to the feedback meeting include circulating a written report of the results to each employee in the group and requesting each employee to provide feedback and suggestions for action either in a one-on-one session with the manager or even anonymously in writing. In some cultures where employees typically have a limited decision-making role, it may even be appropriate for action planning to be the exclusive domain of managers. These alternative approaches may be effective, for example, in many Asian cultures, where the relationship between employees and managers is more formal than it is in the United States.

Due to these necessary variations, corporate direction for feedback and action planning should specify the principles rather than the required steps for the process. The global team member for each country is in the best position to advise on the most appropriate format for survey feedback and action planning in that country.

When a survey is administered to only a small sample of employees, feedback and action planning generally take place at a high level in the company. Therefore, extensive training on conducting feedback sessions is generally not necessary.

Conclusion

There are great challenges and also great benefits to multinational surveying. The results of a multinational opinion survey can provide a global perspective on employee views as well as pinpoint differences between countries and geographical regions. This global employee perspective complements the global data available on a company's operations, revenues, and success in the marketplace.

The keys to success in multinational surveying are careful planning, awareness of and sensitivity to cultural differences in all stages of the project, and an effective team of survey facilitators representing all countries and/or regions to be surveyed. The process will take time to hone, so that it is efficient and productive. It is important to learn from both successes and failures, continually training the members of the global team and updating the survey process to reflect changes in the company and the new issues that arise over time.

References

Boyacilliger, N., & Adler, N. (1991). The parochial dinosaur: Organizational science in a global context. *Academy of Management Review, 16,* 262–290.

Hansen, C. D., & Brooks, A. K. (1994). A review of cross-cultural research on human resource development. *Human Resource Development Quarterly, 5*(1), 55–74.

Hofstede, G. (1980). *Culture's consequences: International differences in work-related values.* Newbury Park, CA: Sage.

Hoppe, M. H. (1993). The effects of national culture on the theory and practice of managing R&D professionals abroad. *R&D Management, 23,* 313–325.

Huo, Y. P., & Randall, D. M. (1991). Exploring subcultural differences in Hofstede's Value Survey: The case of the Chinese. *Asia Pacific Journal of Management, 8,* 159–173.

Kets de Vries, M.F.R. (1994, May). Toppling the cultural Tower of Babel. *Chief Executive,* pp. 68–71.

Myers, A., Kakabadse, A., McMahon, T., & Spony, G. (1995). Top management styles in Europe: Implications for business and cross-national teams. *European Business Journal, 7,* 17–27.

Pennings, J. M. (1993). Executive reward systems: A cross-national comparison. *Journal of Management Studies, 30,* 261–280.

Randall, D. M. (1993). Cross-cultural research on organizational commitment: A review and application of Hofstede's Value Survey Module. *Journal of Business Research, 26,* 91–110.

Randazzo, R. (1994, October). *Creating a global mindset.* Paper presented at the Conference Board Human Resources Conference, New York.

Riordan, C. M., & Vandenberg, R. J. (1994). A central question in cross-cultural research: Do employees of different cultures interpret work-related measures in an equivalent manner? *Journal of Management, 20,* 643–671.

Satow, T., & Wang, Z. M. (1994). Cultural and organizational factors in human resource management in China and Japan: A cross-cultural and socioeconomic perspective. *Journal of Managerial Psychology, 9*(4), 3–11.

Shenkar, O. (1995). *Global perspectives on human resource management.* Upper Saddle River, NJ: Prentice Hall.

Smith, P. B. (1992). Organizational behaviour and national cultures. *British Journal of Management, 3,* 39–51.

Webber, R. A. (1969, May-June). Convergence or divergence. *Columbia Journal of World Business,* pp. 75–83.

CHAPTER 13

Linking Survey Results to Customer Satisfaction and Business Performance

Jack W. Wiley

Of all the recent developments surrounding the use of employee surveys, perhaps none is more exciting than the advent of linkage research. Linkage research involves integrating and correlating data collected from employees with data in other key organizational databases. The purpose of linkage research is to identify those elements of the work environment—as described by employees—that correlate, or *link*, to critically important organizational outcomes such as customer satisfaction and business performance. Obviously, the stronger the linkage between employee survey results and other key measures of organizational effectiveness, the greater the value of employee survey efforts. (Note that I refer in this chapter to *employee surveys* specifically to distinguish them from other types of organizational surveys, such as surveys of customer satisfaction.)

I have several purposes in this chapter. The first is to review the literature that examines the linkage between employee satisfaction, customer satisfaction, and business performance. (Note that in this context, I use the phrase *employee satisfaction* as a generic label for the types of measures typically included in an employee opinion

---

Note: I am indebted to my colleagues Scott Brooks, Emily Hause, and Stephanie Kendall for their helpful contributions to the writing of this chapter.

survey.) Second, I introduce the Linkage Research Model. This model is the first to summarize linkages previously reported and to begin to identify variables that moderate or mediate the inter-relationships between employee and customer satisfaction and business performance. Third, I more fully explain and validate the Linkage Research Model through the use of an illustrative study. Fourth, I highlight ways that an awareness of linkage research findings can strengthen the practice of survey research in organizational settings. And finally, I discuss methodological considerations in conducting linkage research.

Review of Past Research

This section reviews qualitative and quantitative research into the relationship between employee satisfaction on the one hand and customer satisfaction and business performance on the other.

Qualitative Research

Many practitioners, relying primarily upon their own observations, have written about the connection between satisfied employees and satisfied customers. For example, reviewing the in-depth profiles of 101 service companies, Zemke (1989) concludes that in many organizations known for exemplary customer service, employees are indeed more satisfied because they are treated with the same respect with which they are expected to treat their customers. In reviewing Xerox's efforts to pursue the Malcolm Baldrige National Quality Award, Tompkins (1992) outlines that company's quest to improve customer satisfaction, a quest directly linked to internal efforts aimed at measuring and improving employee satisfaction. Describing and evaluating key human resource practices of a major hotel chain, Weaver (1994) concludes that "what we've learned is that the only way to put the customer first is by putting the employee first" (p. 112). Weaver notes that the results of employee empowerment, training, and input programs are higher employee retention, higher productivity, and lower hiring costs.

One of the most thoroughly detailed descriptions of case studies supporting the connection between employee satisfaction, customer satisfaction, and business performance is that provided by

Heskett, Jones, Loveman, Sasser, and Schlesinger (1994). Analyzing data from a variety of different service industries, these authors examined such variables as internal management practices, employee satisfaction and loyalty, productivity, value, customer satisfaction and loyalty, growth, and profit. This analysis resulted in a finding they refer to as the "service-profit chain," made up of these sequential links: internal service quality practices lead to employee satisfaction, which leads to employee loyalty and productivity, which leads to externally perceived service value, which leads to customer satisfaction and loyalty and ultimately to sales growth and profit. The authors describe an audit process that an organization can undertake to enhance its effectiveness, and techniques for measuring and correlating employee and customer satisfaction and business performance are key to this process.

Quantitative Research

While the articles referenced above address a belief that many intuitively hold—that customer satisfaction and business performance are positively linked to employee satisfaction—large-scale quantitative research supporting this belief was nonexistent until the work published by Benjamin Schneider and his colleagues (some of which is described later). In part, this may be a result of the practical difficulties associated with implementing the required research design.

Most linkage research studies employ a similar research design. Typically, employee and customer survey data are gathered as part of strategic human resource and marketing research efforts, and business performance measures are obtained from existing archival databases. In order to correlate these databases—a requirement for conducting linkage research—organizations must be able to aggregate these measures to an appropriate and common business unit level. For example, survey data gathered from individual employees (or customers) might be aggregated at the retail store level.

In practice, the exact level of aggregation may vary depending on the nature of other measures obtained. If customer satisfaction results exist only at the district level (and not the individual retail store level), in order to link that data statistically to business performance data, it becomes necessary to also aggregate the business performance data to the district level. Sample size will thus equal the number of organizational units for which common data are available. The studies summarized below have implemented this type of design.

Conducting research in a branch bank setting, Schneider, Parkington, and Buxton (1980) reported a positive and statistically significant relationship between how favorably customers viewed interactions with bank employees and how favorably bank employees described certain aspects of their work setting. More specifically, when employees felt that a strong customer service imperative existed, customers were more likely to see employees as courteous and friendly. Schneider and Bowen (1985) replicated and extended these findings, showing that when employees describe certain human resource practices (for example, work and career facilitation) in more positive terms, customers report higher service quality. Schneider and Bowen also reported a relationship between turnover intention and customer service, that is, employees were less inclined to leave when customers reported high service quality.

Approximately ten years after the original research by Schneider and his colleagues, Walt Tornow and I were able to replicate their findings by demonstrating that employee and customer satisfaction linkages existed in two additional work settings: district offices of a business services company and a chain of retail stores (Tornow & Wiley, 1991; Wiley, 1991). We also extended the research design to incorporate another set of outcome measures: unit business performance.

The research conducted in the business services district office setting (Tornow & Wiley, 1991) indicated a positive relationship existed not only between employee and customer satisfaction measures but also between these measures and key measures of district office business performance (for example, contract retention). In other words, those district offices achieving better business performance also had more highly satisfied customers and employees. However, the retail store chain research (Wiley, 1991) indicated that while employee and customer satisfaction were positively correlated, unit business performance, measured by net income, was not related to employee satisfaction and, in fact, was negatively correlated with many measures of customer satisfaction. The conclusion was that, for this particular work setting, those store managers who emphasized achieving the highest levels of store business performance apparently did so at the expense of higher customer satisfaction ratings.

Other researchers have also examined the interrelationships between employee and customer satisfaction and performance. Three such studies focused specifically on the employee-customer link and, in all three cases, produced findings corroborating the previous research. Working in the branch system of a major banking organization, Jones (1991) replicated the previous work of Schneider and his colleagues by finding positive and significant relationships between branch employees' descriptions of their working environment and the satisfaction levels of branch customers. Upon reviewing some of the more detailed findings of his study, Jones concluded, as Schneider had previously, that "good management and sound human resource practices are associated with both satisfied employees and satisfied customers" (p. 41).

Ashworth, Higgs, Schneider, Shepherd, and Carr (1995) conducted their research in the field setting of a large insurance company. Aggregating data at a regional level, they found significant and positive correlations between an employee-based customer satisfaction index (that is, a measure of employees' opinions of the emphasis placed on customer service and key human resource practices), overall customer satisfaction ratings, and customers' intention to renew their insurance policies. Particularly intriguing about this research was the fact that data were collected in each of four successive quarters. This allowed for a time-lagged correlational analysis, which suggested that changes in managerial practices and the work environment preceded changes in customer perceptions and intentions.

Finally, in another study conducted in a branch bank setting, Johnson (1995) also reported significant and positive relationships between employee perceptions of service practices and customer perceptions of quality practices. More specifically, this research established a positive link between employee service orientation, certain management practices (for example, training employees in delivering quality service), and customer ratings of both overall satisfaction and satisfaction with specific facets of service delivery (for example, problem solving).

Additional linkage research studies have also incorporated measures of performance. Working in a school setting, Ostroff (1992) reported many positive relationships between employee (teacher) satisfaction, performance (student achievement test scores), and customer (student) satisfaction. Her work also includes a very impressive discussion of the distinction between the individual versus the organizational level of analysis in examining the satisfaction-performance relationship. In the large branch system of an automotive credit company, Johnson, Ryan, and Schmit (1994) found a variety of employee survey measures (for example, workload and stress, and training and development) to be positively and significantly associated with customer satisfaction and negatively and significantly correlated with employee turnover. In addition, their research also showed certain employee survey measures (for example, job and company satisfaction, work group and teamwork) to be significantly and positively associated with such key business performance measures as lower loan delinquency, higher market share, and higher business volume. Angle and Perry (1981), focusing on organizations offering bus services, found employees' stated commitment to the organization to be associated with organizational adaptability and lower employee turnover and tardiness rates but not with measures of organizational efficiency (such as operating costs).

Linkage Research Model

In reviewing the general business literature, the various studies that my colleagues and I have performed, and particularly the research that has examined the components of employee satisfaction associated with customer satisfaction, and ultimately, business performance, I have drawn the following conclusions:

- Employee and customer satisfaction are strongly and positively linked.
- A leadership value system, easily observed by employees and emphasizing customer service and product quality, is fundamental to this linkage.
- Specific practices that the organization and its managers derive from this value system include providing employees with the support, resources, and training required to perform

their jobs effectively, involving them in decisions that affect their work, and empowering them to do what is necessary to meet customer objectives and expectations.

- Employee retention is positively related to customers' satisfaction with the quality of service they receive.
- Quality and customer satisfaction have long-term positive relationships with customer retention, market share, and profitability.
- Certain practices that increase short-term sales and profits may do so at the expense of employee and customer satisfaction.
- Investment in practices that support quality and employee and customer satisfaction is a long-term business strategy, not a quick-fix solution.
- As the leadership value system, over time, continues to be regarded as the foundation for achieving higher customer satisfaction and stronger business performance, it becomes self-reinforcing.

The linkages just described are summarized in Figure 13.1, which shows the Linkage Research Model. The model is derived from past research that has established the existence of various linkages between employee and customer satisfaction and business performance. The model ties the research findings together in a way intended to be more comprehensive than the results of any single study. This new model suggests that the more certain leadership values and practices are present in a given work environment, the more energized and productive the workforce. In turn, the more energized and productive the workforce, the greater the satisfaction of customers and the stronger the long-term business performance of the organization.

Special note should be given to the moderating affect of work characteristics and the mediating influence of time. Our research, as well as the research of others, shows that the relationship between employee and customer satisfaction and business performance can be moderated by certain characteristics of the work setting. Such characteristics include closeness of customer contact (Brown & Mitchell, 1993), job volume or work with a transaction orientation (Lundby, Dobbins, & Kidder, 1995), and size of the organization (Paradise-Tornow, 1991). Research also suggests that

Figure 13.1. Linkage Research Model.

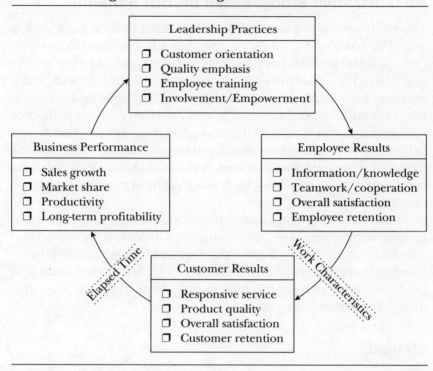

managers emphasizing customer results can negatively impact business performance, particularly short-term profitability. Conversely, managerial emphasis can be placed on short-term profitability (for example, via cost cutting) in a way that detracts from achieving more satisfied customers. Thus, as noted by Heskett, Jones, Loveman, Sasser, and Schlesinger (1994), it is over the longer perspective that a focus on customer results is beneficial to business performance.

What follows is a description of an illustrative study in which my colleagues and I have been involved. It examines employee satisfaction, customer satisfaction, and business performance linkages and supports the Linkage Research Model. After presenting and discussing this study, I highlight the implications of the model for conducting employee surveys.

An Illustrative Study: Retail Branch Banking

The study setting is a large Midwestern retail branch banking system. The bank's leadership was interested in conducting a census (that is, a 100 percent sample) survey of employees in all of its 133 branches. The objectives of the survey were to (1) provide management with a greater understanding of employee opinions, values, expectations, and needs; (2) apply survey results to influence management decision making and planning and to identify priorities for change; (3) compare opinions of bank employees to financial services industry norms; and (4) provide a baseline measurement against which to track progress in organizational development activities.

The leadership team knew that a branch-level customer satisfaction survey would also be completed at about the same time (the fourth quarter of the calendar year) and were extremely interested in integrating the two databases. The leadership team also made available certain key measures of branch business performance for this linkage research.

Method

We collected data through two surveys and from existing business performance information.

Employee Survey

The design of the employee survey was guided by the Linkage Research Model and by other information needs of the bank's management team. Thus, the content of the resulting survey included most of the variables contained in the Linkage Research Model but did not achieve total overlap. In its final form, the survey contained seventy-nine scaled items, which, based on factor analysis and internal consistency analysis, reliably measured opinion on the following fifteen topics, or *themes:* leadership, customer orientation, quality emphasis, employee training, involvement/empowerment, communication, confidence (in the bank), recognition, immediate manager, work/family (balance between these interests), diversity, pay and benefits, career development, job satisfaction, and company satisfaction. Across the system of 133 branches, 2,422 employees completed the survey, a response rate of 80 percent. For the most part, employees completed the survey on company time and in group settings.

Customer Survey

The customer survey contained seventy scaled items, which, based on factor analysis and internal consistency analysis, reliably measured opinion on the following eight themes: bank statements, problem resolution, automated teller machine (ATM), teller, personal banker, physical branch, perceived value, and overall satisfaction. The paper-and-pencil survey was mailed to customers' homes, and 15,455 customers replied, for a response rate of 34 percent, higher than the industry average of approximately 30 percent for surveys distributed through the mail (Bursek & Remenschneider, 1995).

Business Performance

After considerable discussion with bank executives and internal subject matter experts, we decided to focus on two key measures of business or operational performance: (1) teller transactions/full-time equivalent, a measure of the volume of transactions handled by tellers in relation to the number of full-time equivalent teller staff; and (2) productivity ratio, computed as the amount of branch bank revenue generated for every dollar of personnel expense. The business performance measures used were based on year-end data. We believed this approach would provide the most reliable assessment of business performance.

Results

The results show some powerful linkages between employee satisfaction and customer satisfaction and employee satisfaction and business performance, but they also contain some surprises.

Employee Satisfaction Linkages: Theme-Level

The means and standard deviations of the employee survey themes, customer survey themes, and the two business performance measures are presented in Table 13.1.

Table 13.1. Linking Employee Satisfaction to Customer Satisfaction and Business Performance.

Employee Survey (M/SD)	Customer Survey (M/SD)								Business Performance (M/SD)	
	Statements (4.12/.30)	Problem resolution (3.14/.36)	ATM (3.87/.22)	Teller (4.09/.27)	Personal banker (3.93/.30)	Physical branch (4.04/.27)	Perceived value (3.40/.23)	Overall satisfaction (3.92/.30)	Teller transactions (4001.93/632.12)	Productivity ratio (291.95/50.86)
Leadership (3.11/.30)	.25	.17	.21				.16	.16		
Customer orientation (2.80/.36)	.44	.35	.47	.24	.26	.24	.24	.35		.19
Quality emphasis (3.52/.29)	.17								.17	
Employee training (3.36/.23)	.25	.18	.25	.17	.19	.23	.19	.25	.22	
Involvement/ empowerment (3.60/.27)		.15							.28	
Communication (3.28/.27)	.42	.37	.40	.23	.26	.27	.28	.33		.19
Confidence (3.65/.34)	.55	.45	.53	.35	.35	.31	.39	.45		.21
Recognition (3.12/.38)									.16	
Immediate manager (3.65/.36)									.16	
Work/family (3.22/.29)	.21	.17	.27			.18	.15	.17		
Diversity (3.72/.26)	-.22	-.16	-.19	-.24	-.28	-.22	-.21	-.24	.25	
Pay & benefits (3.18/.26)										
Career development (2.02/.05)										
Job satisfaction (3.83/.25)	.22	.16	.16	.18	.19	.15	.28	.20	.15	
Company satisfaction (3.33/.34)	.39	.32	.37	.19	.18	.16	.25	.28	.19	.17

Note: The customer survey and employee survey databases were constructed so that the highest score (5) applied to the most favorable result. Means were computed on the basis of branch averages. Correlation coefficients are presented only when they achieve statistical significance. Correlations $\geq .14$ are significant at $p \leq .05$; correlations $\geq .19$ are significant at $p \leq .01$.

Correlations between the employee and customer survey themes show a generally strong positive relationship to exist between employee and customer satisfaction. Of the 120 possible correlations, 61 are positive and statistically significant. The pattern of positive correlations to customer satisfaction is strongest for the employee survey themes of customer orientation, communication, and confidence. Employee survey themes that achieve more moderately positive correlations are employee training, job satisfaction, and company satisfaction. Notably absent as predictors of customer satisfaction are the themes of recognition, immediate manager, pay and benefits, and career development. Finally, a surprising and bothersome pattern of negative correlations with customer satisfaction resulted for the employee survey theme of diversity (see the discussion below).

Correlations between the employee survey themes and business performance measures are positive, though on average, more moderate in strength than the employee survey–customer survey link. In addition, the pattern of correlations differs notably for the two business performance measures. On the one hand, the productivity ratio—a broad-based measure of total branch productivity—is most strongly correlated to those same employee survey themes most strongly correlated to customer satisfaction. On the other hand, the measure of teller transactions is most strongly correlated to the employee survey themes of involvement/empowerment, diversity, and employee training as well as immediate manager and recognition. That significant correlations would exist between teller transactions and such themes is quite understandable. First of all, tellers represent a large percentage of the employee population of any particular branch. Secondly, it stands to reason that as a group they would be more productive in circumstances where they felt better trained, more involved in decision making, and more properly recognized for their efforts and where they enjoyed more positive relations with their immediate manager.

As mentioned above, a surprising finding was the pattern of negative correlations between the employee survey theme of diversity and the customer survey themes. Bank executives and human resource professionals were particularly concerned about this, given the organization's emphasis on supporting and reinforcing practices associated with recruiting and retaining a more diverse workforce. This concern led to important secondary analyses, the results of which are presented in Table 13.2.

Table 13.2. Linking Diversity and Customer Satisfaction.

Customer Survey	Nondiverse Branches ($n = 31$)[a]	Diverse Branches ($n = 30$)[b]
Statements	−.62	.20
Problem Resolution	−.42	.04
ATM	−.53	.15
Teller	−.57	.12
Personal Banker	−.66	.16
Branch	−.49	.12
Value	−.59	.22
Overall Satisfaction	−.63	.15

[a]All correlation coefficients are significant at $p \leq .01$.
[b]No correlation coefficients are significant at $p \leq .05$.

The employee survey theme of diversity is not, of course, a measure of employees' actual racial or ethnic diversity. Rather, it is a measure of the extent to which employees perceive the organization and its managers as accepting, supporting, and developing employees of diverse backgrounds. We asked the bank for the number and percentage of minority employees at each branch. Using this data, we created two roughly equal-sized subgroups: (1) nondiverse branches, those with a minority population of 6.5 percent or less ($n = 31$ branches) and (2) diverse branches, those with a minority population of 22 percent or more ($n = 30$ branches).

The results (Table 13.2) clearly indicate that in nondiverse branches, the employee survey theme of diversity is significantly and negatively correlated to all customer survey themes. However, in the diverse branches, the theme of diversity is positively, though not significantly, related to all customer survey themes. From these results it would appear that the original pattern of negative correlations is, in fact, artifactual. The negative relationship between diversity and the customer survey themes is influenced by the fact that a majority of the diverse branches are concentrated in one specific geographical region where customer satisfaction in general is lower. Also, employees in nondiverse branches are not likely to report high organizational acceptance and support for employees of diverse backgrounds, which may in part be due to the relative absence of diverse employees at those branches.

Interestingly, in the nondiverse branches, other patterns of negative correlations were found between employee and customer survey themes. More specifically, the nondiverse branches achieving higher customer satisfaction ratings were generally also ones where employees had greater dissatisfaction with pay and benefits, recognition, and their immediate manager. This could result from employees' expecting greater reward and recognition for their exceptional performance (that is, for achieving higher customer satisfaction ratings) and holding their immediate manager responsible when such was not forthcoming. The same pattern of correlations did not hold true for employees in diverse branches.

Employee Satisfaction Linkages: Item-Level

In general, while theme-level correlations can be very revealing, in-depth analysis at the individual survey item level can add pertinent details that further illustrate theme-level dynamics. Table 13.3 displays the employee survey items most highly correlated to the customer survey theme of overall satisfaction and to the two business performance measures. This more detailed analysis shows that the higher-rated branches are those where employees

- Have greater confidence in the ability of senior management and greater confidence that the bank will reach its goals
- Have a clearer understanding of bank goals and objectives and have the necessary training and information to perform their jobs well
- See the branch as more focused on and successful in delivering high-quality service to its customers
- Experience a greater sense of involvement in decision making and more authority to do what is necessary in serving the customer
- Have a greater sense of pride in the bank and its products and services

Customer Satisfaction–Business Performance Linkage

The correlations for the final linkage—customer satisfaction and business performance—are presented in Table 13.4. Considering the results for all branches ($n = 133$), the conclusion seems simple,

Table 13.3. Employee Survey Correlates of Customer Satisfaction and Business Performance.

Employee Survey Theme	Item	Customer Survey Overall Satisfaction	Business Performance Teller Transactions	Productivity Ratio
Customer orientation	Overall, how satisfied are customers with the quality of service they receive?	.47		.19
	The bank is doing a good job of providing service to its customers.	.37		.19
Employee training	I have the training I need to perform my current job effectively.	.22	.23	
	The bank has the right training programs to help me improve the skills I need for my job.	.15	.26	
Involvement/ empowerment	Employees are encouraged to participate in making decisions which affect their work.		.32	
	I have the authority I need to do what is necessary to serve my customers.		.25	.16

Communication	Senior management gives employees a clear picture of the direction in which the company is heading.	.40		.20
	How satisfied are you with the information you receive about what's going on in the company?	.30		.18
	Other departments in the bank keep us informed about things that affect us.		.31	
Confidence	I have confidence in the bank's ability to reach our goal of being a top-performance organization.	.45		.19
	I have confidence in the future of the bank.	.36		.18
	I'm proud to tell people I work for the bank.	.34		.24
	Senior management has the ability to deal with the challenges we face.	.50		.18

Note: Correlations ≥ .14 are significant at $p \leq .05$; correlations ≥ .19 are significant at $p \leq .01$.

Table 13.4. Linking Customer Satisfaction and Business Performance.

Customer Survey	All Branches (n = 133)		Metro Branches (n = 87)		Nonmetro Branches (n = 46)	
	Teller Transactions $M = 4001.93$ $SD = 632.12$	Productivity Ratio $M = 291.95$ $SD = 50.86$	Teller Transactions $M = 4221.74$ $SD = 511.78$	Productivity Ratio $M = 299.95$ $SD = 49.76$	Teller Transactions $M = 3586.22$ $SD = 633.62$	Productivity Ratio $M = 276.83$ $SD = 49.97$
Personal banker	-.40	-.18			-.37	
Teller	-.37	-.22			-.40	
ATM	-.16		.25	.25	-.38	
Statements	-.24				-.25	
Problem resolution	-.23			.20	-.32	
Physical branch	-.34	-.20			-.38	
Perceived value	-.38	-.15			-.35	
Overall satisfaction	-.31				-.39	

Note: Correlations presented are significant at $p \leq .05$.

namely, that customer satisfaction and business performance are, for the most part, negatively and significantly related.

The idea that branches with higher customer satisfaction tended also to be the branches achieving poorer business performance was quite problematic for bank executives, especially those responsible for branch operations. The question they posed was whether or not this pattern of findings would describe both metro branches (those located in greater metropolitan areas, $n = 87$) as well as nonmetropolitan branches (those located in smaller towns and rural settings, $n = 46$). The analysis produced in answer to that question, shown in columns two and three of Table 13.4, reveals that the overall negative pattern of correlations between customer satisfaction and business performance holds only for nonmetro branches and only for the business performance measure of teller transactions. In metro branches, business performance is significantly and positively related to customer satisfaction with ATMs (both performance measures) and problem resolution (the productivity ratio only).

Previous analyses had determined that customer satisfaction was higher in the smaller, nonmetro branches. Discussions with internal subject matter experts suggested it was likely that, relatively speaking, those branches were less busy and less pressured and therefore could more readily provide a higher level of personalized service. These same conditions, however, would naturally result in less production per unit of time. This hypothesis is supported by a comparison of the means of the business performance measures for the two types of branches. Especially relevant is the comparison for teller transactions, showing tellers in metro branches ($M = 4221.74$) to be notably busier than their counterparts in nonmetro branches ($M = 3586.22$).

While branch location clearly moderates the customer satisfaction–business performance link, it does not consistently moderate the linkages between employee satisfaction and customer satisfaction or employee satisfaction and business performance. There are, however, a few exceptions. In nonmetro branches, for example, the employee survey theme of career development is negatively and significantly related to all customer survey themes. In metro branches, almost the opposite holds true: career development is positively and significantly related to five of eight customer survey themes. A probable explanation is that employees in nonmetro branches, who are further removed from bank headquarters, view their career development opportunities as more limited than those of their metropolitan counterparts. Frustration with career development opportunities appears heightened for employees in those nonmetro branches that achieve higher customer satisfaction ratings.

Similarly, in metro branches, both measures of business performance are consistently linked—in a significant and positive way—to various employee survey themes. The same pattern does not hold true in nonmetro branches, where significant relationships are largely absent. As mentioned previously, the business performance measures are notably higher for metro branches. It would appear that as work volume increases, the impact and/or the effectiveness of managerial and human resource practices plays an increasingly important role in achieving stronger business performance.

Overall Study Conclusions

In simple terms, this illustrative study shows that those branches where employees hold more favorable opinions of the bank and key aspects of their work environment are generally branches with higher customer satisfaction and productivity. Among smaller, nonmetro branches, however, customer satisfaction is lower in branches where tellers are busier and thus provide less personalized service to customers. Bank human resource professionals and line managers used the linkage research results to help them focus their survey follow-up and action planning efforts on those survey results shown to be the best predictors of branch customer satisfaction and business performance.

Support for the Model

This study also offers support for the Linkage Research Model. Clearly, the more present the leadership practices of customer orientation, quality emphasis, employee training, and involvement/ empowerment (see Figure 13.1), the more satisfied are bank employees. The average correlations of the employee survey results for these leadership practices with the results for the themes of job satisfaction (average correlation = .51) and company satisfaction (average correlation = .59) support this conclusion. Further, the leadership practices are strongly related to customer results. In fact, the themes of customer orientation, quality emphasis, and employee training (all of which are leadership practices) and communication (largely a measure of senior management communication practices), along with the themes of job satisfaction and company satisfaction, produce strong (indeed, the highest) correlations with the customer survey overall satisfaction theme.

Study findings likewise indicate leadership practices to be significantly related to business performance measures. Again, the themes of customer orientation, quality emphasis, employee training, involvement/empowerment, and communication—along with job satisfaction and company satisfaction—account for the majority of the significant correlations to teller transactions and productivity ratio. The link in the model for which this study provides the least support is the customer results–business performance link. In actuality though, the special secondary analyses, showing how this relationship differs for metro versus nonmetro branches, exemplifies the model's allowance of the moderating influence of work characteristics on key linkages.

Using the Linkage Research Model

The Linkage Research Model carries at least two strong implications for conducting employee surveys in general. One addresses survey content; the other how to best use survey results.

Choosing Survey Content

Decisions about themes or topics to include in an employee survey have a direct bearing on the probability that survey results will predict outcome measures such as customer satisfaction and business performance. Survey themes that have regularly shown a relationship to these outcome measures include the four themes that measure leadership practice: customer orientation, quality emphasis, employee training, and involvement/empowerment. Table 13.5 illustrates the types of questions subsumed under these leadership practices themes.

Based on the research to date, I suggest that the more an employee survey contains such internal practice measures of organizational effectiveness as are shown in Table 13.5, the more likely it

Table 13.5. Predictor Survey Themes and Illustrative Survey Items.

Customer Orientation	Quality Emphasis
Where I work, customer concerns get resolved quickly.	We are continually improving the quality of our services.
Policies and procedures are designed to be user-friendly to customers.	Providing quality service gets higher priority than keeping costs down.
Where I work, there is a strong emphasis on customer service.	Where I work, day-to-day decisions demonstrate that quality is a top priority.
Where I work, we deliver service to customers in a timely fashion.	Where I work, we set clear performance standards for service quality.
Overall, our customers are satisfied with our products and services.	How do you rate the overall quality of work done in your work group?

Employee Training	Involvement/Empowerment
New employees are given the training necessary to perform their jobs effectively.	I have the authority to do what's necessary to effectively serve my customer.
I receive enough training to help me continually improve my job performance.	Employees are encouraged to participate in making decisions which affect their work.
I receive adequate training on my company's products and services.	Sufficient effort is made to get the opinions and thinking of people who work here.
I am given a real opportunity to improve my skills.	When employees have good ideas, management makes use of them.
I am satisfied with the opportunities for training and development that are provided to me.	I am encouraged to take initiative and calculated risks.

is that survey results will be linked to key outcomes. Noticeably absent from this list of more consistent predictors are such traditional "employee relations" topics as compensation and benefits. I am certainly not arguing that measuring such topics is a mistake. Clearly, the content of an employee survey should be designed to achieve the overall objectives of the survey program. The implication is simply this: to the extent that being able to predict organizational outcomes is a driving objective of the survey program, loading the survey content with the themes contained in the Linkage Research Model is highly recommended.

Establishing Survey-Based Priorities for Action Planning

It is a reasonable assumption that most organizations engaging in employee opinion surveys have a commitment to take action on at least a few of the critical priority areas that may be suggested by the survey results. However, identifying the critical priority areas can often be a troublesome task for management teams, and it is not unusual for them simply to focus their action planning efforts on the survey themes with the lowest ratings. For example, if a survey measured twelve themes, then the team might be tempted—in a mechanical and arithmetic-driven way—to focus action planning only on the two or three lowest-rated themes.

However, linkage research suggests that such a strategy probably will not produce the best return on management's investment of action planning and organizational development resources. Once employee survey predictors of outcome measures have been identified, it makes sense to focus action planning efforts on strengthening aspects of the working environment represented by those predictors. This strategy is prudent even when the predictor themes receive, relatively speaking, favorable ratings.

Following this strategy allows an organization to develop further in ways already demonstrated to have an impact on effectiveness. To be sure, in any given organization, there may be extremely important reasons to focus action planning efforts also on survey themes not linked to outcome measures. Nevertheless, once employee survey linkages to outcomes have been established, knowledge of them can help organizations focus on those follow-up activities in the work environment that will most directly influence customer satisfaction and overall business performance.

Special Considerations in Linkage Research

Clearly, linkage research is a strategic exercise that produces many insights and can greatly benefit organizations that properly utilize linkage research findings. Even so, there are a number of special considerations in conducting this type of research.

Data Aggregation

In linkage research, the unit of analysis is not the individual but the organizational unit. While special care should always be exercised in aggregating individual respondent data, for this application it is a necessary and appropriate practice (Schneider, 1990) because customer satisfaction and business performance are typically measured only at the organizational unit level and the resulting action plans are developed primarily for the group level.

In addition, Ostroff (1993) theorizes that individual perceptions may be influenced by group-level variables, such as climate, which can result in uniformity of individual responses within a single group. This view also supports data aggregation. However, one note of caution is sounded by James (1982), who recommends assessing this uniformity by testing within-group versus between-group variance before aggregating.

Finally, if the research so requires, business units may even be combined into larger macro units (see, for example, Ashworth, Higgs, Schneider, Shepherd, and Carr, 1995). Although increased aggregation results in reduced sample size and therefore a loss of statistical power and a loss of specificity in reporting for lower-level units, these disadvantages are offset by the ability to discuss and utilize linkage research results in the broader organizational context.

Moderator Variables

As in other types of research, the relationships between the variables in linkage research are often influenced by situational characteristics. For example, Lundby, Dobbins, and Kidder (1995) found that the relationship between the climate for service and the climate for productivity differed depending on whether the employee position was high or low volume (that is, whether it was, respectively, a bank teller position or loan officer position). Job volume is not the only work characteristic to moderate such relationships. Brown and Mitchell (1993) report that degree of client contact influenced the relationship between the perception of organizational obstacles and the perception of customer satisfaction. Indeed, the branch banking case study presented earlier illustrates that branch location (metro versus nonmetro) moderates the customer satisfaction–business performance relationship.

The moderating influence of work characteristics is an important element of the Linkage Research Model. Its inclusion strengthens the predictive power of the model and allows a more accurate description of organizational realities. As Schneider (1991) points out, relationships between variables in linkage research are probably not simple. In my consulting experience, discussions with internal subject matter experts are often the richest source of hypotheses to explain these complex relationships. Understanding the influence of moderators may even offer new insights into such apparently counterintuitive findings as employee or customer attitudes that are negatively related to business performance measures (see, for example, Wiley, 1991; Paradise-Tornow, 1991).

Time-Lagged Correlational Analysis

Surveys, of course, are typically the source of measures of leadership and managerial practices and employee and customer satisfaction. In linkage research, such data are most frequently analyzed using correlational techniques. These techniques have many strengths, but they also possess limitations—they demonstrate neither causality nor directionality. These limitations are often disregarded in the literature.

One means of expanding the functionality of correlational analysis is to assess time lag. An excellent example is the work by Ashworth, Higgs, Schneider, Shepherd, and Carr (1995), who collected employee and customer satisfaction data across four successive quarters. Correlations between employee satisfaction and customer satisfaction were found to be higher in successive quarters than in concurrent quarters, indicating the directionality of the relationship. As previously noted, Ashworth, Higgs, Schneider, Shepherd, and Carr's analysis suggested that changes in managerial practices and the work environment preceded changes in customer perceptions and intentions. More such research will help us better establish cause and effect. It will also enable us better to detect short-term versus long-term impacts of various changes in organizational practices.

Family Error Rates

Another issue in linkage research, also emerging from its reliance on data collected through surveys, is that of family error rates. Customer and, especially, employee survey instruments often contain many individual survey items. Applying correlational techniques to the resulting databases naturally produces large intercorrelation matrices. An attendant problem is that when such large numbers of correlations are generated and examined, some of the significant relationships found will be due merely to chance. The danger is that these results will be incorrectly interpreted and perhaps even inappropriately used as the basis for action planing.

Several solutions to this potential problem exist. One solution when examining large numbers of correlations is to adopt a more strict probability level. Another solution is to build themes (more technically referred to as scales) and to correlate theme scores rather than individual item scores. This approach has the related advantages of increased validity and reliability, which are inherent in the use of themes (versus single items) as measures of the constructs under consideration. A third solution, which will become more practical as linkage research and practice develops further, is to use planned comparisons. That is, as the nature of the relationships among the variables in the Linkage Research Model becomes better understood, this knowledge can be used to drive theoretical and strategic analysis of linkage research data.

Range Restriction

In order for measures to be significantly correlated, they must truly vary. This basic statistical tenet can have unintended consequences for linkage research studies that are repeated over time within a single organization. For example, if an employee survey result indicates that employee perceptions of customer service are significantly and positively related to customer satisfaction, management may conclude that the organization should increase the emphasis placed on providing the best possible customer service. As this tactic is progressively implemented within the organization (perhaps through new or additional selection, training, and reward programs), the amount of variability in employee perceptions regarding customer service should decline. As perceptions of customer service become more uniform throughout the organization, the employee-based measure of customer service will eventually no longer correlate significantly with customer satisfaction. The absence of a significant correlation may thus lead management to the wrong conclusion regarding the value of the increased emphasis on customer service. As opportunities for replicating linkage research studies within a single organization increase, this type of "error in logic" may occur unless researchers are alert to the issue of range restriction.

The Satisfaction-Performance Paradox

Researchers have long searched to establish empirically the intuited relationship between employee satisfaction and performance. Generally, these investigations have led to mixed, conflicting, or disappointing results (Iaffaldano & Muchinsky, 1985; Petty, McGhee, & Cavender, 1984). The conviction surrounding the existence of this relationship has not, however, disappeared. A wealth of popular business books and case studies continue to assert that happier employees make for more productive employees.

Linkage research, by addressing this presumed relationship at the organizational rather than the individual level, has created a body of research that shows consistent support for the existence of a satisfaction-performance relationship. It thus seems paradoxical that such a stable relationship is found at the aggregated business unit level when only mixed findings emerge at the individual level.

There are, however, several possible explanations that in combination may help explain this seeming paradox. First, unit-level performance criteria are generally very well defined and reliably measured and are not subject to the rating biases typically associated with individual-level performance measures. Second, individual-level attitudes have been shown to be related to "citizenship behaviors" that can be considered to contribute to unit-level performance (Schneider, Gunnarson, & Niles-Jolly, 1994). Third, many of the studies referenced in this chapter were conducted in banking or other retail organizations. In such organizations, service behaviors of employees (for example, courtesy) may be more closely related to attitudes than are performance behaviors in other less service-oriented industries. In essence, the dynamics driving relationships at the business unit or organizational level can be markedly different from the dynamics at the individual level.

Even if identification of consistent satisfaction-performance relationships at the individual level continues to elude researchers, the robustness of findings at the aggregated level will undoubtedly persist. From an organizational development perspective, research at the aggregated level addresses the questions of satisfaction and performance at the level best matched to the group-level interventions practitioners typically employ as remedies. Linkage research can thus be thought of as validating the diagnostic value of employee surveys. It recognizes that high-performance organizations require employees to be actively involved in providing quality and value to customers. As a result, linkage research speaks more to organizational climate and quality processes than it does to the older motivation-flavored attitude research.

Conclusion

Survey practitioners are indebted to Benjamin Schneider and his colleagues for being the first to establish the statistical linkages between employee and customer satisfaction survey results. Even though this groundbreaking research was published approximately fifteen years ago and has since been extended to include key measures of business performance, linkage research is still an emerging research and practice area.

More research is needed to further establish and build upon the Linkage Research Model presented here, which identifies the organizational practices—as described by employees—that predict higher levels of organizational performance. This is an extremely important strategic area of focus for organization-based practitioners as well as for consultants and academics. The knowledge derived from such research can significantly advance our field's understanding of certain prerequisites of organizational effectiveness.

Properly conceived and conducted, organizational survey programs clearly represent a healthy exercise for many organizations. Benefits accrue to those who know how to properly follow up and take action based on survey results. Linkage research holds great promise for enriching the use of surveys: first, by suggesting appropriate topics to include in organizational surveys and, second, by guiding managers in their action planning efforts into those areas that represent the greatest potential for developing high-performance organizations.

References

Angle, H. L., & Perry, J. L. (1981). An empirical assessment of organizational commitment and organizational effectiveness. *Administrative Science Quarterly, 26,* 1–13.

Ashworth, S. D., Higgs, C., Schneider, B., Shepherd, W., & Carr, L. S. (1995, May). *The linkage between customer satisfaction data and employee-based measures of a company's strategic business intent.* Paper presented at the Tenth Annual Conference of the Society for Industrial and Organizational Psychology, Orlando, FL.

Brown, K. A., & Mitchell, T. R. (1993). Organizational obstacles: Links with financial performance, customer satisfaction, and job satisfaction in a service environment. *Human Relations, 46*(6), 725–757.

Bursek, M., & Remenschneider, C. (1995, May). First in service. *Quirk's Marketing Research Review,* pp. 26, 28.

Heskett, J. L., Jones, T. O., Loveman, G. W., Sasser, W. E., & Schlesinger, L. A. (1994). Putting the service-profit chain to work. *Harvard Business Review, 72,* 164–174.

Iaffaldano, M. T., & Muchinsky, P. M. (1985). Job satisfaction and job performance: A meta-analysis. *Psychological Bulletin, 97,* 251–273.

James, L. R. (1982). Aggregation bias in estimates of perceptual agreement. *Journal of Applied Psychology, 67,* 219–229.

Johnson, J. W. (1995, May). *Linking management practices and service orientation to customer satisfaction.* Paper presented at the Tenth Annual Conference of the Society for Industrial and Organizational Psychology, Orlando, FL.

Johnson, R. H., Ryan, A. M., & Schmit, M. (1994, April). *Employee attitudes and branch performance at Ford Motor Credit.* Paper presented at the Ninth Annual Conference of the Society for Industrial and Organizational Psychology, Nashville, TN.

Jones, J. W. (1991). In search of excellent customer service. *Bank Management, 67*(2), 40–41.

Lundby, K. M., Dobbins, G. H., & Kidder, P. J. (1995, May). *Climate for service and productivity in high and low volume jobs: Further evidence for a redefinition of service.* Paper presented at the Tenth Annual Conference of the Society for Industrial and Organizational Psychology, Orlando, FL.

Ostroff, C. (1992). The relationship between satisfaction, attitudes, and performance: An organizational level analysis. *Journal of Applied Psychology, 77,* 963–974.

Ostroff, C. (1993). Comparing correlations based on individual-level and aggregated data. *Journal of Applied Psychology, 78,* 569–582.

Paradise-Tornow, C. A. (1991). Management effectiveness, service quality, and organizational performance in banks. *Human Resource Planning, 14,* 129–140.

Petty, M. M., McGhee, G. W., & Cavender, J. W. (1984). A meta-analysis of the relationships between individual job satisfaction and individual performance. *Academy of Management Review, 9,* 712–721.

Schneider, B. (1990). The climate for service: Application of the construct. In B. Schneider (Ed.), *Organizational climate and culture* (pp. 383–412). San Francisco: Jossey-Bass.

Schneider, B. (1991). Service quality and profits: Can you have your cake and eat it, too? *Human Resource Planning, 14,* 151–157.

Schneider, B., & Bowen, D. E. (1985). Employee and customer perceptions of service in banks: Replication and extension. *Journal of Applied Psychology, 70,* 423–433.

Schneider, B., Gunnarson, S., & Niles-Jolly, K. (1994, Summer). Creating the climate and culture of success. *Organizational Dynamics,* pp. 17–29.

Schneider, B., Parkington, J. J., & Buxton, V. M. (1980). Employee and customer perceptions of service in banks. *Administrative Science Quarterly, 25,* 252–267.

Tompkins, N. C. (1992, November). Employee satisfaction leads to customer service. *HRMagazine,* pp. 93–95.

Tornow, W. W., & Wiley, J. W. (1991). Service quality and management practices: A look at employee attitudes, customer satisfaction, and bottom-line consequences. *Human Resource Planning, 14,* 105–116.

Weaver, J. J. (1994, February). Want customer satisfaction? Satisfy your employees first. *HRMagazine,* pp. 110, 112.

Wiley, J. W. (1991). Customer satisfaction: A supportive work environment and its financial cost. *Human Resource Planning, 14,* 117–128.

Zemke, R. (1989, Autumn). Auditing customer service: Look inside as well as out. *Employee Relations Today,* pp. 197–203.

CHAPTER 14

Federal Government Surveys
Recent Practices and Future Directions

Marilyn K. Gowing
Anita R. Lancaster

This chapter describes survey practices in the civilian and military areas of the federal government. We present both overall trends and case studies of recent practices in certain agencies, and we conclude with a discussion of future directions for government survey practitioners.

The federal government is the nation's largest employer. Its total civilian employment in 1994 was 2,050,172 individuals in approximately 900 occupations in over fifty agencies and departments. Over 40 percent, 840,000, were civilian employees of the U.S. Department of Defense. In addition, the military services include 1.4 million full-time active-duty military officers and enlisted personnel and 1.3 million part-time reservists. Another 750,000 people work for the U.S. Postal Service, a quasi-governmental organization.

It is important to note that the federal government sponsors

Note: The views expressed in this chapter are those of the authors and do not reflect the positions of the U.S. Office of Personnel Management or the U.S. Department of Defense.

voluminous survey research. We have chosen to focus primarily on recent federal surveys of likely interest to private-sector practitioners. For that reason, many well-known, ongoing government-sponsored surveys, such as the U.S. Department of Commerce's CENSUS and the National Science Foundation Survey of Doctoral Recipients, are not included here. Our reporting of detailed methodological and analytical issues is also limited due to space restrictions.

Federal government surveys typically collect data for one or more of the following reasons: (1) in support of statutory requirements (for example, CENSUS); (2) in support of personnel selection, training, and placement programs (for example, the Multipurpose Occupational Systems Analysis Inventory—Close-ended [MOSAIC] of the U.S. Office of Personnel Management [OPM]); (3) for policy formulation purposes (for example, the Post-Retirement Income Survey of the Department of Defense and the National Education Longitudinal Study of 1988 and study follow-up surveys of the U.S. Department of Education; (4) for program evaluation purposes (for example, the sexual harassment surveys of the U.S. Merit Systems Protection Board); and (5) in support of assessing organizational climate, culture, and practices (for example, the OPM's Organizational Assessment Survey).

Across these five areas, survey efforts in the last two categories are currently burgeoning. This is primarily due to three recent federal governmentwide initiatives: the National Performance Review, the Government Performance and Results Act of 1993 (GPRA), and Total Quality Leadership (TQL)/Total Quality Management (TQM) programs.

Briefly, the National Performance Review (NPR) is a Clinton administration initiative to "reinvent" the culture of the federal government—putting customers first, empowering the workforce, cutting red tape, and streamlining bureaucratic systems (National Performance Review, 1993). This initiative has prompted federal survey researchers to define the dimensions underlying a high-performing, reinvented government and also to use the dimensions underlying high performance in private-sector companies as benchmarks whenever possible. It has also spurred a proliferation of customer satisfaction surveys as agencies try to determine if customer needs are being met.

The GPRA requires each federal department to establish corporate-level performance goals and outcome measures. Departments are required to submit strategic plans to the Office of Management and Budget (OMB) by September 30, 1997, and to prepare an annual performance plan in support of their 1999 fiscal year budgets. Each department has also identified a set of performance measures that will be used to evaluate each corporate goal; since GPRA mandates that the measures must be based on existing data sources, plans call for considerable use of survey data.

Total Quality Management/Total Quality Leadership programs emphasize the importance of gathering cultural and climate information to assess the degree of employee empowerment and customer focus. These programs emanate out of the work of W. Edwards Deming and J. M. Juran that shaped quality initiatives in the private sector.

Recent Survey Practices in Civilian Government Agencies

Surveys in the federal government vary dramatically in terms of their degree of technical sophistication. Survey programs within a particular agency may range from those focusing on organization-specific issues to those covering topics of national interest (for example, the Bureau of Labor Statistics' Occupational Employment Statistics survey of approximately 600,000 nonfarm establishments). This section provides a brief introduction to some agency-specific programs and a few in-depth case studies as examples of recent survey efforts within the government.

Diversity Assessment at the Environmental Protection Agency

The Environmental Protection Agency (EPA) has adopted a "change management triad" with diversity, Total Quality Management, and strategic planning serving as the "three pillars" of its change management strategy.

The EPA hired an external contractor to work with its Cultural Diversity Task Force in developing the EPA Cultural Diversity

Employee Survey, which was intended to help the agency understand issues and concerns arising from cultural differences among employees. To prepare survey questions, the contractor convened focus groups composed of a mix of people with different ethnic, racial, gender, and professional discipline backgrounds. Other questions were designed in-house after a literature review. The final survey instrument asked for background information, regarding such matters as age, sex, race, national origin, and tenure; recruitment, hiring, and promotion responsibilities; and professional discipline. It also asked for opinions about organizational practices and employee treatment, covering such areas as fair hiring, record of recruiting minorities and women, existing barriers, preferential treatment, fair share of training, equal access to training, adequacy of training, presence of mentors, promotion opportunities, awards and recognition, performance appraisal, work climate, supervisory and staff relations, professional and support relations, discrimination, and sexual harassment.

The written survey was distributed to all employees in the Washington, D.C., headquarters in February 1992, and 69 percent of them completed it. The survey results have been used as a needs assessment for structuring the action plan of the Cultural Diversity Task Force (U.S. Environmental Protection Agency, 1992; U.S. Environmental Protection Agency, 1993).

Survey Programs of the U.S. Office of Personnel Management

The U.S. Office of Personnel Management conducts numerous surveys each year. In this section, an overview of two surveys is provided.

Survey of Federal Government Employees

The Survey of Federal Employees, conducted by the OPM, was the first major survey of the workforce since 1983. The survey was distributed to a randomly selected sample of white-collar federal employees between mid November 1991 and early February 1992. Surveys were mailed to approximately 57,000 employees, and nearly 32,000 surveys were returned, a response rate of 56 percent.

The survey was designed "to provide policy-makers with information about federal employees . . . employees' satisfaction with their jobs, supervisors, and organizations; performance management; training; work schedule arrangement; leave benefits; and dependent care responsibilities and the ways employees accommodate these requirements" (Office of Systems Innovation and Simplification, U.S. Office of Personnel Management, 1992, p. 1).

Subject matter experts, with the assistance of psychologists and survey researchers, created the survey questions, which were pretested on a variety of employee groups. The final questionnaire contained 184 items.

Organizational Assessment Survey

The Organizational Assessment Survey was constructed by the OPM in 1994 to assist governmental agencies and departments in evaluating their progress in reinventing their cultures. The survey items were developed after a comprehensive literature review of the dimensions underlying high-performance organizations in the public and private sectors (Schneider, 1993). Survey items from past OPM surveys (the Leadership Effectiveness Survey and the Survey of Federal Employees) were added for historical comparison purposes, and survey items that tapped the dimensions underlying the Malcolm Baldrige National Quality Award and the President's Award for Quality and Productivity Improvement were also included.

The Organizational Assessment Survey also includes items used by some of the Fortune 100 companies (for example, Ford Motor Company) as well as items for which private industry averages are available. Therefore, a given federal agency or department can compare its organizational profile with the average profile of other governmental agencies and with the profile of some of the best in business. The 244-item survey assesses eighteen dimensions: rewards/recognition, training/career development, innovation, customer orientation, leadership and quality, fairness and treatment of others, communication, employee involvement, work environment/ quality of work life, balance between work and family/personal life, supervision, teamwork, diversity, social responsibility, job security/ commitment to workforce, strategic planning, performance measures, and use of resources. Reliabilities for these factors range from .69 to .93, with the exception of use of resources (reliability of .19, due in part to the small number of items).

Survey results for the public sector seem to be less favorable than comparable private-sector data. The results obtained from one large public agency for eighteen identical questions covering a broad array of job-related facets revealed that the proportion of employees who answer favorably is lower—by 7 percentage points, on average. The differences ranged from a 19-point disadvantage on overall satisfaction to a 1-point advantage on a question about work group cooperation.

The Organizational Assessment Survey has been administered to portions of the U.S. Marshal's Service and the U.S. Coast Guard. It has also been administered to all employees in the U.S. Mint (see the following discussion) and the U.S. Office of Personnel Management. Major portions of the Organizational Assessment Survey have been included in a survey given by the Internal Revenue Service to all 100,000 of its employees. In each case, the participating agency was assisted by psychologists from the Office of Personnel Management.

Partnership Assessment at the U.S. Mint

President Clinton issued Executive Order 12871 in 1993, calling for agencies to create labor-management partnerships with their unions. These partnerships were intended to develop high-performance organizations providing top-quality service. *Partnership assessment* was the term used to describe a survey-based assessment of organizational culture undertaken with the support of management and formal unions (Kraft, Schneider, Reck, Chia, & Pettibone, 1995).

In 1994, the U.S. Mint asked the Personnel Research and Development Center of the OPM to assist it in assessing its organizational climate and culture. The Mint chose to use the OPM-developed Organizational Assessment Survey (OAS), described above. However, the survey was customized by modifying language to fit the Mint context, adding items in some areas, and developing items to assess additional organizational and respondent characteristics (such as location).

Survey results were provided to the Mint as both dimension scores and individual survey item scores. Seventeen follow-up focus groups were then held around the country—nine with employees, four with first-line supervisors, and four with managers and executives. The purposes of the focus group effort were (1) to verify that the survey results were reflective of the U.S. Mint as a whole, (2) to gain insight into what was going on in the Mint that accounted for the survey results, and (3) to develop recommendations for improving the Mint in the needed areas. The survey results and focus group information were presented to Mint management, unions, and other staff as themes (major concerns related to a given organizational dimension) and recommendations for improving the Mint. That report was used by the Mint to develop action plans to implement organizational changes (for example, training program and policy changes) and to promote a climate and culture conducive to a high-performing organization.

Employees received information about the survey results in a letter from the director of the Mint. At eight locations, a site committee was established. These site committees consisted of the head of the office at that location, the union president and one or two other union officers and stewards, the director of training for the location, a representative from personnel, and other staff. Each site committee prioritized the recommended actions for that location.

Assessment of Culture at the U.S. Postal Service

In 1990, the U.S. Postal Service created a strategic plan for the period from 1990 to 1995. The plan had three major components: financial stability, customer satisfaction, and commitment to employees. The U.S. Postal Service's Employee Opinion Survey (EOS) was created in 1991 to measure the service's commitment to employees.

The Postal Service contracted with a consulting firm to assist in survey construction, administration, analysis, and report preparation. In the summer of 1991, the Postal Service held forty-one focus groups in ten cities to determine the appropriate content areas for the survey. Both bargaining and nonbargaining employees were included (89 percent of the postal workforce is covered by union agreements). The Employee Opinion Survey contained items arising from these focus groups as well as about forty "standard" items provided by the contractor.

In November 1991, the survey was pilot-tested in five divisions and four departments at Postal Service headquarters. The survey was administered to all career employees (that is, 729,000 full-time continuing employees) in April 1992. Follow-up census survey administrations occurred in August 1993 and 1994. The contractor prepared a national report and over 700 separate reports in hard copy with accompanying electronic copies (on Bernoulli disk). These reports were provided to the manager of each facility for use in action planning. Action plans were prepared in each year after a survey administration.

An early factor analysis based on the 1992 data identified twelve organizational climate factors (job attitudes and employee commitment, working conditions, career development and training, employee-management relations, employee treatment and participation, leadership and supervision, performance management, recognition and reward, communications, quality focus, customer satisfaction, and management of change). Reports showed the percentages of favorable and unfavorable responses for each question under each of the twelve factors.

Twenty of the survey questions were chosen to be the basis of the Employee Opinion Index, the average percentage favorable on those twenty items. The twenty items were selected because they were representative of the entire survey and because they pertained to actions within the control of local managers.

Along with each report of EOS results, the Postal Service distributed the *Employee Opinion Survey Feedback and Action-Planning Guide,* to assist managers and employees in understanding the survey findings and in implementing survey-based changes. In 1995, for the first time, the Postal Service tracked the type of survey communications and follow-up provided by unit managers (that is, those who manage the very largest post offices and the mail-processing plants).

The Postal Service is in the forefront of the federal government agencies and departments using climate surveys in that executive compensation is partially determined by changes in a unit's Employee Opinion Index. The Postal Service expects this practice, begun in 1994, to result in line managers' and employees' taking extra effort to understand and implement changes in response to the Employee Opinion Survey.

Survey Programs of the
U.S. Merit System Protection Board

Employee opinion surveys conducted by the Merit Systems Protection Board are based on federal governmentwide samples. Some representative studies include *Whistleblowing in the Federal Government: An Update* (Carlyle, 1993); *Federal Blue-Collar Employees: A Workforce in Transition* (van Rijn, 1992); *Working for America: A Federal Employee Survey* (Redd, 1990); and *Why Are Employees Leaving the Federal Government?* (van Rijn, 1990). The board's recent work has involved employee perceptions of an organizational glass ceiling for women and minorities.

Recent Survey Practices in
the U.S. Department of Defense

During World War II, the Department of Army pioneered sample survey research in its efforts to learn the views of soldiers for policy formulation purposes (Stouffer & Associates, 1949). By the end of World War II, the sample survey was an established research tool for social scientists in the government.

Over the past several decades, Department of Defense (DOD) surveys have included

- Large-scale sample surveys (50,000+) sponsored by senior defense officials to obtain data for policy formulation and program evaluation
- Periodic sample surveys for the purpose of monitoring changes over time
- Surveys to evaluate specific programs or policies
- Ongoing surveys in support of occupational analysis programs across the military services

Due to the size of the DOD, sponsorship of defense surveys is decentralized, and hundreds of surveys are conducted each year by the military services and other defense organizations for their own specific purposes. Departmentwide surveys also gather information across the military services and from civilian personnel and dependents. These surveys are considerably fewer in number and are usually administered to large samples (150,000+) from the four military services and often the Coast Guard, which is part of the U.S. Department of Transportation. When a survey involves more than one service, it is often developed, fielded, and analyzed by the Defense Manpower Data Center, the data repository and research arm of the Office of the Secretary of Defense.

Regardless of where DOD surveys originate, the populations surveyed may be defense civilians, active-duty military, reservists, and/or retirees. Spouses and dependents of active-duty members, reservists, and retirees are also surveyed, but far less frequently. They may be surveyed in conjunction with military members, reservists, or retirees, but they are also surveyed separately (as in, for example, the Armed Forces Adolescent Survey). Occasionally, and in conjunction with OMB approval, DOD surveys cover non-DOD members of the public.

Given the costs of conducting large-scale sample surveys, DOD surveys typically are designed to address multiple objectives, for example, assessing employee attitudes toward pay, job satisfaction, likelihood of staying in the military, and organizational climate.

As in other governmental agencies, separate assessments of organizational *processes* are becoming more widely used within DOD. For example, there has been considerable emphasis in recent years on measuring organizational climate to facilitate an understanding, at the base and unit level, of equal opportunity issues. In addition to service-specific climate surveys, since 1990, the Defense Equal Opportunity Management Institute has fielded the Military Equal Opportunity Climate Survey, covering over 330,000 defense personnel (Landis, 1990).

These surveys are generally administered at the request of a military commander. Since they are voluntary, confidential, and administered to entire work units, the results are summarized by unit and are used by unit leaders to identify equal opportunity and organizational climate issues. Most units have equal opportunity advisers who work with the leadership to develop action plans.

Finally, as in other federal departments, DOD sample survey research has been spurred on by federal-level initiatives for reinventing government and for establishing customer standards. "Customers" are typically internal, for example, a survey might address the customer satisfaction of military members with their medical treatment facilities and programs. As mentioned, given the size of the DOD, survey efforts are largely decentralized, and these types of surveys are consequently proliferating.

DOD Departmentwide Survey Efforts

In the mid 1970s, responsibility for surveys that involved more than one service was centralized at the Defense Manpower Data Center (DMDC). Since then, many surveys have been undertaken on behalf of the Office of the Secretary of Defense on a wide range of issues. For example, the DMDC's omnibus personnel surveys are periodic and include longitudinal components. The DMDC also conducts a wide array of surveys to meet the needs of senior defense officials on the topics of, for example, sexual harassment, race/ethnic harassment, banking services, military recruiter quality of life, relocation services, and health beneficiaries' use and satisfaction with health services.

The DMDC is responsible for reviewing all survey research that involves more than one service, regardless of where the survey originates or whether it is done by defense researchers or contractors. Two examples of recent DMDC survey efforts follow.

1992 Surveys of Officers and Enlisted Personnel and Their Spouses

In recent years, the most important among the DMDC's surveys of military personnel are the six continuing periodic surveys of active-duty officers and enlisted personnel and their spouses and of reserve officers and enlisted personnel and their spouses. The DMDC conducted these surveys in 1992 and 1993. They were administered across all services, and statistical inferences can be made to the entire military population.

For the active-duty surveys, four separate samples were drawn: longitudinal, enlisted recruiters, regular active-duty members, and reserve full-time support active guard/reserves. Spouses of military participants in each of these four samples were also surveyed. The active-duty sample was about 96,830. This included a basic sample of 75,346 active military, 12,000 from the longitudinal component (from the 1985 sample), 5,484 reserve personnel on active duty, and 4,000 military recruiters. The response rate on the active-duty survey was 62 percent. About 65,000 spouses also received surveys, and their response rate was 37 percent.

For the reserve survey, four samples were drawn—longitudinal respondents (10,000), unit members (55,579), military technicians (6,117), and individual mobilization augmentees (5,087). Spouses in each of these four samples were also sampled. The overall member sample was 76,783, and their response rate was 50 percent. The spouse sample was 21,148, and about 30 percent responded.

These periodic surveys are a rich source of data on active-duty military and reserve families, and they are the only data source that allows family comparisons across services. Even key demographic data such as marital status, number of times married, and number of dependents are important since they provide a comparison to summary data obtained from the department's administrative personnel records.

Key areas assessed in the 1992 survey were the background and characteristics of military families, individual and family readiness for separation and deployment, and issues relating to child care, Operations Desert Shield/Desert Storm, the military work environment, military career choice, and retention.

Data from these periodic omnibus surveys are used for a number of major purposes and for innumerable special analyses. For example:

- The data identify and quantify problems that require legislative relief.
- The data are used in congressional testimony on topics of interest to members of Congress (for example, use of food stamps by military personnel).
- The data are used for program evaluation (for example, use of and satisfaction with family support programs and morale, welfare, and recreation programs).
- The longitudinal component enables trend analyses (for example, analyzing the extent to which military members are satisfied with housing and pay today compared to fiscal year 1985–86).
- Because the sample sizes are large and response rates adequate, ongoing analyses can be performed at fairly fine levels

in support of special issues (for example, analyzing the extent to which required maintenance of up-to-date wills and powers-of-attorney vary across the services and by military pay grade groupings).

Sexual and Racial/Ethnic Harassment Research

The DMDC has conducted the most comprehensive research on sexual harassment in the government. In 1988, using Merit System Protection Board (MSPB) research as a model and benchmark, the DMDC conducted an active-duty military survey designed to measure the frequency of sexual harassment, the context and location in which sexual harassment occurs, and effectiveness of DOD and military service programs to eliminate, prevent, or reduce sexual harassment (Martindale, 1990). The survey was administered to about 38,000 active-duty members, including members of the Coast Guard. The response rate was about 60 percent.

Twenty-two percent of active-duty military (including Coast Guard members) reported experiencing one or more incidents of sexual harassment in the previous twelve months. Females were almost four times as likely to experience sexual harassment as males: 64 percent versus 17 percent, respectively. This finding is somewhat higher than the MSPB's 1987 research in which 42 percent of women and 14 percent of men in the federal government reported experiencing one or more sexual harassment incidents (Storey & Crum, 1988).

In 1995, the DMDC launched efforts to (1) replicate the 1988 research (Form A) by fielding a comparable survey to 40,000 active-duty personnel (including Coast Guard personnel); (2) field a new survey (Form B) to a sample of 40,000 active-duty personnel (including Coast Guard personnel), a survey that would expand the MSPB behavioral scale considerably; probe for attitudes toward the complaint process, reprisal, and training; and provide the opportunity to link harassment to outcomes measures such as health status; and (3) conduct a survey (Form C) of 10,000 personnel that would obtain data to link the 1988 and 1995 sexual harassment behavioral scales. In particular, Form B builds on research in the private sector that attempts to define sexual harassment behaviors at a finer level of detail than the MSPB behavioral scale and to define sexual harassment constructs and structures and the dimensions of the behaviors within the constructs (Gelfand, Fitzgerald, & Drasgow, in press; Fitzgerald, Gelfand, & Drasgow, in press). Results will be available in the spring of 1996. Finally, during 1996, the DMDC will field the first, large-scale sample survey to determine racial/ethnic harassment incidence rates among military members on active duty. Results will be available in the fall of 1996.

Recent Practices in U.S. Army Personnel Surveys

The U.S. Army has a long history of survey research. In 1943, the Army began conducting an ongoing survey of active-duty Army personnel. Since 1958, this has been referred to as the Army Sample Survey of Military Personnel (SSMP). The SSMP is conducted semiannually, in the spring and fall. It samples 10 percent of officers and 2 to 3 percent of the enlisted force. Examples of the spring 1995 topics include attitudes about housing; training; morale, welfare, and recreation programs; satisfaction with the Army; promotions; current duty assignment; and equal opportunity. Individual data on career development and mentoring, sexual harassment, and likelihood of staying in the Army were also collected.

During 1991 and 1992, the Army also conducted the Survey of Total Army Military Personnel (STAMP). Mailed to 51,000 active-duty personnel, National Guard personnel, and reservists, it permitted comparisons of those mobilized or deployed with those who were not. It covered the following topics: climate and morale; organizational commitment; leadership; training needs; stress; reenlistment/career plans; personal, family, and economic difficulties in deployment; adequacy of preparation for mobilization/deployment; and advice to others on joining the Army. This survey was a follow-on effort to the 1990 Army Career Satisfaction Survey that provided pre- and post-Operations Desert Shield/Desert Storm data and pre- and post-downsizing data.

The Army also has several large-scale surveys under way that will move from pilot to operational stages in 1996 and 1997.

- The Civilian Biennial Survey, designed to evaluate organizational climate and civilian management processes.
- The Longitudinal Research on Officer Careers survey, a cross-sectional sample with a panel that evolved out of research at the U.S. Military Academy on integration of women into the

Army. It assesses assignments, for example, and job satisfaction, respect and recognition received, quality of supervision, perception of Army life, spousal information, economic issues, leadership and organizational issues, and the impact of downsizing. Although it is in the pilot stage, data on about 20,000 officers have been collected since 1988.

- The Army Career Transition Survey, which asks departing service members for demographic information and about their satisfaction with the Army, reasons for leaving, and so on. The Army has been pilot-testing this survey since 1991.

The Army also sponsors a number of smaller-scale surveys on narrowly targeted subjects and for specific populations. One recent targeted-subject survey concerned uniforms for the twenty-first century. More often, the purpose of special surveys is to explore issues within a specific Army population such as a career field (for example, there have been surveys of chaplains and chaplains' assistants, medical specialists, foreign area officers, nurse corps, noncommissioned officers, and reserve technicians).

The Army Research Institute (ARI) provides technical survey assistance and screens and approves surveys developed for administration to Army personnel. In recent years, the ARI survey center has been involved in about fifty surveys annually. Other than in its occupational analysis program, the Army has no plans for fielding personnel surveys electronically, since the nature of the Army's mission precludes respondents' having personal computers and associated local and wide area networks in the field. The Army can use electronic surveys in its occupational analysis program because that program involves fixed geographical sites.

Recent Practices in U.S. Navy Personnel Surveys

In the last few years, the U.S. Navy's survey center at the Navy Personnel Research and Development Center (NPRDC) in San Diego, California, has conducted a number of large-scale, Navy-wide surveys. For example, the annual Navy-Wide Personnel Survey of active-duty enlisted personnel and officers was conducted from 1990 to 1994. Core questions have been repeated each year, and special items on topics of interest to senior officials have been added from time to time. The sample is approximately 4 percent of enlisted personnel and 11 percent of officers. Data are weighted to represent pay-grade groups. Examples of topics assessed are assignments; voluntary education; family support and child care programs; morale, welfare, and recreation programs; housing; and training. Also included in the Navy-wide Personnel Survey are items related to organizational climate assessment, job satisfaction, and attitudes toward force reductions and base closures, fraternization, sexual harassment, and equal opportunity.

The Navy has surveyed reservists separately from the active-duty force. For example, in 1991, the Naval Reserve Survey was conducted at the conclusion of Operations Desert Shield/Desert Storm primarily for the purpose of measuring topics related to the mobilization: reserve career intentions, reasons for leaving the reserves, type of civilian employer and job, employer's personnel policies during Desert Shield/Desert Storm, and so on. Included in the final analyses were 10,881 respondent cases.

In the last few years, the Navy's survey center has also developed the Total Quality Leadership Climate Survey to assist Navy organizations' efforts in Total Quality Leadership (TQL). This 164-item instrument assesses six constructs: general organizational climate, work team functioning, worker motivation, job characteristics, TQL implementation, and TQL support. The instrument is administered in both a paper-and-pencil and computerized mode. Scoring is done at the Navy's survey center.

Recently, due to policy changes that have mandated the collection and reporting of equal opportunity data at unit levels, the Navy has vigorously pursued equal opportunity survey research. The Navy's Command Assessment Team Survey System (CATSYS) essentially allows local commanders, at the unit level, to identify and understand equal opportunity and sexual harassment issues, but standardized data must be collected and reported up through the unit's chain of command (Rosenfeld & Edwards, 1994). The Navy Equal Opportunity/Sexual Harassment (NEOSH) survey was developed for the purpose of standardizing the data collection. A biennial survey first fielded in 1989, it contains about 100 items that measure Navy members' perceptions of the equal opportunity climate, such as leadership, discipline, and opportunities for advancement. Another 100 items measure the occurrence of sexual harassment and related issues.

Like the other services, the Navy also provides technical assistance in the development of surveys for special topics and populations. For example, the survey center developed and fielded the Navy New Recruit Survey during 1990 and 1991 and again in 1994. Eight areas were assessed: reasons for joining the Navy, influences from family and friends, parent background, advertising awareness, advertising influence, recruiter contact, special enlistment incentives, and job interests (Robertson, 1993).

Also, the Navy survey center develops and fields a number of surveys on specific populations or specific topics. Recent surveys include

- Family quality-of-life surveys for the Navy and the Marine Corps
- Surveys evaluating services provided at morale, welfare, and recreation facilities
- Surveys to estimate pregnancy rates, since work restrictions exist for Navy women who are pregnant (for example, they must be transferred off ship prior to the twenty-first week and are restricted to nonhazardous work)
- A survey to assess quality-of-life issues and permit development of models to predict the effect of quality-of-life issues on such military outcomes as performance, retention, and personal readiness

Recent Practices in U.S. Air Force Personnel Surveys

The U.S. Air Force historically has conducted both large-scale paper-and-pencil surveys and smaller surveys for targeted purposes (for example, tracking relocation costs incurred by military personnel who move). In addition, about ten years ago, the Air Force began using contractor support to provide computer-assisted telephone interviews (CATI) of its personnel on issues where data were needed quickly.

Since 1991, the Air Force survey center at Randolph Air Force Base in San Antonio, Texas, has conducted over 100 surveys a year. These mostly are smaller targeted surveys, occasionally using CATI technology. A number of the targeted surveys have asked service members about Air Force internal services and programs. There have been

- Surveys on occupational and geographical assignments (for example, officer and spouse surveys on the foreign country occupational exchange program)
- Enlisted personnel and officer surveys of attitudes about the Air Force assignment system
- A survey of officers who had attended intermediate and senior schools, regarding their experiences and subsequent assignments
- Officer and enlisted personnel surveys regarding Air Force performance appraisal systems
- A survey of F-16 pilots regarding being stationed in Korea
- A survey of Air Force recruiters regarding quality-of-life issues associated with their assignment as recruiters
- An survey assessment of the special monetary exit incentives developed for downsizing
- An Air Force climate survey
- A survey for the Air Force surgeon general to determine health care beneficiaries' attitudes and opinions
- A needs assessment survey conducted by the Air Force Family Support Center of those using its services
- A survey of Air Force personnel regarding their use of and satisfaction with Air Force public affairs products

Recently, senior Air Force leaders decided to conduct a large-scale personnel survey, their first since 1990. The Air Force decision to offer its large surveys in an electronic as well as a paper-and-pencil format is noteworthy because (1) the Air Force is the first military service to do so and (2) that choice dramatically reduces the costs typically associated with large-scale sample surveys (for example, printing, mailing, and data compilation costs). The survey, conducted in 1994, asked respondents about personal recognition and about their assessment of housing, performance appraisals, base-level services, and the promotion system. The survey is a census of about 750,000 Air Force active-duty officers and enlisted personnel, civilians, reservists, and individuals serving in the Air National Guard. It is currently being configured for administration again in 1995. The software undergirding this effort is a modified off-the-shelf database product for creation of survey programs and distribution of the programs over electronic networks or on floppy disks. Use of this technology is logistically possible because most Air Force personnel are assigned to bases and the Air Force has local and wide area computer network technology in place.

Conclusion

Although federal government organizations are declining in terms of size and budget, it is not clear that this translates into shrinking survey programs. At the Department of Defense, downsizing has resulted in a reexamination of everything from the basic DOD mission to day-to-day business practices. Civilian agencies are also reexamining their missions. For example, both military and civilian organizations are determining what portions of their businesses can be privatized or outsourced. Data to help senior government managers make important strategic decisions are frequently not available from the standard central data repositories and personnel administrative records Increasingly, these managers are turning to survey data to provide the necessary information for management.

The rising costs of large-scale paper-and-pencil surveys have provided an impetus for governmental survey researchers to investigate the use of automated survey administration and analysis. We described some pioneering efforts by the Air Force in this area. Much can be learned from these initial experiences, such as the best use of automated controls to ensure that only the sampled respondent can log on and complete a survey and effective ways to deal with the introduction of viruses onto survey diskettes. Many software products now exist that are easily adapted for use in automated survey administration (see Chapter Nine).

Today's emphasis on governmental reinvention, changing the culture to one that empowers employees and focuses on customers, requires ongoing monitoring of organizational culture at the agency and departmental levels and on a governmentwide basis. While there will always be a need for agency-specific surveys due to the diversity of agency business practices, we recommend that agencies work together in survey consortia on areas of common interest such as the assessment of cultural change (Morris & Lo Verde, 1993). Organizational surveys will be more meaningful if a common core of constructs and related items is adopted, along with a standardized instrument that allows agency-to-agency comparisons and benchmarking to the best in business. We believe the Organizational Assessment Survey holds promise for supporting such a consortia effort. In effect, the public sector needs to establish its own Mayflower Group for organizational assessment.

Finally, to further aid the consortia approach, there should be a central repository of survey information within the federal government. For example, when an organization is beginning a survey effort, there should be a central place for staff to locate and review item pools related to the survey objective. A centralized repository of survey information and data would also facilitate interactions with public-sector survey researchers. In the current governmental era of downsizing and streamlining, survey research has never been more critical. Organizing governmental survey information and building bridges to private-sector survey research efforts would be a major professional contribution.

References

Carlyle, J. J. (1993, October). *Whistleblowing in the federal government: An update.* Washington, DC: U.S. Government Printing Office.

Executive Order 12871 (1993, October 1). Labor-management partnerships. *Federal Register, 58*(192), 52201–52203.

Fitzgerald, L. F., Gelfand, M., & Drasgow, F. (in press). Measuring sexual harassment: Theoretical and psychometric advances. *Basic and Applied Social Psychology.*

Gelfand, M., Fitzgerald, L. F., & Drasgow, F. (in press). The latent structure of sexual harassment: A cross-cultural confirmatory analysis. *Journal of Vocational Behavior.*

Kraft, J. D., Schneider, J. L., Reck, M., Chia, W., & Pettibone, C. (1995, March 31). *Assessing the climate and culture of the United States Mint: The key to becoming a high performing organization.* Washington, DC: U.S. Office of Personnel Management.

Landis, D. (1990, January). *Military equal opportunity climate survey: Reliability, construct validity and preliminary field test.* Oxford: Center for Applied Research and Evaluation, University of Mississippi.

Martindale, M. (1990, September). *Sexual harassment in the military: 1988.* Arlington, VA: Defense Manpower Data Center.

Morris, G. W., & Lo Verde, M. A. (1993). Consortium surveys. In P. Rosenfeld, J. E. Edwards, & M. D. Thomas (Eds.), *Improving organizational surveys: New directions, methods, and applications* (pp. 122–142). Newbury Park, CA: Sage.

National Performance Review. (1993). *From red tape to results: Creating a government that works better and costs less.* Washington, DC: Author.

Office of Systems Innovation and Simplification, U.S. Office of Personnel Management. (1992, May). *Survey of federal employees.* Washington, DC: Author.

Redd, H. C. III. (1990, June). *Working for America: A federal employee survey.* Washington, DC: Merit Systems Protection Board.

Robertson, D. W. (1993, November). *Navy new recruit survey.* San Diego, CA: Navy Personnel Research and Development Center.

Rosenfeld, P., & Edwards, J. E. (1994, September). Automated system assesses equal opportunity. *Personnel Journal, 73*(9), 98–103.

Schneider, J. (1993). *Organizational process dimensions underlying effective organizations: Dimensions to include in OPM's organizational assessment survey.* Washington, DC: U.S. Office of Personnel Management.

Storey, R. H., & Crum, J. L. (1988). *Sexual harassment in the federal government: An update.* Washington, DC: U.S. Merit Systems Protection Board.

Stouffer, S. A., & Associates. (1947–1950). *The American soldier: Studies in social psychology in World War II* (Vols. 1–4). Princeton, NJ: Princeton University Press.

U.S. Environmental Protection Agency. (1992, November). *Cultural diversity challenges for EPA: A strategy for bold action.* Washington, DC: Author.

U.S. Environmental Protection Agency. (1993, May). *United States Environmental Protection Agency headquarters cultural diversity survey final report.* Washington, DC: Author.

van Rijn, P. (1990, May). *Why are employees leaving the federal government?* Washington, DC: Merit Systems Protection Board.

van Rijn, P. (1992, December). *Federal blue-collar employees: A workforce in transition.* Washington, DC: Merit Systems Protection Board.

CHAPTER 15

Ethical Concerns and Organizational Surveys

Marshall Sashkin
Erich P. Prien

The Society for Industrial and Organizational Psychology has the goal of promoting "human welfare through the various applications of psychology to all types of organizations." SIOP members do this through playing three major roles: they are "scientists who derive principles of individual, group, and organizational behavior through research; consultants and staff psychologists who develop scientific knowledge and apply it to the solution of problems at work; and teachers who train in the research and application of I-O [Industrial-Organizational] Psychology" (Society for Industrial and Organizational Psychology, 1995, p. iii). In the general sense, actions of I/O service providers are ethical when consistent with the values and principles stated and assumed in these definitions. Actions that deviate from these values and principles are ethically suspect.

I/O psychologists, especially those who are members of SIOP, are expected to know and follow these general guidelines. Additional guidelines are available in a variety of publications (American Psychological Association, 1990, 1992). Even more specific are

---

Note: The views expressed here are those of the authors in their private capacities and do not necessarily reflect or represent the views of the Society for Industrial and Organizational Psychology or the respective organizations with which the authors are affiliated.

the *Specialty Guidelines for the Delivery of Services by Industrial/
Organizational Psychologists* (American Psychological Association,
1981) and the principles exemplified in the SIOP *Casebook on Ethics
and Standards for the Practice of Psychology in Organizations* (Lowman,
1985). Guidelines can help practitioners attain the ethical practice
goals we believe most practitioners strive to achieve. All guidelines,
however, leave considerable room for interpretation. Moreover,
they are frequently difficult to apply to the specific situations confronting an I/O practitioner.

Thus, our focus in this chapter is pragmatic. We focus specifically on the consultant's ethical obligations when conducting organizational surveys, and we provide many examples, including some
from our own professional practice, to put meat on the bones of
ethical practice. We provide a set of specific principles, short summaries of specific behaviors that the ethical practitioner will always
avoid. Our aim, however, is not just to offer general rules and
guidelines but to encourage readers to think about the ethical
problems and issues that are faced by anyone involved in organizational survey activities.

Designing, administering, and interpreting organizational
surveys does not require legally certified expertise, so just about
anyone who wishes to do so can, regardless of his or her skills and
qualifications or the lack thereof. Persons in virtually all walks of
life and all occupations and positions can and have engaged in
the practice. This makes it all the more important for those of
us who are experts to distinguish ourselves ethically as well as
professionally.

Nevertheless, it is unlikely that any professionals in this field
have conducted a zero-defect practice; the challenge of remaining
perfect for decades is probably impossible unless one is comatose.
Moreover, being ethical requires close personal attention to one's
own and others' expectations. Ethics define which actions are
"right" and which are "wrong," and such definitions cannot be
determined (or challenged) by science. The views and advice we
give here are not based on scientific research but on our practical
experience. While, between us, our experience covers more than
fifty years and quite a few organizations, we make no claims as to
the scientific truth or universal applicability of what we have to say
about ethics. Yet our experience has shown us the professional and
client expectations of "right" behavior that we discuss here.

As one result of that experience, we have come to distinguish two kinds of unethical behavior, and that distinction is central to our discussion. First, there are some unethical behaviors that are, in essence, the unintentional consequences of what might best be thought of as errors committed by *blunderers*. These errors may be due to oversight, lack of foresight, overzealousness, ignorance, or outright stupidity. Indeed, the practice that created the ethical problem may have been intentional, even though the unethical result itself was unintentional. Such blunders must be detailed and understood if practitioners are to avoid making them.

Second, there are ethical transgressions that result from intent. These are committed by *bounders,* consultants who know exactly what they are doing and are well aware that their actions are not ethical.

Last of all, as in so many aspects of life, there are also gray areas, involving matters in which individual consultants must try their best to base their actions on sound ethical judgments despite the complexity of the situation.

In keeping with our practical focus, we discuss the practices that can cause ethical problems according to the sequence in which they are likely to be encountered in the consulting activities surrounding organizational surveys, following this somewhat simplified five-step outline:

- Initiating the survey project
- Developing the survey and the project
- Administering the survey
- Interpreting and reporting results
- Using or applying survey results

Thus, the chapter follows the basic flow of survey practice activities, beginning with the initial consultant-client contact. Whether initiated by the client or agreed to by the client in response to a consultant overture, this event is perhaps the first occasion on which an ethical problem may arise. Each succeeding stage of the process also presents specific opportunities for both the ethical problems that we define as blunders and those attributable to bounders.

Finally, although much of what we have to say concerns the seamy side of organizational survey work, we do not mean to imply

384 Organizational Surveys

that most or even much of that work is characterized by ethical problems. Unethical practices are, we believe, relatively *uncommon;* we concentrate on the seamy side only for the purpose of providing the guidance that may help us all stay on the sunny side.

Initiating the Survey Project

When an organizational survey is initiated, practitioners may encounter ethical problems when they contract to perform the survey and when they obtain client commitment.

Contracting

In organizational consulting, in addition to any obligations to individuals, the consultant must keep in mind his or her obligation to the *organization.* It is at least a blunder to treat a single individual or group as the sole client when an entire organization is involved, especially when (as in all surveys) information is collected that might reflect badly on an individual or group. Client organization members should know from the start just what information the consultant will provide and in what form. This makes it far easier, later on, to avoid problems of unethical disclosure.

In developing an initial consulting relationship, it is absolutely essential that the consultant develop an appropriate understanding of the client organization. To persuade a client to participate in an experiment or to accept features of a survey that will provide the consultant with another publication but not advance the client's interest is, at least, in the gray area of ethical practice. While it is often appropriate to include some experimental items or a section with a unique format in a questionnaire, there must always be a valid rationale and the client must be informed.

Similarly, it is generally inappropriate for the consultant to take actions based on his or her personal views and values, unless the consultant knows that those actions are consistent with what the client wants and needs. This admonition is not meant to imply that the consultant is only a hired hand but that there is a boundary line between an ethical practitioner-teacher and the client's continuing accountability for the operation and effectiveness of the organization.

PRINCIPLE: You shall not place your own interests above those of your client.

An early issue in developing a contract is defining the roles and expectations of the client and the consultant. What activities are the responsibility of the consultant? For what actions will the client take primary responsibility? Allowing a project to start without clearly defined roles and expectations is an ethical blunder. It sets the stage for later blaming on the part of one or both parties, each of whom may honestly feel that the other has not fulfilled his or her contract. Such a circumstance is far less likely if clear role expectations have been defined in advance.

In particular, the consultant should disclose fees and costs, or at least how fees will be calculated, prior to the project's start. This step is especially relevant for survey work, since consultants' roles and services may vary widely, depending on the nature of the survey activities they are involved in. (Are they responsible for data analysis? Do they have a role in interpretation? Are they involved in reporting and feedback activities?) Because consultant activities vary so much, so do consultant costs; a client should be aware whether the project costs include only basic descriptive statistics in a report consisting of data tables or whether an in-depth analysis and group-by-group comparison will be provided along with detailed narrative commentary and the consultant's presence at feedback sessions. It is a blunder to allow the client to *assume* what is and is not included in the cost of a project. Such blunders are, we believe, relatively common.

When the consultant is an academic or a senior external consultant and will involve students or junior colleagues in the project, that arrangement should be explicit. For example, if the consultant plans to give a student primary responsibility for data collection and analysis, the client should know this in advance. The client should not be surprised at the involvement of an unknown student or assistant.

Still another situation in which role clarity may have ethical implications occurs when the client is a student of the consultant. Our favored advice in that situation is to avoid consulting with one's students. At the least, a consultant should not contract with a client who is currently enrolled in a class or seminar being taught by the consultant, as this places both client and consultant in a potential ethical dilemma. That is, it gives the appearance that a quid pro quo has been arranged: a good grade in exchange for a consulting fee. Putting oneself in such a situation is a blunder even in the best of circumstances. Any relationship in which the consultant has power over the client is to be avoided.

PRINCIPLE: You shall not in fact or in appearance engage in quid pro quo exchanges with students or others over whom you could exercise power.

When explaining what the client might expect as possible survey outcomes, the practitioner must exercise prudent caution. He or she should be realistic in linking outcomes to the use of a particular questionnaire or a specific survey feedback intervention program. Such claims should be reasonable and correspond to what can rationally be expected. Claims such as, "improvement in morale leading to 10 percent increases in productivity," or, "reducing turnover from 40 percent to 5 percent," and so forth are so outside of the realm of what is reasonable to expect that a client or another practitioner may safely conclude that these are the utterances of a bounder.

PRINCIPLE: You shall not make extravagant claims in the absence of scientific evidence to document them.

The ethical issues in this area, however, are often more subtle than simply making false promises. Consultants now know that setting expectations can have a major effect on what actually happens in any organizational consulting project (Eden, 1992; King, 1974), and this factor is of special importance in organizational survey work. Creating expectations among members of the organization that a survey will have substantial impact on management decisions and organizational operations when, in fact, top management has neither the intent nor the interest in any such effects, is counterproductive. The typical result is that organization members feel disappointed and disillusioned and blame management for letting them down. Our point, of course, is not that all organizational surveys should or must lead to substantial management-supported changes, only that consultants must make sure that survey publicity is faithful to management's expressed intentions.

At certain times, it is illegal to survey employees to obtain information intended for use in union avoidance efforts. A consultant who does not care what the client proposes to do with survey data may be engaging in action that is illegal as well as unethical. It is wise to have at least a nodding acquaintance with prevailing labor law. When conducting a consultation including a survey in the context of current, pending, or anticipated labor contract negotiations or a union organizing campaign, the prudent consultant will seek legal counsel.

PRINCIPLE: You shall not violate the law in conducting organizational survey work.

Gaining Client Commitment

Consulting lore has it that the right point of entry into the client system is the person who has a budget line to commit to the project. In fact, this is not as self-serving a criterion as might seem at first glance. That is, the consultant must look for both psychological and practical indicators of client commitment. If it is clear that the client does not have the resources to pursue the project (and financial resources are not necessarily the most important resources), then it may be an ethical blunder to go ahead; expectations aroused and unfulfilled often do more harm than good.

Sometimes it is the human resource function of the organization that has the budget to conduct a survey but has only a vague commitment from line management to make use of the results. The wise consultant explores line management's commitment directly, if at all possible. In sum, the issue of client commitment can generate ethical issues in the gray area. One way to avoid this ethical ambivalence is to strive to assess and make explicit all commitments, of both the client and the consultant, early on.

PRINCIPLE: You shall not proceed without the client's informed commitment.

Developing the Survey and the Project

Several ethical issues come to the fore as the survey is developed. Two are of special broad importance. The first has to do with the use of survey items and materials that were developed by others. The second is actually a set of issues, centered on technical considerations in survey development and reflected most of all by the consultant's technical expertise (or lack thereof).

Using Others' Materials

In responding to opportunities for consulting, there is always the temptation (and fairly common practice) of making use of available material—perhaps doing some revising and editing. Material that is presented in the literature or in a text where the intent of the authors is to educate and inform may very well be available for consultants' use. However, the very thought of such use should automatically trigger two actions. The first action should be a formal request to the author (unless there is an explicit statement to the effect that the material is in the public domain or that permission to use the material is automatically granted). For example, some consultants make use of survey systems, paying a license fee in return for a library of items and scales on various topics.

The second automatic action should be to attribute the material to the source in a manner consistent with the originator's or owner's specification. Whether one has permission or no permission is required, using materials without attribution is the act of a bounder.

PRINCIPLE: You shall not provide material to a client as if it is your own work when that is not the case.

Lifting and using scales or whole questionnaires, even if not under copyright or if the material states that it may be used by others, is not good practice. We have seen consultants draw on others' published work frequently, in both appropriate and inappropriate ways. Using one or a few questionnaire items *similar* to those developed by someone else or attributed to published sources is not plagiarism, especially if the items deal with issues of common, general interest and do so in straightforward prose. There may be an infinite number of ways to ask the same question, but after reading enough examples, they all begin to look very much the same.

However, *copying* portions of someone else's questionnaire is, indeed, plagiarism when done without the original author's permission and without specific attribution. For example, the Job Descriptive Index (JDI), developed by Smith, Kendall, and Hulin (1969), has in its creators' view been so widely plagiarized, as well as edited in ways that may seriously distort its validity, that they have begun to assert their copyright and threaten legal action against those who use the JDI without permission (P. C. Smith, letters to E. P. Prien, April 3, 1995, and June 19, 1995). (If you are interested in using the JDI, write to the Test Fund of the Department of Psychology, Bowling Green State University, Bowling Green, OH 43403.)

A simple ethical rule of thumb when thinking about using existing survey materials, other than materials purchased from owners or publishers, is *"Always ask first."*

PRINCIPLE: You shall not plagiarize others' survey questionnaires.

Possessing Competence and Experience

The survey practice area provides many opportunities for individuals to respond to overtures of potential clients, offering as evidence of their competence only general academic credentials. It is deceptively attractive to announce one's availability for this sort of consulting work. If the opportunity to conduct a survey arises, an individual may feel he or she need only consult the extensive reference material on the practice of organizational development and change. Authors such as Argyris (1970), Burke (1994), and Nadler (1977) provide considerable practical guidance on organizational development consultation practice in general and organizational surveys in particular.

The ethical issue here is whether someone without technical qualifications and training in organizational surveys can go to the library and acquire all he or she needs to know to conduct an organizational survey project. In our view, the crucial question is one of technical skill. An aspiring consultant may have completed basic academic preparation in the form of a course on scaling or measurement but may still lack the competence to engage in organizational survey work. Blindly following advice found in a text or an article does not represent competent practice. A client has the right to expect a basic level of practical experience on the part of the consultant, as would be acquired through graduate work in survey research or under the guidance of experienced professionals.

PRINCIPLE: You shall not misrepresent your relevant competencies and "fake it" to sell a client.

Another category of basic technical skills that the practitioner should possess is the knowledge of measurement properties of instruments. This includes an understanding of reliability, validity in its different forms, reading level, and language usage plus other instrument properties that have an effect on both responses made by individuals and the interpretation of results.

To make claims about the measurement properties of an instrument in the absence of solid evidence is the act of a bounder. One trick we have observed is to fake the validation of an instrument. Such false validation may take different forms. It may represent a criterion group as an ideal or it may represent the validation criterion as management's expectations. In either case, the content may possess face validity but be otherwise meaningless.

PRINCIPLE: You shall not use questionable methods to create the impression that a survey instrument is reliable or valid.

Making Inappropriate Claims of Reliability and Validity

Practitioners generally would like to be able to tell the client that the questionnaire being used is reliable and valid. One way to achieve this goal, of course, is simply to select and use (legally) an instrument for which there is evidence of both reliability and validity. But proof of reliability and validity is difficult to come by when one creates one's own questionnaire.

Another way to show evidence of reliability is to compute test-retest reliability or calculate split-half reliabilities. The average inter-item correlation among the items on a scale (Cronbach's alpha) gives a measure of how well the scale items "hang together." Internal consistency, however, does not demonstrate, as does test-retest reliability, that items or scales yield consistent scores when the administration is repeated. This is not necessarily a serious problem, since organizational surveys usually assess relatively labile *states* rather than stable *traits*. Internal consistency is, then, a meaningful measure of reliability for most surveys.

Another common validation approach is to obtain some initial data and perform a factor analysis. If the items factor relatively cleanly into the defined scales, it is often asserted that the instrument has a degree of construct validity. While this may be true, it may also simply be the case that the consultant has done a good job of writing items that fit the dimensions intended.

If the client raises questions about the measurement properties of items, scales, or questionnaires, it is unethical to argue that those kinds of questions are irrelevant and that the only concern is how the instrument looks to the people in the organization. Despite the standard admonition that face validity is no validity, we have seen survey consultants assert that all validity is in the eye of the user and is context-defined. To assert that the only relevant test of validity is how the materials look to clients is essentially nonsense. It is an unethical action attributable to a bounder.

PRINCIPLE: You shall not misrepresent the reliability, dimensionality, or validity of survey questionnaire scale scores.

We raise these issues not to suggest that those conducting survey work in organizations must be technical gurus. None of what we have said should be taken as either insistence that consultants develop their own surveys or that there is anything wrong with use, through permission or purchase, of one of the many specific survey instruments currently available. However, we do believe that consultants engaging in organizational survey work should have the technical competence needed to construct sound survey instruments. With limited competence, consultants are likely to blunder, and if they are totally unaware of the sorts of problems and issues just reviewed, they may make crucial blunders. One who has no technical competence but nonetheless engages in this sort of organizational consulting is a bounder.

Administering the Survey

There are three issues that must be addressed if ethical responsibilities are to be met in administering organizational surveys. The first is anonymity of respondents. The second concerns the voluntary nature of participation. The third deals with the control of data.

Respondent Anonymity

Standard practice is to assure survey respondents of the anonymity of their responses. Whenever such assurances are given, they must be honored unless there is a compelling reason for not doing so. (We discuss specific examples of such reasons later.) Even when not explicitly stated, anonymity is so often assumed that when responses are not to be treated anonymously, respondents should be informed of this decision.

As a general rule, it is best to maintain the anonymity of survey respondents. The promise of anonymity often makes it easier to gain survey participation, since it is clear that an anonymous individual cannot be punished for expressing views distasteful to management. The ethical point of ensuring anonymity is to protect the individual respondent.

Many tricks have been used to secretly identify respondents: invisible ink, coded envelopes, and multiple demographic items and classifications are just a few examples. Practices of the past involved such devices as identification codes hidden in questionnaire spines or margins. In mail surveys, the respondent might be identified by a special code in the return address, the color of the paper or envelope, or the position of the stamp. All of these—and all other—secret methods for identifying respondents without their knowledge and acquiescence are generally recognized as the unethical practices of bounders.

More subtle anonymity problems arise when, for example, individual supervisors want to know who might be a secret "troublemaker." Such supervisors might, for example, personally administer a survey or simply be in the survey room to surreptitiously watch so as to be able to identify an individual's questionnaire. Managers and supervisors should not be present when surveys are administered and should certainly not be the ones responsible for administering a survey to their own groups or units; it is the ethical responsibility of a consultant to make sure that appropriate administration procedures are followed.

A different sort of failure to maintain anonymity sometimes occurs when respondents are invited to write in answers. Unless the responses are screened and "sanitized," that is, edited and typed by a person or service outside the organization, it may be possible for individuals to be identified simply by their use of language or handwriting. This is why open-ended responses should never be fed back in their original unedited form. Bounders' efforts to subvert anonymity are, these days, quite rare. More common are the sort of blunders just described.

An individual anonymity problem (or the perception of one) may result if a group of respondents is very small. Thus, many consultants do not process group analyses for groups with fewer than a certain number of members (ten is a common standard).

Overall, ethical standards for ensuring anonymity of respondents and guaranteeing that no retribution can be exacted for responses on a survey require that (1) individual participants must not be identified on the survey form; (2) the survey administrator must not be able to link specific questionnaire forms to individual respondents; (3) all responses must be processed off-site by an independent contractor; (4) once coded and entered into a data set, the original questionnaires must be destroyed; (5) scores for groups smaller than a certain number must not be provided; and (6) group scores must not be available to persons other than the group members and their managers and higher-level executives.

PRINCIPLE: You shall not compromise the anonymity of respondents.

In addition, it is possible that the consultant might obtain from the survey information that is of crucial value to the organization but that also identifies a person or group and clearly has the potential to damage that person or group. For example, as a result of certain survey questions, a consultant might be led to make inquiries that suggest there has been serious financial fraud in one division of the organization. Our general view is that in such circumstances, what the consultant has learned should be presented, confidentially, to top management. Promises of anonymity are, we believe, voided when there is evidence of illegal or dangerous behavior. Keep in mind that the real client in the consultation is the organization. When there is reason to believe that the client is in material danger, the consultant is ethically justified in advising top management of this fact, even if individuals' anonymity is then compromised. By material danger we mean that client system members are in clear physical or psychological danger or that the client system is in clear financial danger. Even then, ethical practice requires that before the consultant acts in such cases, he or she obtain a second opinion from an informed co-professional.

A personal example may be helpful here. One of us conducted an organizational survey some years ago in a medium-sized manufacturing firm. On one form, there was a write-in comment threatening the physical safety of the CEO, to wit: "I'm going to get the president." In hindsight, we believe it would have been appropriate to attempt to identify this individual, who obviously had a personal grievance serious enough that he or she might have posed a physical danger to the CEO. Such identification would have been possible, since the surveys were coded by organizational group and there were only fifteen people with this particular group code. For example, an intervention could have been conducted by holding counseling interviews with each of the fifteen group members. That might have avoided the later confrontation that occurred when the individual came to work with a loaded firearm and had to be removed.

PRINCIPLE: You shall not compromise confidentiality without a
    second opinion.

Coercing Respondents

While requiring survey participation may seem high-handed, it is not unethical as long as respondents remain anonymous. If respondents are provided with copies to complete and return, it is simple for anyone to elect not to participate: he or she simply discards the questionnaire. Even in a group assembled to fill out a survey, a person can always fake responding and then turn in a blank form.

A much more serious problem is the coercion of responses,

rather than respondents. That is, supervisors and managers may believe that their groups or units must "look good" if their careers are to advance. Thus, they informally encourage subordinates to give favorable responses. When this is done by means of a pizza party or pep rally, it is a questionable practice that should be discouraged. However, managerial "encouragement" often takes on the characteristics of outright coercion and for a specific reason. It is not an uncommon practice for top management to hold supervisors and line managers accountable for employee morale and its improvement. We learned after the fact of this practice in one setting: we found that line managers were trying to manage the outcome of the survey so as to mitigate anticipated negative actions against them by top management if their units had "poor" scores.

The consultant should emphasize to the client the need to let managers and supervisors know that such coercive actions are not permitted and will not be tolerated. In addition, the consultant should emphasize that managers or supervisors should not be permitted to be present in the room when surveys are administered or to see the completed questionnaires (as we discussed above). This problem can also be addressed by explaining to respondents exactly how their anonymity is guaranteed. Such public knowledge may further reduce the possibility of unethical private actions.

PRINCIPLE: You shall not permit or facilitate the manipulation of responses by supervisors or managers.

Control of Data

Administering the survey effectively and ethically is in large part a matter of planning data collection, making that plan clear to participants, carefully supervising the data collection process, and controlling data once they have been gathered. We have already touched on the importance of control of the data in discussing anonymity and coercion of respondents. Ethical practice requires that raw data be accessible only by the consultant and the consultant's representatives. If the consultant is internal to the organization, an outside contractor should be part of managing the data collection process. This does not necessarily mean that survey administration must be done by outsiders, simply that data processing should normally be external to the organization.

PRINCIPLE: You shall not cede control over survey data to anyone, inside *or* outside of the organization.

Interpreting and Reporting Results

> There are three kinds of lies: lies, damned lies, and statistics.
> —Mark Twain, *Autobiography*

When it comes to interpreting the results of an organizational survey, the consultant faces at least three specific ethical concerns. First, he or she must select statistical analyses and presentations that make interpretation of the data clear and that do not mask results or make misinterpretation easy, whether intentionally or not. Next, the consultant must determine the client's level of understanding, so as to design data presentations that will be meaningful to the client. Finally, the consultant must consider how to facilitate the use of the data by the client, so that the client becomes less dependent on the consultant for interpretation and application.

Consultants can use statistical analysis of results properly to inform the client or misuse statistical analysis and thus confuse the client. The use of inappropriate statistics and the confusion of statistical significance with practical significance are technical blunders that may have serious ethical implications. When done intentionally, they are the unethical actions of bounders. And the use of statistics to create client dependency on the consultant or to deliberately lead the client to the next stage of a contractual relationship of financial benefit to the consultant is surely the act of a bounder.

PRINCIPLE: You shall not misuse statistics to sell consulting services.

Using Statistics Appropriate to the Data

To select appropriate statistics, consultants must possess a basic understanding of descriptive statistics and of the meaning of *sig-*

nificance with respect to results and differences. Results should be reported in ways that make errors of interpretation on the client's part less likely. For example, when results are reported in crudely rounded whole numbers, at one extreme, or in calculations carried out to four or five decimal places, at the other, the results may well be misunderstood by the client. Gross rounding may obscure real and important differences; excessive precision may imply a scientific basis for differences that are in fact trivial. These technical blunders may not be made with the intent to deceive but may lead nonetheless to erroneous conclusions on the part of the client.

The lack of understanding that leads a consultant to ignore important characteristics of the data is more than just a blunder. It is an example of the consultant's lacking the expertise needed to engage in this consulting activity in the first place.

PRINCIPLE: You shall not present statistics that hinder understanding.

Even worse are the actions of a consultant whose presentation of data clouds real differences, hides certain results, or exaggerates other results to further the consultant's self-interest. The aim may be to cover up an error, to perpetuate the consultation, or to further the consultant's aims of self-aggrandizement. Or the consultant may be trying to guarantee a positive evaluation of past consulting activities. In all of these cases, the consultant is a bounder engaged in intentionally unethical activities.

PRINCIPLE: You shall not lie with statistics.

Finally, consultants must pay attention to the fundamental distinction between statistical and practical significance. Scientists have a tendency to attach significance to any result that meets a .05 level of significance. However, for data from large samples (which are frequently the case in survey work), almost any difference will be statistically significant.

In the real world of business and industry (and of government and nonprofit organizations, too), resources are always scarce, and priorities must be based on estimates of potential effect and return on investment. It is unethical for a consultant to report without careful qualification even extreme levels of statistical significance when the differences found are, in practical terms, meaningless due to very large sample size. When the consultant purposely emphasizes statistically significant yet practically meaningless differences in order to "validate" his or her survey, to "prove" a point of theory, or to "prove" the positive effects of his or her actions, then the consultant is a full-blown bounder.

PRINCIPLE: You shall not exaggerate the practical meaning of statistical significance.

Giving Presentations That the Client Understands

In most client-consulting relationships, the consultant will deal with several audiences. They will include executives, internal consultants (most of whom will have professional competencies), and various employee groups, who may be empowered to develop and implement constructive action plans but who will typically have little or no experience in interpreting survey data or statistical analyses. Identifying audience competencies is essential if one is to avoid blunders.

In preparing material for various client audiences, some consultants engage in smoke-and-mirrors activity. They might, for example, report the data using very complex or sophisticated statistical analyses that only they can understand and interpret. The none-too-subtle message, of course, is that the client really needs the consultant. This is not a blunder, but the act of a bounder seeking to exploit the dependency of a client. In this same vein, bounders may intentionally present survey results in a way that serves their aim of continuing the project (if you can't find a problem, make one!) or expanding business with the client. Lest the reader think that this philosophy and practice does not actually exist, we assure you that it does.

PRINCIPLE: You shall not attempt to extend the consulting contract by striving to appear indispensable as an interpreter of survey results.

Teaching the Client to Understand the Results

The reporting of results is yet another situation in which an ethical organizational survey consultant takes on the role of teacher. It is incumbent on the consultant to see that an adequate degree of statistical understanding exists and, if not, to provide it to the appropriate client system members.

Especially unethical is the practice of the data dump. Only a bounder would drop the data in the client's hands and then abandon the project. Sometimes such a consultant may perform a data dump out of frustration, when results are complex and he or she is unable to see any clear meaning in them or figure out how to help the client use them. Another possibility is that the project budget limit has been reached and the consultant is no longer able to bill for fees. An ethical consultant, however, will provide at least a minimum of interpretive assistance, whether or not the client can afford it.

An ethical consultant, in this or any other area, aims to have a positive impact. This generally means making the client more capable of independent action and less dependent on external consultation. The achievement of that aim is the appropriate point of closure. In contrast, the unethical bounder intends to become so important to and needed by the client that the project (and the associated consulting income) will continue indefinitely.

Of course, real life is rarely as dramatically black or white as our statements would seem to imply. So we would also point out that simply to recite the results and verbally tell the client what is already written in the report is also insufficient and probably both a technical and an ethical blunder (since it denies the full value and use of the results to the client, who has paid for that value and use). To act as a teacher with respect to the meaning of statistical results and their interpretation, as a catalyst in the process of interpretation, and as a guide in planning and implementing actions based on the results, while simultaneously working one's way out of the project, is the optimum solution.

PRINCIPLE: You shall not leave the client without the ability to use the survey results to the benefit of the organization.

Using or Applying Survey Results

The ethical issues that develop at the action planning stage of an organizational survey consultation often involve the actions of management rather than those of the consultant. That is, the consultant may have obtained a clear commitment toward action based on the findings. Even so, management may decide against any actions. Although we see this as an ethical issue, it cannot be attributed to the consultant.

One thing the consultant can do is to make sure that promises are not made that the survey will lead to outcomes that are unlikely or impossible. Such promises are the acts of bounders; they are detectable by the same simple test that applies in so many other areas of life: if it sounds too good to be true, it probably is.

PRINCIPLE: You shall not make unreasonable promises about outcomes.

There is another common area in which ethical issues arise, an area in which consultants can reasonably expect to have some influence. Despite efforts to maintain anonymity, it is not uncommon for some individuals to be identified as the source of "problems." This is particularly likely in the case of the supervisor or manager whose direct reports clearly identify the boss as the problem.

The consultant must strike a delicate balance between protecting the reputation of the accused individual (could the accusation could be deliberate character assassination?) and protecting the organization and its members from the alleged transgressor. Thus, knowledge of the accusation must be highly restricted. The depth of the ensuing investigation will depend on the seriousness of the charge. That "Jones spends his lunch hour gambling" may require only a mental note on the part of the director of human resources. That "most women here are terrorized by Smith's jokes and gropes" calls for an investigation to proceed in discrete stages until the situation is understood and resolved.

We here repeat what we stated earlier: only a bounder would become involved in a survey project in which the explicit aim was to identify "problem personnel" or "troublemakers" so they could be punished or removed. In general, an ethical consultant will not undertake an organizational survey project when management's central interest is the attitudes and behavior of individuals rather than of groups and the organization as a whole.

PRINCIPLE: You shall not conduct surveys to identify and convict individuals.

In general, we think that ethical issues are less likely to arise at this last stage of organizational survey consultations if two factors have been present from the start. First, the emphasis should from the beginning be on groups and the organization as a whole and not on individual behavior. Second, the broadly stated purpose should from the beginning be on identifying and solving problems for improvement and not on punishing or eliminating "problem" people or groups. If these two characteristics have been part of the explicit initial expectations defined by the consultant and the client, the consultant is less likely to be confronted with the sorts of issues just discussed.

Conclusion

In this chapter, we have attempted to present our collective experiences with the ethical issues in conducting organizational surveys as consultants. We have drawn on our own blunders as well as our successes and on the blunders and achievements of colleagues. We hope that our discussion may prove helpful in guiding the work of others.

When carried out so as to be of maximum benefit to the client, the survey consultant's assignment is neither simple nor easy. It may thus be deceptively easy for a practitioner looking to simplify or lighten his or her task to manipulate clients and to act in ways that serve his or her own self-interests when consulting with a client who does not possess the expertise to evaluate and challenge a practitioner. Putting into practice the cynical adage "Blessed are those who possess much brass, for they shall exchange it for gold" may yield short-term profits but also long-term grief for both client and consultant. "Do good and you will do well" seems to us to be the wiser aphorism.

But this advice applies primarily to the bounder, the consultant who yields to temptation and knowingly crosses the line to engage in actions that do not merely raise ethical questions but violate the principles of ethical conduct. It is easy to condemn such actions since they present a clear instance of inappropriate behavior. It is more difficult to deal with the ethical issues that arise out of blunders.

Looking back on our discussion, the reader may observe that there are really two sorts of blunders. Some blunders are the result of ignorance, if not incompetence. Indeed, in many cases, ignorance *is* incompetence. Such blunders are also easy to inveigh against. Yet, as Socrates pointed out, the essence of wisdom is realizing how little one actually knows. So, before blaming the ignorant for their ignorance, it would be well to understand that awareness of ignorance is not always a simple or obvious matter.

Other blunders, however, involve making the wrong ethical choices when faced with issues in the oft-cited gray areas.

We believe that no matter how intent one may be on conducting an ethical practice, in the real world one is bound to make some blunders—of both types. Thus, our goals for consultants are more modest than perfection. We believe that it is possible to avoid unethical conduct, the actions of a bounder, while also minimizing blunders brought about through ignorance or error. All of us are human, and, in degree, we will all blunder at times. Nevertheless, we should all heed the following capstone principle for organizational survey practitioners, which is drawn from the advice of Hippocrates to medical practitioners:

PRINCIPLE: You shall do no harm to the client organization or to the individuals in it.

References
American Psychological Association. (1981). Specialty guidelines for the delivery of services by industrial/organizational psychologists. *American Psychologist, 36,* 664–669.

American Psychological Association. (1990). Ethical problems of psychologists. *American Psychologist, 45,* 390–395.

American Psychological Association. (1992). Ethical principles of psychologists and code of conduct. *American Psychologist, 47,* 1597–1611.

Argyris, C. (1970). *Intervention theory and method.* Reading, MA: Addison-Wesley.

Burke, W. W. (1994). *Organization development: A normative view* (2nd ed.). Reading, MA: Addison-Wesley.

Eden, D. (1990). *Pygmalion in management: Productivity as a self-fulfilling prophecy.* San Francisco: Lexington Books.

King, A. S. (1974). Expectation effects in organizational change. *Administrative Science Quarterly, 19,* 221–230.

Lowman, R. (Ed.). (1985). *Casebook on ethics and standards for the practice of psychology in organizations.* College Park, MD: Society for Industrial and Organizational Psychology/American Psychological Association.

Nadler, D. A. (1977). *Feedback and organization development: Using data-based methods.* Reading, MA: Addison-Wesley.

Smith, P. C., Kendall, L. M., & Hulin, C. L. (1969). *The measurement of satisfaction in work and retirement.* Skokie, IL: Rand McNally.

Society for Industrial and Organizational Psychology. (1995). *Membership directory.* Bowling Green, OH: Author.

Name Index

Subject Index